T0303318

Frame It Again

Framing effects are everywhere. An estate tax looks very different to a death tax. Gun safety seems to be one thing and gun control another. Yet, the consensus from decision theorists, finance professionals, psychologists, and economists is that frame-dependence is completely irrational. This book challenges that view. Some of the toughest decisions we face are just clashes between different frames. It is perfectly rational to value the same thing differently in two different frames, even when the decision-maker knows that these are really two sides of the same coin. *Frame It Again* sheds new light on the structure of moral predicaments, the nature of self-control, and the rationality of cooperation. Framing is a powerful tool for redirecting public discussions about some of the most polarizing contemporary issues, such as gun control, abortion, and climate change. Learn effective problem-solving and decision-making to get the better of difficult dilemmas.

José Luis Bermúdez is Professor of Philosophy and Samuel Rhea Gammon Professor of Liberal Arts at Texas A&M University. His many books include *The Paradox of Self-Consciousness*, *Thinking without Words*, and the highly successful textbook *Cognitive Science*, now in its third edition.

JOSÉ LUIS BERMÚDEZ

FRAME IT AGAIN

NEW TOOLS FOR RATIONAL DECISION-MAKING

CAMBRIDGE
UNIVERSITY PRESS

CAMBRIDGE
UNIVERSITY PRESS

University Printing House, Cambridge CB2 8BS, United Kingdom

One Liberty Plaza, 20th Floor, New York, NY 10006, USA

477 Williamstown Road, Port Melbourne, VIC 3207, Australia

314–321, 3rd Floor, Plot 3, Splendor Forum, Jasola District Centre,
New Delhi – 110025, India

79 Anson Road, #06–04/06, Singapore 079906

Cambridge University Press is part of the University of Cambridge.

It furthers the University's mission by disseminating knowledge in the pursuit of education, learning, and research at the highest international levels of excellence.

www.cambridge.org
Information on this title: www.cambridge.org/9781107192935
DOI: 10.1017/9781108131827

© José Luis Bermúdez 2021

First published 2021

Printed in the United Kingdom by TJ International Ltd, Padstow Cornwall

A catalogue record for this publication is available from the British Library.

ISBN 978-1-107-19293-5 Hardback

Cambridge University Press has no responsibility for the persistence or accuracy of URLs for external or third-party internet websites referred to in this publication and does not guarantee that any content on such websites is, or will remain, accurate or appropriate.

Contents

Figures

Tables

Acknowledgments

I am very grateful to the American Association of Learned Societies for a Fellowship allowing me to devote myself to writing this book during the 2018–2019 academic year, and also to the Department of Philosophy and College of Liberal Arts at Texas A&M for allowing me to take up the Fellowship. Thanks are due also to the National Endowment for the Humanities for a Summer Stipend, which I held in the summer of 2018.

I greatly appreciate having had the opportunity to present three lectures on framing to the Institut Jean Nicod at the École Normal Supérieure in Paris, and I learned much from discussing the ideas in this book with audiences at the European Society for Philosophy of Psychology, the Foundations of Normativity project at the University of Vienna, the Logos Research Group at the University of Barcelona, and the Department of Philosophy at UC San Diego. An early draft of the first seven chapters was discussed at an enjoyable retreat with faculty and students in the Philosophy Department at Davidson College, North Carolina.

Chapter 7 draws on my "Frames, rationality, and self-control" (in J. L. Bermúdez, Ed., *Self-Control, Decision Theory, and Rationality*, Cambridge University Press, 2018). That paper originated in a workshop at Texas A&M that was funded by a grant from the Templeton Foundation via the Philosophy and Psychology of Self-Control project at Florida State University, directed by Al Mele.

Three anonymous referees for Cambridge University Press gave very helpful comments on the manuscript. I thank them, and also Michael Schmitz, Richard Pettigrew, and Al Mele, who commented on individual chapters. Clare Palmer read every chapter, several on multiple occasions, greatly improving style and content.

Finally, I would like to thank the editorial team at Cambridge University Press: Ilaria Tassistro, David Repeto, and, especially, Janka Romero, who signed the book up and commented on almost every chapter.

Priming the Pump: Framing Effects and the Litany of Human Irrationality

This is a book about frames and framing effects. So, let's start with some examples, to get a preliminary feel for what is at stake here. I will present five framing effects, without much by way of discussion or analysis. In each of these cases, people come to view a single outcome in very different ways, depending on how it is framed.

The first three cases are experimentally induced in a lab. They display the framing effects cleverly and very clearly, even though they are not the most celebrated cases of experimental framing effects such as the celebrated Asian disease paradigm, which we'll look at in more detail in Chapter 2.

The fourth example shifts the emphasis away from the laboratory. It is an idealized version of familiar real-life cases with which most of us are painfully familiar. When faced with temptation, decision-makers struggle to stick to the plans they have committed themselves to as the moment of truth draws near. We'll look at cases of temptation and self-control in much more detail later on (in Chapter 7), but the point I want to make here is that how we frame the path of virtue (or the path of temptation) can determine whether or not we manage to exercise self-control.

The final example completely changes tack. We go back to the shadowy world of the ancient Greek tragedies, where history and myth blend. It is a famous passage from the first play in Aeschylus's trilogy *The Oresteia*, where the chorus looks back to Agamemnon's fateful dilemma at Aulis. From a psychological point of view, it is exponentially more complex than either the three experimental cases or the self-control/temptation example (and certainly doesn't lend itself to experimental replication). Despite that (or really, because of it), we will come back to it many times in the course of this book, as I believe that the power and importance of frames becomes much clearer when we see how they function in the really hard cases. The easy cases have received too much attention, which has skewed our understanding of frames and framing effects.

Without digressing too much, at this stage the only goal is to understand the cases and come to a (perhaps provisional!) conclusion about what they reveal, and whether what is going on is rational or irrational. It might be a good idea to make a note of your thoughts, so that you can come back to your immediate reactions to these examples when we are further along in the book.

Framing Effect 1: Rating Basketball Players

Irwin Levin at the University of Iowa asked subjects to evaluate how well basketball players were performing, based on information he provided about their shots over a period of time.[1] He presented the information in two different ways. For one group, it was presented positively, as they were told the percentage of shots that the player made successfully. For a second group the information was presented negatively, in terms of the percentage of shots that the player had missed. These are of course different ways of framing the same facts about how the player played. Yet Levin found that the same players were consistently ranked more highly by subjects in the positive frame than they were in the negative frame.

Framing Effect 2: Negotiating Contracts

Margaret Neale and Max Bazerman (from Arizona and MIT respectively) asked a class of 102 undergraduates studying Business Administration at the University of Texas to simulate an industrial negotiating situation.[2] The students had to imagine that they were negotiating with union representatives on behalf of a fictional company (Townsford). Their job was to negotiate a settlement, but they also had the option of giving up and going into binding arbitration – a much riskier strategy.

They were divided into two groups. Both groups were presented with information about the different priorities and settlement-points of management and the union on five different issues. For one group the information was presented positively (from the perspective of the company).

[1] Reported in Levin, Schneider, and Gaeth 1998.   [2] Neale and Bazerman 1985.

Students in the positive frame were given numbers corresponding to the total gain to company if the company were to settle at that point. They were also told:

> Any union concession from their current position will result in gains for the company. Please remember that your primary objective is to maximize such gains for the company. I cannot emphasize the importance of these gains to Townsford enough. It is mandatory that you, as Townsford's representative, secure such concessions from the union to increase these gains to a meaningful level.

Students in the negative frame were given exactly the same numbers, but those numbers were presented in the form of losses rather than gains. This group was told:

> Any concessions beyond those granted will represent serious financial losses to the company. Please remember that your primary objective is to minimize such losses to the company. I cannot emphasize the severity of this situation enough. It is mandatory that you, as Townsford's representative, secure the necessary concessions from the union to reduce our losses to a tolerable level.

Obviously, there is no difference in the objective information possessed by the two groups. Contract negotiations are what is called a zero-sum game. A gain to the company is a loss for the union, and a gain to the union is a loss for the company.

Still the group in the positive frame were much more likely to negotiate a settlement, whereas the group in the negative frame were more willing to take the riskier option of abandoning the negotiation and submitting to a binding arbitration.

Framing Effect 3: Sacrifices for the Common Good

As game theorists know well in theory, and the rest of us in practice, many social situations have the form of a *social dilemma*.[3] Social dilemmas occur when collective disaster is the result of individuals behaving perfectly rationally to promote their self-interest. Open range grazing in the American West is a famous example. It had its heyday in the second half of the nineteenth century. Any rancher could graze their animals on open rangeland and each individual farmer had an obvious incentive to put as many of their animals on the land as they could. Why not, since the grazing is free? But of course, if too many farmers do so, then the

---

[3] Brewer and Kramer 1986.

rangeland is destroyed for everyone.[4] Open range grazing is an example of a commons dilemma (often called *tragedy of the commons*[5]). In the simplest form of commons dilemma individuals have to decide what share to take for themselves of a shared resource (as in the open range case, where the open range is the shared resource).

Another type of social dilemma comes with the provision of public goods. A public good is a good that benefits everyone, at least potentially (such as university education, or state-funded healthcare in a single-payer system, such as the United Kingdom's National Health Service). In public good dilemmas, individuals have to decide how much (if anything) to contribute to maintaining a public good. Such dilemmas can arise for private groups – residents of an apartment block deciding whether to increase the maintenance charge to pay for a new roof, for example. But they also arise in debates about taxation levels. In the United States, for example, local governments sometimes hold referendums on increasing property taxes to pay for additional local services, or improved schooling. Each resident and each voter is confronted with a public good dilemma.

Marilyn Brewer (UCLA) and Roderick Kramer (Stanford) ran a study to test whether subjects would respond differently to a collective choice problem depending on whether it was presented as a commons dilemma or as a public good dilemma. The experimental task was cleverly designed to induce the tension between individual good and common good that characterizes all social dilemmas. Subjects were told that there was a common resource pool of points. All the subjects had access to the common pool and were instructed to maximize their own points total while maintaining the common resource as long as possible. In one condition (the *public good condition*), subjects were given points and then had to decide what proportion to contribute back to the pool, while in the *commons dilemma condition* subjects had to decide how many points to take from the common pool. The outcomes were identical across the two conditions in terms of points. And so the monetary rewards to the subjects

[4] Limited forms of open range grazing persist in some western states in the United States and Canada, but when a state such as Texas is described as an open range state, what this typically means is that landowners do not have a legal obligation to fence their animals and, for example, keep them off public roads. The "golden age" of open range grazing was brought to an end in the United States in the last years of the nineteenth century by a combination of over-supply and over-grazing, compounded by a very severe winter in 1886–87.

[5] The phrase originated with the Victorian economist William Forster Lloyd, but was popularized by the ecologist Garrett Hardin in an influential paper of the same name published in 1968.

were the same. There is no difference, for example, between starting with 1,000 points and contributing 250 points to the common pool, on the one hand, and starting with 500 points and taking 250 points from the common pool. Either way you end up with 750 points.

Still, the two groups behaved very differently. It turns out the subjects left more points in the common pool in the commons dilemma condition than they were prepared to contribute to the common pool in the public good condition. Apparently, people are much less willing to contribute points to the common pool than they are to leave points in the common pool. Forgoing a gain is easier than taking a loss, it seems, even when the experiment is designed so that there is no difference in outcome, but only a difference in how the outcome is framed.

Framing Effect 4: The Battle against Temptation

It is easy to make commitments in advance, but hard to live up to them when the time comes to follow through in the face of temptation. The basic phenomenon should be familiar to anyone who has taken out a gym membership or made a New Year's resolution to lose weight. At a safe (temporal) distance the long-term outcome of being fit and slim is far more attractive than the short-term prospect of an extra hour in bed, or the mid-morning snack. And yet when the alarm goes off or the stomach starts rumbling hours after breakfast and hours before lunch it is a different story. The immediate reward suddenly seems far more attractive than the long-term outcome. Self-control is hard. In fact, one might wonder how it is even possible.

We need to exercise self-control because preferences change over time. In the indeterminate future, being fit and slim is much more attractive than the prospect of a snack. But when the snack is right there, it seems much more appealing than being fit and slim at some indefinite time in the future. This type of *preference reversal* occurs because of how people discount the future. If I have a high discount rate, then I care relatively little about the future. But if I have a low discount rate, then I care very much about what happens in the future. The problem is that people do not typically have constant discount rates. Much experimental evidence suggests that the discount rate for a given event changes as the event approaches. If I decide on a Friday to fast until lunchtime on the following Thursday, then I probably have a high discount rate on Friday and over the weekend for the breakfast that I am planning to forgo on Thursday morning. As the week goes on, though, my discount rate for the breakfast falls. And by the time I wake up on Thursday morning it is very low indeed. In the meantime, though, my discount rate for the long-term goal of being slim and fit has not really changed at all. And so the short-term prospect of eating breakfast comes to seem more important than the long-term goal of being slim and fit. That is how temptation strikes!

Sometimes we succumb to temptation. But often we don't. Why not? There is a vast literature on this, from self-help manuals to experimental studies on how rats respond to delayed rewards. Crucially, though, whether we succeed in exercising self-control can be due to how we frame the different possible actions and outcomes when faced with temptation. If it is a simple choice between eating breakfast and sticking to my fasting plan, and if my changing discount rates have led to a preference reversal, then I may well end up chowing down on my breakfast. But what if I attach a special importance to actively resisting temptation? This might lead me to a different way of framing the act of holding out for the long-term reward of being fit and slim. For example, if I frame it as the act of being resolute – and I like the idea of being resolute – then it fits with my self-conception. And being resolute now may well make it more likely that I'll be resolute in the future. For all these reasons I might well prefer being resolute in the face of temptation to having breakfast, especially if I frame having breakfast as succumbing to temptation.

As we'll see in Chapter 7, there is experimental evidence that self-control often works like this. But really this is a framing effect. All I've done is reframe the outcomes and reconceptualize the decision problem. In this situation there is no difference between being resolute in the face of temptation and forgoing breakfast. And succumbing to temptation is the same as eating breakfast. The outcomes are the same. Only the framing changes.

Hopefully, by this point you will have started to wonder whether framing effects are always irrational. On the face of it, self-control is a good thing. In fact, it seems more irrational to succumb to temptation and abandon a long-term plan. So, it seems odd to make it irrational to escape temptation by reframing outcomes. This is a case where framing seems to be a tool for rational thought and rational action.

Framing Effect 5: Agamemnon at Aulis

And now for something completely different. The last framing effect I want to present comes from Greek tragedy. As I mentioned earlier, it sits far away from the experimental studies of framing discussed up to now and, although I will come back to it in much more detail in Chapter 6, I want to put it on the table now to introduce some of the complexities and richness of the framing phenomenon.

The chorus in Aeschylus's tragedy *Agamemnon*, the first play in the *Oresteia* trilogy, tells the story (familiar to his audience from many other sources) of the Greek leader Agamemnon at Aulis. Agamemnon is leading the Greek fleet against Troy to avenge the abduction of Helen by Paris. While the fleet is becalmed at Aulis, the prophet Calchas interprets a portent – two eagles swooping down to kill and eat a pregnant hare. As Calchas interprets the portent, it reflects the displeasure of the goddess Artemis at the prospect of innocents being killed at Troy. The lack of wind has the same source. The only solution, says Calchas, is for Agamemnon to sacrifice to the goddess his own daughter Iphigenia.

In a powerful and memorable passage, the chorus recalls Agamemnon's anguished cry:

> And I can still hear the older warlord saying,
> "Obey, obey, or a heavy doom will crush me! –
> Oh but doom *will* crush me
>   once I rend my child,
>   the glory of my house –
>   a father's hands are stained,
> blood of a young girl streaks the altar.
> Pain both ways and what is worse?
> Desert the fleets, fail the alliance?
>   No, but stop the winds with a virgin's
> blood,
>   feed their lust, their fury? – feed their
> fury! –
> Law is law! –
>   Let all go well."[6]

With apologies to Aeschylus (excellently translated by Robert Fagles), Agamemnon might more prosaically be described as in the grip of a framing effect. There is a single option, bringing about the death of Iphigenia, that Agamemnon frames in two different ways – as *Murdering his Daughter*, on the one hand, and as *Following Artemis's Will*, on the other. His alternative is *Failing his Ships and People* (by refusing to make the sacrifice).

Agamemnon's dilemma is that he evaluates the death of Iphigenia differently, depending on how it is framed. He certainly prefers

---

[6] Aeschylus, *Agamemnon*, lines 205–16, translated by Robert Fagles.

Following Artemis's Will to *Failing his Ships and People*. At the same time, though, he prefers *Failing his Ships and People* to *Murdering his Daughter*. But he knows, of course, that *Following Artemis's Will* and *Murdering his Daughter* are the same outcome, differently framed.

By way of a taster for what lies ahead, my view is that the last two examples of framing effects (the battle against temptation and Agamemnon at Aulis) are fundamentally different from the first three. They are more complex both because the decision-situations are more multifaceted and because they engage reasoners' motivations, emotions, and values in deeper ways. It is here that we need to look properly to understand the power of frames; to see how there can be rational framing effects; and to appreciate how these rational framing effects can and should be part of good decision-making.

But it is standardly (almost universally, in fact) believed that it is completely irrational to be susceptible to any kind of framing effect. And one of the reasons that frames and framing are held in such low esteem (from the perspective of rationality) is that people have focused primarily on the first group of framing effects – the ones revealed by experimental psychologists and behavioral economists. And there is a very good reason for this focus. The initial experimental work on framing effects was part of a very significant narrative about human irrationality that emerged in the last decades of the twentieth century. Looking at how that narrative emerged gives useful and important background. We turn to it now.

The Litany of Irrationality

Every once in a while, experiments and ideas emerge from a narrow university context and take on a life of their own. One such complex of experiments and ideas has become a powerful narrative in the popular imagination. This narrative emerged originally from experiments on the psychology of reasoning and decision-making and then was subsequently reinforced from areas as apparently divergent as behavioral finance and cognitive neuroscience.

Researchers from these areas and others have converged on the basic idea that human beings are fundamentally flawed reasoners, regularly contravening the basic principles of rationality. Laboratory experiments seem to show that even highly educated and trained individuals regularly and systematically commit egregious fallacies, flouting fundamental laws of logic and basic principles of probability. Some of the experiments are abstract, but many are not. And expertise seems to be no guarantee of success. Doctors evaluating the probability that patients who test positive for a disease really have that disease seem to fare no better than mathematically sophisticated undergraduates in Ivy League schools doing basic tests of logical competence, or MBA candidates assessing investment strategies.

Some of the leading researchers on human reasoning have made drastic claims (in a typically understated academic style). Richard Nisbett, in one of the earliest salvoes in what became known as the rationality wars, said that his and other psychological experiments had "bleak implications for human rationality."[7] The cognitive psychologists Daniel Kahneman (joint winner of the 2002 Nobel Prize in economics) and Amos Tversky summed up their early work on statistical reasoning by saying "for anyone who would wish to view man as a reasonable intuitive statistician, such results are discouraging."[8] Others have been more breathless. The title of journalist David McRaney's best-selling book *You Are Not So Smart* speaks for itself. Likewise, *Predictably Irrational: The Hidden Forces That Shape Our Decisions*, written by the cognitive psychologist and behavioral economist Daniel Ariely.[9]

This is not just an "academic question." According to the dominant narrative, poor reasoning and irrational decision-making are particularly acute when it comes to finance and investing. Behavioral economics and behavioral finance are, in essence, academic disciplines founded on the premise that market participants are fundamentally irrational when it comes to spending and investing. This basic premise has become well-established among finance professionals and others who make their living in and around financial markets. The websites of major investment companies such as Vanguard offer introductions to behavioral finance for retail investors and investment professionals.[10] The personal finance sections of bookstores and websites are packed with books that offer to help save investors from themselves. A great example (and a very well-written

---

[7] Nisbett and Borgida 1975.   [8] Kahneman and Tversky 1972.

[9] McRaney 2011 and Ariely 2008.

[10] The Vanguard site for financial advisors, for example, contains video tutorials on how investors make decisions and how financial advisors can incorporate "behavioral coaching" into their practice. See the Advisor's Alpha section of the Vanguard advisors' website at https://advisors.vanguard.com/VGApp/iip/site/advisor/researchcommentary?page=A dvisorAlpha (accessed 3/28/16).

and thought-provoking book) is *The Little Book of Behavioral Investing: How Not To Be Your Own Worst Enemy* by James Montier.[11]

This is what I call the *litany of human irrationality*.[12] The dominant narrative that human reasoning is fundamentally flawed is built on a frequently recited and repeated invocation of experiments and studies. But these experiments and studies are narrowly focused and much more equivocal than generally thought. They have also been over-interpreted. If the case for human irrationality were really as powerful as it has been taken to be, then it would be a miracle that we ever managed to develop financial and economic systems sophisticated enough to allow investors to go astray as spectacularly as they are supposed to do. So I, like quite a few others, think that this is an area where a degree of skepticism is badly needed.[13]

In any event, while many participants in the "rationality wars" have taken aim at different aspects of the litany of human irrationality, one central part of the litany has been left completely untouched. This is the role of frames and framing in human reasoning, as illustrated in our five examples. We tend to value things as a function of how we frame them. The way in which we look at the world influences how we evaluate our different options and the outcomes that they might bring about. In many cases shifting frames leads us to change how we evaluate things. And this is what leads to framing effects. In a typical framing effect we find ourselves valuing the same thing differently depending upon how we frame it. From the perspective of the psychology of reasoning and behavioral finance (and just about everybody else) susceptibility to framing effects is Exhibit A in the narrative of human irrationality. And even the

---

[11] Montier 2010.

[12] I owe a terminological debt to Björn Lomberg, who writes about the environmentalist litany in his book *The Skeptical Environmentalist* (Lomberg 2001).

[13] Early push-back against the litany came from the philosophers Elliot Sober 1978 and L. Jonathan Cohen 1981, each of whom objected to the basic idea that there could be an experimental demonstration of human irrationality (for example, by arguing that the basic idea of irrationality only makes sense against the background of shared rationality). For further broadsides and commentary from a philosophical perspective see Stich 1990 and Stein 1996 respectively. Objections to the litany have also come from an evolutionary perspective, with authors such as Gigerenzer 1991 arguing that performance on probability tests drastically improves when the tests are presented in terms of frequencies rather than probabilities, which reflects how our brains evolved to deal with probabilistic information. A related objection to the litany comes from the rational analysis approach first developed by the psychologist John Anderson 1990, which starts from the basic premise that the mind is well adapted to its environment. Oaksford and Chater 2007 use rational analysis to explain (away) many of the key data points from the litany.

most dedicated opponents of the litany of irrationality have nothing positive to say about framing effects.

The basic message of this book, however, is that this way of thinking about frames and framing effects is fundamentally mistaken. Framing is completely unavoidable and, while framing effects can sometimes be irrational, they often are not. In fact, framing can be a powerful tool for rational decision-making and problem-solving. Using frames is one of the best tools we have for rational self-control, and it is also key to social cooperation and collaboration.

What Are Frames?

This book is about frames and framing. However, there is no chapter entitled "What are frames?" This is deliberate. The concept of framing is used in many different contexts and in many different disciplines. I am sure that there is no single way of thinking what a frame is that all those who work with the concept would agree upon. The concept of a frame is itself something that can be framed in many different ways, one might say. Trying to give a watertight definition is surely a fool's errand.

So, for example, we certainly find the concept of a frame in experimental psychology and behavioral economics, as we'll see in more detail in Chapters 2 and 3. But what psychologists and economists think of as a frame is rather different from the type of framing envisaged by, for example, the cognitive linguist George Lakoff in his best-selling book *Don't Think of an Elephant: Know Your Values and Frame the Debate*.[14] Economists and experimental psychologists often study how people are influenced by positive versus negative ways of characterizing outcomes. Will you react differently to something that is presented as a direct loss that you might incur (a drop in your wealth from $1,500 to $1,000, for example), as opposed to a gain that you forgo (say, a lost opportunity to increase your wealth from $1,000 to $1,500)? Lakoff, in contrast, is interested in the cognitive metaphors that structure how we think and speak about thorny moral and political issues. His interest is much more in political messaging. In a classic behavioral economics experiment there is a neutral outcome (a level of wealth, for example) that can be characterized in different ways. Not so much for the kind of framing metaphors that Lakoff is interested in. As we will see in the concluding chapters, when issues get sufficiently complicated, there are

[14] Lakoff 2004.

no neutrally characterizable outcomes. Every description of, say, abortion embodies a particular frame and narrative. Even trying to describe abortion in the way it might be described in a medical textbook will be viewed as embodying a particular stance, which illustrates what I will call the illusion of frame-neutrality.

Many sociologists, political scientists, and communication theorists look at how frames work in communicative contexts – similar in focus to cognitive linguists such as Lakoff, but different in emphasis. They think that linguistic frames are not just metaphors. They function also as mechanisms to perpetuate stereotypes and reinforce power structures, so many social scientists think. The analysis of how news is framed is a key part of media studies and media analysis, itself carried out in different ways by different groups within academia. The issue here is not just how a particular news story is presented (the "slant" that one newspaper or TV station might give to the story), but also how items are selected as newsworthy in the first place.

To add to the confusion, frames are often discussed without being labeled as such. I think of the great German logician and mathematician Gottlob Frege as a pioneer of the idea that how we frame the world determines how we think about it and act within it. One of Frege's great insights was the notion of sense (*Sinn* in German), which he also called *mode of presentation* (*Art des Gegebenseins* in German, literally meaning *way of being given*). Here are two typically Fregean examples. It makes a difference whether you think about the number 2 as the smallest prime number or as the square root of 4. It makes a difference whether you think about the planet Venus as the Morning Star or as the Evening Star. Thinkers can take different cognitive perspectives on a single object and those cognitive perspectives can lead them to reason and to act in very different ways. As I bring out in Chapter 5, Frege's ideas are very important in articulating a framework for thinking about the rationality of framing.

In short, frames are discussed and deployed very differently in psychology, economics, linguistics, sociology, political science, and philosophy. Even a simple catalog of all the different ways that people talk about and appeal to the framing concept would be a book-length study – and one that, as far as I know, nobody has undertaken. It would be futile to try to give a definition that will capture all and only the ways of thinking about frames that would feature in the as yet unwritten *Book of Frames*. But nor, on the other hand, is it just a linguistic accident that the word "frame" keeps coming up in broadly similar contexts.

Ludwig Wittgenstein, who was an inveterate opponent of philosophers' attempts to provide necessary and sufficient conditions for key concepts, introduced the idea that certain key concepts might function by family resemblance, rather than having a core meaning that can be stated in a definition. His favorite example was the concept *game*. There is no single feature shared by everything that would be correctly classified as a game, but any game is similar in some key respect to some other games. The unity of the concept *game* is secured by a complex pattern of similarities holding within and across sub-groups of games (multi-player games, solitary games, competitive games, word games, and so on).

I am sure that Wittgenstein is right about games, but not so sure that what he says applies to the concept *frame*. A better model comes, I think, from the fourth century BC philosopher Aristotle, who single-handedly pioneered the systematic study of language and reasoning (among many other things). Aristotle distinguished two categories of words – *synonyms* and *homonyms*. Two words or expressions are synonyms when they have the same meaning, while a word is a homonym if it has multiple unrelated meanings. So, to take examples that have stood the test of time, "bachelor" and "unmarried man" are synonyms, while the word "bank" is a homonym (referring either to a financial institution or to the side of a river, depending upon context). If we think about the multiple ways that people talk about frames, I think it's clear that we are not dealing with a case of synonymy. The expression "mode of presentation," as used by Frege, does not have the same meaning as the word "frame," used by Amos Tversky, for example. But nor is the word "frame" functioning as a homonym when it is used by sociologists as opposed to behavioral economists.

Fortunately, Aristotle can help. He suggested that there is a special category of homonyms. These are homonyms where the multiple meanings share a common core, or what is sometimes called a focal meaning.[15] There is a common semantic thread, as it were, that runs through the different meanings. This common semantic thread relates them, without collapsing them into one. On Aristotle's picture, this type of word or concept is unified by more than family resemblances, without having a single meaning that might be captured by a simple definition. I think

---

[15] The expression *focal meaning* is due to Owen 1960, which is an important paper on Aristotle's theory of meaning. Other Aristotle scholars have acknowledged Owen's insight, but proposed different terminology. See Shields 1999, for example, who prefers to talk about core-dependent homonyms.

that *frame* and *framing* function in this way. They are used in fundamentally different, non-synonymous ways, but at the heart of those there is a single core.

The best expression of this core that I have encountered comes from an important book published in 1974 by the sociologist Erving Goffman. In *Frame Analysis*, Goffman explores the basic idea that individuals and groups use frames as ways of organizing their experience. He works with a very general definition. For him, frames function as "schemata of interpretation" that allow individuals "to locate, perceive, identify, and label."[16] Each of the ways of thinking about frames discussed above (and all of those that we will be looking at in this book) have this basic characterization at their core – as their focal meaning, in the Aristotelian sense. They can each be viewed as taking this core idea of a schema of interpretation that allows individuals to locate, perceive, identify, and label – and then developing and expanding it in divergent (and often incompatible) ways. Different things can count as schemata of interpretation. They can have different sources. And they can function very differently.

The topic of this book is the rationality of frames. Now that we have said something about frames, it is time to turn to rationality.

Background: How We Reason vs. How We Ought to Reason

Continuing with Aristotle, he is often quoted as having said that "man is a rational animal." In fact, it's not clear that the phrase "rational animal" actually originated with Aristotle, as opposed to later Stoic philosophers and Aristotle's own commentators and interpreters in the Middle Ages. But no matter – it's a useful phrase and a good place to start.

The first thing to say is that talking about rational animals is fundamentally ambiguous. In one sense, when we talk about rationality we are talking about a process – the process of reasoning. In this sense, rational animals are distinctive because they solve problems by reasoning; because they can think about abstract concepts such as justice and truth; and because they are capable of reflecting on themselves and their place in the world. This is a descriptive conception of rationality – rationality as a process. In the descriptive sense, when we say that human beings are rational animals we mean that human beings are distinctive because they engage in certain types of reasoning.

---

[16] Goffman 1974, p. 21.

In another sense, when we talk about rationality we are talking about an aspiration, an ideal. Rational animals are distinctive in this sense because they understand that thinking and reasoning are subject to standards. Rational thinkers know that they are bound by the laws of logic and other basic principles of sound reasoning, such as the probability calculus. What makes them rational thinkers is that they aspire to abide by those laws and principles. This is a normative conception of rationality. From a normative perspective to say that human beings are rational animals is to say that they are distinctive because they understand (at some level) that reasoning is governed by ideal standards, and they strive to respect those ideal standards.

If we are looking, as the medieval Aristotelians were, for what is distinctive of human beings, then we need to focus on rationality in the normative sense of striving to follow standards rather than the process-driven, descriptive sense. Researchers in comparative psychology and cognitive ethology have identified many types of non-human animal behavior that seem best understood as resulting from mental processes of reasoning. It seems clear that non-human animals are not automata responding blindly and rigidly to external stimuli, although it is not easy to understand the type of reasoning that non-human animals are engaged in.[17] To the best of my knowledge, though, there is no experimental or field evidence that animals besides language-using humans are rational in the second, normative sense.

In any event, in the human case there is clearly a constant tug-of-war between rationality as process and rationality as ideal. It is not news that we all often reason in ways that fail to respect ideal standards. According to the litany, these are not just occasional misses. The litany is supposed to show that the ideal standards are regularly and spectacularly contravened, so that the normative principles of rationality are more honored in the breach than in the observance. In effect, what the litany says is that the overwhelming evidence from everyday life and scientific studies is that human beings are *ir*rational animals.

The litany is typically embedded in a much richer narrative. According to one version of this richer narrative there are distinctive patterns in our widespread departures from ideal rationality. Manifest irrationality has, as it were, its own rationale. This is where experimental psychology and

---

[17] I have tried to clarify some of the issues in Chapters 6 and 7 of my book *Thinking Without Words* (Bermúdez 2003a). See also the essays in the aptly named collection *Rational Animals?* (Hurley and Nudds 2006).

behavioral finance are reinforced by other disciplines. According to influential evolutionary psychologists our departures from the canons of normative rationality have a solid evolutionary explanation. Irrationality is not a random phenomenon. Instead it occurs because what we are actually doing when we reason is applying cognitive short-cuts and rules of thumb that actually helped our ancestors to survive in the physical and social environments they had to deal with. Those cognitive short-cuts and rules of thumb (often called *fast and frugal heuristics*) sometimes yield the same results as classical normative theories of rationality, but more often they diverge.[18]

So-called dual-process (or dual-system) theories offer a second way of interpreting the litany.[19] The key idea here is that problem-solving can engage either of two separate and distinct reasoning systems. Different authors draw the distinction between the two systems in slightly different ways, but the basic contrast is between a fast and intuitive System 1 and a slow and deliberate System 2. Table 1.1 gives some of the characteristics

Table 1.1 *System 1 and System 2 reasoning compared*

System 1	System 2
Fast	Slow
Intuitive	Analytic
Automatic	Controlled
Concrete	Abstract
Implicit	Explicit
Pattern recognition and mental short-cuts	Rules-based
Shared with animals	Uniquely human
Reflects specialized knowledge-bases	Linked to general intelligence
Evolutionarily old	Evolutionarily recent

[18] A classic example is the work of the evolutionary psychologists Leda Cosmides and John Tooby. See, for example, Cosmides 1989 and Cosmides and Tooby 1992. For an introduction see §8.3 of *Cognitive Science: An Introduction to the Science of the Mind* (Bermúdez 2020). For more on fast and frugal heuristics see Gigerenzer, Todd, and Group 1999, Gigerenzer and Selten 2001, and Gigerenzer and Gaissmaier 2011.

[19] For influential presentations see for example Stanovich and West 2000 and Kahneman 2011. Evans 2008 defends dual-process theory against some of the most prominent objections.

typically taken to distinguish the two systems and the types of reasoning that each employ.

Both System 1 and System 2 can be mistaken, of course. But, as Table 1.1 shows, only System 2 is supposed to be explicitly guided by normative ideals of rationality. Our characteristic departures from ideal rationality typically occur when System 1 is engaged.

Plainly, therefore, the litany of human irrationality only makes sense against a background of normative theories of ideal reasoning. Such normative theories are developed in many different places. The most prominent are formal logic, statistics, decision theory, and game theory.

Logicians study forms of deductive argument, distinguishing those that are valid from those that are invalid. Logically correct reasoning deploys argument forms that preserve truth – where it is impossible for the premises of the argument to be true and the conclusion false. The laws of logic are intended to be completely general, holding whatever the subject matter.[20]

Statisticians focus on cases where conclusions are supported by evidence but not entailed by that evidence. They look at different ways in which hypotheses are supported by evidence, and how strong a conclusion it is legitimate to draw from limited evidence. Issues here include how probability is to be understood and estimated, as well as how rational thinkers should update their beliefs when new evidence comes in.[21]

Decision theorists explore how rational thinkers ought to choose when confronted with a range of possible actions. Decision-making can take place in many different conditions. Sometimes the outcomes of each possible action are known with certainty. Sometimes decision-makers know only the probabilities of each potential outcome. And sometimes not even the probabilities are known. Different canons of rational choice apply in each case.[22]

Game theorists look at the problems and challenges emerging from situations involving collective action – interactions where there are multiple participants and the outcomes are fixed by the actions of all participants. These situations typically cannot be modeled just by decision theory, because the different outcomes depend not just on what each chooser does and how the world turns out, but crucially on how other participants behave and their expectations about other players.[23]

---

[20] For informal introductions to the issues logicians grapple with, see Read 1995 and Priest 2000.

[21] Statistics is not an area that lends itself to informal introductions, but a good place to start is with the volumes on Statistics and Probability in Oxford University Press's useful Very Short Introductions series – Hand 2008 and Haigh 2012 respectively.

[22] For a short overview see Chapter 1 of Bermúdez 2009. For more detail see Resnik 1987, Binmore 2009a, or Peterson 2009 (which also contains material on game theory).

[23] Binmore 2007 is a good place to start. For a more technical and shorter overview see Leyton-Brown and Shoham 2008, which is an abridged version of Shoham and Leyton-Brown 2008.

This book will engage with all of these areas. On the negative side we will look at how framing is supposed to be fundamentally illogical, driving thinkers to make irrational decisions and to weigh evidence incorrectly. As already hinted, these charges need much closer scrutiny. On the positive side we will look at some of the ways that framing can help tackle problems left unsolved by classical normative theories such as decision theory and game theory. So, for example, classical decision theory cannot explain the rationality of self-control. Nor can classical game theory explain why rational agents often choose to cooperate and collaborate in certain basic types of social interaction. We'll see that bringing frames into the picture yields important insights into how agents actually resist temptation and how they end up cooperating with each other.

But showing that framing effects are useful falls a long way short of showing that they can be *normatively* rational – as opposed to descriptively rational. The controversial claim that I want to make is that being sensitive to how things are framed *can* be perfectly rational *in the normative sense*. I emphasize the word "can" for a reason. According to both proponents and opponents of the litany, framing effects are both widespread and invariably irrational. It would be absurd to respond to this by saying that it is *always* rational to be susceptible to framing effects. What we will be exploring in this book is that there are *some* cases where it is perfectly rational to be sensitive to frames – and indeed, where it might even be irrational *not* to be sensitive to frames. What makes this interesting is that these are very important cases – both practically and theoretically.

Here's the plan for the book. As I said earlier, one reason why frames and framing are typically looked down upon (from the perspective of rationality) is that people have focused primarily on the first group of framing effects that we looked at right at the beginning of this chapter – the framing effects revealed by experimental psychologists and behavioral economists. We will start out by looking at these.

First, the case for the prosecution. Chapter 2, "Framing: The Classic Experiments," reviews some of the most influential experiments that have driven discussions of framing and primed the litany of irrationality. Chapter 3, "Where the Rubber Hits the Road: Investors, Frames, and Markets," extends the discussion to investing behavior and the financial markets, looking at classic examples of the kind of irrational framing that investment advisors warn against (while at the same time often succumbing to it). And then in Chapter 4, "Juliet's Principle," I summarize the case for the irrationality of framing, based on the fundamental claim that it is irrational to allow oneself to evaluate differently two or more different ways of framing the same outcome, when one knows that that is what they are ("a rose by any other name would smell as sweet," in other words).

With that review in place, the remainder of the book will be spent exploring cases like Agamemnon at Aulis and the self-control example, starting in Chapters 5 and 6. In Chapter 5, "Rational Frames?," I introduce and discuss in more detail a range of framing effects of the type that I offer as candidates for rational framing effects. Then in Chapter 6, "Agamemnon and Climate Change," I develop a framework for how those framing effects work and why they can be rational. These two chapters are the theoretical heart of the case for the defense.

With that theoretical framework in place, I turn to more detailed examples and applications. Chapter 7 ("Framing Temptation and Reward: The Challenges of Self-Control") will take us back to self-control. In Chapters 8 ("Chickens and Chariot Races: Framing in Game Theory") and 9 ("Fair's Fair: Framing for Cooperation and Fairness") we will look at game theory and how frames can work there. We will focus particularly on how games can be framed from the perspective of the individual (the "I"-frame) or from the perspective of the group (the "we"-frame), and how this framing can affect what counts as a rational solution to the game. And then in Chapters 10 and 11 we look at what happens in the sort of discursive deadlock that occurs both privately in personal dilemmas and publicly in debates about controversial topics such as, say, abortion, gun control, and immigration. In Chapter 10 ("Getting Past No: Discursive Deadlock and the Power of Frames") I diagnose discursive deadlock as rooted in clashes of frames. And then in Chapter 11 ("Opening the Door to Non-Archimedean Reasoning") I show how a rational, frame-sensitive reasoner can tackle both public and private discursive deadlock.

2

Framing: The Classic Experiments

What I call the litany of human irrationality is a catalog of examples of widespread breakdowns in human reasoning. The litany reflects literally decades' worth of experiments and research into human reasoning. Framing effects are one of its chief exhibits. Any discussion of framing and decision-making needs to start by looking very carefully at the experimental literature and how it has been interpreted.

The experiments show that outcomes and scenarios can be framed in different ways and that these different frames affect how people evaluate and react to those outcomes and scenarios. Some of these framing effects exploit tight connections between framing and how risk is evaluated and perceived. It turns out that people tend to be much happier to take risks when they are faced with possible losses, and more resistant to risk when faced with possible gains. And in fact, as the experiments show, people will react differently to the same outcome when it is framed in terms of a possible loss as opposed to a possible gain. This is the aspect of framing that has made it such an influential concept for behavioral economics and behavioral finance, because of its potential significance for individual investor decisions and large-scale market behavior (the subject of Chapter 3).

Who Lives and Who Dies: The Asian Disease Paradigm

The best place to start is probably the single most famous experiment in the literature on framing – the Asian disease paradigm developed by the extraordinarily influential cognitive psychologists Amos Tversky and Daniel Kahneman (who subsequently, and after the death of Tversky, won a Nobel Prize for his contributions to psychology and economics). Like many influential experiments it is beautifully simple – and seems very clear cut (deceptively so!).

Tversky and Kahneman worked with two large groups of subjects, each containing around 150 students at Stanford and at the University of British Columbia.[1] The first group was presented with the following problem:

Imagine that the United States is preparing for the outbreak of an unusual Asian disease, which is expected to kill 600 people. Two alternative programs to combat the disease have been proposed. Assume that the exact scientific estimates of the consequences of the programs are as follows:

- *If program A is adopted then **200 people will be saved***
- *If program B is adopted then there is 1/3 probability that 600 people will be saved and 2/3 probability that **no people will be saved***

Which of the two programs would you favor?

The overwhelming majority of subjects preferred program A over program B – 72 percent as opposed to 28 percent

The second group of subjects was presented with a subtly reformulated version of the same problem. The basic cover story was word-for-word identical, but the scientific estimates of the consequences were now phrased in terms of lives lost rather than lives saved.

Imagine that the United States is preparing for the outbreak of an unusual Asian disease, which is expected to kill 600 people. Two alternative programs to combat the disease have been proposed. Assume that the exact scientific estimates of the consequences of the programs are as follows:

- *If program C is adopted then **400 people will die***
- *If program D is adopted then there is 1/3 probability that nobody will die and 2/3 probability **600 people will die***

Which of the two programs would you favor?

The second group also saw a significant majority favoring one program. But they went in the opposite direction to the first group: 78 percent of the subjects in group 2 favored program D while only 22 percent favored program C.

Most people confronted with the Asian disease results and similar experiments have the same reaction. The problem, though, is that the

---

[1] See Tversky and Kahneman 1981 for the original presentation.

consequences of program A are exactly the same as the consequences of program C. Likewise for program B and program D. If there are 600 people and 200 survive then that's exactly the same as 400 of the 600 dying. And if, as in program B, there is a 1/3 chance that everybody survives and a 2/3 chance that nobody survives, then that's exactly the same as program D, where there is a 1/3 chance that nobody dies and a 2/3 chance that everybody dies. And it is not just that they just happen to be the same outcome. It is a matter of logic that they are the same. If you start with 600 people and only 200 survive, then 400 die, and vice versa.

So, the experiment seems to provide a very clear-cut example of a framing effect. The two groups react very differently, although they are each presented with a choice between the same two outcomes. There is no difference between the problems besides how they are framed. The first problem is phrased in terms of survival. It uses the survival frame. The second is phrased in terms of death. It uses the mortality frame. This is widely held to be the canonical example of a framing effect.

Tversky and Kahneman used what psychologists call a between-subjects design. That means that there were different people in the two groups, so that no single subject was actually presented with the two different frames (as they would be in a *within-subjects design*). And so, no subjects found themselves in the awkward position of simultaneously preferring program A (= C) to program B (= D) and preferring program D (= B) to program C (= A). But the between-subjects effect is sufficiently striking and strong to suggest that a typical person would most likely respond differently to the problem depending upon how it is framed. Moreover, the Asian disease framing effect has been replicated in a within-subjects design.[2]

So, the Asian disease paradigm reveals an obvious and striking framing effect. But there is even more going on, as emerges as soon as one asks what possible explanation there could be for evaluating the two frames differently. Even if you think (as most people do – but wait until Chapter 5 to hear from a minority of dissidents) that there cannot be any *rational* grounds for preferring one frame to another, there still has to be some kind of explanation. It seems unlikely that the experimental subjects are being totally arbitrary, after all. The most obvious factor is the way the two problems are structured as choices between a certain outcome (200 surviving/400 dying) and a risky outcome (a 1/3 probability of 600 surviving/0 dying and a 2/3 probability of 0 surviving/600 dying).

[2] See Kühberger 1995, for example.

The fact that each choice involves weighing a risky outcome against a certain outcome brings in a whole new set of issues to do with individual attitudes to risk. As Tversky and Kahneman interpreted their own results, subjects respond differently in the two different frames because each frame primes a different attitude to risk. In the survival frame subjects are risk-averse. That means that they opt for the certain outcome over the risky one. In contrast, when the problem is framed in terms of mortality, subjects are risk-seeking. They prefer to take a chance rather than live with the certain outcome. Tversky and Kahneman have an interesting explanation of why the two frames prime different attitudes to risk. And it turns out that their account is much more broadly applicable. In fact, their analysis of how we view risk differently depending on whether we are looking at losses or gains turns out to be a cornerstone of behavioral finance.

More on frames, risk, losses, and gains later. First, though, we need to take a look at some other examples of experimentally induced framing effects to confirm that we find substantial framing effects even when risk is taken out of the picture.

Lean Meat and Success Rates

Psychologists studying framing effects have identified many cases of what they term *valence-consistent shifts*. The valence of a frame is whether it is presented in a positive light or a negative light. A valence-consistent shift is a framing effect that is driven purely by the valence of the frame. Valence is certainly a factor in the Asian disease paradigm. It is positively valenced to talk about people being saved and negatively valenced to talk about people dying. But it is not easy to disentangle the role of valence in the overall framing effect because of the complexities introduced by the choice between a risky outcome and a certain outcome. Fortunately there are many experiments showing what seem to be purely valence-driven framing effects.

We looked briefly at one example in the Introduction. Framing Effect 1 illustrated how people evaluate basketball players differently depending on how their performance is reported. If players' levels of accuracy are reported with a positive valence (in terms of the percentage of shots that were successful) then they tend to be ranked more highly than when the accuracy levels are reported with a negative valence (in terms of the percentage of shots that were unsuccessful).

Here is another example that may strike a chord with meat-eaters and supermarket shoppers! Irwin Levin and Gary Gaeth looked at how labeling affects consumer evaluations of ground beef (minced beef, for British readers). Their subjects were asked to rate ground beef on a number of dimensions – greasy vs. non-greasy; bad-tasting vs. good-tasting; low-quality vs. high-quality; lean vs. fat. In an earlier study Levin had looked just at evaluations based on verbal descriptions and shown a significant framing effect when subjects were asked to evaluate hypothetical purchases of ground beef on the same dimensions. In that study subjects rated beef that was labeled as 25 percent lean significantly higher than beef labeled as 75 percent fat. In fact, they consistently thought that 25 percent lean beef was leaner than 75 percent fat beef!

Levin and Gaeth's innovation was to compare framing effects when subjects simply had a verbal description and when they actually tasted the beef.[3] They used exactly the same dimensions of evaluation as the earlier experiment and also employed a between-subjects design. So in each condition (the verbal description condition and the tasting condition) there were two groups of subjects. One group was given the positively valenced frame (25 percent lean), and the other the negatively valenced frame (75 percent fat). What was really striking was that they found a framing effect in each condition. It is true that the effect was less powerful in the tasting condition, but even when the subjects had a chance to taste the beef there was still a significant effect: Subjects liked the taste of beef that was labeled as 25 percent lean better than identical beef labeled as 75 percent fat. And it made no difference whether the beef was tasted before or after the subjects were given the valenced frame.

There are other very clear-cut examples of valence-driven framing effects. Describing outcomes in terms of success rates rather than failure rates is a great way of changing how subjects evaluate things. This has been shown in a wide range of areas from job placement programs to condom use.[4] Here is a nice example from a well-known study by Dennis Duchon, Kenneth Dunegan, and Sidney Barton.[5] In another between-subjects design a group of over 100 engineers and scientists from a large engineering firm were randomly assigned to one of two groups. Subjects in each group were presented with the following vignette.

[3] See Levin and Gaeth 1988. The earlier study, which looked just at evaluations based on verbal descriptions is reported in Levin 1987.
[4] For job placement programs see Davis and Bobko 1986. Condom use was studied in Linville, Fischer, and Fischoff 1993.
[5] Duchon, Dunegan, and Barton 1989.

> *As R&D manager one of your project teams has come to you requesting an additional $100,000 in funds for a project that **you** instituted several months ago. The project is already behind schedule and over budget, but the team still believes it can be successfully completed. You currently have $500,000 remaining in your budget unallocated, but which must carry you for the rest of the fiscal year. Lowering the balance by $100,000 might jeopardize flexibility to respond to other opportunities.*

The vignette ended differently for the two groups. Both groups were given the information that the ratio of successes to failures was 60:40 (i.e. 60 percent of previous projects had succeeded while 40 percent had failed). But for one group the information was given in a positively valenced frame (with the team described as having a 60 percent success rate). The other group had a negatively valenced frame. They were told that the team had a 40 percent failure rate. Both groups were asked to assess the likelihood that they would fund the request on a Likert scale from 1 (Reject) to 5 (Fund) with 3 being Uncertain.

The valence-driven framing effect was significant. In the positive frame the average response was 3.97, compared to only 3.50 in the negative frame. On the Likert scale that is the difference between Lean to Fund (4) and Uncertain (3.5). Two other interesting features of the experiment have been less frequently discussed. First, the framing effect extended to participants' risk assessment. Subjects in both groups were asked to assess how risky they thought it would be to fund the request, also on a 1 to 5 Likert scale. The average response in the positively valenced frame was 3.01, contrasted with 3.34 in the negative frame. So, subjects thought that it was riskier to fund a team with a 60 percent success rate than one with a 40 percent failure rate.

Second, the experimenters also asked subjects to rate themselves according to their style of decision-making, on a 7-point Likert scale with Intuitive at one end and Rational on the other. There was no statistically significant relation between reported degree of rationality and susceptibility to framing effects. Engineers who think of themselves as hard-nosed rational decision-makers seem no less likely to be influenced by how the problem is framed than the ones who think of themselves as intuitive decision-makers (and yes, there were some of these – responses ranged from 1 to 7!).

Framing Effect 2 from Chapter 1 showed that the gain/loss framing effect has ramifications not just for the explicit judgments that people make but also for how they interact with each other. Recall that students studying Business Administration at the University of Texas were asked to simulate a negotiation with union representatives on behalf of a fictional company. Once again all the relevant information (about the respective starting positions of management and union, as well as the costs to the company) was presented in two frames. In one frame (the loss frame) the students were told how much everything would cost the company, while in the other (the gain frame) they were told how much the company would save. The end result of the experiment was that students in the gain frame behaved differently from students in the loss frame. Students in the gain frame were much more likely to negotiate a settlement than they were to opt for binding arbitration. The new twist in Framing Effect 2 is that it brings risk back into the picture. Negotiating a settlement is the "safe" option, as opposed to the risky option of opting for arbitration (who knows what those arbitrators might come up with?). The next section will give more insight into what is going on here.

Risky Choices, Losses, and Gains

With these nice examples of valence-driven framing clearly in view it's time to go back to the Asian disease paradigm. We already have a good sense of what it tells us about how people value outcomes framed as losses versus outcomes framed as gains. Now it's time to look at how those valuations are affected by the presence or absence of risk. This is where things start to get really interesting!

As with lean versus fat and success rates versus failure rates, the two frames in the Asian disease paradigm are differently valenced. In general, talking about saving lives is positively valenced, while talking about deaths is negatively valenced. But there's an extra twist. If you think about it as a difference between lives lost and lives saved then you see that this is really a special type of valence. The positive valence comes from framing the outcome as a gain (lives saved), while the negative valence comes from framing the outcome as a loss (lives lost).

Now, recall the basic choice that the subjects were given in each of the two frames. They were asked whether they would choose a program with a known outcome or a program that could have two different outcomes, where the probability of each outcome is given. So really the subjects have two different prospects. If they choose program A (in condition 1) or program C (in condition 2) then they are choosing a certain prospect – that is, their choice has a known outcome. But if they choose program B (in condition 1) or program D (in condition 2) then they are choosing a risky prospect. Decision theorists often think of risky prospects as lotteries. Take program B, for example. If program B is implemented then there is a 1/3 probability that 600 people will be saved and a 2/3 probability that nobody will be saved. Another way of describing this would be to say that choosing to implement program B is basically choosing one of the tickets in a three-ticket lottery. The lottery is very simple. One of the tickets corresponds to 600 people being saved, while two correspond to nobody being saved. The person choosing obviously doesn't know which ticket is which.

So, in the Asian disease paradigm each group of subjects was asked to choose between a certain prospect and a risky prospect. The certain prospect and the risky prospect are equivalent in a very important sense. To put it in the language of decision theory and economics, the two prospects had the same *expected value*. This is one of the most fundamental concepts in formal theories of rationality, so it is worth spending time getting clear on it.

Expected value is a very basic way of comparing certain prospects and risky prospects. To get an intuitive feel for the idea imagine that you are lucky enough to play the following game multiple times. A benevolent stranger tosses a coin. If it lands heads then she will give you $10, while if it lands tails then she gives you nothing. If you play sufficiently many times then (assuming that the coin is fair) you will win approximately half of the tosses and lose approximately half of them. Differently put, as you continue playing the game the proportion of your wins and your losses will eventually become equal. More precisely, as you continue playing the game the proportion of your wins will converge on 50 percent. You will win half the time and lose half the time. So, averaging it all out over time, your average win on each coin toss is $5 (although of course, there are no individual coin tosses that pay out $5). So, in an intuitive sense, the value of each coin toss is $5.

Now look at it another way. Each coin toss is a (risky) prospect with two possible outcomes – either you win $10 or you win $0. Assuming that the coin is fair those two outcomes are equally likely. So it seems reasonable to think that the value of the coin toss is the average of the two outcomes. Once again we get $5. This is the expected value of the coin toss. It doesn't matter whether you toss the coin once or a thousand times. Each coin toss has the same expected value, namely, $5.

So, how does this let us compare certain prospects and risky prospects? Well, it's not hard to work out the expected value of being given $5 for sure. The expected value is $5. That means that the expected value of the risky prospect of a coin toss that pays out $10 on heads and $0 on tails is the same as the expected value of the certain prospect of being given $5 for sure.

We've looked at a very basic risky prospect – a coin toss with two equally likely outcomes. We got the expected value by averaging out the values of the individual outcomes (adding them and then dividing by two). Obviously we can follow the same strategy for more than two outcomes, provided that the outcomes are equally likely. But what if (as in the Asian disease case) the outcomes are not equally likely? We just need to make a small adjustment. We can't average out the values of the individual outcomes. But we can still add them up, *provided that we take the probability of each outcome into account*. So consider the prospect offered by program B. There are two outcomes – 600 lives saved and 0 lives saved – with probabilities 1/3 and 2/3 respectively. Discounting by the probabilities we get 600 × 1/3 = 200 and 0 × 2/3 = 0. Adding them gives 200. So the expected value of this prospect is 200 lives saved. This is the same as the expected value of the prospect offered by program A. So, program A and program B have the same expected value.

"OK, that's all very well," I hear you say – "but I'd much rather have $5 than an even chance of $10 or $0. And I'm definitely more comfortable with a program that saves 200 lives for sure than with one that has a 1/3 chance of saving 600 and a 2/3 chance of saving nobody. So as far as I'm concerned it's irrelevant that program A and program B have the same expected value, or that $5 for sure has the same expected value as an even chance of $10 or $0." A lot of people would share your view. Technically you (and they) are *risk-averse*. It is intuitively obvious what risk-aversion is, but it will be helpful for the following to have a technical definition.

We can define what it is to be risk-averse (and, by extension, what it is to be risk-neutral or risk-seeking) through the concept of a *certainty equivalent*. This is a concept that applies to risky prospects. Sticking for the moment to prospects with purely monetary outcomes, the certainty equivalent of a risky prospect is a sum of money such that you are indifferent between the prospect of getting that sum of money for sure and the risky prospect. One way to see what is going on here is to go back to the idea that a risky prospect is a lottery. What's the maximum that you would pay for a ticket to that lottery? That's your certainty equivalent for the risky prospect. So, if you'd be happy to pay up to $3 for a chance to buy a ticket to the two-ticket lottery where one ticket wins $0 and the other ticket wins $10, then $3 is your certainty equivalent for the risky prospect.

Now we have an easy way to understand different attitudes to risky prospects. To see what your attitude to risk is we compare your certainty equivalent for a risky prospect with the expected value of that prospect. There are three possibilities. Either your certainty equivalent for the risky prospect is the same as its expected value. Or it is lower. Or it is higher. Let's look at these in turn.

Risk-neutral
Suppose that your certainty equivalent for the risky prospect is exactly the same as the prospect's expected value. All you care about is the expected value – $5 or 200 lives saved. It doesn't matter how you get there. The fact that one prospect is risky and the other is not risky is not important to you. So you are risk-neutral. You neither avoid risk, nor pursue it. All you care about is expected value.

Risk-averse
Suppose now that your certainty equivalent is lower than the risky prospect's expected value. In essence you value the risky prospect at less than its expected value. That means that you are negative about the fact that the risky prospect is risky. In other words, you are averse to risk.

Risk-seeking
Suppose that your certainty equivalent is higher than the expected value. So you value the risky prospect at more than its expected value. In effect you are prepared to pay a premium in order to take part in the lottery. You actively pursue the risky prospect. You are risk-seeking.

It is helpful to have a visual way of representing attitudes to risk. To do that we need to introduce a new concept – the concept of utility, which is one of the most important concepts for thinking about rational choice and action in economics and the other social sciences.

Utility and Attitudes to Risk

So far we have been talking about expected value. This is not the sense of "value" with which people talk about moral value or aesthetic value. It is much narrower than that. As we've seen, the expected value of a gamble is really its expected return – which might be measured in lives saved, for example, as well as in cold, hard cash. But we've already seen from the discussion of different attitudes to risk that how we think about outcomes is not just a function of the returns that we expect from them. If you are risk-seeking or risk-averse then in an important sense you attach a differ-ent value to a lottery than you do to its expected value. So, a risk-averse person's certainty equivalent for a lottery is less than the lottery's expected value, while the risk-seeking person's certainty equivalent is higher. The standard way of putting this in decision theory and economics is to say that the risk-averse agent attaches less *utility* to a lottery than she does to its certainty equivalent. Her certainty equivalent is less than the lottery's expected value because she attaches a higher utility to the lottery's expected value than she does to the lottery itself. The risk-seeking agent assigns utility in the opposite way. She assigns a higher utility to the lottery than to its expected monetary value.

What exactly is utility? We will come back to this controversial question.[6] In economics utility is standardly taken to be simply a measure of preference, as revealed in choice. That is, to say that an agent assigns a higher utility to P over Q is simply to say that they would choose P if they had a choice between P and Q. For many social scientists, in contrast, the concept of utility has an explanatory role to play. The fact that an agent assigns a higher utility to P than to Q doesn't simply describe her choice of P over Q. It explains it. Her assigning a higher utility to P over Q is the reason why she chooses P rather than Q. For the moment I propose standing back from these debates. We can introduce the concept of utility to capture how the choices of an agent who is not completely risk-neutral reflect more than just the expected values of the different possible outcomes. The concept may or may not do more than that, but for the moment it does not matter.

The point of introducing utility is that economists typically represent the difference between being risk-averse and being risk-seeking through the shape of an agent's utility curve. A utility curve is simply a curve that plots the utility an agent assigns to a given commodity. To keep it simple for the moment, we can let that commodity be money – or, more precisely, the expected monetary value of a risky situation (understanding risk in a broad sense, so that the outcome of receiving $50 for sure counts as a risky outcome).

Now imagine a graph that has expected monetary outcome on the *x*-axis (horizontal) and utility on the *y*-axis (vertical). On that graph we are going to represent how agents with different attitudes towards risk think about a simple lottery that offers a 50 percent chance of $50 and a 50 percent chance of $100. Let's call that lottery L. Again for simplicity, let's assume that each type of agent assigns the same utility to each of the two

---

[6] For an introduction and further references see Chapter 2 of my book *Rationality and Decision Theory* (Bermúdez 2009) and Okasha 2016. For historical background on the concept of utility see Broome 1991a.

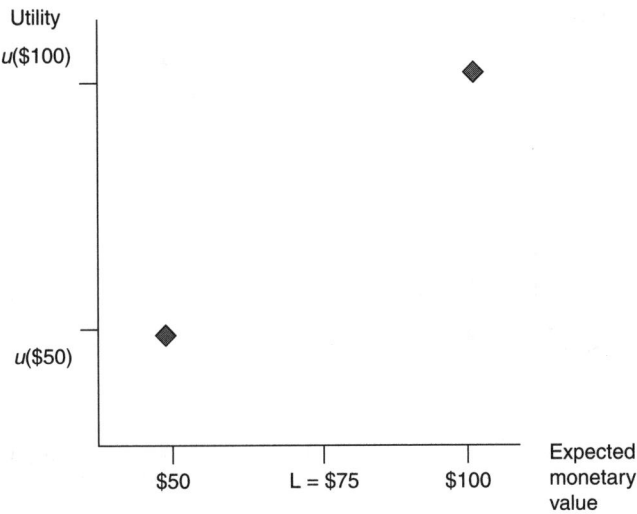

FIGURE 2.1 Representing an agent's attitude to risk

Note: Expected monetary value is represented on the *x*-axis and the utility the agent assigns to expected monetary outcomes is assigned on the *y*-axis. We are looking at attitudes to a lottery that offers a 50% chance of $50 and a 50% chance of $100. The expected monetary value of that lottery is $75. So we start by representing the utility that the agent assigns to the outcomes of receiving $50 and $100 respectively. These are labeled as *u*($50) and *u*($100). The question we are interested in is the utility *u*(L) that the agent assigns to the lottery L with expected monetary value of $75.

possible outcomes – to receiving $50 and to receiving $100. Call these *u* ($50) and *u*($100) respectively. Our starting point then is as represented in Figure 2.1.

What we are interested in is the utility *u*(L) that agents with different attitudes to risk assign to the lottery L with an expected monetary value of $75. That will tell us about the shape of the agent's utility curve.

We know that perfectly risk-neutral agents care only about expected monetary outcomes. They are completely indifferent to the degree of risk involved. This means that risk-neutral agents assign utilities in a way that is directly proportional to expected monetary value, with risk appearing nowhere in the equation. So, risk-neutral agents have utility curves that are really straight lines, representing the fact that they assign utility in a way that is directly proportional to expected monetary outcome. Since the expected value of the lottery is midway between the expected value of $50

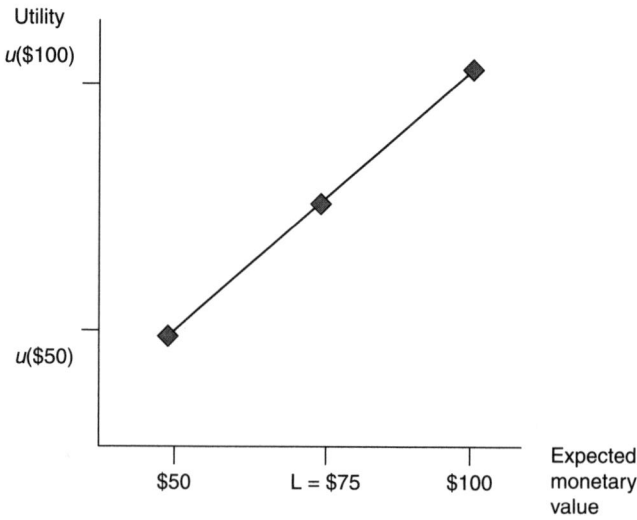

FIGURE 2.2 Utility for agents who are risk-neutral
Note: An agent who is risk-neutral assigns utility in a way that is directly proportional to expected monetary outcome. So the utility curve of a risk-neutral agent is in fact a straight line. It is linear.

and the expected value of $100, its utility will be midway between the utility the agent attaches to $50 and the utility she attaches to $100.

The situation from the perspective of a risk-neutral agent is shown in Figure 2.2. In the standard terminology, risk-neutral agents have **linear** utility curves.

How about risk-averse and risk-seeking agents? It will be easier to do this in two stages. We can start by looking at the relation between utilities, lotteries, and certainty equivalents for risk-averse and risk-loving agents respectively. And then we can extrapolate to their utility curves.

The defining feature of a risk-averse agent is that her certainty equivalent for a risky gamble is less than the expected value of that gamble. So, in this case her certainty equivalent might be $70, if she is only slightly risk-averse, or $60, if she is very risk averse. Let's take it to be $65 and mark it on the graph as CE(L) in Figure 2.3 (which includes the risk-neutral line for reference).

The risk-averse agent assigns the same utility to receiving $65 for sure as the risk-neutral agent assigns to lottery L. This is indicated by the dotted horizontal line in Figure 2.3. The horizontal distance

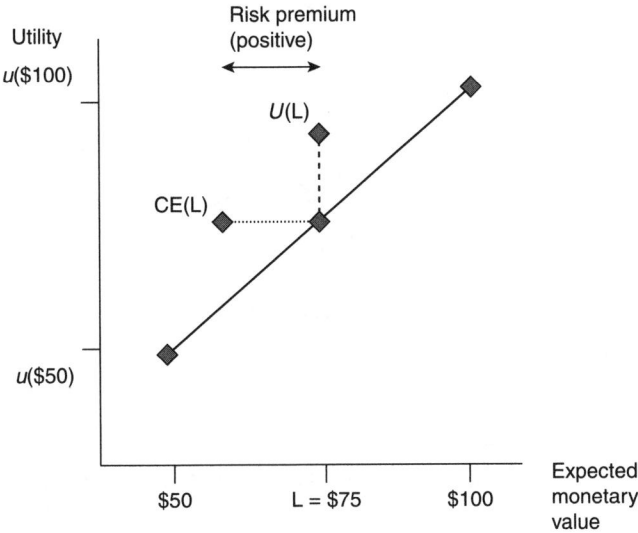

FIGURE 2.3 Utility for a typical risk-averse agent
Note: The linear utility curve of a risk-neutral agent is included for reference. The certainty equivalent for the lottery L is denoted by CE(L), with the dotted horizontal line indicating the extent of the agent's risk premium. The risk premium is positive for risk-averse agents. The dashed vertical line illustrates how a risk-averse agent prefers a certain outcome of $75 to a lottery with an expected value of $75.

between the certainty equivalent of L (i.e. CE(L)) and the expected monetary value of L is called the *risk premium*. It is, in effect, the amount of money that a risk-averse person would need to be paid in order to participate in a lottery with a given expected monetary value – the compensation for the risk, as it were. By the same token, the utility that the risk-averse agent attaches to the expected monetary value of L (i.e. to $75) is greater than the utility attached to the lottery with $75 as its expected monetary value. In other words, it is a mark of risk-aversion to prefer $75 for sure to a lottery with an expected value of $75. This is indicated in Figure 2.3 by the dashed vertical line leading from the risk-neutral line to *u*($75).

Risk-seeking agents are basically the mirror image of risk-averse agents. Whereas risk-averse agents' certainty equivalent for lottery L is less than its expected value of $75, risk-seeking agents have certainty

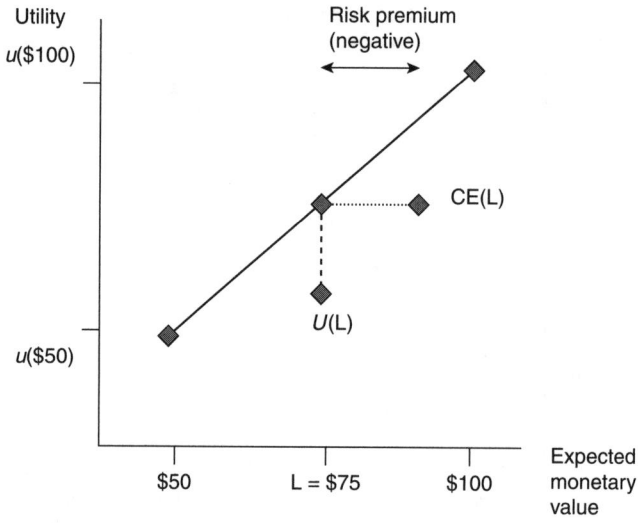

FIGURE 2.4 Utility for a typical risk-seeking agent
Note: The linear utility curve of a risk-neutral agent is included for reference. The certainty equivalent for L is denoted by CE(L), with the dotted horizontal line indicating the extent of the agent's risk premium. The risk premium is negative for risk-seeking agents. The dashed vertical line illustrates how a risk-seeking agent prefers a lottery with an expected value of $75 to a certain outcome of $75.

equivalents for L that are higher than L's expected monetary value. So the situation for risk-loving agents is as depicted in Figure 2.4.

Whereas risk-averse agents have a positive risk premium, the risk premium for risk-loving agents is negative. That means that they are prepared to pay to take a risk – as opposed to requiring compensation for doing so. And, as one might expect, the risk-seeking agent would rather participate in a gamble with an expected value of $75 than they would receive $75 for sure. So, whereas in Figure 2.3 the dashed line from risk-neutrality to u(L) goes upwards, it goes downwards in Figure 2.4.

Drawing a line through the relevant points for risk-averse and risk-seeking agents allows us to represent their utility curves, as in Figure 2.5.

The precise degree of curvature and the particular values on each axis do not really matter for representing the difference between being risk-averse and being risk-seeking. What matters is the general shape of the curve. The risk-averse curve in Figure 2.5 has the property of being

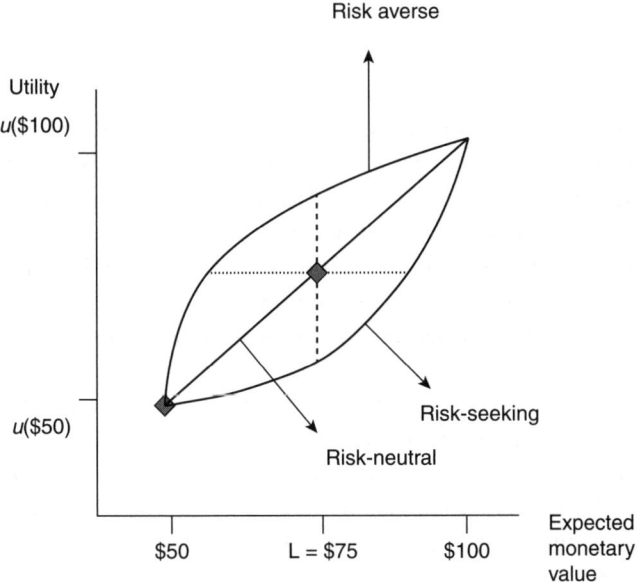

FIGURE 2.5 Utility curves and attitudes to risk: a summary
Note: Risk-neutral agents have linear utility curves, while risk-aversion is characterized by a concave utility curve. The utility curves of risk-seeking agents are convex.

concave. The risk-seeking curve has the opposite property of being **convex**.[7] This is a general property of these two different attitudes to risk. Just as all risk-neutral agents have linear utility curves, so too do all risk-averse and risk-neutral agents have concave and convex utility curves respectively.

In fact, this is the standard understanding within economics and decision theory of different attitudes to risk.

- To be risk-neutral is to have a *linear* utility curve.
- To be risk-averse is to have a *concave* utility curve.
- To be risk-seeking is to have a *convex* utility curve.

---

[7] "Concave" and "convex" have precise mathematical definitions reflecting properties of the utility functions that are being graphed. We don't need to go into those details. Just think of a concave curve as one that has the following property: A line between any two points under the curve will only go through points that are themselves under the curve. A convex curve lacks that property.

Rationality and Risk

This is a book about rationality. So, I should emphasize that, from the perspective of rationality, there is no correct attitude to risk. It is not intrinsically irrational to be risk-seeking. Casino gamblers may be irrational in all sorts of ways, but not because they value a gamble more than they value its certainty equivalent. And the kind of prudence often displayed by people who are risk-averse may be a virtue in all sorts of ways, but it doesn't make them any more (or less) rational than their risk-neutral or risk-seeking friends. It's up to you how much you are prepared to pay for a lottery ticket – or whether you choose to get involved with the lottery at all.

This is because your attitude to risk reflects your choice of certainty equivalent, and there are no right or wrong answers about the certainty equivalent of a given risky prospect. It's just a matter of how you personally strike a balance between a certain prospect and a risky prospect. In this respect a risky prospect's certainty equivalent is very different from its expected value (continuing with the convenient simplification that expected value is purely monetary). If we know how much each of the different outcomes pays out, and we know how probable each outcome is, then the expected value is a simple arithmetical fact. There's no room for discussion about the expected value of the coin toss gamble we have been discussing. Whatever your attitude to risk, that gamble has an expected value of $5. But your certainty equivalent is entirely up to you. It's a matter, an economist might say, of your personal utility function, and there's no right or wrong about that (as long as you make choices in a way that is internally consistent and conforms to a small number of basic axioms). You might be so risk-averse, for example, that your certainty equivalent is $0. This would be unusual, but not irrational. Or you might love gambling on coin tosses so much that your certainty equivalent is $10. Likewise – unusual but not irrational.

Still, that doesn't mean that people can't be irrational when confronted with risky choices. It might be the case, for example, that attitudes to risk can be easily manipulated, so that people can be induced to switch from being risk-averse to being risk-seeking without any good reason. And that brings us back to the Asian disease experiments, because that is exactly what the experiments are standardly taken to show – that people are inconsistent in their attitude to risk, valuing risky prospects differently depending on whether they are framed as losses or as gains.

To see how this is supposed to work we need to think about the attitudes to risk displayed in the two conditions. We've already seen that the basic concept of expected value can be applied, using the "currency" (for want of a better word) of lives saved. In each condition the two programs have the same expected value. And in each condition the choice is between a certain prospect and a risky prospect. So now we have all the pieces in place to look at attitudes to risk, using the concepts just developed.

Look again at condition 1. The dominant preference here is for the program that saves 200 lives for sure (a certain prospect), as opposed to the risky prospect that has an expected value of saving 200 lives. This is intuitively risk-averse. It also fits the technical definition. If you assign greater utility to saving 200 lives for sure than to a risky prospect that has an expected value of saving 200 lives then your certainty equivalent for the risky prospect must be less than 200 lives. But that is just what it means to be risk-averse – you have assigned to a risky prospect a certainty equivalent that is less than the prospect's expected value.

Now look at condition 2. Here the dominant preference is for the risky prospect with a 1/3 probability that nobody will die and a 2/3 probability that everybody will die. The expected value here is 400 deaths. Greater utility is assigned to the risky prospect than to a certain prospect with the same expected value. As before, this seems intuitively to be risk-seeking behavior and it also fits the technical definition. If you assign higher utility to a risky prospect than to a certain prospect with the same expected value this means that your certainty equivalent for the risky prospect must be greater than its expected value, which is just what it means to be risk-seeking.

So now we can get a full picture of what is going on in the Asian disease paradigm. The striking effect is not just that preferences change because of how the outcomes are framed – as happens with different ways of labeling the fat content of beef or the ratio of success to failures in evaluating team performance. This is not just an "ordinary" preference reversal. What we also get is a framing-induced shift from one attitude to risk to another – from being risk-averse to being risk-seeking.

Subjects choose the certain prospect (program A) over the equivalent risky prospect (program B) when the prospects are framed in terms of gains (lives saved). But when the prospects are framed in terms of losses (total deaths, or lives lost) then they choose the risky prospect over the equivalent certain prospect. So the pattern seems to be: subjects are risk-averse for gains and risk-seeking for losses.

This brings us back to the rationality theme. I stressed earlier that there is no correct attitude to risk, from the perspective of rationality. Being risk-seeking is no less (and no more) rational than being risk-averse. And there is nothing special about risk-neutrality. In fact it might even be rational to be risk-averse in some contexts and risk-seeking in others. As it happens, variable attitudes to risk are very common. Because insurance companies need to make a profit, insurance premiums are fixed at a level that means that only risk-averse people will buy them. The company can only make money over time if the consumer pays a premium to avoid the risky prospect of confronting an uncertain world without insurance. Since the insurer in effect takes the risky prospect on, their profit depends upon the expected value of the premium exceeding the expected value of the risky prospect. So, from the perspective of expected value, the consumer would have been better off taking the risk rather than paying the premium. Anybody who voluntarily buys insurance is displaying risk-aversion. And obviously, casinos and lotteries are set up so that only risk-seekers will participate. But would it be obviously irrational to buy insurance in the morning and then purchase a lottery ticket in the afternoon? I'm not convinced. We'll come back to this later.

But even if it does turn out to be rational to be risk-seeking in some contexts and risk-averse in others, the Asian disease paradigm seems problematic on a much deeper level. On the face of it, it appears deeply irrational to flip between being risk-averse and being risk-seeking depending upon how the relevant prospects are framed. We'll look at this in more depth in the next chapter, where we look at how framing and risk-aversion can play out in the financial markets. We'll see that the situation is very complex. Before we get there, though, I want to look at some more examples of how framing can induce fundamental shifts in attitudes to risk.

Fuel to the Flames: More Experiments on Framing Risk

The basic pattern of many experiments in this area should be clear by now, as should the main elements of the theoretical background. So we can move a little more briskly through some of the high points of the literature on framing effects in attitudes to risk. You might like to answer the problems yourself and make a note of your answer before reading on. My hunch is that even after the earlier discussion most of the people reading this book will answer in line with the experimental subjects.

Here is one of my favorites, also from the team of Kahneman and Tversky.[8] It follows their standard pattern. Here is the first choice:

A. A sure gain of $2,400
B. A 25% chance of gaining $10,000 and a 75% chance of gaining nothing

And here is the second:

C. A sure loss of $7,500
D. A 75% chance of losing $10,000 and a 25% chance of losing nothing

Which did you choose in each case?

If you chose A in the first problem and D in the second then you are not alone. In fact you are in the company of 84 percent of the experimental subjects in Choice 1 and 87 percent in Choice 2. Unlike the Asian disease experiments this was a within-subjects design rather than a between-subjects design. So each of the 150 experimental subjects actually made both choices.

As before, Choice 1 is the gain frame and Choice 2 is the loss frame. But there is a subtle difference from the Asian disease experiments. The two prospects in Choice 1 do not have the same expected (monetary) value. The expected value of the prospect in A is $2,400, while the expected value of the prospect in B is $2,500 (i.e. 25% of $10,000). So, A is very emphatically the risk-averse choice. An A-chooser must have a certainty equivalent for the risky prospect in B that is not just lower than its expected value, but lower by at least $100. In contrast, the two prospects in Choice 2 have the same expected value. So, choosing D in Choice 2 definitely counts as risk-seeking.

So far this looks like a minor variation on the Asian disease experiments. We have a risk-averse choice in the gain frame and a risk-seeking choice in the loss frame. What this experiment adds, though, is another route to showing how this pattern of choices can come out as irrational. Since this is a within-subjects design we can aggregate the two choices and look at the overall financial position that subjects end up in. By making both choices you are in effect choosing a portfolio, and aggregating the two choices gives the value of the final portfolio. So we can compare the dominant pattern of choices (A and D) with the obvious alternative (B and C).

---

[8] The experiment is reported in Tversky and Kahneman 1981.

Here is how they come out:

A & D A 25% chance of gaining $2,400 and a 75% chance of losing $7,600[9]

B & C A 25% chance of gaining $2,500 and a 75% chance of losing $7,500[10]

To choose A & D rather than B & C is to take what is called the *dominated* portfolio. A & D is dominated because, however things turn out you will be worse off with A & D than with B & C. Think about it as two lotteries, each with four tickets – one winning ticket and three losing ones. The prize for the winning ticket is lower in the A & D lottery than in the B & C lottery – and the penalty for the losing tickets is greater. It doesn't make much sense to choose a lottery where the upside is smaller and the downside is greater! But that's exactly what the majority of Kahneman and Tversky's subjects did! Only 3 percent of the 150 students they studied chose B & C, while 73 percent chose A & D. But what could be more irrational than choosing an obviously dominated portfolio?

Well, you might say, it's hardly obvious that the B & C combination dominates the A & D one. How could one reasonably expect undergraduates at Stanford and the University of British Columbia to work it out? It's true that they were told that the two choices were concurrent, which seems like a good clue that one should look at the overall position. But still – it certainly requires more thought than figuring out that if beef is 25 percent lean then it is 75 percent fat, or that a 60 percent failure rate is the same as a 40 percent success rate. As far as the litany of human irrationality is concerned, though, this is all just grist to the mill. It's true that people are not very good at aggregating when making complex choices. But that's just another sign of irrationality!

To see how this argument might go, consider the following nice set of experiments from the economist Richard Thaler, one of the founders of behavioral economics and behavioral finance (and recipient of the 2017 Nobel Prize for economics), and his collaborator Eric J. Johnson from the Columbia School of Business.[11] They raise the ante by posing and

[9] You get this result as follows. From A you have a sure gain of $2,400. So adding that to the outcomes in D gives a 25% chance of $2,400 (i.e. the sure gain minus $0) and a 75% chance of losing $7,600 (i.e. the sure gain minus $10,000).

[10] You can do this one. See the previous note and plug in the new numbers.

[11] The following studies are described in Thaler and Johnson 1991. See also Thaler 1999.

comparing two Kahneman and Tversky-type problems. I am going to call them Problem 1 and Problem 2.

Let's start with Problem 1, a within-subjects design in the standard format. Here is your first choice:

A. A sure gain of $1,500
B. A lottery determined by the toss of a fair coin, yielding $1,950 if the coin lands heads and $1,050 if it lands tails.[12]

And here is the second:

C. A sure loss of $750
D. A lottery determined by the toss of a fair coin, yielding a loss of $525 if the coin lands heads and a loss of $975 if it lands tails.

You know the drill by now. In both choices the expected values are the same. The majority of subjects make the risk-averse choice in the gain frame and the risk-seeking choice in the loss frame. So far, nothing new.

Now the same subjects are confronted with Problem 2. This problem has a different format, but I'm sure that you will spot the change in frames, though. Here is the first part of Problem 2.

> Imagine that you have just won $1,500 in a lottery. You have the opportunity to participate in a second lottery, determined by the toss of a fair coin. If the coin comes up heads you will win $450, while if it comes up tails you will lose $450. Would you take part in the second lottery after having won in the first – Yes or No?

And now for the second part:

> Imagine that you have just lost $750 in a lottery. You have the opportunity to participate in a second lottery, determined by the toss of a fair coin. If the coin comes up heads you will win $225, while if it comes up tails you will lose $225. Would you take part in the second lottery after having lost in the first – Yes or No?

Stop and think about the relation between the prospects in Problem 1 and Problem 2.

Hopefully you've noticed that the two problems really just present the same set of prospects in a different way. More accurately, in different frames – here we have frames within frames! With respect to your eventual

---

[12] I have changed the numbers to bring them more into line with our other examples. The original experiments were more in the $30 range.

financial position there's no difference between taking a sure prospect of $1,500 and declining to gamble further if you have already won $1,500 in an earlier lottery. And so on for the other prospects.

What's interesting and intriguing, though, is that the new framing induces yet more preference reversals. Thaler and Johnson found that a substantial number of participants switched from being risk-averse in the gain frame in Problem 1 to being risk-seeking in the gain frame in Problem 2. In Problem 1 they preferred the certain prospect of $1,500 to the lottery, but the very same subjects were prepared to participate in the second lottery in Problem 2, effectively signing up for the same lottery that they had just rejected. There was also a reversal in the loss frame. Whereas in Problem 1 subjects in the loss frame typically made the "textbook" choice of the risk-seeking gamble, when the prospects were reframed in Problem 2 over 50 percent switched over to the (risk-averse) certain prospect.

What could be going on here? It's obviously not just an issue of the loss frame vs. the gain frame, because the new reversals take place within each frame. So it must have something to do with the major difference between Problem 1 and Problem 2, which is that the choices in Problem 1 are presented simultaneously while those in Problem 2 are presented successively. In Problem 1 you are given a choice without any specified starting point, whereas in Problem 2 you have a starting point (either a gain of $1,500 or a loss of $750) and then you are presented with a choice. The starting point frames how you think about the subsequent choice because it encourages you to frame the eventual outcome in a particular way. Thaler and Johnson describe this in terms of what they call the process of *hedonic editing*, which is a form of *mental accounting*.

In essence, they suggest, people think about successions of losses and gains in ways that make eventual outcomes seem as pleasant (or: as minimally unpleasant) as possible. Losses are unpleasant. So people find it psychologically difficult to aggregate them. This makes the second part of Problem 2 particularly challenging. Anyone contemplating the risky prospect has to deal with the possibility of a loss of $225 on top of a loss of $750. You could say that this adds insult to injury. In any event, according to Thaler and Johnson's theory, it explains why people tend to switch from being risk-seeking in the loss frame in Problem 1 to being risk-averse in the loss frame in Problem 2. They just can't handle the possibility of a "double whammy."

When it comes to gains people also tend to segregate (i.e. they tend to consider a sequence of gains separately, rather than amalgamating them and consider the total gain). But for completely the opposite reason. Gains are segregated because they are enjoyable and so people want to have more opportunity to enjoy the pleasure of having them. Lumping the gains together would take away some of the pleasure. And that, according to Thaler and Johnson, is why the risky prospect looks more attractive in Problem 2 than it does in Problem 1. It invites subjects to think about the possibility of doubling up on the delights of winning.

Still, you might reasonably ask why the most salient outcomes should be the two just considered. What about the other outcome in each of the risky prospects in Problem 2. Why do people focus primarily on the outcomes where there is either a double gain or a double loss? Why do these, as it were, drown out the outcomes where a gain is followed by a loss, or a loss followed by a gain? Thaler and Johnson have an answer. They claim that these are cases where people tend to aggregate, rather than segregate. If you gain $1,500 and then lose $450 then you are inclined to aggregate and conceptualize (frame?) your end-point as a net gain of $1,050. And if you lose $750, but follow that up with a gain of $225 then here you aggregate and frame the end-point as a net loss of $525.

So, from the perspective of hedonic editing, the "mixed" cases (where you win some and lose some!) look much more like the outcomes in Problem 1. They don't have the extra psychological impact of the outcomes that involve a double gain or a double loss. So, the theory goes, the way that the prospects are framed in Problem 2 makes it much easier for people to focus disproportionately on the double outcomes rather than the mixed ones. That means that the risky prospect in the gain frame starts to seem more attractive than the certain prospect (even though people tend to be risk-averse for gains, when the decision problem is not presented in stages). By the same token, in the loss frame the risky prospect looks much worse than the certain one (even though people are typically risk-seeking for losses).

From a psychological point of view the hedonic editing proposal seems acute and insightful. From the perspective of rationality, however, it looks troubling. If what she ends up with is a certain amount of money, why should a rational agent care how she got there? How can it make a rational difference whether a loss was followed by a gain, or whether the final monetary position was the result of two gains (or two losses). Surely, one might think, a rational agent would care only about the destination, not about the journey. If we really do engage in hedonic editing, as Thaler and Johnson suggest, then doesn't that simply provide more fuel for the flames of the litany of irrationality?

3

Where the Rubber Hits the Road: Investors, Frames, and Markets

We now have all the machinery we need to move out of the laboratory and into the world of investments and markets. It's time to look at some key exhibits from studies of investor behavior in behavioral economics and behavioral finance. It turns out that the concepts introduced in Chapter 2 (framing effects, hedonic editing, and varying attitudes to risk depending on whether gains or losses are on the horizon) really help make sense of puzzling questions about how individuals make their investment decisions and how financial markets work.

As before, we will spend much of the time identifying and explaining patterns of choices and patterns of behavior. But running through the background is the recurrent theme that these patterns of choice are fundamentally irrational. The picture that emerges is one of powerful and persistent illusions driving investor and market behavior. As we'll see, framing effects are at the root of these illusions. In fact, these framing effects are ultimately intensified versions of those encountered in Chapter 2. Unsurprisingly, when money is at stake the concepts of loss and gain become incredibly important.

Here are two much-studied phenomena that both appear to be driven by framing effects.

- The *disposition effect* is a robust phenomenon in individual investors of all levels of skill and experience. The disposition here (to borrow from the title of a famous paper by Hersh Shefrin and Meir Statman in the *Journal of Finance*) is the disposition "to sell winners too early and ride losers too long."[1] When investors need to liquidate part of their

---

[1] Shefrin and Statman 1985.

44

portfolio they tend systematically to sell securities that have registered a gain, ignoring the overall balance of the portfolio and the often considerable tax advantages that come with realizing losses. Several different types of framing underlie the disposition effect.

- *Myopic loss-aversion* is a theory proposed by Shlomo Benartzi and Richard Thaler to explain the so-called *equity premium puzzle*.[2] Investors expect and receive a significant premium for holding equities (stocks) as opposed to relatively risk-free investments such as government bonds. This premium is much higher than would be predicted by standard models of risk-aversion. For Benartzi and Thaler, a particular type of framing explains the divergence between what they think of as the rational equity premium (the level of premium that would be appropriate if you had a rational perspective on the relative risks and returns of equities and government bonds) and the actual equity premium.

The disposition effect and the theory of myopic loss-aversion have been much studied since they were first proposed in the 1980s and 1990s respectively. Much of the work has employed laboratory experiments (like those considered in Chapter 2). But there have also been very thought-provoking empirical studies of investor behavior "in the wild," as it were. Looking at the theory, experiments, and empirical studies together gives a rich picture of how framing structures investment decisions and how people think about money more generally.

"Selling Winners, Riding Losers": Framing and the Disposition Effect

The disposition effect is the tendency that investors have not to realize losses – holding on to losing investments in the (often vain) hope that the losses will eventually be recouped. In his book *Beyond Greed and Fear*, Hersh Shefrin refers to this as "get-evenitis."[3] The disposition effect is one of the prime exhibits of behavioral finance – an (allegedly) irrational habit that is destructive to people's wealth and that is grounded in a range of different framing effects.

Loss-aversion is often cited as a (partial) explanation of the disposition effect. Loss-aversion is the phenomenon of not wanting to realize a loss. So, if you need to liquidate assets (in order to buy a house, for example)

---

[2] Benartzi and Thaler 1995.   [3] See Shefrin 2002.

and you have a choice between selling a security that has gained $x and one that has lost $x in the same period, then loss-aversion predicts that you will sell the winner and hang on to the loser, *all other things being equal*. But the qualification is important. There are all sorts of other things to take into account. Most obviously – how one thinks the two securities will do in the future. It would be pretty silly to sell a losing security that you have good reason to think is fundamentally under-valued in order to hang on to one that you think is fundamentally over-valued (as long as you are working within a time horizon that makes it reasonable to think that there will be a reversion to true value). There are also potential issues to do with transaction costs, taxes, and so forth.

For these reasons it is inconceivable that there could be some sort of general principle to the effect that a rational agent should always sell losers and hang on to winners. Professional investors often talk about "taking profits." It stretches the bounds of plausibility that they are always irrational to do this. So a presentation of the disposition has to be more subtle than simply talking about selling winners and riding losers. If there is a disposition effect at all, it needs to be a tendency to sell winners and ride losers *even when an impartial observer might reasonably think it makes better sense to sell the loser*. And spelling this out is not an easy thing to do.

Fortunately, in their original paper Shefrin and Statman present the disposition effect much more subtly than it is standardly reported. They discuss investor behavior in the face of two features of the United States tax code – the tax-deductibility of capital losses and the so-called "wash-sale rule." As in many tax codes, the IRS allows capital losses to offset capital gains. So, prudent investors might be expected to review their portfolios towards the end of the tax year with a view to minimizing their overall tax bill by realizing some capital losses. This is often called *tax loss harvesting*.

But there are potential costs to tax loss harvesting. The IRS's *wash-sale rule* effectively bars you from claiming a tax deduction for a realized capital loss if you purchase a "substantially identical" security within a 30-day period after the original sale.[4] So, tax loss harvesting will put you out of the relevant section of the market for at least 30 days, which might in the overall scheme of things cost you more than you would save in taxes. As Shefrin and Statman point out, however, there are legal ways of

---

[4] I cannot resist complaining about this terminology in the US tax code. There is no sense in which two things can be substantially identical. Either they are identical, in which case there is only one thing. Or they are not. There is no intermediate setting, any more than one number can be substantially a multiple of another.

circumventing the wash-sale rule. Investors can use *tax swaps*. Tax swaps exploit the fact that, as the IRS typically interprets the wash-sale rule, two securities can have very similar return profiles without counting as substantially identical. The example they give is the two banks Citicorp and Chemical Bank. At the time they were writing, these two securities looked rather similar in their histories, returns, and prospects. And so, they suggest, a savvy investor could harvest a tax loss by selling their Chemical Bank stock while simultaneously purchasing an equivalent amount of Citicorp stock. They would not be breaching the wash-sale rule, because Citicorp and Chemical Bank shares are not "substantially identical," but the investor is in effect taking on an equivalent investment.

One might wonder about the example, given the rather divergent histories of Citicorp (which effectively became insolvent in the financial crisis of 2008 and had to be bailed out) and Chemical Bank (which acquired Chase Manhattan in 1996 and is now the largest US bank by assets under the name JPMorgan Chase). But of course the real issue is not how things actually turned out over the next 30–40 years, but how a reasonably well-informed and rational investor in December 1985 might have expected them to turn out within their own investment horizon, given the information available. Shefrin and Statman claim that "the tax swap offers an alternative which stochastically dominates the decision to continue holding Chemical Bank."[5] In other words, given the available information an investor who makes the tax swap is financially better off (because of the tax write-off) than an investor who doesn't, while both are looking at exactly the same expected returns. So why, Shefrin and Statman ask, do investors find it so hard to engage in tax loss harvesting?

It's all a matter, they claim, of how the situation is framed. This brings us back to the ideas about mental accounting and hedonic editing from Chapter 2. It may be the case that, from the perspective of an ideal investor, there is no substantive difference between the expected return from holding Chemical Bank and Citicorp respectively at the moment when an investor is considering the tax swap, but real-life investors tend not to look at the numbers that dispassionately. As Kahneman and Tversky have emphasized for many years, people tend to think relatively, not absolutely.[6] What people typically value are changes relative to a

---

[5] Shefrin and Statman 1985, p. 780.
[6] This is a basic tenet of Kahneman and Tversky's *prospect theory*, which they developed to systematize and explain their experimental findings. We will look at it in more detail in Chapter 4.

starting point, rather than absolute positions on a scale. With respect to investments, rather than valuing a particular level of wealth, what they care about is how their wealth has changed relative to a particular reference point. In this case the reference point is the purchase price of the stock. That determines how investors frame the situation. And within that frame swapping Chemical Bank for Citicorp is not a neutral exchange between two securities with similar expected returns. Rather, they think about it in terms of mental accounts – closing the Chemical Bank account at a loss in order to open a new Citicorp account. And thinking about it in that way gives the transaction a very negative valence that makes it hard to implement.

But it is possible to change the frame, and so make the tax swap seem more attractive. Shefrin and Statman quote an anecdote from Leroy Gross's manual for stockbrokers that brilliantly illustrates the power of frames. Gross first explains the problem, as he sees it:

> Investors who accept their losses can no longer prattle to their loved ones. "Honey, it's only a paper loss. Just wait, it will come back." Investors who realize losses must admit their folly to the IRS when they file that itemized tax return. For all those reasons and more, investors as a whole are reluctant to take losses, even when they feel that to do so is the right course of action.[7]

And here is his solution:

> When you suggest that the client close at a loss the transaction you originally recommended and invest the proceeds in another position you are currently recommending, *a real act of faith has to take place*. The act of faith can be more easily effected if you make use of some transitional words that I call "magic selling words."
>
>   The words that I consider to have magical power in the sense that they make for a more easy acceptance of a loss are these: *"Transfer your assets."*[8]

In other words – frame it so that it is not taking a loss! Here is how it is supposed to work:

> The two separate transactions (moving out of the loss and moving into a new position) are made to flow together by the magic words "transfer your assets." The prospect thought he was making a single decision, switching one investment into another. He was not being asked to think in terms of selling XYZ and collecting the proceeds, and then having to think of any different ways to reinvest the proceeds.[9]

[7] Gross 1982, p. 150.   [8] Gross 1982, p. 150.   [9] Gross 1982, p. 152.

This is a powerful illustration of how framing can create the disposition effect and (something that is much less frequently discussed) how shifting the frame can eliminate the effect.

There is another framing effect at work besides the mental accounting of losses. In a series of papers Nicholas Barberis has explored the role of *narrow framing* in investment decisions.[10] Narrow framing occurs when an agent is faced with a risky choice and evaluates the risks it involves independently of other existing or foreseen risks. A simple example would be taking a single investment decision completely on its own terms, rather than looking at it in the context of one's portfolio as a whole. Consider the Chemical Bank/Citicorp example again. The tendency to the disposition effect diminishes when investors focus less on the single transaction itself, looking at it instead as part of an overall investment strategy.

Suppose, for example, that you have a general investment strategy of trying to maintain diversification across different market sectors. So you need to maintain a certain percentage of your wealth in financial stocks. From that perspective it really does not matter whether you hold Chemical Bank or Citicorp. And even if you are focusing on losses and gains, rather than absolute levels of wealth, then it will be losses and gains across the portfolio as a whole, rather than the specific loss involved in closing a single position. So you will be less likely to be traumatized by the prospect of selling. In effect, the narrower one frames an investment decision, the easier it is for loss-aversion to gain traction – while the broader one's frame, the less scope there is for the disposition effect to take hold.

The Disposition Effect in the Wild

The framing studies in Chapter 2 were all laboratory studies, often performed on students. These studies are thought-provoking and conceptually rich, but they are undeniably artificial. You might well wonder how robust the basic results are when we move outside the controlled environment of a university study and look at how investors behave in their natural habitats. Fortunately, there is a small but growing literature that has examined the disposition effect in the wild.

Terrance Odean published a classic study in the *Journal of Finance* in 1998.[11] He examined the records of 10,000 individual accounts held at

---

[10] See, for example, Barberis and Huang 2008 and Barberis and Xiong 2009.

[11] Odean 1998. Ben-David and Hirshleifer 2012 also look at brokerage data, exploring the probability of selling as a function of profit/loss.

one of the large US discount brokerages in the period from 1987 to 1993, looking at all the stock sales that took place in the period and assessing them both from a tax liability perspective and from the perspective of future performance. These are individual investors, sophisticated enough to be trading on their own account with a discount brokerage, but typically not professionals. Odean's methodology was very interesting. Whenever one of the investors in the sample sold a stock he looked at the investor's entire portfolio and classified each stock into one of four categories, based on the difference between its purchase price and its price on that day. Stocks that were actually sold were classified either as *realized gains* or *realized losses*, while stocks that were left in the portfolio were classified either as *paper gains* or as *paper losses*. Doing this gave him a snapshot of the state of each investor's portfolio whenever they sold a stock. He then aggregated all of the snapshots across the 10,000 accounts over the six-year period to look at two ratios for the entire sample – the proportion of gains realized (PGR) and the proportion of losses realized (PLR). Here are the two equations:

$$PGR = \frac{Number\ of\ realized\ gains}{Number\ of\ realized\ gains + Number\ of\ paper\ gains}$$

$$PLR = \frac{Number\ of\ realized\ losses}{Number\ of\ realized\ losses + Number\ of\ paper\ losses}$$

In essence, the PGR measures the extent to which investors took profits – i.e. *sold winners*. If you look at all the gains that were available to them on the sum total of all trading days, then the PGR is the proportion of those available gains that were actually cashed in. In contrast, the PLR measures the extent to which investors cut their losses. If you look at all the losses summed up over all investors and all trading days, then the PLR measures the proportion of those losses that were realized – i.e. *the proportion of losers sold*.

Odean's principal finding is that the PGR significantly exceeded the PLR – i.e. that the investors in the sample took profits more frequently than they cut losses. The PGR was 14.8 percent, while the PLR was 9.8 percent, which is a huge difference (just over 50 percent). On the face of it this looks like strong empirical confirmation of the disposition effect. Still, as observed earlier, the disposition effect is a tendency to sell winners and ride losers *even when an impartial observer might reasonably think it makes better sense to sell the loser*. So we need to be sure that the investors in the sample did not have good reasons for taking profits rather than cutting losses.

It would be hard to claim that the disposition effect is at work if the investors actually had good reasons to think that their losing positions would do better going forwards than their winning stocks – perhaps, for example, they all had a well-founded belief that stock prices would revert to some sort of mean. Of course, there's really no way of finding out what was going through investors' heads when they were planning their trades, but a useful proxy is to examine how the stocks in question actually did. The *ex post facto* evidence here is pretty clear, since the average return over the following 12 months from the winning stocks that were sold was 3.4 percent higher than the average return from the losing stocks that the investors in the sample retained. Granted, this is not conclusive, since some investors have a horizon investment longer than a year. But still, it is a striking difference, and on the one-year time horizon the disposition effect definitely cost the investors money.

Here is another possible explanation. Perhaps the investors were simply rebalancing their portfolios, selling stocks in order to realign their portfolio to match their basic asset allocation strategy – they might sell winning stocks, for example, when those stocks had come to take up too great a proportion of the overall portfolio. This is what a prudent investor might have done when internet stocks increased so drastically in value in the run-up to the bursting of the dot-com bubble at the turn of the millennium. In order to eliminate rebalancing as a potential cause Odean looked at a restricted sample. Since investors who rebalance typically only sell a portion of their holdings of a particular stock, rebalancing trades can be taken out of the equation by restricting the sample to trades where the entire holding is sold. Since Odean found that the effect persisted even when the sample was restricted in this way, it seems that rebalancing is not the explanation.

Odean's data aggregate over the entire group, so there is no way of disentangling whether the disposition effect varies in strength across different types of investor. This question is addressed in an interesting paper by Ravi Dhar and Ning Zhu published in *Management Science* in 2006.[12] They used the same basic technique as Odean, looking at investor accounts in one of the major discount brokerages. They had basic demographic information, together with complete trading records, for just under 8,000 investors. Using the same measures as Odean (PGR and PLR) they studied how the disposition effect varied according to income, expertise, and trading frequency. Here are the basic findings:

[12] Dhar and Zhu 2006.

- Of the investors in the sample, 80.3 percent displayed some form of disposition effect.[13]
- The major demographic difference was between high-income and low-income investors (with a diminished effect for high-income investors who, the authors hypothesize, are better placed to get advice from financial planners and tax professionals).
- Investors classified as professional/managerial were only slightly less prone to the disposition effect than non-professionals.
- Investors who traded more frequently were less prone to the effect.

In sum, four out of five investors exhibited the disposition effect to some extent, with the most significant attenuating factors being a high income level and frequent trading.[14]

The Equity Risk Premium Puzzle

So, the disposition effect shows how important framing effects are when investors come to sell their investments in equities (stocks). But in fact framing effects go even deeper than that. According to an influential account originally proposed by Shlomo Benartzi and Richard Thaler, framing effects have a role to play in answering the basic question of why investors buy equities in the first place! To see what is going on here we need to begin with the so-called equity risk premium puzzle.

The equity risk premium is the extra compensation that investors require to hold risky assets, such as equities, rather than safe assets, such as government bonds. This extra compensation comes in the form of a higher return over time for equities as opposed to bonds. But there is a puzzle – the extra compensation that investors have been receiving seems disproportionately large relative to standard models of how investors (and people in general) evaluate risk. Stocks have historically returned much more than it would seem they ought to. Why is that?

---

[13] Interestingly from the perspective of framing, Dhar and Zhu present this as 19.7% of the sample not displaying the disposition effect!

[14] Some of the investors in the Dhar and Zhu study seem to have been fairly sophisticated, but none were professional traders. What happens when it comes to people who buy and sell securities for a living? Do they also reveal the disposition effect? Work by Ryan Garvey and Anthony Murphy suggests that they do. See Garvey and Murphy 2004. The disposition effect has also been studied in other markets. See, for example, the influential study of condominium prices in downtown Boston during the 1990–97 boom–bust cycle in Genesove and Mayer 2001.

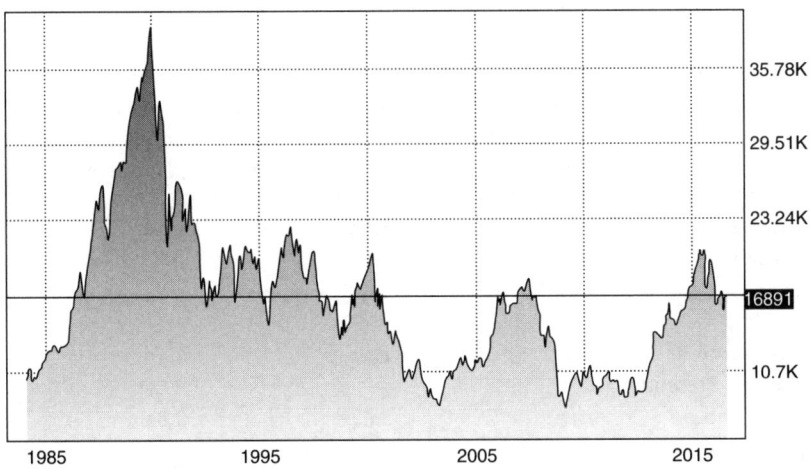

FIGURE 3.1 The NIKKEI 225 Japanese stock market index from 1984 to August 2016, with the value on August 31, 2016 marked in black
Downloaded from www.tradingeconomics.com on August 31, 2016.

Let's begin at the beginning, with the obvious point that equity markets can be dangerous places. Individual stocks, and the market as a whole, can go down as well as up. And once down, they can stay down. When I wrote the first draft of this chapter in September 2016, the Japanese stock market index the Nikkei 225 was trading at well below half of its all-time high, which was reached over 25 years earlier in December 1989.[15] Figure 3.1 shows how the Nikkei 225 fared in that interval. It is a cautionary tale.

When you compare the rollercoaster ride of Figure 3.1 with the slow but safe and steady returns of a typical government bond then it is obvious why investors expect a higher return for holding equities over bonds (and, by and large, they receive it – just not if they happened to buy into the Japanese market in the closing months of 1989).

Still, when you look at the US stock market over long historical periods, the magnitude of the equity risk premium is striking. The first people to draw attention to it and see how puzzling it is were Rajnish Mehra and

[15] As it happens, that market peak was more or less the same time as I made one of my earliest stock market investments – in a managed fund focusing on the Pacific and heavily exposed to the Japanese market. It wasn't a large investment, but I am still hanging on to it (and despite having had over 25 years to grow it still isn't a large investment). Make of that what you will.

Table 3.1 *Measuring the magnitude of the equity risk premium in the United States*

Data set	Real return on a market index (%) Mean	Real return on a relatively riskless security (%) Mean	Equity premium (%) Mean
1802–2004 (Siegel)	8.38	3.02	5.36
1871–2005 (Shiller)	8.32	2.68	5.64
1889–2005 (Mehra–Prescott)	7.67	1.31	6.36
1926–2004 (Ibbotson)	9.27	0.64	8.63

From Mehra 2008, where it is Table 2.1.

Edward Prescott in an article in the *Journal of Monetary Economics* in 1985. In a review article published in 2008 Mehra provided updated numbers confirming his and Prescott's initial analysis. Table 3.1 is taken from the 2008 paper and shows the magnitude of the premium for periods going back as far as 1802.

To get a sense of the magnitude of the premium, compare the outcome of investing $1 in equities in 1802 with the return that you would have had from putting $1 in a riskless government security. The $1 put in the stock market in 1802 would have grown to $655,348 in real terms (i.e. taking inflation into account) by 2004, while the $1 invested in Treasury Bills would only have grown to $293 in the same period (again in real terms).

And this is not just a US phenomenon. Table 3.2 shows the equity risk premium in a range of other economies. Note the negative returns on "riskless" securities, due no doubt to the effects of inflation (since these are real returns that take inflation into account).

All the evidence suggests, then, that there is a significant and robust equity risk premium. But what's the puzzle? Mehra and Prescott's insight back in 1985 was that standard economic models of how people think about risk completely fail to predict an equity risk premium this large. Most people are risk-averse (when it comes to investments), but very few people are as risk-averse as they would have to be for the equity risk premium to be as large as it is.

Table 3.2 *The equity risk premium in a range of economies outside the United States*

Country	Period	Mean real return		
		Market index (%)	Relatively riskless secur-ity (%)	Equity premium (%)
United Kingdom	1900–2005	7.4	1.3	6.1
Japan	1900–2005	9.3	−0.5	9.8
Germany	1900–2005	8.2	−0.9	9.1
France	1900–2005	6.1	−3.2	9.3
Sweden	1900–2005	10.1	2.1	8.0
Australia	1900–2005	9.2	0.7	8.5
India	1991–2004	12.6	1.3	11.3

Dimson, Marsh, and Staunton (2002) and Mehra (2007) for India.
From Mehra 2008, where it is Table 2.2.

Recall from Chapter 2 that attitudes to risk are typically understood in economics through the shape of a consumer's utility curve. People who are risk-averse have utility curves that are concave (as in Figure 2.5, for example). This graphical way of representing risk-aversion also provides a way of measuring degrees of risk-aversion. A consumer's degree of risk-aversion is indicated by how curved their utility curve is. More risk-averse consumers have more curved utility functions. This is because the more curved a utility function is, the greater the gap will be between an investment's expected value and its certainty equivalent. This is illustrated in Figure 3.2.

Thinking about degrees of risk-aversion in terms of the curvature of utility curves offers a precise way of measuring risk-aversion. This is the Arrow-Pratt risk-aversion coefficient, which in effect measures how the slope of a consumer's utility curve changes as magnitudes increase.

The details are not important for now.[16] The important thing is how curved a utility curve would have to be in order to require the level of

---

[16] For completeness, though, the Arrow-Pratt risk coefficient is reached by dividing the second derivative of the equation for the utility curve by the first derivative, and then changing the sign – i.e. $-\frac{u''}{u'}$. This gives a measure that is constant up to affine transformation of the utility function.

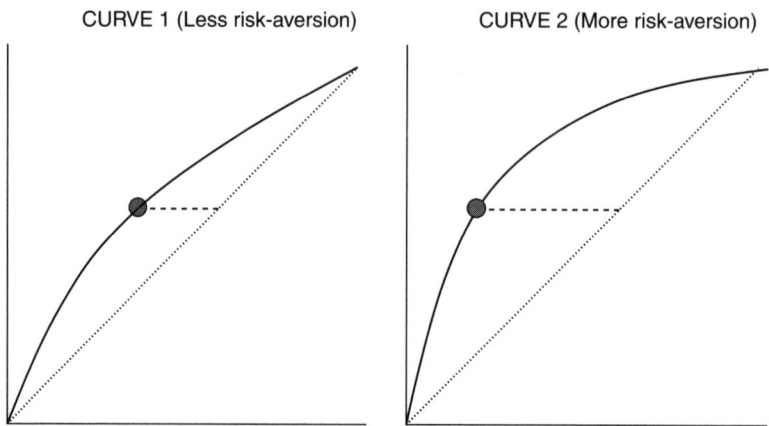

CURVE 1 (Less risk-aversion) CURVE 2 (More risk-aversion)

FIGURE 3.2 How the curvature of utility curves indicates degrees of risk-aversion

Note: Both utility curves are compared to the risk-neutral curve, which is indicated by the dotted line. The dot indicates the certainty equivalent of a given investment and the risk premium is indicated by the dashed line marking the horizontal distance between certainty equivalent and expected value. The more curved the line is, the greater that horizontal distance is, and so the more risk-averse the consumer is.

compensation for taking on risk reflected in the equity risk premium. The short answer is that it would have to be very curved indeed – so curved, in fact, that it is not clear that anyone is that risk-averse. Mehra and Prescott's analysis in their original 1985 paper suggested that the equity risk premium that they found would have required a risk-aversion coefficient of over 30. For comparison, models in modern portfolio theory containing a parameter for the risk-aversion coefficient typically place an upper bound on that parameter of 10, while received wisdom is that most investors range between risk coefficients of 2 and 4.

To give you a sense of how the different risk-aversion coefficients play out, here is a powerful illustration from a paper by Gregory Mankiw and Stephen Zeldes on the equity premium puzzle in the *Journal of Financial Economics*.[17] Consider the following gamble. A fair coin is going to be tossed and if it comes up heads you will receive $50,000, while if it comes up tails you will receive $100,000. What a wonderful opportunity, you might reasonably think. The worst case scenario is that you get $50,000

[17] See Mankiw and Zeldes 1991.

and you've got an even chance of $100,000. So how much would you pay for that opportunity? What would your certainty equivalent be, in other words? It will obviously be a function of how you think about risk. More technically, your certainty equivalent will be determined by your coefficient of risk-aversion.

Menkiw and Zeldes calculated the certainty equivalents that would be generated by different coefficients of risk-aversion. Somebody with a risk-aversion coefficient of 1 would have a certainty equivalent of $70,711, while the certainty equivalent would drop to $58,566 for a coefficient of 5. For someone with a risk-aversion coefficient of 30, though, the certainty equivalent of the risky gamble would be $51,209. In other words, this would be being so incredibly averse to risk that you would not be prepared to pay $51,210 for a chance to play a game in which you have a 50 percent chance of winning $50,000 and a 50 percent chance of winning $100,000. Surely very few people are *that* averse to risk. Just ask yourself whether you would be prepared to toss a fair coin where you will lose $1,210 if it comes up heads but gain $48,790 if it comes up tails! Of course, you might just happen to be that risk-averse. In that case, you can ask yourself whether you think that you are representative of equity investors in general.

Myopic Loss-Aversion

But if risk-aversion does not explain the equity risk premium, then what does? Shlomo Benartzi and Richard Thaler's theory of *myopic loss-aversion* argues that the demand for such a high risk premium ultimately comes from a combination of two factors. The first is loss-aversion. The second is the frequency with which investors evaluate their portfolios. They come together as follows. If investors have a *myopic* perspective (that is, if they are short-sighted when it comes to their investment time horizons) then they will check their portfolios more frequently, which means that they will have to confront the reality of loss more frequently. And that in turn means that their inherent aversion to loss is given more opportunity to kick in.

To emphasize again, loss-aversion is importantly different from risk-aversion. Risk-aversion is measured by the shape of an individual's utility curve – the greater the curvature, the greater the degree of risk-aversion. Loss-aversion, on the other hand, means that an investor, or other type of agent, will react to losses differently from gains. This is because losses are more psychologically impactful than gains. The negative *dis*value attached to losing a certain sum of money is higher than the value attached to gaining that same sum of money. Someone who is loss-averse will be more upset by losing $1,000 than they will be happy when they gain $1,000. In fact, there is experimental evidence suggesting that attitudes to losses and gains differ by a factor of around 2. So, the disvalue of losing something that one actually possesses is around twice the value of gaining that thing in the first place.[18]

Volatility is what makes the connection between loss-aversion, frequency of evaluation, and risk. Risky assets, such as equities, are typically highly volatile. Over a period of time their prices display a high variance above and below their mean price for that period. In modern portfolio theory, risk is typically equated with volatility, but there is no need to go that far. All that we need is the intuitive point that risky assets tend to go up and down. The more frequently you look at your investments the more likely you are to run into one of the down spells. So the more likely you are to experience the negative effects of a loss, even if it is just a paper loss.

For Benartzi and Thaler, then, the equity risk premium is the compensation that investors demand for taking on the pain of looking at investments that have not done well. And the premium is as high as it is because investors have the unfortunate habit of looking at their portfolios frequently and myopically. Frequency and myopia are in fact two different things, although they often get run together in the literature. Myopia is the important thing for understanding the equity risk premium. Losses and gains are measured relative to evaluation horizons. The longer your evaluation horizon, the less likely you are to be troubled by fluctuations and variance.[19] But myopic investors have short time horizons, which is why they see a loss where a more phlegmatic investor with a longer time horizon might simply see a fluctuation. Of course, for many people the length of their investment time horizon is driven by the frequency with which they check their portfolio, but it need not be like that. Someone

---

[18] For empirical studies of loss-aversion (and its close cousin the endowment effect) see the empirical studies in Kahneman, Knetsch, and Thaler 1990. They found, for example, that subjects who had just been given a mug and were then offered the opportunity to trade it for a pen of equal (monetary) value, were not only unwilling to make the trade, but actually wanted a premium of around twice the value of the mug before parting with it. See also Carmon and Ariely 2000 for an even more extreme illustration with basketball tickets (admittedly, not just any old basketball tickets – tickets for the NCAA Final Four!).

[19] And your evaluation horizon is not the same as your investment horizon. If you are a 40-year-old investing for retirement then your investment horizon is 25 years, or thereabouts. But you would be wise to evaluate your portfolio more frequently than that (if you want to give yourself the opportunity to change your overall investment strategy, for example).

investing for the long haul with a Buffett-like tenacity might still choose to check their portfolio on a daily basis.

In their paper, Benartzi and Thaler explore the relation between investment time horizon and the equity risk premium. The approach was very clever. They started off by assuming an investor with the kind of preferences revealed in the various experiments and studies that we have been looking at in this chapter and the last one. So, their typical investor is risk-averse for gains and risk-loving for losses. They also started off from the premise (experimentally supported) that people typically look at things relative to a given reference point, rather than in absolute terms – and that they are loss-averse (i.e. that they feel the pain of a given loss significantly more than they feel the joy of a corresponding gain). This framework allowed them to accommodate the experimental evidence as to how people actually make choices.[20]

Then they explored a data set giving the historical returns for equities and bonds month-by-month in the period 1926–90.[21] Extensive sampling from the data set allowed them to calculate the return distribution for different evaluation horizons over the entire period, starting with a one-month evaluation period and then increasing by a month at a time. They did this for equities and for bonds. Plugging the return distribution for a given evaluation period into the preferences allowed them to calculate how a typical investor might have valued each investment class for a given evaluation period. In other words, for a given *n*-month investment period, they worked out how a typical investor (as defined by the various experimental studies of choice behavior we have been looking at) would have evaluated a portfolio composed solely of equities relative to a portfolio composed solely of bonds in a massive number of *n*-month periods over the entire 65-year span from 1926 to 1990.[22] Think of this retrospectively, so that investors are taking stock of how their investments have fared over a given *n*-month period. The results of the comparison are shown in Figure 3.3.

The key to understanding the equity risk premium is the point at which the two lines cross. This is the point where the investor is

---

[20] Benartzi and Thaler basically assumed that their typical investor has the preference structure described by Kahneman and Tversky's prospect theory. We will look at prospect theory in more detail in Chapter 4.

[21] The data set comes from the CRSP (the Center for Research in Security Prices) at the University of Chicago Booth School of Business. Note that Benartzi and Thaler used bonds rather than Treasury Bills as the comparison class.

[22] They took 100,000 samples for each *n*-month period (obviously with replacement – i.e. allowing the same *n*-month period to be sampled more than once).

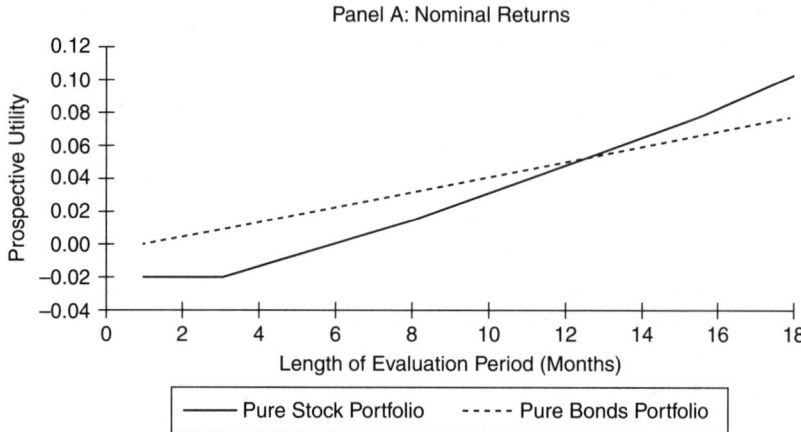

FIGURE 3.3 How Benartzi and Thaler think that a typical investor would evaluate a portfolio composed solely of stocks vs. a portfolio composed solely of bonds
Note: The prospective utility values are arrived at by massive sampling of the CRSP database over the period 1926–1990, as described in the text.
Figure 1 from Benartzi and Thaler 1995 (p. 84).

indifferent between the equity portfolio and the bond portfolio (and so values them the same). As Figure 3.3 shows, the indifference point is reached with an evaluation horizon of just over 12 months. So, even though equities have massively outperformed bonds over the entire 65-year period, when that long period is broken down into 12-month segments then the bond portfolio looks just as attractive as the equity portfolio. This is a little clearer when put the other way around. When one looks just at 12-month evaluation periods, then the actual equity premium (the amount by which equities have outperformed bonds over the period) is exactly the level of compensation for holding equities that would be demanded by an investor with the type of preferences that people display in experimental studies.

The reason that Benartzi and Thaler propose this as a satisfying explanation of the equity risk premium is that, they claim, *the typical investor has an evaluation period of around 12 months.* In support of this they mention the following:

- Investors typically file their taxes on annual basis
- Investors tend to receive their most comprehensive reports from their brokers, investment funds, and retirement accounts annually

- For institutional investors, annual reports from companies are much more important than quarterly earnings reports.[23]

If this is right, then the equity risk premium is explained exactly as Benartzi and Thaler propose – by a combination of loss-aversion (reflected in the prospect theory preferences) and myopia (reflected in the 12-month evaluation period).

The Benartzi and Thaler explanation of the equity risk premium is very theoretical, and rests upon some significant assumptions (e.g. the typical period of evaluation). But other scholars have found empirical support for the theory of myopic loss-aversion. Here are some highlights.

- Noting that much of the experimental support for the theory of myopic loss-aversion comes from student populations, Michael Haigh and John List tested the theory with professional traders from the Chicago Board of Trade (CBOT).[24] Subjects were asked to invest some portion of a 100-unit endowment in a lottery with a 2/3 probability of returning 2.5 times the stake, and a 1/3 probability of returning nothing. In the frequent feedback condition subjects made nine separate decisions with immediate feedback on each occasion, while in the infrequent feedback condition, subjects made three decisions (each of which remained in force for three plays). The feedback in the infrequent condition was aggregated over the three plays, rather than given for each play individually. The theory of myopic loss-aversion predicts that subjects should be prepared to bet more with infrequent feedback than with frequent feedback.[25] Not only is this what Haigh and List found, but they also found that the effect was much greater among the professional traders from the CBOT than among a control group of undergraduate students (from the University of Maryland).
- Kristoffer Eriksen and Ola Kvaløy looked at yet another population of investors – professional investment managers. Using the same paradigm as Haigh and List, Eriksen and Kvaløy found strong evidence of myopic loss-aversion among the investment managers. Interestingly, the effect was more pronounced when the managers

[23] Benartzi and Thaler 1995, p. 83.
[24] Haigh and List 2005, using an experimental paradigm originally developed in Gneezy and Potters 1997.
[25] Because the more frequent the feedback the higher the demanded return – or alternatively, the less money staked on a given return.

were investing clients' money than when they were investing their own.[26]

- Boram Lee and Yulia Veld-Merkoulova looked at data from a survey of 2,000 Dutch households to explore myopic loss-aversion in the field, with an average of eight years' investment history for each investor. Consistent with the theory of myopic loss-aversion, they found a strong (negative) correlation between frequency of portfolio evaluation and the proportion of equities in the portfolio. In other words, the more frequently they were confronted with the reality of investment loss, the less they valued the return from equities (which is another way of saying – the higher the compensation they demanded from the equity part of their portfolio).[27]

Framing, Myopia, and Loss

The theory of myopic loss-aversion is certainly ingenious and seems to fit the data well.[28] But in what sense does it involve framing? There is nothing frame-dependent about loss-aversion *per se*. We've certainly looked at framing effects involving loss-aversion, but in all those cases framing came in because subjects seemed to evaluate an outcome differently depending on how it was reached. And for investors to be myopic is a matter of how frequently they check and review their portfolios. Where is the framing in that?

Actually, I think that there are at least three different ways in which framing is implicated in the theory of myopic loss-aversion. They are:

- How the starting point of evaluation is framed
- How the end-point of evaluation is framed
- How the risk of an investment is framed.

Some of the framing effects are more subtle than others. Let's take a look.

The key notion in the theory of myopic loss-aversion is the idea of a period of evaluation – the typical interval at which investors check the

---

[26] Eriksen and Kvaløy 2010.   [27] Lee and Veld-Merkoulova 2016.

[28] Not all commentators have been convinced, however. Benartzi and Thaler's original analysis is challenged in Durand, Tee, and Lloyd 2004. Blavatskyy and Pogrebna 2009 and 2010 argue that many of the experiments using the Gneezy and Potters paradigm only show myopic loss-aversion in the aggregate (as opposed to showing it for a majority of individual investors). They explicitly exempt Haigh and List from this charge, however. And this criticism would also seem to leave the Lee and Veld-Merkoulova survey analysis untouched.

status of their portfolios and review progress. Benartzi and Thaler plausibly argue that most investors check and review annually. But not everyone who checks and reviews annually will necessarily be myopic in the right sort of way to generate the equity risk premium (or maybe it is the wrong sort of way!). Both the starting point and the end-point need to be framed in a way that will engage the investor's aversion to loss. After all, if you don't have a loss then there is nothing to be averse to.

So, suppose that you are a typical small investor holding equities, perhaps in a defined contribution retirement account, or with another type of tax-protected account (e.g. an IRA in the United States or an ISA in the United Kingdom). You review your investments every year. What would it take for you to be myopically loss-averse? Obviously, the Benartzi and Thaler proposal depends upon you encountering a loss in sufficiently many one-year periods for your instinctive aversion to loss to kick in and require the substantially higher return characteristic of the equity risk premium. But for that to happen it must be the case that you take the starting point of your evaluation to be the previous evaluation date – say, the previous December, if, like most investors, you typically review and check towards the end of the financial year. But it certainly doesn't follow from the fact that you review annually that you will assess performance over a one-year period. Most investment brokers provide enough information for you to assess the performance of your portfolio at many different time intervals. It's up to you to choose the interval – or, in other words, how you frame the starting point of evaluation.

It would be perfectly open to you, for example, to look at the annualized rate of return from your portfolio since you opened the account. Looking at annualized rates of return flattens out many of the spikes (both upside and downside) – and it does this more effectively the longer you have held your portfolio. So, unless you really have been spectacularly unfortunate or ill-advised, you won't see any losses. Even in the worst years (2008, say, or 2002) what you will see will be a dip in your annualized rate of return. Here is a nice illustration.

The year 2008 was a truly awful one for equity investors. From December 2007 to December 2008 the Dow Jones Industrial Average fell 33.986 percent (even with dividends reinvested).[29] Anybody reviewing and checking their portfolio on a December-to-December basis would rightly have been distraught. Framed on a year-on-year basis it is hard to gloss this performance as anything but awful, and the psychology of loss-aversion

---

[29] I am using the Dow Jones Industrial Average Return Calculator at dqydj.com.

would surely kick in in full force. But suppose (for simplicity) that you had held your investment since January 1990 and that when you carried out your annual investment review in December 2008 you framed your starting point and progress by looking instead at the annualized rate of return of your portfolio (with dividends reinvested). Then you would have seen a drop in the annualized rate of return from 12.043 percent to 8.95 percent. That is not great, for sure. But from a psychological point of view it would seem to fuel loss-aversion much less than the idea of a 33.986 percent year-on-year loss.

And of course the starting point only gives half of the frame. How one looks forward is just as important as how one looks backwards. If you are treating the moment of evaluation as a fixed reference point then things will look very different than if you look at it as a snapshot within a larger investment horizon. Taking a longer-term view lessens the blow of paper losses. It creates opportunities for portfolio rebalancing, for example. Many value investors believe in some form of reversion to the mean over time. So an equity that has fallen in price over the last 12 months might be framed as an investment opportunity – as being priced below fundamental value in a way that could generate excess returns over time when (and if) the market reverts to its long-term function as a weighing machine (to borrow Benjamin Graham's famous phrase). This way of thinking about their portfolios is not open to myopic investors, because of how they frame the end-point of evaluation, treating the moment of evaluation as a fixed end-point, rather than a fluid stage in a long-range process.

This relates directly to the idea of narrow framing, which affects how risk itself is framed.[30] Narrow framing occurs when outcomes are framed in a way that screens out the context. So, for example, an investor might focus on an individual security, rather than their entire portfolio, losing the smoothing effect that comes with taking a more all-encompassing view. Narrow framing magnifies the psychological impact of losses, even paper losses. Think back to the discussion of hedonic editing and mental accounting in Chapter 2. Losses are psychologically impactful, and the more of them there are the greater the impact. Someone who frames outcomes narrowly may find many individual losses as they review their portfolio, with accompanying psychological trauma, whereas someone who frames their outcomes in a portfolio-wide way might find the impact of individual losses mitigated by the overall health of their portfolio, and/ or by gains elsewhere.

[30] Barberis and Huang 2008; Barberis and Xiong 2009.

And even taking a portfolio-wide perspective might count as narrow framing, because an ideal investor might be advised to consider their equity investment portfolio within the broader context of their total wealth, and other assets, such as their principal residence, for example. Stock market risk is not the only kind of risk. Inflation, interest rates, property prices, and exchange rates all have risks associated with them. So, even if one loses money within one's investment portfolio as a whole, taking these other risks into account might blunt the psychological impact of those losses. I might take comfort in the thought that, although my stock market investments have gone down, increasing house values have raised my overall net worth. Or I might reflect on how much worse things might have gone had I been heavily invested in fixed income securities such as bonds.

So, to sum up, empirical evidence for the disposition effect and the theory of myopic loss-aversion suggest that several different types of framing drive investment decisions. It matters greatly how changes in wealth are framed – relative to a shifting reference point, rather than absolutely. Likewise, how investors evaluate the success or failure of individual investments depends very much on how they frame their horizon of evaluation – where they start from and how far into the future they look. It also depends on how broadly they cast their net – on how much they contextualize individual investments within their portfolio as a whole, and then on how much they consider their portfolio in the context of all the other risks that they confront.

So, with all this evidence on how framing drives behavior clearly in view, our next step is to look at what people have said about the rationality of framing. We've looked at the descriptive piece. The normative piece will be the subject of the next chapter.

4

Juliet's Principle

It's time to take stock. We have seen many examples of framing effects. Some are nicely revealed in the laboratory. Others appear when we look closely at financial markets and investments. Still others run through everyday life. These framing effects have a reasonably well understood basis in the brain.[1] They seem to be as real as real can be. So now we need to start tackling a fundamental issue. This has come up on many occasions, but up to now we have kept on putting it to one side. So far, we have focused on reporting framing effects and understanding what they involve. But, even though I have been trying to be dispassionate and neutral, it should be clear to everyone that framing effects have not had a good press. The issue for now, and it will occupy us in one form or other for the rest of this book, is whether and how this is justified. Are framing effects always a negative? Are people susceptible to them always irrational?

The economists, psychologists, and neuroscientists whose work we have been considering tend to take a very unequivocal view. As we saw right at the beginning of the book, framing effects are prime exhibits in the litany of irrationality. Sometimes when I am reading articles on framing effects I can almost hear the sound of experimenters crying "Gotcha!" as they find subjects who switch, for example, from being risk-averse to being risk-loving as the frame changes. And there is a very good reason for this. The dominant way of thinking about rationality and rational decision-making in the social sciences leaves absolutely no room for susceptibility to framing effects to be anything other than the height of

[1] For more details, see the Appendix, "Frames in the Brain."

66

irrationality. When experimenters explore framing effects, they tend to do so against the backdrop of a normative theory of how rational thinkers and rational agents *ought* to make decisions. This normative theory goes by many names – expected utility theory, Bayesian decision theory, rational choice theory. But at the heart of the theory is a simple principle. This is often called the principle of extensionality (I'll explain the terminology in due course). I have a different name for it.

Shakespeare's Juliet famously mused – "What's in a name? That which we call a rose / By any other name would smell as sweet." Of course, she is talking specifically about the names "Montague" and "Capulet" (Romeo's and hers, respectively). But there is a more general point. What we call things shouldn't affect how we value them. Nor, by extension, should our valuations depend upon how we describe different courses of action or their alternative possible outcomes. So, with apologies to Shakespeare, I will co-opt the name *Juliet's principle* for the principle that rational thinking should be frame-independent.

The first part of the chapter sketches a basic outline of Bayesian decision theory. I show how decision theory codifies and regiments a very natural and intuitive way of thinking about how people can and should go about deciding what to do and how to choose. As it is standardly developed, Bayesian decision theory has Juliet's principle as an almost immediate consequence. But of course, there is an obvious conclusion to draw from the many experiments and results that we have been looking at in the last few chapters. They all seem to show that Bayesian decision theory is really not a very good description of how people actually go about making decisions. So, if what we are interested in is a model, not of how rational agents *ought* to reason, but rather of how flesh-and-blood agents actually do go about making decisions, then we need to look elsewhere. This was well understood by Amos Tversky and Daniel Kahneman who between them did so much to reveal how huge the gap is between Bayesian decision theory and the psychological realities of everyday life. Tversky and Kahneman developed what they called *prospect theory* as a way of trying to bridge the gap.

Prospect theory is not supposed to be a theory of how rational choosers *ought* to choose. It is descriptive, not normative. In fact, it was originally designed (and then subsequently fine-tuned) in order to systematize Kahneman and Tversky's experimental studies of the vagaries of human decision-making. And so, unsurprisingly, it has no place for Juliet's principle. Instead, it incorporates a subtle account of the mechanics and machinery of framing. Looking at that account in the second part of the chapter provides a useful counterweight to the prescriptions of Bayesian decision theory. By the end of the chapter we will have a good sense of how Juliet's principle is honored both in the breach and in the observance.

What's in a Decision?

Before getting into the details of decision theory and prospect theory let's start by thinking more generally about decisions and actions. Experimental psychologists, economists, and other social scientists largely share an abstract picture of the different stages of decision-making. We can think of this as a schematic outline, as it were, of what goes into a typical decision. This schematic outline sets the framework for more precise theories and models of decision-making. Bayesian decision theory and prospect theory are really just different ways of putting flesh on the same set of bones.

In thinking about decision-making, we can start from the end and work backwards. In most cases the aim of decision-making is simply deciding what to do. This typically involves selecting an action from a range of possible actions. So, we can say that the end-point of decision-making is action selection. But on what basis are actions selected?

The standard, and very plausible, view is that the crucial determinant of action selection is how each of the different available actions is valued. Valuing an action, in turn, is standardly thought to be a two-step process. First, the decision-maker needs to calculate the possible outcomes of each action. In many cases, of course, an action will have different possible outcomes depending on how the world turns out. Second, the different possible outcomes of each action need to be assessed and compared. In very general terms, the "currency" for that assessment/comparison is how the different possible outcomes individually further the decision-maker's goals and values. And it is not enough simply to calculate the possible benefits of a given course of action. The costs of each action also need to be factored in. So too does the likelihood of the world turning out in ways that lead a particular action to produce one set of costs and benefits rather than another.

But these calculations do not take place in a vacuum. Before any of this can take place the decision-maker needs to develop a framework for decision-making. The very first step is identifying the parameters of the decision. At a minimum that means working out what the different possible courses of action are. But typically, it also involves identifying factors that, although they are not directly within the decision-maker's

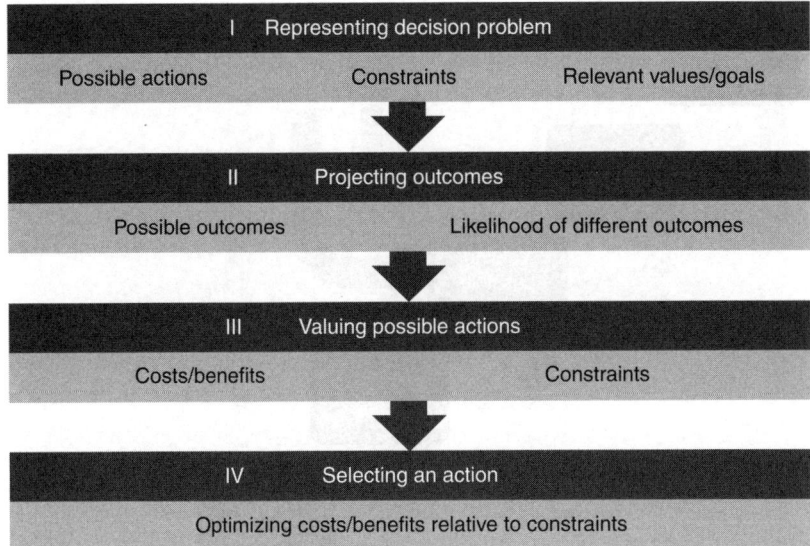

FIGURE 4.1 A schematic representation of the different stages in decision-making

control, will nonetheless affect the outcomes of different possible actions. Decision-makers need to situate what they can do relative to constraints imposed by the environment in which they are operating. Sometimes those constraints are fixed, imposed by physical features of the environment, for example. In others, they are more dynamic. Things are very different, for example, when the decision-making environment contains other agents.

So, flipping the order around so that we follow the actual process of decision-making, there are four main steps in decision-making. These are depicted in Figure 4.1.

Of course, Figure 4.1 is very schematic. It presents, as it were, a template for thinking about how decisions are made. Many real-life cases of decision-making will skip one or more of the steps. Sometimes the shape of the decision problem is given, for example – it is just obvious what the available actions are, and how they are to be compared. But a complete account of decision-making will have to include all of the dimensions that we have identified.

There is one respect, though, in which the process depicted in Figure 4.1 oversimplifies. It only flows in one direction. There are no feedback loops and so no indication of how each of the steps can be influenced and structured by learning. Learning requires

Frame It Again

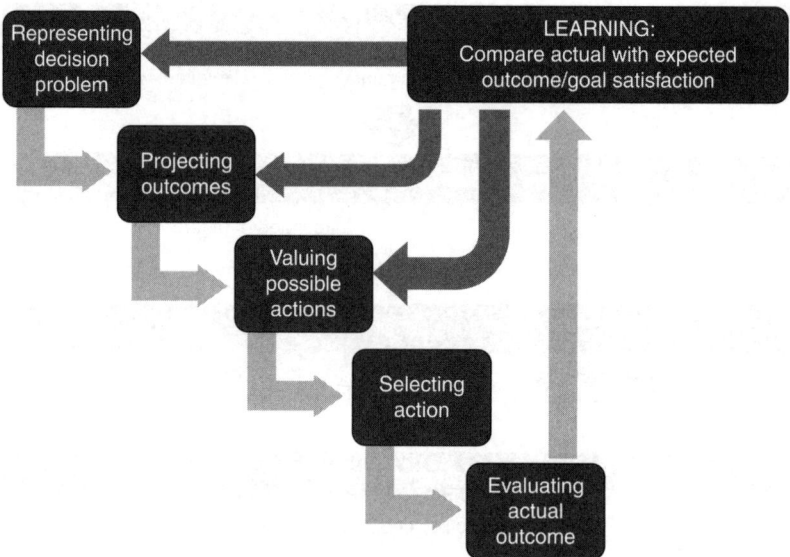

FIGURE 4.2 A schematic illustration of feedback channels in decision-making

mechanisms for evaluating outcomes and then comparing actual results to expected results. The gap between expectation and reality is an error signal. Closing the gap (and diminishing the error) means making changes in the tools used and/or the information brought to bear in earlier steps, as illustrated in Figure 4.2.

Again, this is a schematic diagram, intended to show the different elements that a full account of decision-making needs to illuminate, rather than a blueprint for every instance of decision-making.

On this schema, the basic components of decision-making are pretty simple. In very general terms, to make a decision is to select one of a range of possible actions. Actions are typically compared through their different possible outcomes, with those outcomes in turn evaluated in terms of how each of them are judged to further the agent's goals, interests, and values. The canonical development of this general schema is Bayesian decision theory (also known as expected utility theory, or rational choice theory). This theory sets the normative framework for most discussions of rationality in the social sciences. It is standardly thought to be definitive of individual rationality, and hence the touchstone against which framing effects are measured.

Working with Utilities and Probabilities

The framework for Bayesian decision theory is set by the general schema just sketched out. It is designed to set standards of rationality for a certain family of decision problems.[2] These are decision problems where an agent has available a fixed number of possible courses of action. Each of these different courses of action has a different outcome (or a range of different possible outcomes) depending on the different ways in which things might turn out. In other words, the agent can do one of a number of things, the results of which will depend upon certain factors that are outside her control.

Many decision problems involve what is known as *decision-making under certainty*. Imagine that you are ordering a main dish in a restaurant. You have a number of different courses of action available to you – basically, as many as there are main dishes on the menu (in addition to the course of action of not ordering anything, if that is a viable option for you). Assuming that you are in a well-stocked and competently run restaurant you may be confident that the outcome of each possible course of action is that you would receive the item ordered. Here it does not make sense to think of the outcomes depending upon the state of the world. Each action has only one possible outcome.

Let us suppose, in contrast, that you like living dangerously (in a gastronomic sense) and you choose to visit *The Pot-Luck Inn*, a restaurant famous for its selective approach to its own menu. *The Pot-Luck Inn* has a menu with only two dishes – a meat dish and a vegetarian dish. However, each dish is prepared by a different chef. The two chefs hate each other and are never in the kitchen at the same time. So, if the vegetarian dish is available, the meat dish will not be, and vice versa. Customers who choose a dish that is not available are asked to leave the restaurant. As far as this decision problem is concerned there are two relevant states of the world. In one state of the world the meat chef is in the kitchen and in the other the vegetarian chef is in the kitchen. Plainly, each of your available courses of action will have a different outcome depending upon which state of the world holds. If you order the meat dish and the meat chef is in the kitchen then you will get the dish you ordered. If you order the meat dish and the vegetarian chef is in the kitchen then you are just plain out of luck.

---

[2] A classic introduction to Bayesian decision theory is Chapter 1 of Luce and Raiffa 1957. For more up-to-date perspectives see Peterson 2009 and Allingham 2002 (in the OUP Very Short Introductions series).

So, we need to distinguish between decision problems where there is only one relevant state of the world and decision problems where there is more than one relevant state of the world – or, put another way, between decision problems where each available course of action is believed to have only one outcome and decision problems where there are available courses of action with more than one outcome. Deciding what to do in a situation of decision-making under certainty is relatively straightforward. You know what the outcome will be for each of the available actions, and so all that you need to do is consult your preferences over those outcomes. The concept of *utility*, which we have already encountered, is the currency that Bayesian decision theory uses to measure the strength of preferences. Basically, numerical values are assigned to outcomes in such a way that quantitative relations between those numbers reflect differences in the degree to which those outcomes are valued. As you might expect, the general principle here is to choose the action with the highest utility. In other words, rational agents in a situation of decision-making under certainty will maximize utility.

The second kind of decision problem (where actions have more than one possible outcome) is more complex. To see how Bayesian decision theory deals with it, let's flesh out the example a little more. After a chaotic beginning, the chefs at *The Pot-Luck Inn* have settled between them that the vegetarian chef will work on average 4 days a week, while the meat chef will only work an average of 3 days. The menu clearly describes the arrangement that the chefs have made, but gives no guidance on the day-by-day schedules of the two chefs. Ordering a meal at *The Pot-Luck Inn* is a paradigm example of what decision theorists call *decision-making under risk*. You have, broadly speaking, two possible courses of action. You can order the meat dish or order the vegetarian dish. The outcome of your order depends upon which state the world happens to be in – the state in which the vegetarian chef is in the kitchen or the state in which the meat chef is in the kitchen. You do not know which state actually holds. But you are not flying completely blind, since you have some basic information about the probabilities of the two different states of the world. You know that there is a probability of 4/7 that the vegetarian chef will be in the kitchen and a probability of 3/7 that the meat chef will be in the kitchen.

What rational decision-makers will choose depends not just on the probabilities of the different potential states of the world, but also on their preferences over the different possible outcomes. Obviously, if I prefer a vegetarian meal to a meat meal then I would be well advised to order from the vegetarian menu, since it is more likely that the vegetarian chef is in the kitchen on any given day. But if my liking for meat signifi-cantly outweighs my liking for vegetables, then it will make sense for me to order meat, even though the vegetarian state of the world is more probable.

If you have assigned a numerical value to the utility of an outcome, and you know the probability of the state of the world in which that outcome will occur, then you can calculate the *expected utility* of that outcome. All you need to do is to multiply the utility of the outcome by the probability that it will come about. With that in hand, you can then calculate the expected utility of an action. The expected utility of an action is the sum of the expected utility of all of its possible outcomes. Here is the formula for the expected utility (EU) of an action A, where A has n outcomes. Each outcome is designed by O_i and occurs with probability p_i.

$$\mathrm{EU(A)} = \sum_{i=1}^{n} p_i u(O_i)$$

The formula says that the expected utility of A is given by adding together the utilities of each of its different possible outcomes, with the utility of each outcome O_i weighted by the probability p_i that it occurs.

So, if you assign m units of utility to having a vegetarian dinner and n units of utility to having a meat dinner, then you can easily calculate the expected utility of the two actions available at *The Pot-Luck Inn*. The expected utility of ordering a vegetarian meal is 4/7 m + 3/7 × 0 (since you have a 4/7 chance that you will get what you ordered and a 3/7 chance of getting nothing). The expected utility of ordering a meat dish is 3/7 n + 4/7 × 0 (since you have a 3/7 chance that you will get what you ordered and a 4/7 chance of getting nothing).

So, which should you choose? Well, it depends of course on the relation between m and n. You should choose meat if the expected utility of choosing meat outweighs the expected utility of choosing the vegetarian meal – that is, if 3/7 n > 4/7 m or (multiplying both sides by 7) if 3 n > 4 m. Simplifying further, a rational agent will choose meat provided that the utility n that they assign to the meat outcome is greater than 4/3 m, where m is the utility that they assign to the vegetarian outcome. This is just a special case of the general principle of expected utility theory, which is that a rational agent will always choose the action that has the highest expected utility.

The important point here is that Bayesian decision theory really makes rationality into a matter of internal consistency. The theory doesn't have anything to say about how much utility you should assign to meat dishes as opposed to vegetarian dishes – or to anything else for that matter. Nor does it say where you should get your information about probabilities. It takes utilities and probabilities as given and then defines the rational choice as the one that maximizes utility when the different ways the world could turn out are taken into account.

Of course, it would be reasonable to ask where utilities and probabilities come from. The short answer is that the existence of probability and utility assignments is guaranteed for agents who make choices that are internally consistent in certain very basic ways. So, this gives a deeper sense in which Bayesian decision theory is a theory of consistency. Let me explain, because it will be important for seeing why Bayesian decision theory is committed to Juliet's principle.

The great breakthrough in the development of decision theory came in 1944 when Johann von Neumann and Oskar Morgenstern proved a *representation theorem* for their version of expected utility theory.[3] Working within an environment in which all probabilities were objective and known by decision-makers, they took as their starting point a decision-maker who makes choices that obey a small set of basic axioms – or, alternatively put, whose preferences over possible actions obey the basic axioms. They then showed that it will always be possible to work backwards from those choices/preferences in order to obtain a utility function for that decision-maker. Moreover, and this is the really important point, when that utility function has been defined, the decision-maker's choices will always come across as maximizing expected utility, relative to objectively known probabilities. What this shows, ultimately, is that maximizing expected utility is equivalent to making choices that are internally consistent in certain basic ways dictated by the axioms of decision theory.

Leonard Savage built upon this representation theorem in his 1954 book *The Foundations of Statistics*.[4] Savage added what are called "personal probabilities" or "subjective probabilities." The von Neumann/Morgenstern utility theorem is proved relative to objective probabilities

[3] Frank Ramsey was the first economist to sketch out a representation theorem in his paper "Truth and probability," published the year following his early death at the age of 26 (Ramsey 1931). For an accessible presentation of the theorem in von Neumann and Morgenstern 1944 see Chapter 4 of Resnik 1987.
[4] Savage 1972 is the second edition of *The Foundations of Statistics*. This is not a book for the faint-hearted. Chapter 1 of Ahmed 2014 presents the basics of Savage's theory.

of the sort that one might encounter playing gambling games or picking colored balls out of urns. But of course, most decision-making does not take place in the world of urns, dice, and cards. Savage showed how to prove a representation theorem that worked backwards from suitably consistent choices to generate a probability function as well as a utility function, still with the property that the choices made come out as maximizing expected utility. In other words, if your choices meet the consistency requirements imposed by the axioms, then it will be possible to define both a utility function (defined over the different possible outcomes of your actions) *and* a probability function (defined over different possible states of the world) so that you come out as always maximizing expected utility relative to those two functions.

In any case, here's another way of putting the point that explains why the representation theorems are called what they are. In effect, what these theorems show is that the machinery of expected utility theory can function as a way of representing choices that meet certain constraints of internal consistency over time. This will turn out to be very important for understanding why Bayesian decision theory is committed to Juliet's principle.

Juliet's Principle and Bayesian Decision Theory

Let's start with two quotes. The first is from a review paper by Amos Tversky and Daniel Kahneman published in 1986. They are discussing how framing effects bear upon Bayesian decision theory. They observe the incompatibility between framing effects and Bayesian decision theory, and draw a stark conclusion.

> Because framing effects and the associated failures of invariance are ubiquitous, no adequate descriptive theory can ignore these phenomena. On the other hand, because invariance (or extensionality) is normatively indispensable, no adequate prescriptive theory should permit its violation. Consequently, the dream of constructing a theory that is acceptable both descriptively and normatively appears unrealizable.[5]

Juliet's principle (which they more prosaically call the principle of invariance, or the principle of extensionality) is, in their words, "normatively indispensable" – that is, it is a non-negotiable requirement of rationality. And so, given how widespread framing effects are, that simply means that

---

[5] Tversky and Kahneman 1986, p. S272.

there is an ineliminable gap between the normative theory of rationality and a descriptive theory of how we actually reason. No theory can do both jobs.[6]

The second quote is from the famous economist Kenneth Arrow. Arrow is much more explicit about what exactly Juliet's principle involves.

> A fundamental element of rationality, so elementary that we hardly notice it, is, in logicians' language, its extensionality. The chosen element depends on the opportunity set from which the choice is to be made, independently of how that set is described. To take a familiar example, consider the consumer's budget set. It is defined by prices and income. Suppose income and all prices were doubled. Clearly, the set of commodity bundles available for purchase is unchanged. Economists confidently use that fact to argue that the chosen bundle is unchanged, so that consumer demand functions are homogeneous of degree zero in prices and income. But the description of the budget set, in terms of prices and income, has altered. It is an axiom that the change in description leaves the decision unaltered.[7]

Arrow makes his point very crisply. From the perspective of economics what fundamentally matters for individual consumers is their respective budget sets. A consumer's budget set is basically all the different bundles of goods and services that they can purchase relative to their income. Arrow's point is that it really doesn't matter how those goods and services are labeled. A washing machine and a meal out are still a washing machine and a meal out however one labels them. And, as he observes, pricing is really just another form of labeling. What matters is purchasing power, and that remains constant even if, say, all of the numerical values are doubled, so that the consumer earns twice as much while everything else costs twice as much. But how do we get from Bayesian decision theory to Juliet's principle? I think that we can reconstruct (at least) two reasons explaining why Juliet's principle has seemed to so many to be, in Arrow's phrase, "a fundamental element of rationality."

The first reason is a little technical. To appreciate it, let's look briefly at the version of Bayesian decision theory proposed by Leonard Savage in *The Foundations of Statistics*. As mentioned earlier, Savage provided the first really systematic development of expected utility theory and his model

---

[6] My book *Decision Theory and Rationality* (Bermúdez 2009) goes into much more detail on the different tasks that a theory of rationality can be called upon to perform, and the tensions that this creates.

[7] Arrow 1982, p. 5.

remains a touchstone. It turns out that Juliet's principle is an almost trivial consequence of the machinery that Savage develops.

There are four basic elements in Savage's theory. First, there are *states of the world*. A state of the world is a detailed specification of the world – what a contemporary philosopher might term a possible world. As Savage puts it, "a state is a description of the world leaving no relevant aspect undescribed."[8] In Savage's theory, probabilities are assigned to states of the world. So, the personal probability function is defined across states of the world. Second, there are *events*. Events are sets of states (or what we might think of as sets of possible worlds. So, for example, the event of a ball breaking the window is the set of all states (possible worlds) in which a ball breaks the window. Some events are what Savage calls *consequences* (what we have been calling outcomes). This is the third element in the theory. Consequences are, like events, sets of states. But they are individuated in terms of how they come about and what the agent is doing, as well as what happens in them. So, within the event of a ball breaking the window, we might distinguish those states in which I threw the ball (that would give one consequence/outcome) and those in which someone else threw the ball (part of the same event, but a different consequence/outcome). Finally, Savage has a distinctive way of thinking about *acts*. An act, on his theory, is a function that assigns a consequence (outcome) to every state of the world. The intuitive idea here is that we can identify anything you do with the consequences that it brings about. But the particular consequences that come about because of what you do are determined by the state the world is in. Savage proposes to capture that dependence elegantly by identifying acts with functions from the set of states to the set of consequences.

So, the basic elements of Savage's theory are states, events, consequences, and acts. Why is this important? Because of how he understands them. If we take states of the world as basic, then events and consequences are sets of states, while acts are functions from states to consequences. Since functions are standardly understood by mathematicians as themselves sets, this means that the basic elements of the theory are sets. So, in particular, this means that probabilities and utilities are assigned to sets. Probabilities are assigned to the sets of states that count as events. So, for example, one might assign a probability of 0.7 to the event of it raining tomorrow, where that event is understood as the set of all possible worlds in which it is raining. And utilities are assigned to outcomes. The starting

[8] Savage 1972, p. 13.

point for the representation theorem is the agent's preferences over all possible acts. Since acts are functions, and hence are sets, the objects of preferences are also sets.

But if preferences, utilities, and probabilities are all defined over sets, then Juliet's principle is an immediate consequence. This is because it means that Savage's decision theory is formulated within set theory and the so-called axiom of extensionality is the most basic axiom of set theory.[9] Within set theory, the extensionality axiom says that there cannot be two different sets with the same members. Or, in other words, the identity of a set is fixed by its members – irrespective of how the set itself might be described, or how the members themselves might be described. Juliet's principle certainly holds within set theory and so, if Bayesian decision theory is formulated set theoretically, then the principle would seem to carry over automatically to Bayesian decision theory.

It is not clear from the context, but I am fairly confident that this is what Arrow meant by saying that extensionality is an axiom of the theory of rationality. Still, though, you would be forgiven for finding this a less than compelling argument for Juliet's principle. After all, the principle is being derived more from characteristics of the surrounding theory than from the nature of decision theory and rational choice. Given how important Juliet's principle is, can we find more convincing reasons for taking susceptibility to framing effects to be a paradigm of irrationality?

Here is a second argument that may be more convincing. Recall from the last section what the representation theorems of Bayesian decision theory show. They reveal that making choices that maximize expected utility is ultimately equivalent to having preferences over actions that are internally consistent in a special sense. They are internally consistent because they obey a small set of axioms. In an important sense, therefore, the normative force of the principle of maximizing expected utility stands or falls with the normative force of the basic axioms. So, Bayesian decision theory's claim to lay down what is to count as rational decision-making ultimately rests upon the claim of those basic axioms to be principles of rationality. This is important for thinking about Juliet's principle, because Juliet's principle seems to be required if the basic axioms are to do their work. Let me explain.

There are numerous different axiomatizations of Bayesian decision theory, but they tend to share common elements. A very standard

---

[9] For more details, see any introduction to axiomatic set theory, such as Suppes 1960 or (my personal favorite) Enderton 1977.

requirement is that preferences be *transitive*. What this means is that, if you prefer A to B and you prefer B to C, then you should prefer A to C (where I am assuming that preferences are strict, so that preferring A to B rules out being indifferent between A and B). Someone whose preferences fail to be transitive typically has what are called *cyclical preferences*. The name speaks for itself. Non-transitive preferences are cyclical because the preference relation keeps circling back to the beginning. Someone with cyclical preferences finds themselves preferring A to B and B to C and C to A and A to B . . . and so on indefinitely.

Transitivity certainly is a pretty plausible candidate to be a requirement of rational decision-making and rational choice. One reason for thinking so is that someone with cyclical preferences can find it impossible to make a choice in certain situations. Suppose, for example, that you have to choose one thing from the set {A, B, C}. If you prefer A to B and B to C and your preferences are transitive then your choice is clear. You should pick A. But what should you do if you have the cyclical preferences described in the previous paragraph? You certainly shouldn't pick A, because you prefer C to A. But you shouldn't pick C either, because you prefer B to C. And nor is B a viable option, since you prefer A to B. So, it looks as though someone with cyclical preferences won't be able to choose anything from the set {A, B, C} – at least, not if they stick to the plausible principle that you shouldn't choose something if there is something else available that you strictly prefer to it.

Another reason often put forward for transitive preferences being a requirement of rationality is the so-called money-pump argument. The basic idea here is that someone with intransitive preferences lays themselves open to accepting a series of trades that will eventually bankrupt them. Here is how it works. Suppose that you (strictly) prefer A to B, B to C, and C to A. Then an ingenious and unscrupulous decision theorist (who is often assumed in the literature to be Dutch, for reasons that are not clearly understood!) will be able to milk you of everything you possess.[10] Suppose that you are in possession of C. Then, since you strictly prefer B to C, you should be prepared to pay some sum of money to exchange C for B. The same reasoning will lead you to be ready to pay in order to swap A for B, since you strictly prefer A to B. But now, given that you have a cyclical preference for C over A, you should be excited about the prospect of

---

[10] The Dutch reference comes in because a money pump is closely related to what are (probably unfairly) known as Dutch books, where a Dutch book is a series of bets that is guaranteed to leave you worse off.

paying to swap A out for C. Eventually, of course, you will have gone around the circle so many times that you have been completely bankrupted.[11]

It is true that some people have argued that it can be perfectly rational to have non-transitive preferences.[12] We will come back to this. The important point for now is that Bayesian decision theory requires that preferences be transitive. There is a simple reason for this. Contravening Juliet's principle opens the door to intransitive preferences. Let's look at this using a nice example that we will be coming back to in Chapter 6 – Agamemnon at Aulis (Framing Effect 5 from Chapter 1).

Recall that the prophet Calchas interprets the portent of two eagles swooping down to eat a pregnant hare as requiring Agamemnon to sacrifice his daughter Iphigenia to the goddess Artemis. For Agamemnon (as I am interpreting him) there is a single outcome that he frames in two different ways – as *Murdering his Daughter*, on the one hand, and as *Following Artemis's Will*, on the other. The alternative is *Failing his Ships and People* (by refusing to sacrifice his daughter). Agamemnon's dilemma is that he evaluates the death of Iphigenia differently, depending on how it is framed. He certainly prefers *Following Artemis's Will* to *Failing his Ships and People*. At the same time, though, he prefers *Failing his Ships and People* to *Murdering his Daughter*. On one way of looking at the matter, this gives him cyclical preferences. His preferences are cyclical because he simultaneously prefers *Failing his Ships and People* to *Murdering Iphigenia* and *Murdering Iphigenia* to *Failing his Ships and People*. This is an exotic example, but the basic point generalizes. To be in the grip of a framing effect is to value some thing or outcome differently depending upon how it is understood or described. And on the face of it, that seems to lead naturally to cyclical preferences. So, if transitive preferences are a requirement of rationality, then so too must Juliet's principle be a requirement of rationality.

But still, that's not the only way of looking at the situation. Someone might wonder whether Agamemnon's preferences have been accurately represented. As I have described things, there is a single outcome (the death of Iphigenia) that Agamemnon frames in two different ways. And it is only if we think of the death of Iphigenia as a single outcome that

---

[11] For a critical discussion of money pump arguments see, for example, Schick 1986, Levi 2002, and Ahmed 2017.

[12] The moral philosopher Larry Temkin is a prominent defender of intransitive preferences. See Temkin 1987 and 1996, for example, and Vorhoeve 2013 for critical discussion.

Agamemnon comes out with cyclical preferences. We can only represent Agamemnon as having cyclical preferences if he both prefers *Murdering Iphigenia* to *Failing his Ships and People* and *Failing his Ships and People* to *Murdering Iphigenia*. There is no cycle or intransitivity if we instead represent Agamemnon's preferences in a more fine-grained way, so that instead of talking about a single outcome that is framed in two different ways we think of him as having preferences over two distinct objects. The first object is *Following Artemis's Will*. The second object is *Murdering his Daughter*. If these are distinct objects, so that Agamemnon can evaluate them differently then there is no intransitivity. If we think about it in that way, then Agamemnon has a perfectly transitive set of preferences over three distinct objects, rather than a cyclical set of preferences over two distinct outcomes.

I am deliberately using the neutral term "object" rather than "outcome" because I do not want to say that different frames create different outcomes. There is a fairly standard response when people come up with apparent counterexamples to transitivity or other decision-theoretic axioms. One can always get rid of an apparent counterexample by redefining the outcomes.[13] As a general strategy, this works better for some cases than for others. But here I simply point out that Agamemnon is perfectly aware that *Following Artemis's Will* and *Murdering Iphigenia* are not different outcomes. They are really just different ways of thinking about the same basic outcome – the death of Iphigenia. That is why Aeschylus's *Agamemnon* is a Greek tragedy, not a comedy of errors. We

---

[13] The classic example is Savage's *sure-thing principle*, which was famously challenged by the Nobel-winning French economist Maurice Allais. In a paper published in 1979, Allais came up with an example (the so-called Allais paradox) where many have thought it is perfectly rational to contravene Savage's principle (Allais 1979). The sure-thing principle basically says that if you prefer A over B then your preference should continue to hold even when the choice between A and B is embedded in a more complex decision situation (and vice versa). So, for example, if you prefer sorbet to ice cream then you should prefer a gamble in which you have a 50% chance of chocolate cake and a 50% chance of sorbet to a gamble in which you have a 50% chance of chocolate cake and a 50% chance of ice cream. The chocolate cake outcome is the same in the two gambles (it's a sure thing, in a sense). So, it should be irrelevant to how you choose between them and a rational agent will be guided only by the fact that they prefer sorbet to ice cream. The basic point of the Allais paradox is that how people react to an outcome can be affected by the other outcomes in which it is embedded to create what are sometimes called complementarity effects. But, as has often been pointed out, it is always possible to eliminate the complementarity effects by holding that there is no single outcome across the two cases. For more discussion of this general strategy see, for example, Broome 1991b Chapter 5, and Weber 1998.

will revisit this example in Chapter 6, and see there that Agamemnon is really best described as having what I will call *quasi-cyclical preferences*.

So ... What Really Happens When People Make Decisions?

Bayesian decision theory is a beautifully clear and clean mathematical theory. It reduces decision-making to a small set of axioms and a single principle. But it is hard to apply it to the messy complexities of the real world. Even the founder of modern decision theory had his doubts. Savage himself pointed out that the version of decision theory that he developed in *The Foundations of Statistics* only applies straightforwardly to what he calls "small worlds." In part that is because the key mathematical result requires an implausible starting point. In order to prove the fundamental representation theorem you have to assume that the decision-maker whose preferences and utilities you are trying to represent has a complete set of preferences over all available actions. But sometimes you have no idea how you will react in a given situation until you get there. And in part it is because Bayesian decision theory is in the last analysis a theory of consistency – the axioms of decision theory basically provide a recipe for making choices that are internally consistent. Savage (quite reasonably) did not think that consistency is always a virtue. Your previous choices may not be a good guide – or indeed any guide at all. After all, surely preferences can change rationally.

Still, these doubts notwithstanding, Bayesian decision theory has a good claim to being the best candidate for laying down norms for rational decision-making. But it is not the only game in town. There are many versions of non-expected utility theory out there.[14] These are typically proposed as ways of making Bayesian decision theory more psychologically realistic by modifying or replacing one or more of the axioms that seem to have counter-intuitive consequences. But of course, as the term "non-expected utility theory" suggests, there is a cost, which is losing the expected utility principle. And decision theorists who propose alternatives to Bayesian decision theory are often either coy or ambiguous about what they are actually proposing. Are they offering an alternative *normative* theory? That is, are they proposing a new set of basic axioms and principles that they think better capture what it is to be a *rational* decision-maker? Or, alternatively, are they really just changing the subject and

---

[14] For reviews see Starmer 2000, Schmidt 2004, and Sugden 2004.

offering theories intended as better *descriptions* of how people actually reason?

Prospect theory is a conspicuous exception. It shows no such ambiguity. It was explicitly proposed by Amos Tversky and Daniel Kahneman as a way of accommodating and explaining an enormous array of experimental results on human reasoning and decision-making (many, but not all, coming out of their own labs). The main reason for focusing on it here is that the importance of framing in decision-making is absolutely at the heart of the theory. Here's a passage that we have already looked at once before that makes this absolutely plain.

> Because framing effects and the associated failures of invariance are ubiquitous, no adequate descriptive theory can ignore these phenomena. On the other hand, because invariance (or extensionality) is normatively indispensable, no adequate prescriptive theory should permit its violation. Consequently, the dream of constructing a theory that is acceptable both descriptively and normatively appears unrealizable.[15]

Tversky and Kahneman accept that Bayesian decision theory tells us how we should reason. They agree with the orthodox view that Juliet's principle is a basic demand of rationality. What prospect theory offers is (they think) a more accurate account of how people actually go about solving decision problems. Prospect theory is a descriptive theory of decision-making – warts and all.

The basic elements of Bayesian decision theory are probabilities and utilities. These are defined over outcomes and states understood in ways that are completely frame-independent. Combining probabilities and utilities in accordance with the expected utility principle gives the rational solution to a given decision problem. The rational course of action is the action with the greatest expected utility, where the utility of an action is the sum of the utilities of its different possible outcomes, discounted by their probability. Prospect theory offers a very different picture of how decision-makers solve decision problems. Whereas the Bayesian model has just one stage, prospect theory identifies two stages, each of which diverges substantially from the prescriptions of decision theory.

First there comes an editing stage. This involves interpreting the different possible outcomes – coding them in terms of gains and losses relative to a neutral starting point, for example; discarding extremely unlikely outcomes; and canceling out components that are shared by different

---

[15] Tversky and Kahneman 1986, p. S272.

outcomes. The editing phase is really a construction of the decision problem (whereas decision problems in Bayesian decision theory are just taken as given). The editing phase is a breeding ground for framing effects.

The editing phase can involve a number of different operations. These operations fix how the outcomes are viewed and hence directly structure the decision problem. In effect the editing phase introduces a whole layer of interpretation and conceptualization that is completely absent from Bayesian decision theory. Editing often simplifies the decision problem. In their original 1979 paper in the journal *Econometrica* where prospect theory was first proposed, Kahneman and Tversky identified six distinct editing operations. Here are three of the most important operations from the perspective of framing. In the first two cases I have related the editing operations back to more real-life examples, including some of the framing effects discussed in earlier chapters. The examples Kahneman and Tversky give of these operations tend to be from their own experiments, and I have used one of these to illustrate the third editing operation.

Coding

As we observed when looking at how people can flip from making risk-averse choices to making risk-seeking ones, often what matters to people is what they perceive as gains and losses, rather than absolute quantities. Gains and losses are themselves conceptualized relative to a neutral starting point. So, for example, what drives the disposition effect identified by Shefrin and Statman (and reviewed in Chapter 3) is that investors frame sell/hold decisions in terms of the original purchase price of a given security. The purchase price is the neutral starting point, relative to which investors identify losses and gains. In the theory of myopic loss-aversion, in contrast, the neutral starting point is fixed by the frequency with which investors review their portfolios and their respective investment horizons. The coding part of the editing phase fixes this neutral starting point. As we will see shortly, this sets the frame relative to which the value of different outcomes is fixed.

Segregation/aggregation

It makes a difference when one evaluates different prospects whether outcomes are considered separately or together (i.e. whether they are segregated or aggregated). Consider the hedonic editing hypothesis from Chapter 2. According to the hedonic editing hypothesis, people have a tendency to segregate both losses and gains. This at least is what the experiments seem to show, but (according to the hypothesis) the reasons are different in each case. People segregate losses because they find it less disagreeable to consider a number of small losses than the trauma of a single large loss. They segregate gains, on the other hand, because they would rather spread the pleasure out than take it all at once! This process of segregating/integrating outcomes is part of how decision problems are framed in the editing phase.

Cancellation

How one reacts to decision problems that unfold over time often depends upon how one decomposes the different outcomes. It can really matter, for example, whether one combines the different stages of the decision problem or considers them sequentially. Here is Kahneman and Tversky's own example. Consider a two-stage game in which there is a 75 percent chance that the game ends at the first stage. If the game does continue to the second stage, then you have to choose between (A) a guaranteed $3,000 and (B) an 80 percent chance of $4,000. You make your choice between (A) and (B) before the game starts. Most people when the choice is put like this tend to choose (A), because they prefer what seems to be a certain outcome to a risky outcome. But, of course, (A) is not a certain outcome. If you combine the probabilities across the two stages, then it becomes clear that (A) is really a 25 percent chance of $3,000, and (B) is a 20 percent (i.e. 25 percent of 80 percent) chance of $4,000. And when people are presented with the choice in this form they typically prefer (B) to (A), because they prefer an expected value of $800 to one of $750. The first way of framing the choice is described as an example of cancellation because both outcomes share the first stage, and so decision-makers see it as irrelevant to the choice and hence cancel it out.

So – coding, segregation, and cancellation are all operations that can take place in the editing phase. They fix how the decision problem is framed.

Once the decision problem has been edited, the next stage is selecting a particular action. For prospect theory this is not simply a matter of computing expected utility. It cannot be, because the basic currency of prospect theory is not given by probabilities and utilities. Probabilities are themselves subject to a type of editing. Even when objective probabilities are known for particular outcomes, these are weighted by a decision function π that reflects the impact of that probability on the overall value of the prospect. This decision function fundamentally changes the behavior of probabilities, and they no longer obey the axioms of the probability calculus. So, for example, there is no requirement that $\pi(p)$

and $\pi(1-p)$ sum to 1. And the π function systematically overweights low probability events, so that $\pi(p) > p$ where p is, say, the probability that your next plane flight will be attacked by terrorists, or that your house will be subject to a home invasion. The insurance and home security industries thrive on this property of the decision weight function!

Finally, prospect theory replaces the concept of utility with the concept of value. The word "value" has a technical meaning in prospect theory, different from the meanings that we have already looked at. It has nothing to do with value in the moral or artistic sense. Nor is it to be equated with value in the sense of expected monetary value. Kahneman and Tversky's concept of value is intended to do the same job as the concept of utility – namely, to capture how people make choices between outcomes that reflect more than the expected (monetary) value of those outcomes. But the value functions of prospect theory behave very differently from the utility functions of classical economics and Bayesian decision theory.[16]

We have already looked at examples of utility curves. So, for example, in Chapter 2 we saw that people who are risk-averse have concave utility curves with diminishing marginal utility, whereas risk-seekers have convex utility curves with increasing marginal utility.[17] Things look very different in prospect theory. The basic idea in prospect theory is that people have an S-shaped value curve, as depicted in Figure 4.3.

The S-shaped value curve is intended as a general psychological model of how and why people make the choices that they do. It has some very important properties.

First, it is a fundamental tenet of prospect theory that value is relative not absolute. What people value are changes relative to a starting point, rather than absolute positions on a scale. So, for example, rather than valuing a particular level of wealth, what they care about is how their wealth has changed relative to a given starting point (the beginning of the calendar year, say, or the time at which they made a particular investment). Whereas utility is standardly measured on a scale from 0 to 1, set by the least and most preferred outcomes respectively, the value of an outcome is set by how much it deviates from a neutral starting point set in the editing phase. So, the S-shaped curve is defined in terms of a reference point, which is the origin of the two axes. *The quantity being measured increases to the right of the origin and decreases to the left.* Gains to the right. Losses to the left.

---

[16] For more illustrations and discussion of the relation between prospect theory and utility theory see the essays in Kahneman and Tversky 2000.

[17] See Figure 2.5 for illustrations.

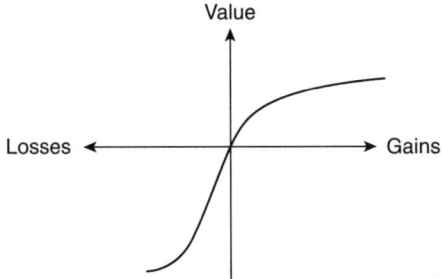

FIGURE 4.3 The S-shaped curve of prospect theory
Note: The curve is intended to represent the value function of a typical individual. Unlike the utility curves of classical decision theory and economics, value is defined over gains and losses relative to a starting point (located at the origin of the graph). Moreover, the value function includes negative disvalue, as well as positive value.

Second, prospect theory takes negative disvalue into account as well as positive value. As has already emerged in this chapter, the utility functions of classical decision theory and classical economics basically function as representations of preferences over outcomes, so the bottom of the utility scale is given by the least preferred outcome, to which we by convention assign a utility of zero. But once you start thinking about the objects of value as changes relative to a reference point, then it makes sense to start thinking not just about the positive value that you attach to some outcome (roughly, how much you like them), but also about the negative disvalue that other outcomes have (how much you *dis*like them). Both of these are defined relative to the reference point, which is neutral between value and disvalue. *Value is represented above the reference point, and disvalue below it.* Value up. Disvalue down.

Third, the S-shaped value curve has the *loss-aversion* property built into it. One of the basic psychological facts discussed in Chapters 1 and 2 is that losses are more psychologically impactful than gains. The degree of (negative) *dis*value attached to losing a certain magnitude (e.g. a sum of money, say, $1,000) is higher than the degree of (positive) value attached to gaining that same magnitude. This is reflected in the S-shaped curve being asymmetrical. In particular, the value function is steeper for losses than for gains. This means that the same horizontal distance (i.e. the same magnitude of loss or gain) corresponds to a much greater vertical distance below the reference point than above it – i.e. the same magnitude is

Frame It Again

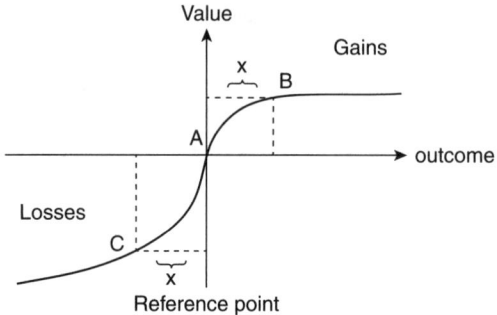

FIGURE 4.4 Representing loss-aversion in the S-shaped value curve of prospect theory

Note: If *x* is a given magnitude of change (say, $1,000), then the value the agent attaches to gaining *x* is represented by the vertical distance from A to B, while the value the agent attaches to losing *x* is represented by the vertical distance from C to A. The shape of the curve reflects the tendency to attach a greater disvalue to losing a given sum than the value attached to gaining that same sum. In other words, prospect theory predicts that I will be much more upset about losing $1,000 than I will be pleased by gaining $1,000.

Drawing by Marc Oliver Rieger.

disvalued much more when it is lost than it is valued when it is gained, as indicated in Figure 4.4.

Finally, the S-shaped curve has built into it both diminishing marginal value and diminishing marginal disvalue. This is easy to appreciate in the case of wealth. Consider a given change in wealth – say, gaining $1,000. Most people think about this gain the same way. The less money they have the more they value it. So, the difference between having $5,000 and having $6,000 is much more significant than the difference between having $100,000 and having $101,000. The same holds for losing $1,000. Most people would feel a $1,000 loss that takes their wealth down from $6,000 to $5,000 much more than a loss that reduces their wealth from $101,000 to $100,000. Diminishing marginal (dis)value is represented in the S-shaped curve by the value and disvalue functions both being steepest near the reference point and getting progressively shallower the further away from the reference point they get.

So now we have in front of us two very different theories. The first is Bayesian decision theory, widely held to define what it means to be a rational decision-maker. Bayesian decision-makers maximize expected utility. That is, they choose the action with the highest expected utility, where the expected utility of an action is the sum of the utility attached to its different possible outcomes when those utilities are discounted by the probability that the relevant outcome will occur. Thanks to the representation theorems we can be sure that decision-makers who maximize expected utility will have transitive preferences and obey certain basic axioms of rationality such as the sure-thing principle. And we know that Bayesian decision theory is committed to Juliet's principle as a basic requirement of rationality, holding that it can never be rational for one's valuation of an outcome to change as a function of how it is framed.

The second theory is prospect theory. This is a very different kind of theory. It is not an account of how rational agents ought to reason. The founders of prospect theory accept Bayesian decision theory (and so Juliet's principle) as a normative theory of rationality. They offer prospect theory as an account of how people actually do reason, taking as their starting point the basic fact that people regularly breach the basic principles of Bayesian decision theory – particularly Juliet's principle. Prospect theory, therefore, offers a psychological model of what, from the perspective of Bayesian decision theory, are fundamentally flawed decision-making processes.

So, the picture that emerges is very much in line with what in Chapter 1 I called the litany of irrationality. Bayesian decision theory tells it the way it ought to be. Prospect theory tells it the way it is. Framing effects are fundamentally irrational – but at the same time inescapable. This stark contrast between ideal norms and messy reality sets the agenda for the rest of the book. It's time to start pushing back. Framing effects can be perfectly rational. We'll start to see how and why in the next chapter.

5

Rational Frames?

This is where we are after the first four chapters. On the one hand, it looks as though we fall prey to framing effects everywhere we turn, from super-market shelves to our retirement accounts. On the other hand, accepted theories of how to make rational choices all hold that being susceptible to how outcomes are framed is a paradigm of irrationality. The psychologists Amos Tversky and Daniel Kahneman make this dilemma very vivid. They offer us two theories – expected utility theory and prospect theory. One (expected utility theory) is a normative theory – a theory of how rational agents are supposed to make decisions and navigate practical problems. The second (prospect theory) is a descriptive theory – a theory that has built into it much, if not all, of the irrationality condemned by the normative theory. And there is no chance, they clearly state, of bringing the two theories into harmony. The reality, they think, is that practical reasoning is irremediably irrational. And so, we have fuel for what I earlier called the litany of irrationality.

We have a conflict between how things are and how things are sup-posed to be – between the descriptive and the normative. Obviously, the force of the conflict depends upon the *accuracy* of the descriptive claims being made, and the *legitimacy* of the normative theory against which those descriptive claims are being evaluated. Anyone unhappy with how the litany of irrationality plays out in this context has, broadly speaking, two available strategies. They can take issue with the descriptive side of the conflict. Or they can take issue with the normative side – with the justification for what I am calling Juliet's principle. One way of taking issue with the descriptive side of the problem would be to challenge the basic data, by identifying flaws in the original framing experiments, for example. We will look at some examples of this strategy in the first section.

Much more promising, though, is the second strategy, which is to take a hard look at the justification for Juliet's principle. This is what will occupy us for the remainder of this chapter. First, I offer a new set of tools for bringing into clearer focus the question I want to ask about framing and rationality. Doing this will lead us to shift focus to a different type of framing effects from those considered up to now. In the last part of the chapter I develop three examples originally discussed by the philosopher Frederic Schick to illustrate how being susceptible to framing effects *can* be rational. The first two examples come from autobiographical episodes described by the novelist and essayist George Orwell and the existentialist philosopher Jean-Paul Sartre. The third is from Shakespeare's *Macbeth*.

Another Look at the Experiments?

As you might expect, the principal experimental paradigms in the framing literature have been closely scrutinized. Some follow-up experiments have failed to replicate key findings, while others have claimed to identify respects in which the experiments do not deliver on what they claim to deliver.[1] I think it's fair to say that, generally speaking, the critics have gained some traction, but not a lot. The problem they face is that the framing literature is just so huge that all that they can do is chip away at the edges. If doubt is cast on one set of experiments, then promoters of the litany of irrationality can just shift to another set, or develop a variant. Still, although the critical studies might not succeed in their overarching aim of discrediting the basic claims about framing that drive the litany of irrationality, some of them do raise very interesting issues that bring clearly into focus the normative issues at stake.

We can learn a lot from looking at two challenges in particular – the first from Shlomi Sher and Craig McKenzie, and the second from David Mandel. Both point to very important features of practical reasoning and problem-solving, and to a tacit assumption behind objections to allowing how one values things to be affected by how they are framed. Let me start with Sher and McKenzie, whose ideas and experiments have been presented in a series of articles.[2] They challenge a basic assumption of the

---

[1] I will not be discussing failures to replicate in the main text, but more details can be found in the detailed survey of framing experiments in Levin, Schneider, and Gaeth 1998.

[2] Sher and McKenzie 2006, 2008, and 2011.

framing experiments, namely, that the two different framed outcomes are, in their expression, *informationally equivalent*. This assumption is an integral part of the case for the experiments revealing widespread irrationality. What seems to make it so irrational to change one's preferences depending upon how the outcome is framed, is that changing the frame neither adds nor takes away any information from the problem that is presented. In typical experiments, the sums of money typically remain the same across the two frames, as do the numbers of people who will lose their lives. The same holds for the probabilities. Nothing important changes when switching from a gain frame to a loss frame. Or so it seems.

But, Sher and McKenzie ask, are the two options really informationally equivalent across the two frames? We know that the two outcomes are *logically* equivalent, in the sense that it is not possible for one to hold without the other. But that does not necessarily make them *informationally* equivalent. Suppose that something like the following is going on:

> Let A and B be a pair of logically equivalent statements about a choice problem. Suppose in addition that speakers' conversational behavior exhibits the following regularity: speakers, choosing between uttering "A" and uttering "B", are more likely to utter "A" when some background condition C (not explicitly specified in the statements A and B) holds than when C fails. In that case, a listener who hears a speaker say "A" can safely infer a higher probability of C being true than if the speaker had said "B". If knowledge about the background condition C is relevant to the choice at hand, then the speaker's (e.g., experimenter's) utterance of the two logically equivalent statements A and B may with impunity lead to different decisions. (Sher and McKenzie 2006, p. 469)

Preference reversal across frames would not be irrational, they point out, if one of the frames brought into play a background condition that is not brought into play by the other. In that case there might actually be valid reasons for people to switch their preferences.

In fact, that is exactly what they think happens when one looks more closely at some of the classic experiments, and in particular at the language used to describe the options between which subjects are choosing. Sher and McKenzie propose what they call the *reference point hypothesis*. To explain it, let's go back to a classic framing experiment presented in Chapter 2 – the robust result that people evaluate ground beef more favorably when it is labeled as 25 percent lean rather than as 75 percent fat.[3] On the face of it this seems completely irrational. What grounds

---

[3] Levin and Gaeth 1988.

could there possibly be for such valuations, given that there seem to be no differences between being 25 percent lean and being 75 percent fat? Sher and McKenzie, though, deny that the two descriptions are informationally equivalent (even though being 25 percent lean is logically equivalent to being 75 percent fat). On the basis of a range of experiments (none of which has anything to do with framing), they suggest that information is carried by something as simple as how one describes proportions. In particular, they suggest that when one property of the ground beef rather than another is highlighted, this is standardly taken to imply that the proportion of that property is higher than what they call the reference point – which is the norm, or what generally would be expected. So, even though you may have no particular preconceptions about how much fat ground beef should contain, when you are told that it is 25 percent lean you are led to believe that this is leaner than normal – and, conversely, when you are told that it is 75 percent fat you are led to believe that it is fattier than normal. And so, the two frames convey different information in a way that might make the preference reversal perfectly rational. After all, if you are concerned about cholesterol levels, it seems perfectly reasonable to prefer meat that is leaner than normal to meat that is fattier than normal.

Here is another, very different illustration of the same point, this time from David Mandel in a paper in the *Journal of Experimental Psychology* in 2013. Mandel's target is the classic Asian disease paradigm, and in particular the implicit assumption that any rational person will recognize the description of 200 people being saved as equivalent to 400 people dying (relative to a population of 600). Mandel argues that this is simply wrong, given how numerical expressions are typically understood. He argues, drawing on evidence from both linguistics and his own experiments, that numerical expressions are typically not understood precisely. So, he claims, when people hear that 200 people will be saved, this is typically understood as the claim that *at least* 200 people will be saved, rather than as that *exactly* 200 people will be saved. Likewise, the claim in the mortality frame that 400 will die is understood as saying that at least 400 people will die. To support this analysis, Mandel ran a version of the Asian disease paradigm in a between-subjects design. In one condition, subjects were given the standard formulation, while in a second the numbers were made precise by specifying that exactly 200 would die, and so on. As predicted, the framing effect was replicated in the first condition but not observed in the second.

Although I think that both Mandel and Sher and McKenzie raise important criticisms of the framing experiments, they are unlikely to upset the entire paradigm. The mass of the experimental evidence is just too great and too wide-ranging. The main point that I want to extract from them is more general and applies far beyond the particular experiments that they discuss. For me, the take-home message is this: The case for the irrationality of frame-dependent preference reversals rests upon the informational equivalence of the two different framings of the same outcome, and it may be the case that framing something differently can bring new factors into play. If that new information provides a new reason for preferring that option, then the patterns of choices revealed in the framing experiments may in fact be perfectly rational. This in essence will be the starting point for my argument that frame-sensitivity can be both rational and in fact very useful (I emphasize: *Can be*, which is not to say *Must be*). Before embarking on that argument, though, I want in the next section to set out more precisely the principal claim I am trying to establish.

Substitution and Rationality

I will be arguing that it can be perfectly rational to value things differently depending upon how they are framed. In other words, being subject to framing effects is not necessarily a sign of irrationality. But what does this mean? Can we say anything more precise about what it amounts to – and, equally important, what it *does not* amount to? Can we be more specific about what counts as a framing effect? Answering these important questions is the task of this section. The tools that I will be using and developing come from logic and the philosophy of language.

The great eighteenth-century philosopher and mathematician Gottfried Wilhelm von Leibniz, joint inventor of the calculus among other things, was the first to formulate an early ancestor of the principle of extensionality that we looked at in Chapter 4. Leibniz's principle of substitutivity is a principle about sentences and truth (although Leibniz himself was sometimes a little careless in his formulations, not always clearly distinguishing between things and the language we use to talk about them).[4] Here is a standard formulation of the principle of substitutivity:

---

[4] For a classic discussion of Leibniz on logic and language see Ishiguro 1990.

Substitutivity (names)
If *a* and *b* are names referring to the same object, then they may be substituted for each other in a sentence without changing the truth-value of that sentence.

So, for example, since "Jacopo Comin" and "Tintoretto" are both names referring to a single individual (the famous Renaissance painter of the Venetian school), substituting one name for the other will not make a true sentence false, or a false sentence true. "Jacopo Comin was born on September 29, 1518" and "Tintoretto was born on September 29, 1518" both have the same truth-value (true, as it happens).

Hopefully you'll see the connection to Juliet's principle. When we are talking about individual things, the names we use to pick those individuals out do not matter – "a rose by any other name . . . ." Philosophers of language have tended to focus on proper names in thinking about the substitutivity principle. In thinking about framing, though, we need a more general formulation. The two sentences "The packet of ground beef is 25 percent lean" and "The packet of ground beef is 75 percent fat" do not differ because they involve different proper names. They differ in the predicates they each apply to the packet of ground beef. One applies the predicate "– is 25 percent lean" and the other applies the predicate "– is 75 percent fat". The predicates are different, but they are really just two different ways of picking out the same property, namely, the property of containing 25 percent lean meat and 75 percent fat. So, we need a version of the substitutivity principle that applies to predicates. The following serves our purposes.

Substitutivity (predicates)
If two predicates "– is F" and "– is G" both refer to the same property, then they may be substituted for each other in a sentence without changing the truth-value of that sentence.

You might reasonably ask what it is for two predicates to refer to the same property. We can think about it in terms of the objects that the two predicates apply to. In order for two predicates to refer to the same property, they must, at a minimum, apply to exactly the same objects. Philosophers differ over whether this condition is all that is needed for two predicates to refer to the same property, but fortunately we don't need to go in to that here.[5]

---

[5] A good place to start for those who want to explore these debates is the essays in Mellor and Oliver 1997.

Philosophers have devoted a lot of attention to sentences for which these substitutivity principles fail to hold. There are certain, basic types of sentence for which substituting co-referring names, or co-referring predicates, can result in a change of truth-value. Sentences that describe what a person believes are a good and much-discussed example. Consider the following sentence:

(1) Francesca believes that Tintoretto was a famous Venetian painter.

Suppose that (1) is true. Now consider the result of substituting another name for Tintoretto – "Jacopo Comin" instead of "Tintoretto."

(2) Francesca believes that Jacopo Comin was a famous Venetian painter.

There is no reason to think that (2) must be true just because (1) is true. Francesca might not know that Tintoretto's birth name was Jacopo Comin, for example. She might think that Jacopo Comin was a completely different Italian painter with no connection to Venice, for example. Or simply have no idea who he was.

Here is some standard terminology that will be useful for the following. Sentences for which the two substitutivity principles hold are typically called *extensional contexts*. Juliet's principle holds for extensional contexts. Sentences such as (1) and (2), which attribute beliefs, are typically called *intensional contexts*. The same type of reasoning that we used to show that sentences attributing beliefs are not extensional contexts can be applied straightforwardly to attributions of other psychological states. Certainly, valuing fits the bill, as shown by the following pair of sentences.

(3) Francesca values Tintoretto's paintings.

(4) Francesca values Jacopo Comin's paintings.

It is perfectly possible for (3) to be true and (4) false. So, valuation is an intensional context.

When philosophers of language talk about intensional contexts they often talk about them in terms of rationality. Here is a fairly standard definition of an intensional context:

Intensional context
An intensional context allows substitutivity to fail without implying any breakdown of rationality. This occurs in circumstances where the thinker/decision-maker is unaware of the relevant identities.

Look at (3) and (4) again, and suppose that the first is true and the second false. One way of describing the situation here is that it is perfectly rational for Francesca to value Tintoretto's paintings without valuing Jacopo Comin's paintings – provided that she is unaware that Jacopo Comin is Tintoretto. Francesca's lack of knowledge is crucial. Suppose that she does in fact know that Jacopo Comin is Tintoretto. Then it becomes difficult to see how (3) and (4) can have different truth-values. If Francesca values Tintoretto's paintings, and she knows that Tintoretto and Jacopo Comin are in fact the same person, then (one might think) she is rationally committed to valuing Jacopo Comin's paintings. If (3) is true and (4) false, then this can only be because Francesca has temporarily forgotten that Jacopo Comin is Tintoretto, or is suffering from a lapse of rationality.

What has all this got to do with framing? To see the connection let's go back to the Asian disease paradigm. Suppose that Francis is subject to the framing effect, and consider these two sentences.

(5) Francis prefers the certain prospect of 200 being saved out of 600 to the uncertain prospect of a 1/3 probability of all 600 being saved and a 2/3 probability of none being saved.

(6) Francis prefers the certain prospect of 400 dying to the uncertain prospect of a 1/3 probability of none of the 600 people dying and a 2/3 probability of all 600 dying.

The basic datum for the framing effect is that (5) is true and (6) false. The reasoning that we used before to show that "— believes that —" and "— values —" are intensional contexts likewise shows that "— prefers — to —" is an intensional context. So, this tells us how to interpret the framing effect.

If Francis is unaware that the prospect of 200 being saved out of 600 is the very same prospect as 400 out of the 600 dying, and likewise for the two descriptions of the uncertain prospect, then one might think that it is perfectly acceptable for (5) to be true and (6) to be false. After all, Francis and Francesca seem to be in the same position. Francesca does not know that "Tintoretto" and "Jacopo Comin" are both names of the same painter. And Francis just doesn't know that, relative to a population of 600, having 200 survivors is the same as having 400 fatalities. But of course, it is hard to take this suggestion seriously. Francesca has perfectly good reasons for not knowing that Tintoretto's birth name was Jacopo Comin. After all, this is a fairly obscure piece of information that was unknown to art historians for several centuries. Francis has no such excuse, however. A moment's thought should be enough to convince him that the scenario in which 200 out of the 600 survive is exactly the same as the scenario in which 400 out of the 600 die.

So, no doubts are cast upon Francesca's rationality by her ignorance of Tintoretto's birth name. The same cannot be said of Francis, however. He has come up badly short. And, in fairness to our imaginary Francis, he would probably accept this. Certainly, the anecdotal evidence strongly suggests that when people subject to Asian disease-type framing effects have the framing effect pointed out to them, they quickly retract their judgments. In fact, this is one way of looking at David Mandel's experiments briefly reported in the last section. Making it completely explicit that there are *exactly* 200 survivors in one scenario and *exactly* 400 fatalities in the other effectively forces people to think their way to the equivalence of the two scenarios. And that is why the framing effect disappears.

The main thing I want to emphasize is that susceptibility to the experimental framing effects should disappear when (rational) subjects have the relevant equivalence pointed out to them. There is not (or should not be) any temptation for people to stick to their guns when they are reminded that there is no difference between meat that is 25 percent lean and meat that is 75 percent fat. But then that raises an interesting possibility. Are there examples of frame-driven valuations where this does not hold? Are there cases where people might value a given outcome differently depending on how it is framed, and then be rational in sticking to their valuations even in the full knowledge that there is a single outcome that they are evaluating in different ways depending on how it is described and presented? I should emphasize that the issue here is one about rationality. There probably exist people who will stick to their guns in the lean/fat case, just as there are people who believe that the world is flat or that the government has established child slave colonies on Mars (as denied by a NASA spokesperson on June 29, 2017).[6] But there is no case to be made that any of these views could be rationally held.

So, here is the possibility that I want to consider. *Are there cases where subjects are well aware that there is a single outcome framed in two (or more) different ways and yet where they can rationally assign different values to that outcome depending upon how it is framed?*

Since almost nobody has taken this possibility seriously (with one conspicuous exception, to be introduced in the next section), we need entirely new terminology even to formulate it. A basic take-home message from the

---

[6] See www.thedailybeast.com/nasa-denies-that-its-running-a-child-slave-colony-on-mars for the Mars story and https://wiki.tfes.org/Frequently_Asked_Questions for some FAQs answered by the Flat Earth Society.

discussion in this section is that the suggestion goes far beyond taking valuation and preference to be intensional contexts. Intensional contexts do allow a rational decision-maker to value a single thing or outcome differently depending on how it is framed, but only if decision-makers are unaware that they are really just thinking about a single thing or outcome. Within intensional contexts, as soon as decision-makers realize that there is really just a single outcome framed differently where they previously thought that there were two different outcomes, then rationality requires them to bring their judgments into line with each other. If Francesca learns that Tintoretto is the same person as Jacopo Comin, then she has to decide whether she likes his paintings or not. She can't be rational and both like them and not like them.

Here is some new terminology. Let me introduce the notion of an *ultra-intensional context*. To make the contrast clearer, I repeat the definition of an intensional context.

Intensional context

An intensional context allows substitutivity principles to fail without implying any breakdown of rationality. This occurs in circumstances where the thinker/decision-maker is unaware of the relevant identities.

Ultra-intensional context

An ultra-intensional context allows substitutivity principles to fail without implying any breakdown of rationality, even in circumstances where the thinker/decision-maker is aware of the relevant identities.

Let's assume that A = C. To say that preference is an intensional context is to say that a rational person might prefer A to B and B to C, but only if they are unaware that A = C. So, back to Francesca. Francesca doesn't know that Tintoretto is Jacopo Comin and so she can rationally prefer Tintoretto's paintings to Giovanni Bellini's paintings, while liking Bellini's paintings more than Jacopo Comin's paintings. In contrast, to say that preference is an ultra-intensional context is to say that a rational agent might prefer A to B and B to C even if they know perfectly well that A = C.

This means that ultra-intensional contexts allow rational agents to have a form of *cyclical preferences*.[7] I will call these preferences *quasi-cyclical* because they are not strictly cyclical (they do not actually form a circle). It is not the case that, for some A and B, someone can prefer A to B and B to A. But

---

[7] See the earlier discussion of cyclical preferences in Chapter 4. As discussed there, cyclical preferences cannot be transitive. The quasi-cyclical preferences that I am discussing here are not immediately intransitive in the same way.

still, to all intents and purposes there is something approximating circularity. That is to say, there are A, B, and C, such that (if preference is an ultra-intensional context), a rational agent can prefer A to B and B to C, even though they know full well that A and C characterize the same event under different frames.

Many people will find this a very counter-intuitive idea. Certainly, it flies in the face of standard views in economics, psychology, and decision theory – not to mention philosophy. How could it possibly be rational knowingly to value something differently depending upon how it is framed? How could any rational person knowingly and simultaneously think *both* that doing one thing is preferable to doing another *and* that doing the second thing is preferable to doing the first? There seems to be something fundamentally inconsistent and incoherent about anyone who engages with the world like this. Still, I am going to try to persuade you that valuing and preference *are* ultra-intensional contexts.

Just to be clear about what exactly is at stake here, to say that valuing and preference are ultra-intensional contexts is to say that *it can be* rational to have values and preferences that shift according to how things are framed. It certainly does not mean that it is *always* rational to have such values and preferences. And nor does it mean that subjects in the framing experiments are reacting rationally to the choices they are offered. The examples that I will be giving of cases where it seems rational to engage in what I call frame-dependent reasoning are much richer and more complicated than any of the experiments we have looked at. And my arguments for the rationality of frame-dependent reasoning do not, as far as I can see, apply to the experimental subjects.

So, how am I going to establish that preference and valuation are ultra-intensional contexts? We have already seen that cases like the Tintoretto/Jacopo Comin example will not do the job. At best, they can show that valuation and preference are "ordinary" intensional contexts. Completely different strategies are required to show that they are ultra-intensional. I will be adopting a two-pronged approach, spread over this chapter and the next.

First, I will try to loosen the grip of the intuition that it is always irrational to allow preferences and values to vary according to how situations are framed. The best way to do this is by example. I will describe a range of cases where values and preferences do vary in frame-sensitive ways. All that I ask when you read these cases is that you grant that it is at least a possibility that the decision-maker is being rational. The examples are not meant to convince. They are there to prepare the ground by (hopefully) weakening your resistance.

Once we've got the examples clearly in view, the next step is to develop a framework for interpreting them. In Chapter 6 I will explain why I think that the decision-makers in the examples I give are really looking at the situations they face in a perfectly rational manner. The arguments that I offer there are what I hope will seal the deal. But until we get to those arguments, please consider the examples with an open mind!

Frederic Schick's Examples

I mentioned earlier that there is one other person who has approached the idea that valuing and preferring are what I am calling ultra-intensional contexts (although he uses a different terminology). This is the philosopher Frederic Schick, who has written a very thought-provoking series of books that deserve to be much more widely known. In *Understanding Action: An Essay on Reasons, Making Choices: A Recasting of Decision Theory,* and *Ambiguity and Logic,* Schick has forcefully argued that how we view and interpret situations can, and should, affect how we think about them. He does not talk about frames and framing, preferring instead to talk about our "understandings," or how we see things. Nor is his basic focus on rationality. But the basic point that he wants to make is a great starting point for our discussion. And so I will start by presenting some of the examples that he himself gives, giving his own gloss on them and pointing out where that differs from my own emphasis. That will take us to the end of this chapter and set things up for the arguments I will be giving in the next chapter.

Fascists or Fellow Human Beings?

An example that Schick discusses in many places comes from George Orwell's essay "Looking back on the Spanish Civil War," which Orwell wrote three years into World War II, some seven years after his time with the International Brigade fighting in Spain on the side of the anti-fascist Republicans. Orwell's attitude in this later piece is somewhat more ambivalent than his earlier and much better-known *Homage to Catalonia.* I quote in full the passage that Schick discusses, so that the context is clear.

> Early one morning another man and I had gone out to snipe at the Fascists in the trenches outside Huesca. Their line and ours here lay three hundred yards apart, at which range our aged rifles would not shoot accurately, but by sneaking out to a spot about a hundred yards from the Fascist trench you might, if you were lucky, get a shot at someone through a gap in the parapet. Unfortunately the ground between was a flat beet-field with no cover except

a few ditches, and it was necessary to go out while it was still dark and return soon after dawn, before the light became too good. This time no Fascists appeared, and we stayed too long and were caught by the dawn. We were in a ditch, but behind us were two hundred yards of flat ground with hardly enough cover for a rabbit. We were still trying to nerve ourselves to make a dash for it when there was an uproar and a blowing of whistles in the Fascist trench. Some of our aeroplanes were coming over. At this moment a man, presumably carrying a message to an officer, jumped out of the trench and ran along the top of the parapet in full view. He was half-dressed and was holding up his trousers with both hands as he ran. I refrained from shooting at him. It is true that I am a poor shot and unlikely to hit a running man at a hundred yards, and also that I was thinking chiefly about getting back to our trench while the Fascists had their attention fixed on the aeroplanes. Still, I did not shoot partly because of that detail about the trousers. I had come here to shoot at 'Fascists'; but a man who is holding up his trousers isn't a 'Fascist', he is visibly a fellow creature, similar to yourself, and you don't feel like shooting at him.[8]

As Schick emphasizes in many places, Orwell is looking at a single situation through two different lenses, as it were. He is conceptualizing the soldier in two different ways – as a fellow human being, and as a Fascist. It is natural to see this as a framing phenomenon. In one frame, he wants to shoot the solder, but in another he does not.

To connect this example up to the earlier discussion, we have a clear failure of substitutivity. The following sentence certainly seems to be true as a characterization of Orwell's state of mind:

(7) Orwell desires to shoot the Fascist soldier in front of him.

But the following sentence, which differs from it only by substituting another way of referring to the same individual, is false

(8) Orwell desires to shoot the fellow human being holding up his trousers.

But Orwell is perfectly well aware that the Fascist soldier is the fellow human being holding up his trousers. If this were just an ordinary, intensional context, then Orwell's awareness of the identity would rationally require him to make his desires consistent. He is rationally required to decide between the two different frames. He needs to decide whether he is looking at a Fascist soldier, or at a fellow human being, and once he has settled on one frame, then he will know whether or not to shoot. In other

[8] Orwell 1957, pp. 193–94.

words, from the perspective of rational decision-making, the fact that both (7) and (8) are true is an aberration that Orwell needs to resolve.

As I mentioned, Schick does not typically analyze his examples in terms of framing. But I think that he would be sympathetic to this way of describing them, and much of what Schick says is compatible with the way of looking at Orwell's situation that I have just described. So, for example, Schick emphasizes more the process of how Orwell resolves the situation than how Orwell did, or might have, rationally deliberated. In particular, he stresses, how, in Orwell's particular case, the process of making his mind up is a process of shifting how he understands the situation. Consider the following passage:

> Orwell wanted to "shoot at Fascists" and believed he now could do it ... What was it about those pants that got him to put down his gun? Orwell answers that question: "a man holding up his trousers ... is visibly a fellow-creature, similar to yourself." I take it the pants were down to his knees, and that Orwell is saying that someone half-naked and "visibly" human had to be seen as human. Before the man jumped out of the trench, Orwell had seen his firing at him as shooting at a fascist, which he wanted to do. The soldier's half-naked predicament was for him a wake-up call ... He then saw his firing at him as his shooting at a fellow creature, and this he didn't "feel like" doing.[9]

Schick thinks, quite correctly, that Orwell's change of mind is not something that can be easily explained with the standard vocabulary of beliefs and desires, or the machinery of decision theory. His beliefs and desires do not change. What changes, for Schick, is how he (Orwell) *sees* (or, I would say, *frames*) the situation. He writes:

> Orwell's seeing the fascist before him as a fellow human being – his seeing that to shoot would be to shoot a human being – wasn't like seeing he was running. The *seeing* in these cases was conceptual. We might describe it as a conceiving of the action, and this conceptual seeing or understanding calls for being fitted in somehow.[10]

He then summarizes the lesson he draws from the Orwell example as being that such *seeings* and *understandings* need to be built into how we think about action and how we think about decision theory.

In a sense, therefore, Schick's approach is compatible with thinking that the Orwell example really just illustrates an ordinary, intensional context. The importance of frames for him, is that switching frames can resolve a decision problem. My view, on the other hand, is that this

---

[9] Schick 2003, p. 3.   [10] Schick 2003, p. 5.

example offers much more than that. It is a good example of an ultra-intensional context. Orwell is certainly conflicted. He has a difficult decision to make. But his viewing the situation in front of him under two different frames is not a sign that he is irrational. For reasons that will emerge in the next chapter, I do not believe that deliberating rationally *requires* him to eliminate one of the two frames. He can rationally deliberate in the full knowledge that his evaluation of the situation varies according to how he frames it. In fact (something that will be important in the next chapter), Orwell may well be better able to deliberate rationally because his evaluation varies in ways that depend upon how he frames the scene in front of him.

This difference of emphasis between myself and Schick can be most easily seen by switching from talking about desires to talking about preferences. Making this switch allows us to describe how Orwell sees things from a comparative perspective. While Orwell is in the trench, the following statements seem both to be true:

(9) Orwell prefers lowering his rifle to shooting this fellow human being.

(10) Orwell prefers shooting the fascist in front of him to lowering his rifle.

This means that Orwell has a form of what I earlier termed *quasi-cyclical preferences*, given that the fascist is the fellow human being. That is to say, there are A, B, and C, such that Orwell prefers A to B and B to C, knowing full well that A and C characterize the same event under different seeings, understandings, or frames. And in fact, he knowingly has these quasi-cyclical preferences, since he is of course aware that the fascist in front of him and the fellow human being are one and the same.

As previously observed, if a rational decision-maker can knowingly have quasi-cyclical preferences, then that is really just another way of saying that preference is an ultra-intensional context. But for how long did Orwell have the preferences described by (9) and (10). Were his quasi-cyclical preferences just a fleeting aberration? Or something more significant?

Perhaps they were just a fleeting aberration? Perhaps what happened is that Orwell resolved the conflict between (9) and (10) in his own mind, deciding that, when all was said and done, the soldier in front of him was a fellow human being, rather than a fascist – or at least, that that was how he was going to "see," "understand," or "frame" the situation. Orwell's dilemma and its upshot can certainly be described that way. That seems to be how Schick views it. The lesson that Schick draws is that one of the two understandings comes to dominate the other – as he puts it, seeing the soldier was a fellow human being was a "wake-up call" for Orwell. If that is what happened, then by the time Orwell had decided not to shoot (10) was no longer true – realizing that the fascist in front of him was a fellow human being, Orwell stopped preferring shooting the fascist to not shooting the fascist.

But perhaps that is not what actually happened. Perhaps one frame came to dominate the other without the other one disappearing. Perhaps even after Orwell had decided not to shoot the fellow human being holding up his trousers, he still preferred shooting the fascist in front of him to lowering his rifle. That would be a very different state of mind. It would lead him to a very different set of retrospective judgments, for example. So, imagine Orwell looking back on the episode in the scenario I am considering and think about the regrets that he might have had. He might have regretted not shooting this fascist, for example. After all, as he points out in the quoted passage, his guiding purpose in joining the International Brigade was to shoot fascists. But still, he has no regrets about not having shot the fellow human being holding up his trousers. By the same token, think about what he might retrospectively have been proud of. He might have been proud of not having shot a fellow human being holding up his trousers, but still have mixed feelings about not having shot the fascist who was right in front of him.

History does not record which description actually best fits Orwell. The essay gives no clues. And of course, that does not matter. What I want to focus on is an imaginary Orwell (who might or might not be the real Orwell) and whose state of mind is best captured by the second description. What I will be arguing in the next chapter is that this imaginary Orwell could well have been responding perfectly rationally. Before we get there, though, here is a second example from Frederic Schick.

Filial Duty or Vengeance?

Schick often returns to a story from Jean-Paul Sartre's popular essay "Existentialism and humanism," first published in French in 1946 as "L'existentialisme est un humanisme" and translated into English two years later.[11] Here it is:

---

[11] The English translation is Sartre 1948.

I will refer to the case of a pupil of mine, who sought me out in the following circumstances. His father was quarrelling with his mother and was also inclined to be a "collaborator"; his elder brother had been killed in the German offensive of 1940 and this young man, with a sentiment somewhat primitive but generous, burned to avenge him. His mother was living alone with him, deeply afflicted by the semi-treason of his father and by the death of her eldest son, and her one consolation was in this young man. But he, at this moment, had the choice between going to England to join the Free French Forces or of staying near his mother and helping her to live. He fully realised that this woman lived only for him and that his disappearance – or perhaps his death – would plunge her into despair. He also realised that, concretely and in fact, every action he performed on his mother's behalf would be sure of effect in the sense of aiding her to live, whereas anything he did in order to go and fight would be an ambiguous action which might vanish like water into sand and serve no purpose. For instance, to set out for England he would have to wait indefinitely in a Spanish camp on the way through Spain; or, on arriving in England or in Algiers he might be put into an office to fill up forms. Consequently, he found himself confronted by two very different modes of action; the one concrete, immediate, but directed towards only one individual; and the other an action addressed to an end infinitely greater, a national collectivity, but for that very reason ambiguous – and it might be frustrated on the way.[12]

For Sartre, the lesson to be drawn is one about existential freedom. His pupil cannot appeal either to conventional morality or to his own feelings. Conventional morality is too abstract to provide real guidance, he thinks. And he has a subtle objection to his pupil's own suggestion that he be guided by the strength of his feelings. As he puts it, "feeling is formed by the deeds that one does; therefore I cannot consult it as a guide to action."[13] So, the advice Sartre gives his pupil is: "You are free, therefore choose."[14] Not very useful.

On the face of it, we can describe the mental state in which Sartre's pupil finds himself as one with quasi-cyclical preferences. The following two propositions seem to fit Sartre's characterization of the situation (and of course what matters here, as before, is not accurate biography, but presenting a psychologically plausible decision problem):

(11) The pupil prefers avenging his brother's death to remaining with his mother.

(12) The pupil prefers keeping his mother alive and sane to trying to join the Free French.

[12] Sartre 1948, pp. 35–36. [13] Sartre 1948, p. 37. [14] Sartre 1948, p. 38.

These are quasi-cyclical because the only way he has of avenging his brother's death is to join the Free French and the only way he has of keeping his mother alive and sane is to remain with her. His dilemma is, of course, that he is well aware that he has the preferences described by (11) and (12), while knowing full well that they conflict with each other.

As with the Orwell case, Frederic Schick's emphasis is on how the pupil might have resolved the situation. (I say *might*, because Sartre records the advice he gave, but not what the pupil actually did.) As he imaginatively recreates the process by which the pupil might have settled on a course of action, nothing changes in the pupil's beliefs and desires. He continues to believe that going to London to join General de Gaulle is a risky undertaking with an uncertain outcome. Nothing changes in his assessment of how his mother would be affected by his different possible actions. And he continues to have the desires that would give him the quasi-cyclical preferences I have described in (11) and (12). For Schick, this is another illustration of the fact that one's choices are not in general determined by one's desires and beliefs. Beliefs and desires can only drive choice through how situations are seen or understood. And so, he offers examples of how the pupil's understandings may have changed in a way that pushed him towards one course of action rather than another.

> It may have happened like this. He woke up one morning to the sound of marching and unfamiliar music. Some German soldiers were tramping by in the street, singing a German song. It struck him that while his enemies were parading their triumph, he was lying in bed. He then saw his staying at home as a sort of spinelessness. How different this shameful life of his was from that of his friends in the army! He resolved at this moment to join them.
>
> Or perhaps this happened instead. He spoke to his mother one day of leaving. She said not a word, but her face went blank. She looked like a frightened child. He saw that his leaving her as she then was would be an act of abandonment. That jolted him and it made up his mind.
>
> In both scenarios, what eases the quandary is a sort of conversion. No new belief or desire enters but rather a new understanding of the situation.[15]

The question that I want to raise, however, is not about whether Sartre's pupil acquires any new beliefs or desires in the process of resolving his dilemma. I am happy to grant Schick that he does not. My question is whether he *loses* any – or more precisely, whether rationality requires him to lose any.

---

[15] Schick 1991, p. 5.

Let's assume that Sartre's pupil resolves his dilemma in a way that is consistent with the requirements of rationality, settling on one of his two options. The process that Schick describes seems to be a process of restoring consistency. When he visited Sartre, and asked him for advice, the pupil had two inconsistent perspectives on his situation (two different ways of framing it), and so could not settle on one course of action. Subsequently (we assume), he ended up taking one course of action rather than the other. But what did this involve? Schick says that it involved him fixing on one understanding, or frame, rather than the other. But does that mean that the other understanding/frame completely lost its grip on him? Does settling on one way of looking at things mean that one has to stop seeing things the other way?

Or could Sartre's pupil, as a rational decision-maker, have fixed on a course of action and still retained his quasi-cyclical preferences? Could he have rationally settled on avenging his brother's death while still preferring keeping his mother alive and sane to joining the Free French? Or, alternatively, might he have rationally decided to keep his mother alive and sane, while still preferring avenging his brother's death to remaining with his mother? I shall say that yes, he could do this.

Murder or Courage?

Orwell's autobiographical account and Sartre's story about his pupil's dilemma both present us with classical examples of clashes between frames. As I have characterized them, both are cases where decision-makers have quasi-cyclical preferences, because they have very different ways of framing the situation before them. My fundamental question is whether such quasi-cyclical preferences can be rational. Or equivalently – is preference an ultra-intensional context?

A touchstone issue here is how we think about what happens *after* the decision problem is resolved. Can a rational agent persist in holding quasi-cyclical preferences, even after one of the clashing frames has (as it were) won out? The final example I want to consider in this chapter is not discussed by Schick as frequently or in as much depth as the other two we have looked at, but it has the singular virtue of bringing this issue very clearly into focus. It comes from Shakespeare's *Macbeth*.

In Act I, Macbeth, Thane of Glamis, is told by the witches that he will become both Thane of Cawdor and King of Scotland. When the first part of the prophecy is fulfilled (by King Duncan's executing the current Thane and granting the title to Macbeth), Macbeth begins to think about making the second part of the prophecy come true by killing Duncan. Providentially Duncan arrives under Macbeth's roof, and Lady Macbeth encourages her husband to assassinate the King. But still Macbeth has his doubts. On the one hand, he recognizes that killing Duncan would make him King – and surely that's worth the risk:

> If it were done when 'tis done, then 'twere well
> It were done quickly. If the assassination
> Could trammel up the consequence, and catch
> With his surcease success; that but this blow
> Might be the be-all and the end-all here,
> But here, upon this bank and shoal of time,
> We'd jump the life to come.
>
> *(Act I, Sc. 7)*

But, as he immediately recognizes, he has two different obligations to Duncan. He is his host and also his pledged kinsman. On both counts his duty is to protect Duncan, not murder him.

> He's here in double trust:
> First, as I am his kinsman and his subject,
> Strong both against the deed; then, as his host,
> Who should against his murderer shut the door,
> Not bear the knife myself.
>
> *(Act I, Sc. 7, lines 1–7)*

His first reaction is to be swayed by the second set of considerations: "We will proceed no further in this business," he tells Lady Macbeth. She has little patience, telling him to live up to his aspirations, not be like a cat who wants fish but is too frightened to wet its paw.

> Was the hope drunk
> Wherein you dressed yourself? Hath it slept since?
> And wakes it now, to look so green and pale
> At what it did so freely? From this time
> Such I account thy love. Art thou afeard
> To be the same in thine own act and valor
> As thou art in desire? Wouldst thou have that
> Which thou esteem'st the ornament of life,
> And live a coward in thine own esteem,
> Letting "I dare not" wait upon "I would,"
> Like the poor cat i' th' adage?
>
> *(Act I, Sc. 7, lines 35–44)*

Challenging his courage and manliness sways Macbeth:

> I dare do all that may become a man;
> Who dares no more is none.
>
> *(Act I, Sc. 7, lines 46–47)*

And so Macbeth resolves his decision problem (with a little wavering yet to come, when he soliloquizes on the dagger as he approaches Duncan's bedchamber).

So, with apologies to Shakespeare and generations of literary critics, the following two propositions both seem to be true of Macbeth.

(13) Macbeth prefers fulfilling his double duty to Duncan to murdering the King.

(14) Macbeth prefers bravely taking the throne to backing away from his resolution to make the prophecy come true.

He knows, of course, that to fulfill his double duty to Duncan is to back away from his resolution to make the prophecy come true – and likewise that bravely taking the throne is murdering the King. So, he has quasi-cyclical preferences.

Here is Schick's gloss. It follows what by now should be a familiar pattern.

> Macbeth resisted killing the king. He knew that if he killed him today, he would himself be king tomorrow, and he wanted badly to be king. But he saw the killing as a betrayal, and that held him back ... Killing would betray a trust, a trust imposed twice over. He refused to stoop to that.
>
> Lady Macbeth didn't argue with the facts: Of course killing would be betrayal. Macbeth's beliefs were not at issue, and neither was what he wanted. She argued that he was *seeing things* wrong, that his understanding was shameful, that his voice was that of fear. Since he wanted so much to be king, going ahead would be *manliness*: It would be the *bold* thing to do. Backing off would be *cowardice*.[16]

Lady Macbeth artfully brings her husband to see killing Duncan as bravely taking the throne, thus bringing about what in another context might be called a preference reversal.

So far this is familiar terrain. But we are only at the end of the second act of a five-act play, and one of the central themes after the death of Duncan is precisely that Macbeth does not continue to stick firmly to the framing proposed by Lady Macbeth. There are many passages suggesting that his original framing of the killing as a breach of trust persists, and

---

[16] Schick 1997, pp. 25–26.

with it the preference characterized in (13). A famous example comes when he learns that the English army is at the gate.

> I have lived long enough. My way of life
> Is fall'n into the sear, the yellow leaf,
> And that which should accompany old age,
> As honor, love, obedience, troops of friends,
> I must not look to have; but, in their stead,
> Curses not loud but deep, mouth-honor, breath,
> Which the poor heart would fain deny, and dare not.
>
> *(Act V, Sc. 3, lines 22–27)*

Simplifying more than a little, the regret he expresses has its source in the preference reported in (13). He still desires the validation due to one who chooses duty over personal gain ("honor, love, obedience"), but is well aware that he has acted counter-preferentially and placed such validation completely out of reach.

My point, though, is not that Macbeth has somehow switched back from the frame inspired by Lady Macbeth to his original framing. Macbeth is not a weather-vane. The reason we are still reading *Macbeth* is that he remains conflicted. He continues to his death to see the killing of Duncan in both ways: (13) and (14) are no less true of him in Act V than they were in Act II. That is the way it is and, it is hard to avoid thinking, that is the way he wants it to be. Think about how he continues after asking the Doctor attending his wife the following rhetorical question:

> Canst thou not minister to a mind diseased,
> Pluck from the memory a rooted sorrow,
> Raze out the written troubles of the brain,
> And with some sweet oblivious antidote
> Cleanse the stuffed bosom of that perilous stuff
> Which weighs upon the heart?

Perhaps he wishes such medicine (physic) for Lady Macbeth, but certainly not for himself. "Throw physic to the dogs. I'll have none of it," he says, as he straps his armor on. This is not exactly the words or behavior of someone remorsefully trying to turn the clock back. In my view, Macbeth retains quasi-cyclical preferences to the bitter end.

Here, then, are the three main points that I want to take away from this discussion of Schick's own examples.

- Frames (or seeings, or understandings) are fundamentally important for thinking about the springs of action. Difficult decisions are often clashes between different ways of framing the situation that the decision-maker confronts.
- When decision-makers find themselves conflicted between different ways of framing the situation in front of them they can easily find themselves with quasi-cyclical preferences.
- Difficult decision problems are sometimes resolved by the decision-maker's settling on one frame over another, but not always.

From my own perspective, I want to emphasize in addition the following points.

- If preference is what I have termed an ultra-intensional context, then it can be rational to have quasi-cyclical preferences. That is, a decision-maker might rationally prefer A to B and B to C, even though they know perfectly well that A and C are the same outcome framed in two different ways.
- One key indicator that preference is an ultra-intensional context would be if it is rational for decision-makers to retain their quasi-cyclical preferences even after they resolved the decision problems by settling on one frame rather than another.
- One sign that decision-makers have retained quasi-cyclical preferences would be their experiencing regret or similar retrospective emotions.

But still, this all adds up to a lot of Ifs. The basic questions are still in play. Are there good reasons to think that preference is an ultra-intensional context? Can it be rational to have quasi-cyclical preferences? We will finally answer these questions in the next chapter.

6

Agamemnon and Climate Change

We now have a framework for thinking about framing effects and rationality. We saw that framing effects can involve quasi-cyclical preferences. Someone has quasi-cyclical preferences when they prefer A to B and B to C, despite knowing that A and C are different ways of framing the same outcome. So, the question of whether framing effects can be rational is really the question of whether it can be rational to have quasi-cyclical preferences. This chapter presents what I take to be compelling reasons for thinking that it *can* be rational to have quasi-cyclical preferences. To see why, we need to broaden our perspective on decision-making to include factors not typically taken into account by theories of rational choice. I want to focus on two in particular.

The first is the importance, from the perspective of rational decision-making, of properly constructing a decision problem. Except in the simplest cases, decision problems are constructed, not found. Rational thinkers have to work out for themselves what their available actions are and what the outcomes might be. This is itself a process of thinking, which can be more or less rational. One of the factors is how fully and carefully a thinker has thought through the actions and outcomes. There is, I will suggest, a rational requirement of due diligence, and in many cases due diligence can require thinking about actions and outcomes under multiple frames, in a way that gives rise to quasi-cyclical preferences.

The second factor is the role of emotions in decision-making. Theories of rationality tend to view emotions as distractions that interfere with rational problem-solving. On a view that goes back (at least) to Plato and the ancient Greeks, rationality is, quite literally, dispassionate. But valuations and preferences have to come from somewhere. This was recognized by David Hume, in many ways the spiritual father of modern, instrumental theories of rationality, who famously described reason as the "slave of the passions." But what Hume didn't see was how the way that we frame available actions and possible outcomes structures our emotional engagement with them, and so affects our valuations and preferences. Frames can rationally drive emotional engagement in ways that can produce rational preferences that are quasi-cyclical.

Two Sacrifices: Agamemnon and Abraham

For a dramatic example of ultra-intensionality and quasi-cyclical preferences, we can go back to Agamemnon, the ancient Greek king whom we first encountered in Chapter 1. Aeschylus's *Agamemnon*, the first play in his trilogy *The Oresteia*, is set in the aftermath of the Trojan War, whose origins are well known (although almost certainly mythical). Helen, wife of Menelaös, was abducted from their home in Sparta by Paris, son of Priam, King of Troy, while Menelaös was attending a funeral in Crete. Paris took Helen to Troy. Menelaös's brother Agamemnon raised a fleet of 1,000 ships and planned to set sail for Troy to recover Helen. The play is set in Argos, ten years after the beginning of the Trojan War.

Aeschylus's *Agamemnon* begins outside the palace at Argos, with Agamemnon still away and the palace occupied by his wife Clytemnestra and her lover Aegisthus. As they wait for the rumored return of their king, the members of the chorus (all old men of Argos) repeat the familiar tale of how the Trojan War began. They dwell in particular on how the Greek fleet was becalmed at the port of Aulis. While the ships and men waited in vain for the wind to pick up, a dramatic event occurred – two eagles swooping down to kill and eat a pregnant hare. It was clearly a portent, and one that only Calchas, the prophet of Apollo, was able to interpret. The death of the hare and her offspring represented the innocents who would lose their lives at Troy thanks to the two eagle-kings, the sons of Atreus, Agamemnon and Menelaös. The goddess Artemis was displeased at the prospect. There is only one solution, says Calchas: "My captains, Artemis must have blood." The fleet will only be able to sail if Agamemnon sacrifices to the goddess his own daughter Iphigenia.

The chorus picks up the tale (in Robert Fagles's fine translation):

> And I can still hear the older warlord saying,
> "Obey, obey, or a heavy doom will crush me! –
> Oh but doom *will* crush me

> once I rend my child,
> the glory of my house –
> a father's hands are stained,
> blood of a young girl streaks the altar.
> Pain both ways and what is worse?
> Desert the fleets, fail the alliance?
>   No, but stop the winds with a virgin's blood,
>   feed their lust, their fury? – feed their fury! –
> Law is law! –
>   Let all go well." [1]

Scholars of classical tragedy tend not to look at it this way, but Agamemnon seems to be in the grip of a framing effect. There is a single outcome that Agamemnon frames in two different ways. On the one hand, he frames the death of Iphigenia as *Murdering his Daughter*. But on the other, he frames it as *Following Artemis's Will*. He knows full well that these are two different ways of thinking about a single outcome. But he evaluates the death of his daughter differently across the two frames. As the leader of the Greek forces, he certainly prefers *Following Artemis's Will* to *Failing his Ships and People*. At the same time, though, as a father, he prefers *Failing his Ships and People* to *Murdering his Daughter*.

So, we can describe Agamemnon's unfortunate situation in our usual manner. The following sentences are both true of him:

(1) Agamemnon prefers Following Artemis's Will to Failing his Ships and People.
(2) Agamemnon prefers Failing his Ships and People to Murdering his Daughter.

These preferences are quasi-cyclical, since Agamemnon is under no illusions about what *Following Artemis's Will* requires. And, as we observed in the last chapter, if a rational decision-maker can have quasi-cyclical preferences, then preference is an ultra-intensional context. So, the obvious question to ask is: Can Agamemnon rationally have the quasi-cyclical preferences characterized in (1) and (2)?

To help get this question into focus I'd like to propose an imaginary character called Agamemnon-minus. Agamemnon-minus is just like Agamemnon, except that he lacks the psychological depth of Aeschylus's hero. Agamemnon-minus's reaction to hearing Calchas's interpretation is simply to salute, send for Iphigenia, and give the order to his troops to prepare

---

[1] Aeschylus, *Agamemnon* lines 205–16, translated by Robert Fagles.

the sacrificial altar. Agamemnon-minus only frames the situation one way. He cannot see the death of Iphigenia as anything but the necessary response to a divine command. The fact that *Following Artemis's Will* would require him to murder his daughter does not cross his mind.

Agamemnon-minus, as I have characterized him, has a roughly contemporaneous incarnation in the patriarch Abraham.[2] As related in Chapter 22 of the Book of Genesis, God commanded Abraham to sacrifice his son Isaac as a burnt offering on a mountainside in the region of Moriah. The episode is tersely described in verses 6 through 11.

> Abraham took the wood for the burnt offering and placed it on his son Isaac, and he himself carried the fire and the knife. As the two of them went on together, Isaac spoke up and said to his father Abraham, "Father?"
>
> "Yes, my son?" Abraham replied.
>
> "The fire and wood are here," Isaac said, "but where is the lamb for the burnt offering?"
>
> Abraham answered, "God himself will provide the lamb for the burnt offering, my son." And the two of them went on together.
>
> When they reached the place God had told him about, Abraham built an altar there and arranged the wood on it. He bound his son Isaac and laid him on the altar, on top of the wood. Then he reached out his hand and took the knife to slay his son.[3]

Of course, an angel stays Abraham's hand at the crucial moment, but Abraham could hardly have predicted that. What is striking in the biblical tale is Abraham's complete lack of reservation about complying with God's command. Abraham is not conflicted in the manner of Job or some of the famous Old Testament prophets. He simply saddles up his donkey to get the job done. His preferences (as depicted in Genesis 22) are exhaustively described by saying that he prefers *Following God's Command* to *Allowing Isaac to Live*. He is not represented as taking into account the fact that *Following God's Command* amounts to *Murdering his Son*.

Some would say that Agamemnon-minus and Abraham at least have the virtue of being consistent. No doubt, such a person might say, Agamemnon-minus is less profound than Agamemnon and not so well suited to be a tragic hero, and Abraham has the single-minded faith of a zealot. But from the point of view of rationality, profundity and not being a zealot are not what counts. Rationality requires consistency, not tragic

---

[2] More accurately, if Abraham and Agamemnon actually existed, they probably both existed at some time in the second millennium BC.

[3] New International Version.

depth or a rich appreciation of the complexity of the situation. On this way of considering the matter, rationality has nothing to say about the content of one's preferences. The job of a theory of rationality is simply to take whatever preferences you have, and explain what has to hold for those preferences to be consistent and internally coherent.

The classic statement of this approach to rationality is David Hume's famous lines in *A Treatise of Human Nature*:

> 'Tis not contrary to reason to prefer the destruction of the whole world to the scratching of my finger. 'Tis not contrary to reason for me to chuse my total ruin, to prevent the least uneasiness of an *Indian* or person wholly unknown to me. 'Tis as little contrary to reason to prefer even my own acknowledg'd lesser good to my greater, and have a more ardent affection for the former than the latter ... In short, a passion must be accompany'd with some false judgment, in order to its being unreasonable; and even then 'tis not the passion, properly speaking, which is unreasonable, but the judgment. (Hume 1978 [1739–40], p. 416)

Hume is often thought to be the spiritual father of modern rational choice theory, which typically takes itself to be a formal theory of consistent preferences. From this type of Humean perspective, Agamemnon-minus certainly counts as rational in a way that Agamemnon does not.

I am not convinced, though. Agamemnon-minus may be consistent in ways that Agamemnon is not, but why would one think that that automatically makes him a better decision-maker? An important part of being a rational decision-maker is properly understanding the decision problem one faces. And that means understanding what one's options are, and what the different possible outcomes are. At a minimum, it seems to me, Agamemnon-minus has failed to do this. If all that Agamemnon-minus can see is the goddess, the fleet, and his obligations as a leader, then he seems to be missing something very important. His perspective is unidimensional, when the decision problem he faces is multidimensional. I submit that failing to recognize the complexity of the decision situation is itself a failure of rationality. Or, to put it another way, if a theory of rationality requires a rational decision-maker to misperceive the complexity of a decision problem, then that seems to me to be a strike against that theory of rationality.

More on this shortly. But before trying to spell out how exactly to understand the requirement of rationality that Agamemnon-minus seems to be failing on, I want to address a worry that you might have. You might think, to continue the baseball analogy, that I have loaded the bases against Agamemnon-minus by giving him a repugnant set of preferences.

What counts against Agamemnon-minus, as I have characterized him, is not that he is failing to recognize the multidimensional complexity of the decision problem. Rather, the problem is that he has a completely reprehensible lack of concern for his daughter. It's got nothing to do with rationality at all.

Actually though, I would have the same worry about Agamemnon-minus's rationality, even if he were unidimensional in the opposite direction, as it were. If all that Agamemnon-minus can see is his daughter and his obligations as a father, then he is also missing something very important. He is the leader of the Greeks, in charge of a huge armada gathered to avenge Helen's abduction by Paris. The decision problem has a political dimension, as well as a personal one. Ignoring the political dimension and focusing solely on the personal dimension is no less a failure of rationality than ignoring the personal dimension and focusing solely on the political dimension.

The same holds for Abraham. At the time of the Isaac episode, Abraham already had reason to believe himself to be chosen by the Lord. After all, God had already given him specific and unambiguous instructions: "Go from your country, your people and your father's household to the land I will show you. I will make you into a great nation and I will bless you."[4] Had Abraham focused solely on the personal dimension of his situation he would, given this background, have been no less irrational than he was in ignoring it completely.

So, what exactly is the requirement of rationality that Agamemnon-minus and Abraham are failing to meet? The suggestion I'd like to explore is that rationality imposes informational requirements, as well as procedural requirements and requirements of consistency. Standard presentations in decision theory typically take the decision problem as given. They assess what would count as a rational way of solving a fixed decision problem, where the parameters of the decision problem are set in ways completely outside the control of the decision-maker (they are *exogenous*). Here is a very famous and much-quoted example, from Leonard Savage's book *The Foundations of Statistics*, which was the first book to develop a systematic presentation of Bayesian decision theory.

---

[4] Genesis 12, verses 1–2.

Consider an example. Your wife has just broken five good eggs into a bowl when you come in and volunteer to finish making the omelet. A sixth egg, which for some reason must either be used for the omelet or wasted altogether, lies unbroken beside the bowl. You must decide what to do with this unbroken egg. Perhaps it is not too great an oversimplification to say that you must decide among three acts only, namely, to break it into a bowl containing the other five, to break it into a saucer for inspection, or to throw it away without inspection. (Savage 1954, p. 13)

Relative to this specification of the possible acts, Savage identifies two states of the world relevant to his choice between the three acts. In the first state, the egg is good. In the second it is rotten. Each of his three possible acts will have different consequences depending on whether the world is in the first state or the second state. So, the decision problem can be represented in Figure 6.1.

For Savage, and for most subsequent decision theorists, all decision problems that can be tackled through Bayesian decision theory have the same basic structure as the omelet example. The decision-maker has a set of possible acts. Each of those acts has one or more consequences, depending upon the state of the world. Decision-makers have preferences over the different possible consequences and assign probabilities to the different states of the world. Those preferences and probabilities allow the decision-maker to solve the decision problem by identifying the action that maximizes expected utility.

Act	State	
	Good	Rotten
break into bowl	six-egg omelet	no omelet, and five good eggs destroyed
break into saucer	six-egg omelet, and a saucer to wash	five-egg omelet, and a saucer to wash
throw away	five-egg omelet, and one good egg destroyed	five-egg omelet

FIGURE 6.1 Leonard Savage's omelet example in *The Foundations of Statistics*
Note: This is the only example in the book. Table 1 on p. 14 of Savage 1954.

Savage himself was perfectly well aware that making an omelet is hardly representative of the full richness of human decision-making. He is very clear that Bayesian decision theory, as he understands it, is really only applicable to what he called "small worlds." The characteristic of a small world is that it is possible, in his words, "to look before one leaps." That is to say, in a small world one can completely specify the range of possible acts, spell out their consequences, and identify all the relevant states of the world. Most decisions do not, of course, take place in a small world, and Savage recognizes this clearly enough:

> Carried to its logical extreme, the "Look before you leap" principle demands that one envisage every conceivable policy for the government of his whole life (at least from now on) in its most minute details, in the light of the vast number of unknown states of the world, and decide here and now on one policy. This is utterly ridiculous, not – as some might think – because there might later be cause for regret, if things did not turn out as had been anticipated, but because the task implied in making such a decision is not even remotely resembled by human possibility. It is utterly beyond our power to plan a picnic or to play a game of chess in accordance with the principle, even when the world of states and the set of acts to be envisaged are artificially reduced to the narrowest reasonable limits. (Savage 1954, p. 16)

This cautionary perspective on Bayesian decision theory by one of its founding fathers has not been widely appreciated or discussed in the subsequent literature.[5] When we think it through, though, I think that it points us towards the importance of informational requirements of rationality.

Here is a different way of putting Savage's basic point. A small world is a situation in which acts, consequences, and outcomes are clear and unambiguous, even if admittedly a little simplified. There really are only three things one can do with the sixth egg in the scenario he discusses, and there is not a whole lot of room for discussion about the states and consequences spelled out in Figure 6.1. It seems reasonable to think that most people who find themselves in Savage's situation would look at the acts, consequences, and states in more or less the same way.

But of course, most decision problems are not like this. Outside the small world context, decision problems are typically constructed, not given. Decision-makers have to decide for themselves what their available actions are. They need to conceptualize the different results that actions might have, and work out how those different results might depend upon

---

[5] But see Binmore 2009a for a conspicuous and thoughtful exception.

states of the world. Rational decision-making, as standardly understood, has a basic currency. That currency is made up of preference, utility, and probability (as we explored in Chapter 4). But before that currency can be brought to bear, decision-makers first need to fix the outcomes over which they have preferences and to which they assign utilities. They need to identify the respects in which those outcomes can vary. And they need to work out how such variation is contingent upon different ways that events might turn out.

Turning an encountered situation into a decision problem requires active thought and reflection. And those processes of active thought and reflection are themselves subject, I suggest, to standards of rationality. This brings us back to Agamemnon-minus and Abraham. It seems reasonable to say (independent of any particular view about rationality) that the more important a decision, the greater the obligation of care and diligence in setting out the relevant decision problem. But what count as care and diligence here? Again, it seems reasonable to require that decision-makers be sensitive to as many important ramifications of their potential actions as possible. Really, this is just another way of stating the obvious platitude that one needs to think about the consequences of one's actions before acting. If rational agents need to have preferences over (and assign utilities to) the foreseen consequences of an action, then they can reasonably be held to account for not thinking through the consequences carefully enough. This, I claim, is the root of the problem with Agamemnon-minus and Abraham – a lack of care in thinking through the ramifications of their action. They have failed to exercise due diligence in how they have formulated their options and the consequences of those options.

In fact, this gives us a useful label for the requirement of rationality here. I will call it the *due diligence requirement*, which can be stated as follows:

Due diligence requirement
In setting up a decision problem, rational decision-makers need to be appropriately sensitive to as many potential consequences of the different courses of action available to them as possible.

What counts as appropriate sensitivity will of course vary according to context. There is a spectrum. Omelet making is at one end, and deciding whether or not to sacrifice one's offspring is at the other. At this point, though, you might reasonably ask two questions. First, why is the due diligence requirement a requirement of *rationality*? And second, what has this got to do with framing and quasi-cyclical preferences? I will take these questions in order.

The reason for taking the due diligence principle to be a requirement of rationality is not just that it is a precondition for any type of practical reasoning and decision-making. After all, practical reasoning has many preconditions that are not plausible candidates for being requirements of rationality. It is a requirement of common sense, not of rationality, that one not be blind drunk before making an important decision, for example. But the due diligence requirement reflects a very special type of precondition. The way in which one sets up a decision problem directly fixes the content of one's reasoning. It yields the conceptual framework within which practical reasoning takes place, and this conceptual framework can be more or less adequate to the situation one faces. Agamemnon-minus and Abraham (at least as presented in the Book of Genesis) deliberate within a conceptual framework that falls woefully short of the situation within which they find themselves. Their failing is one of rationality because it is a failure of thought. They have just not thought the situation through as carefully as they should have done. And since this is a failure of thought in the service of practical reasoning, it qualifies, I claim, as a failure of rationality.

But what has due diligence got to do with frames? The connection emerges because what one sees as the consequences of an action is often a function of how one frames that action. The consequences of the killing of Iphigenia look very different depending on whether it is framed as an appeasement of Artemis's revulsion for the imminent loss of innocent life at Troy, or as the murder of a blameless young woman. The first framing steers Agamemnon towards focusing on the political dimensions of the action, as something that will make it possible for him to follow through on what he perceives as his obligation to avenge the dishonoring of his brother Menelaös. The second framing leads him to focus more on the undeserved suffering of Iphigenia, as well as on the emotional cost to himself and to his wife Clytemnestra. These are all clearly consequences of the action that he is contemplating, but coming to see them can require coming to conceptualize the action in multiple ways – to view it through multiple frames, in other words.

So, the fact that Agamemnon frames the killing of Iphigenia in different ways can be justified by the requirement of due diligence. The decision he faces is momentous, for him and Iphigenia, of course, but also for the Greeks (not to mention the Trojans). So, it is incumbent upon him to think it through as carefully as he can, which means taking into account all the different perspectives and frames that he can. It is true that the existence of multiple frames leads him to quasi-cyclical preferences. But he got to those quasi-cyclical preferences by satisfying a requirement of rationality, and for that reason (I claim) he is rational in having them.

Agamemnon-minus, in contrast, only sees the killing of Iphigenia in one way. As a consequence, his preferences are not quasi-cyclical. They are consistent in a way that Agamemnon's preferences are not. But he pays a price for that consistency. His perspective is impoverished. Moreover, it is impoverished in a way that leaves him open to censure from the perspective of rationality. He fails to satisfy the due diligence requirement, which is a requirement of reason.

Agamemnon is, of course, a rather unusual case. You might think that a case for the rationality of quasi-cyclical preferences that rests upon a tragic hero from Ancient Greece has a limited applicability. Surely most of our practical reasoning and deliberation is far closer to the omelet-making end of the spectrum than to Aeschylus's dramatic world of divine portents and becalmed fleets. For the moment, I simply note that three examples we explored at the end of the last chapter can all be viewed in parallel terms. Macbeth, Orwell, and Sartre's pupil are all, in their various ways, satisfying the due diligence requirement. Each is trying to come to terms with the multi-dimensional complexity of the decision problem they face, and ultimately that is an important reason for them ending up with quasi-cyclical preferences. I accept, though, that none of these three examples are really taking us all that much closer to omelets. In the remainder of this chapter I turn to a very general argument that will hopefully bring the discussion further toward everyday reality.

Frames and Emotions

According to the argument from due diligence, decision-makers are under a requirement of rationality to think through as deeply as possible all the potential ramifications of the different acts available to them. How one thinks about the consequences of actions is often a function of how one frames (understands/sees/conceptualizes) those actions. That is why applying due diligence can lead, in suitably complex decision problems, to viewing an action under multiple frames. And once one is viewing an action under multiple frames, it is not hard to see how quasi-cyclical preferences might emerge. My claim in the last section was that those quasi-cyclical preferences can inherit the rationality of the process that led to them. Having quasi-cyclical preferences can be rational when those preferences result from satisfying the due diligence requirement.

Even someone convinced by this argument, however, may have questions about the relation between framing and quasi-cyclical preferences. What the due diligence argument really establishes, you might think, is that a rational agent will try to look at her available actions under multiple frames. And doing so may well lead to her having quasi-cyclical preferences. But is there any reason to think that those quasi-cyclical preferences are anything but an aberration? Suppose we grant that Agamemnon has a degree of rationality lacking in Agamemnon-minus, because he frames the killing of Iphigenia both politically and personally, rather than just seeing it under one frame and ignoring the other. Could he not have that degree of rationality without the quasi-cyclical preferences? Could he not appreciate the complexity of the decision problem without falling prey to what many people would think of as inconsistency? Would it not have been *more* rational for Agamemnon to be able to take multiple perspectives on the killing of Iphigenia *without* having quasi-cycling preferences? These are very reasonable questions. To respond to them we need to think more deeply about the relation between frames and quasi-cyclical preferences. How and why does looking at actions and outcomes through multiple frames lead to quasi-cyclical preferences? The remainder of this chapter develops an answer to this question emerging from the complex interactions between framing and emotional engagement.

We can start with a commonsense observation about preferences, one that applies to "ordinary" preferences as well as to quasi-cyclical preferences. Preferences are grounded in valuations. We typically prefer one thing to another because we value it more. The concept of utility is one way of capturing this way of thinking about preferences. One might say, for example, that preferences reflect utility assignments. In other words, decision-makers prefer one thing to another because they assign more utility to it. This is a fairly standard, and broadly commonsense, way of looking at the conceptual framework of decision theory.[6] However, I

---

[6] This is a commonsense observation, but it is not universally accepted. Many economists and some decision theorists accept a version of the theory of revealed preference, according to which preferences are simply revealed in choice behavior and it is a mistake to look for any psychological basis for choice behavior. Utility is a not a psychological notion, but rather a measure of choice behavior. I discuss some of the tensions between revealed preference theory and the idea that decision theory offers a theory of rationality that can guide practical reasoning in my book *Decision Theory and Rationality* (Bermúdez 2009). See also Broome 1991a and Okasha 2016.

want to step back from the language of utility for the rest of this chapter, since utility is usually defined in ways that rule out quasi-cyclical preferences, and instead talk more generally about value, understood as the base of preference.

How does valuation work? Where does it come from? Within decision theory and standard theories of rationality, an agent's valuations are taken as given. This is another aspect of the legacy of David Hume briefly discussed in the last section. From a Humean perspective, practical reasoning is purely instrumental. Agents' valuations (their desires, ends, utility assignments, pro-attitudes – whatever you want to call them) are taken as given. The job of practical reasoning is to find means for satisfying those desires, or achieving those ends. For that reason, there is limited scope for reasoning about valuations themselves (and some would deny that there is any scope at all).[7] Against this type of instrumentalist background, it is not surprising that theories of rationality have had little to say about the origins of valuations – from an instrumentalist perspective, where they come from does not really matter.

Obviously, valuation works through many different mechanisms. I want to focus on a mechanism that seems particularly central. This mechanism is emotional engagement. How we value things is often driven by how we engage emotionally with them. (I am taking emotions in a broad sense here to include moods, valences, and all other affective states.) One of the themes that emerge from the neuroscience of framing is that framing effects can result from the interaction between "hot" and "cold" psychological mechanisms.[8] Whereas cold mechanisms are reason-driven, hot ones are emotion driven. Loss-aversion is a prime example of a hot psychological mechanism. Hot, emotion-driven cognition is widely thought to have a neural basis in subcortical areas such as the amygdala. The neuroscience of framing provides compelling evidence of powerful interactions between framing and emotions. It also raises some deep questions. One is about what, for want of a better phrase, one might term the direction of influence. We can think about the relations between emotional engagement and framing from two different perspectives. On

---

[7] While a broadly Humean approach to practical reason is dominant among social scientists and decision theorists, philosophers have been more critical. For an overview of the debate see Smith 2004. Williams 1979 is a well-known defense of a Humean approach to practical reason. Williams's paper has been much discussed. See McDowell 1995, Parfit 1997, Dancy 2000, Setiya 2004, and Smith 1995, for example.

[8] See the Appendix, "Frames in the Brain," for a survey of recent work on the neuroscience of framing.

the one hand, one can look at how different emotional states affect the way people frame situations and outcomes. The direction here is from emotions to frames. On the other, one can look at how different ways of framing an outcome or situation can affect how one engages emotionally with it. Here the direction is from frames to emotions.

Both directions are interesting and important. For my principal line of argument, I want to focus primarily on the second direction (from frames to emotions) because that will illustrate how framing can drive valuation – and hence how framing something in different ways can lead to quasi-cyclical preferences. But it will be helpful to start with the first direction, which has been studied in a number of different areas in the social sciences, particularly within communication research and political science.

In communication studies, researchers tend (for obvious reasons) to think about frames in terms of messaging (and so much more narrowly than we have been doing, since many of the frames that we have been exploring have little or nothing to do with communication). To frame a message is to highlight certain aspects of the message in a way that directs attention to certain types of information and so primes particular reactions and responses rather than others. Here is a useful characterization of how communication researchers view frames from a paper by Robin Nabi in the journal *Communication Research*:

> A frame is a perspective infused into a message that promotes the salience of selected pieces of information over others. When adopted by receivers, frames may influence individuals' views of problems and their necessary solutions.[9]

Within a communicative context, then, frames are viewed primarily as ways of selecting particular items of information and influencing how that information is used and acted upon. And from that perspective, the idea that emotions can, in effect, function as frames is very attractive, since there is considerable experimental (and of course anecdotal) evidence that emotions can influence how salient information is, and so how we respond to it.

The paper already mentioned by Robin Nabi reports some interesting experiments supporting this general suggestion with respect to drunk

---

[9] Nabi 2003, p. 225. Nabi cites an earlier and helpful definition from Robert Entman in the *Journal of Communication*: "To frame is to select some aspects of a perceived reality and to make them more salient in a communicating text in such a way as to promote a particular problem definition, causal interpretation, moral evaluation, and/or treatment recommendation" (Entman 1993, p. 52).

driving. She primed subjects either with fear or with anger, by asking them to complete a survey on how they felt about drunk drivers – on the assumption that being asked to state their feelings would precipitate the relevant emotion frame and influence their subsequent responses. Fear was primed by using fear-appropriate words in the survey (e.g. "how anxious does drunk driving make you?"). Likewise for anger ("how annoyed do you get at drunk drivers?"). Subjects were asked to complete questionnaires on what they took to be the causes and appropriate responses to drunk driving. Nabi found that subjects in the anger group tended to locate the causes of drunk-driving in the individual, and to favor retributive (punishment-based) solutions, while subjects in the fear group favored societal causes and protective responses. Nabi's interpretation of the results is that they show how emotions can themselves function as frames (in the sense defined in the quoted passage). This is, as it were, the limiting case of how emotions can influence frames.

In many cases, however, emotions and frames need to be clearly distinguished. In an article published in the journal *Political Behavior* in 2008, the political scientists James Druckman and Rose McDermott explored some more complex ways in which emotions can interact with frames.[10] Their work continues the well-known paradigm discussed in earlier chapters, investigating how attitudes to risky choice are affected by whether outcomes are framed as losses or as gains. The basic and much replicated finding, underlying the S-shaped curve in prospect theory, is that people tend to be risk-averse for gains and risk-seeking for losses. Druckman and McDermott found that this basic framing effect can be modulated by emotion. They ran two versions of a standard risky choice paradigm (the Asian disease scenario, and a structurally similar scenario about government grants for community development), using an independent measure of emotional state in a background questionnaire. Interestingly, and somewhat counter-intuitively, Druckman and McDermott found that propensity for risk was directly affected by participants' emotional states in a way that cut across the framing of outcomes in terms of gains or losses. High enthusiasm levels were correlated with increased risk-seeking behavior (which they explain by hypothesizing that positive emotions affect risk perception, making favorable outcomes seem more likely and unfavorable ones less likely). Different types of negative emotion had different effects on risk-seeking behavior: Aversive emotions (such as anger) tended to make subjects more risk-seeking (even when

---

[10] See Druckman and McDermott 2008.

outcomes were framed as losses), while anxious emotions (such as distress) tended to make them more cautious (even when outcomes were framed as gains).

These examples of how emotions can impact framing are instructive. But they do not tell us much about the rationality of framing effects. If anything, they support the view that susceptibility to framing effects is *not* a rational phenomenon. Things look rather different, however, when we consider the opposite direction of influence – when we look at how framing can affect emotional engagement. The point I want to emphasize here is that emotional engagement can vary as a result of differences in framing. This is important because bringing different emotions into play can easily result in differences in valuation, which in turn can be a source of quasi-cyclical preferences. The remainder of this chapter will explore this idea through the complex example of human-caused climate change.

Human-Caused Climate Change

Policy makers, politicians, and concerned citizens have grappled with the challenge of how to communicate the importance of climate change to a public that can easily fail to see the relevance of the problem to their everyday lives; that is unused to thinking about issues with long time horizons; and that is largely ill-equipped properly to understand the science behind the concern. Many have recognized that the challenge is one of framing. It is well documented that facts about the changing climate and environment (rising sea levels, rising temperatures, and so forth) are not persuasive in isolation. They need to be fitted within a narrative that people will find compelling and persuasive. These narratives offer different ways of framing the basic phenomenon of climate change so that it can feature in individual decision-making. We are all constantly making decisions to which climate change is at least potentially relevant – decisions about consumption at every level from the supermarket to large one-off purchases such as cars and houses, for example, as well as political decisions such as voting.

But of course, there are many possible narratives. Here are two that are particularly prominent in public discussions of human-caused climate change. One frame is the disaster frame. One way of presenting climate change in the disaster frame is to highlight extreme weather events, such as heatwaves, wildfires, and coastal flooding together with the associated loss of life and disruption to human habitation. A second frame is the future generations frame. To present climate change in the future generations frame is to emphasize the obligations that we have as individuals and as a society to those who will come later. It is to emphasize climate change not so much as a matter of what is happening now as of the legacy that we leave. The Sierra Club's Our Wild America campaign, launched in 2013, offers a good example of the future generations frame, constantly reiterating that America's public lands are "held in public trust by and for all Americans" (past, present, and future) and using the language of legacy and heritage. For example: "With the Our Wild America campaign, the Sierra Club is doubling down in the fight to preserve our wild heritage in the face of threats from mining, drilling, and climate disruption."[11]

Each of these frames brings a different set of emotions into play. The disaster frame plays directly to emotions of empathy and compassion, which have, as it were, directly salient targets. It also taps into people's fears and, more generally, their complex and ambiguous feelings about the forces of nature. The future generations frame invokes more abstract emotions – an emotional commitment to justice, for example, and a concern with how our actions now might be perceived by our successors. It is not hard to see how a decision problem might be solved differently depending on which of these frames is in play. Someone might have a more direct emotional response to an outcome viewed under the disaster frame, than under the future generations frame, and this might be reflected in the weight that they attach to, say, the fuel consumption figures for the new vehicles that they are considering buying. Thinking about fuel consumption as a contribution to the *Climate Change Disaster* might lead someone to prefer a hybrid car to a gas-guzzling pick-up truck. But someone who thought about fuel consumption as a contribution to the *Climate Legacy* (and who was generally less moved by the plight of future generations than by the plight of contemporaries suffering from natural disasters) might have the reverse preferences. And, of course, those might be the same person. Someone who thought about climate change under both the disaster and the future generation frames could easily have quasi-cyclical preferences.

In fact, even talking about a disaster frame is too monolithic. A lot depends on what sort of disaster climate change is framed as being. Patterns of charitable donations show that the reported cause of a disaster event is a very important determinant of giving behavior. The Disasters Emergency Committee (DEC) is an umbrella organization of 13 charitable

[11] From the Sierra Club website at www.sierraclub.org (downloaded on August 15, 2017).

organizations in the United Kingdom, including such household names as Oxfam, the British Red Cross, and Save the Children. It is interesting and informative to compare the sums of money raised by the DEC in response to natural disasters to the sums raised for human-caused disasters. So, for example, the DEC raised a total of £392 million for their Asian Tsunami Appeal, which began in 2004 (and only closed in 2012), while the 2007 Chad/Darfur appeal to help victims of genocide and ethnic cleansing in the Sudan only lasted until 2008 and raised £13.6 million, almost exactly 1/30 of the Tsunami total. This is a striking disparity, since the difference in the sums raised did not in any sense reflect a difference in total human suffering. The total loss of life from the tsunami was calculated by Oxfam at 169,000, with 600,000 displaced. Estimates for Darfur vary, due to difficulties in gathering information, but a review of mortality surveys published in *The Lancet* in 2010 by Olivier Degomme and Debarati Guha-Sapir came up with a figure of 298,000 excess deaths due to violence and disease.[12] All estimates for displacement are over 1.5 million. So, in purely quantitative terms the human cost of genocide and ethnic cleansing in Darfur seems to be significantly greater.[13]

Psychological studies have replicated this effect. Hanna Zagefka and collaborators presented different groups of subjects with different versions of a fake newspaper article describing the human costs of a famine (Zagefka et al. 2011). In one version, the famine was presented as resulting from drought and natural causes, while in the other it was due to war. Each group responded in a questionnaire and also had the opportunity to donate money. Subjects in the natural disaster group consistently responded more strongly and donated more money. Zagefka and her colleagues hypothesize that victims of natural disasters are perceived as being less responsible for their plight and more willing to help themselves. This is not a view that bears serious scrutiny, but it does seem to be widespread.[14]

So, even within the disaster frame there are further opportunities for viewing climate change within different frames – and hence further opportunities for ending up with quasi-cyclical preferences. Consider, for

---

[12] See Degomme and Guha-Sapir 2010.

[13] For another illustration, compare two campaigns in 2013. The DEC raised £97 million in their appeal for the Philippines Typhoon appeal, compared to £27 million for the war in Syria. All information on DEC appeals is drawn from the DEC website (www.dec.org) and downloaded on August 9, 2017.

[14] For a review of research on the psychology of charitable contributions see Zagefka and James 2015.

example, a decision on whether or not to donate to a disaster relief organization such as the Climate Relief Fund. The Climate Relief Fund was set up to aid victims of global warming. Here is how it explains its mission on its website:

> Global warming has loaded the dice, making extreme weather events more frequent and severe. From super storms to biblical flooding, interminable droughts to devastating wildfires, this new normal is affecting communities everywhere who need our support. And local organizations know best how to help their communities respond, recover, and rebuild.
>
> As we help those in need, we also need to raise awareness about the urgency of climate change. Most disaster relief organizations are not focused on connecting the dots between climate change and extreme weather, and many actively avoid the topic. That's why the Climate Relief Fund shares the stories of disaster victims, so decision makers understand the real effects of inaction.[15]

The Climate Relief Fund is (no doubt intentionally) agnostic on the causes of global warming. So, people who see climate change as predominantly a natural phenomenon (due to naturally occurring weather fluctuations, for example) and who respond in similar ways to subjects in the Zagefka et al. experiments, might prefer donating money to the Climate Relief Fund to giving to another charitable organization that supports victims of war – say, the International Rescue Committee. Such people might frame their donation as supporting an organization that mitigates natural disasters. People looking at climate change within the human-caused frame (and also with the pattern of responses revealed in the experiments), however, might not be so moved. Within the general domain of human-caused catastrophes, they might well prefer to give their limited philanthropic funds to victims of war, rather than to an organization supporting victims of human-caused climate disasters.

Someone who framed climate change in both ways (as a natural disaster *and* as human-caused) could easily end up with quasi-cyclical preferences, since they would be perfectly well aware that Climate Change Relief is both an organization that mitigates natural disasters and an organization supporting victims of human-caused climate disasters. For example, my preferences might look like these:

(3) I prefer supporting Climate Change Relief (*qua* organization that mitigates natural disasters) to supporting the International Rescue Committee (*qua* organization supporting victims of war).

---

[15] Downloaded from www.climate.relief.org on August 9, 2017.

(4) I prefer supporting the International Rescue Committee (*qua* organization supporting victims of war) to supporting Climate Change International (*qua* organization supporting victims of human-caused climate change).

How could I have preferences like these? Well, I might think that the victims of natural disasters are always more deserving of support than the victims of human-caused catastrophe. That would explain (3), provided that I look at Climate Change Relief in the natural disaster frame. But then, switching to the human-caused frame, I might think that nobody deserves support more than the victims of war – which would yield (4).

But still, the fact that I could have such preferences does not show that I would be rational to do so. We need to go back to our main question: Would any of these sets of quasi-cyclical preferences be rational? In thinking about this, it is important to remember that climate change is an incredibly complicated phenomenon. It is perfectly possible to frame it in different ways, each of which reflects part of the complex reality of the phenomenon and yet which jointly give rise to quasi-cyclical preferences. The very existence of the Climate Relief Fund shows the viability of viewing climate change within the natural disaster frame. Likewise for the Sierra Club and the future generations frame. Remaining within the realm of charitable organizations, there are plenty of examples of the viability of viewing climate change within the human-caused frame. Consider 350.org, for example, which describes itself on its website as promoting "online campaigns, grassroots organizing, and mass public actions to oppose new coal, oil and gas projects, take money out of the companies that are heating up the planet, and build 100% clean energy solutions that work for all." This is fairly representative of the genre.

So, the first point I want to make is that these three different ways of framing climate change are perfectly legitimate (and no doubt, of course, there are other legitimate frames). By this I mean that each of them reflects and highlights a genuine aspect of a complex phenomenon.[16] There is nothing wrong with viewing climate change under any of these three frames – as we have seen, each frame is actively promoted by at least one reputable and successful charitable organization. And there is no plausible charge of irrationality to be raised, I think, against someone

---

[16] This would be denied, I suppose, by people who believe that human-caused climate change is a myth. But I am comfortable with the idea that overwhelming scientific consensus secures the legitimacy of a frame.

who adopts one frame over the others. There may be reasons for preferring one frame to another, but that does not make one frame more rational than another – although there is one exception. We find this exception clearly stated in the passage from David Hume that we looked at earlier – the passage that encapsulated the instrumental approach to rationality. Hume writes:

> In short, a passion must be accompany'd with some false judgment, in order to its being unreasonable; and even then 'tis not the passion, properly speaking, which is unreasonable, but the judgment. (Hume 1978 [1739–40], p. 416)

Translating this into our current terminology, we can adapt Hume's point to be that a frame cannot be legitimate if it is based on a false belief. So, applying Hume's criterion would plausibly exclude, for example, any framing of genocide and ethnic cleansing in Darfur on which its victims are held responsible for their own fates. It would also plausibly exclude any way of framing climate change as a natural disaster that absolved humans of all responsibility.

So, if this is right, then there is at least one rationality constraint upon frames. A frame can be legitimate only to the extent that it is not based on (and nor does it straightforwardly imply) false beliefs. No doubt, it would require a lot of work to spell out this requirement precisely. It seems very strong to rule out any false beliefs. Agamemnon's Artemis frame would be a casualty, for example. Perhaps we should restrict the clause to false beliefs that are explicitly contradicted by easily available evidence? It may not be false beliefs themselves that are the problem, but rather the failure to update beliefs in the face of countervailing evidence. A full account needs to balance the undesirability of falsehood with the need for a theory of rationality to respect the constraints of the informational situation in which people find themselves. We will come back to this in Chapter 10.

Does rationality place any other requirements upon frames? In particular, does rationality place any constraints upon framing a situation, outcome, or complicated phenomenon such as climate change in multiple ways? This is the situation that we are most concerned with, because we are exploring the potential rationality of quasi-cyclical preferences that result from knowingly taking multiple perspectives on a single outcome.

In line with the general principle that rationality imposes requirements of consistency, it seems plausible to require that a rational decision-maker not frame an outcome in ways that are straightforwardly inconsistent with each other. So, for example, a rational decision-maker cannot view the death of Iphigenia as an act of murder in one frame, while holding that it is not an act of murder in another frame. Nor can a rational decision-maker hold that climate change is human-caused in one frame, while holding that it is not human-caused in another frame. There is nothing particularly surprising about this. It is just a consequence of the basic requirement of rationality that a rational thinker should not have contradictory beliefs.

I want to emphasize, though, that this requirement of rationality should be interpreted carefully. Consider Agamemnon again. He frames the death of Iphigenia in two ways – as *Murdering his Daughter* and as *Following Artemis's Will*. This is not, on the face of it, inconsistent. The two frames are compatible with each other. The fact that Agamemnon is framing the death of Iphigenia as *Following Artemis's Will* does not mean that he is framing it as *not* being an act of *Murdering his Daughter*. Rather, it means that he is foregrounding one aspect of a complex situation, while another aspect recedes into the background. The murder dimension becomes recessive in his thinking, but that does not mean that he somehow has to force himself to deny that killing Iphigenia would be an act of murder. Likewise, when Agamemnon adopts the *Murdering his Daughter* frame, he is not denying that Iphigenia's death would satisfy Artemis (as interpreted by Calchas). He is, as it were, downplaying the significance of the private dimension of the death of Iphigenia. But downplaying the significance of something falls a long way short of denying that it exists.

More generally, then, we can say that different ways of framing a situation or outcome are consistent when they do not require anyone who holds them simultaneously to have beliefs that contradict each other.[17] This is very much in line with the earlier characterization of a legitimate frame as reflecting and highlighting a genuine aspect of a complex phenomenon. If we think of frames as partial perspectives, then it is not hard to see how different ways of framing an outcome can be consistent. In fact, it is not hard to see how different ways of framing an outcome can complement each other in ways that yield a richer and deeper understanding of a decision problem. If we think (as I think we ought to) that rationality requires us to be as well informed as possible about complex decision problems, then we end up with a similar point to that made earlier in this chapter in what I termed the due diligence requirement.

---

[17] Actually, what I call the No Contradictory Beliefs requirement is more restricted than this. It only applies to what I call *factual propositions*. Rational decision-makers can have non-factual beliefs that contradict each other. More details will come in Chapter 10.

So, to take stock, it seems rationally permissible to view situations and outcomes under multiple frames, provided that those frames are complementary and consistent (i.e. they do not contradict each other) and that none of them are based on false beliefs or comparably dubious sources. In fact, there is a case to be made that, from the perspective of rationality, it can be better to be sensitive to multiple ways of framing a complex outcome, than it is to focus exclusively on a single frame. With this, the argument is almost complete.

The final steps bring us back to the theme of emotional engagement. We have seen numerous examples of how viewing an outcome or situation under different frames can bring different emotional reactions and responses into play. So, let's start by considering the interpersonal situation involving different people adopting different ways of framing a given outcome, and then move to the intrapersonal situation of a single person framing that outcome in different ways.

I take it as a basic starting point that there is nothing intrinsically irrational about responding to something as a function of how it is framed. How I frame an outcome can affect my emotional response by, in effect, priming one emotion over another. We have seen many examples of this. If there is irrationality in this phenomenon, it is not due to the basic fact that emotions are involved, but rather to a perturbing factor, such as the emotional response being driven by some kind of false belief or other failure of theoretical rationality.

So, there is nothing irrational about an individual responding to something emotionally as a function of how it is framed. And nor is there anything irrational about two (or more) different people having different emotional responses to something as a function of how it is framed (subject to the caveat that there is no failure of theoretical rationality in either case). As all the examples of climate change framing show, this is about as common a phenomenon as it is possible to imagine. I want to say also that there is nothing irrational about a single person responding emotionally to something in different ways depending on how it is framed. It is hard to see why it is irrational to have a different emotional response to climate change under the natural disaster frame and under the future generations frame, for example. The first frame might inspire fear and compassion, for example, while the second might evoke a sense of duty and a concern for justice. From the perspective of rationality, I claim, there is nothing wrong with my viewing climate change under these two different aspects, and responding appropriately. Moreover, since it has already been conceded that my valuations can rationally be driven by my emotional responses, it is rationally permissible for me to value (or rather, disvalue) climate change differently, depending on the frame through which I am viewing it.

Now, let's go back to the earlier idea that preferences are grounded in valuations. We have already granted that different emotional responses can (rationally) lead different people to different valuations. Since valuations ground preferences, that means that people with different emotional responses can rationally have different preferences. Let's consider a two-person interpersonal context, so that we have two different people with different preferences resulting from different types of emotional engagement with a complex decision problem. Let's continue assuming, moreover, that there are no confounding factors, such as false beliefs or other failures of theoretical rationality. It is hard to see what grounds there could be for saying that one person's preferences are more rational than the other person's. So (in the absence of confounding factors) we have two equally rational emotional responses, valuations, and consequent preferences. And this remains the case even if the two preferences are opposed to each other – if the first person prefers A to B relative to one frame-dependent emotion-driven valuation, while the second person prefers B to A relative to a second frame-dependent valuation.

Now for the final step in the argument. Once again, let's transpose the interpersonal case just described into an intrapersonal context, so that instead of two different people with opposing preferences we have one person with exactly the type of quasi-cyclical preferences that we have been discussing. What possible reason could there be, given the earlier discussion, for holding that such a person is irrational? If what I've said up to now is sound, then we've already established the following four claims (with the usual caveats that the frames are legitimate, in the sense discussed above, and that there are no false beliefs, or other forms of theoretical irrationality involved):

(i) It can be rationally permissible for an individual to view an outcome or scenario under multiple frames.

(ii) It can be rationally permissible for an individual who views an outcome or scenario under multiple frames to respond emotionally to it in different and frame-dependent ways.

(iii) It can be rationally permissible for how one values an outcome or scenario to be driven by how one responds to it emotionally.

(iv) If one has rationally permissible valuations, then the resulting preferences are rationally permissible.

From (i) through (iv) together, it follows that it is rationally permissible for someone to view a single outcome through multiple frames even when that leads to quasi-cyclical preferences. Of course, that does not mean that quasi-cyclical preferences are *always* going to come out as rational. But we can see how sometimes they will be.

In and of itself, this is an interesting result. It certainly flies in the face of standard ways of thinking about rational decision-making and rational problem-solving. But there's a lot more to be learnt from thinking about frames. The next step is to apply the framework of quasi-cyclical preferences to solving practical problems. We will make a start on this in the next chapter, which will look in more detail at self-control, first discussed in Chapter 1. We'll see how strategies for successful self-control can depend upon framing and quasi-cyclical preferences.

7

Framing Temptation and Reward: The Challenges of Self-Control

Many of the examples of framing that we've been looking at have been dramatic, both literally and metaphorically. It is hard to imagine anything much more dramatic than Agamemnon contemplating the sacrifice of his beloved daughter, or Macbeth grappling with remorse as he fights to retain his ill-won kingdom. It's now time to come back down to earth. It's time to put these ideas about quasi-cyclical preferences and ultra-intensionality to work, so that we can see how framing can be important in everyday decision-making of the sort that we all grapple with on a daily, or near-daily, basis.

My topic for this chapter is individual self-control. The problem here is really one of coordination. How do individuals coordinate their present, past, and future selves over time? How do they stick to their commitments and avoid falling into temptation? In the next chapter we will move from the individual to the group and look at how social groups can come together to collaborate and cooperate. The group case also poses a coordination problem. How do the members of a group coordinate with each other? What happens when the collective interest pulls in one direction and individual self-interest in another?

In fact, the puzzles in the two cases are very similar in abstract structure. As far as orthodox theories of rational choice are concerned, it is hard to see how coordination can be achieved, either within an individual over time or across individuals at a time. The standard theory tells you to maximize from the perspective of the here and now, overriding any conflicting demands that might come from earlier commitments and later rewards (in the individual case) or from the collective benefits of coordinated action (in the group case).

Most challenging for orthodox models of rational choice are those situations where there is a sharp tension between the immediate rewards of maximizing in the here and now, and the greater long-term rewards obtainable by resisting the pull of the immediate. In the individual case, a classic example of resisting the pull of the immediate is to exercise self-control. In the group case, it is through collaboration in circumstances where the pay-offs and benefits are skewed against the cooperative options. But how are these to be achieved? No doubt there are many mechanisms, but I want to focus on how framing can help – in particular, on what happens to the decision problem when we introduce new ways of framing the options and outcomes.

Why Self-Control?

Self-control is a multiply interesting phenomenon. For one thing, it is hard to imagine anything more pragmatically relevant to practical reasoning and rational decision-making, because many (most?) practical decisions, however rational, require a degree of self-control for their implementation. It is not surprising, therefore, that for most of us self-control comes up on a daily basis in one form or another. We are all almost constantly either exercising self-control or failing to exercise it. So, any way of thinking about self-control with the potential to improve our ability to exercise it offers rich dividends.

Given the centrality of the phenomenon, it is not surprising that self-control has been studied from a range of different perspectives across a number of different academic disciplines.

- For philosophers, self-control is typically conceptualized as the opposite of weakness of will. On this way of thinking about it, to exercise self-control is in the last analysis to avoid being weak-willed. From this perspective, which goes back at least as far back as Aristotle, self-control is a character virtue, or at least a character trait. Taking this perspective into account brings into play a long and rich tradition of thinking about action and practical reason.[1]
- For economists and decision theorists, in contrast, self-control tends to be discussed in the context of what is often called dynamic choice,

---

[1] For recent philosophical discussions of self-control and weakness of will see Holton 2009 and Mele 2012. Classic discussions include Davidson 1969, Mele 1987, Pears 1984, and Wiggins 1978.

where the issue is how decisions over time can be integrated with each other. Issues of self-control arise when valuations and utilities at different times conflict. What happens to my plans, for example, when I am confronted by a preference reversal – e.g. when my desire for a long-term good, and concomitant plan to attain it, threaten to be derailed by a short-term temptation? From this perspective, self-control is the property of a pattern of choices over time.[2]

- Psychologists tend to focus on mechanisms – the mechanisms that make self-control necessary (how particular individuals discount the future, for example) and the mechanisms that achieve it. Some psychologists think of self-control as a psychic force, the psychological equivalent of a muscle. Psychologists also consider the practical question of how self-control can be developed and promoted in individuals.[3]

These perspectives are not brought into contact with each other as frequently as they should be. But they are certainly not incompatible, and in one form or another, all come into play in the course of this chapter.

I begin with the ancient Greeks. The classic discussions of weakness of will and self-control that Socrates offers in the early Platonic dialogs set the contours of the intellectual landscape in a way that has not really been improved upon in the subsequent two and a half millennia. Moreover, as we will see at the end of the chapter, Socrates's subtle discussion of choice and action in *Protagoras* offers a suggestive prefiguring of how and why framing is so important.

With the Socratic background in place, I then set up a stripped-down, schematic example for discussing self-control. The example is a very simple sequential choice problem (a problem of decision-making over time) illustrating how even the best-laid plans can be derailed by temptation. This type of problem has been much discussed by decision theorists and economists. This is because it shows very clearly why orthodox theories of rational choice find it hard to explain why self-control is even possible.

---

[2] McClennen 1990 is a classic text, discussed further in Bratman 1999, McClennen 1998, and Gauthier 1997. See also Strotz 1956 and Elster 1979 for influential earlier discussions. The essays in Bermúdez 2018c offer a range of perspectives on decision-theoretic discussions of self-control, from both philosophy and psychology.

[3] The idea that self-control is like a muscle is associated with the ego depletion theory promoted by Baumeister and collaborators (Baumeister, Heatherton, and Tice 1994, and for a recent meta-analysis see Hagger et al. 2010). Walter Mischel's experiments on delay of gratification in children are discussed further below. Influential book-length treatments include Rachlin 2000 and Ainslie 2001.

In many ways, the perspective of contemporary decision theorists and economists is the exact opposite of how Socrates looked at the issues. Socrates operates (in the *Protagoras* for example) with a model of action and motivation that seems to rule out the possibility of considered judgments and plans being overruled when an agent succumbs to temptation. In contrast, modern rational choice theory has a model of action and motivation that makes it hard to see how temptation can be resisted in favor of considered judgments and plans.

In trying to make sense of all this, it helps that the sequential choice problem is formulated so that it is relatively straightforward to bring to bear discussions of self-control and related phenomena from psychology. So, we can use psychological models of how the values of rewards are discounted over time to explain the power of temptation. And we can see the relevance of psychological research into the importance of how rewards are conceptualized and framed. That will lead eventually into a model of how self-control can be achieved through framing.

Socrates: Self-Control and the Science of Measurement

The only philosopher who has had more paradoxes named after him than Socrates is his predecessor Zeno of Elea. But there is a difference between them. Zeno of Elea set out deliberately to create paradoxes, as part of his (puzzling) project of trying to demonstrate the unreality of space, time, and motion.[4] Socrates, in contrast, was not setting out to produce paradoxes, but rather to characterize the realities of our psychological and ethical lives. The Socratic paradoxes are so called because Socrates's sense of psychological and ethical reality is very different from our own – and, for that matter, from that of his contemporaries.

Prominent among the Socratic paradoxes is what is often termed his denial of the possibility of *akrasia*, the Greek word whose principal translations are "weakness of will," "weakness of character," "incontinence," or "lack of self-control."[5] The most famous statement of this view

---

[4] For more on Zeno's paradoxes and their background see McKirahan 2010, ch. 6 and Barnes 1979, ch. 12. Enthusiasts for the paradoxes themselves will want to consult the essays in Salmon 2001.

[5] The Greek word ἀκρασία does not really make an appearance in classical philosophy before Aristotle, so it is strictly speaking inaccurate to talk of Socrates's views (or Plato's views, for that matter) on *akrasia*. But still, the practice is very well established and so I continue it. We find ἀκρασία translated as "weakness of will" by David Wiggins; as "weakness of character" by J. L. Ackrill; as "incontinence" by Terence Irwin; and as

is in the dialog *Protagoras*, named after the famous Sophist with whom
Socrates engages. That dialog contains a lengthy argument for another of
the Socratic paradoxes, often called the unity of the virtues. This is the
thesis that what are typically thought of as separate virtues (courage,
prudence, and so on) are really just one virtue, because they are all
ultimately forms of knowledge. As part of that argument, Socrates argues
that there is no such thing as, in his words, "being overcome by pleasure
and, therefore, though recognizing what is best, failing to do it."[6] What
Socrates appears to be denying is that the phenomenon that Aristotle was
subsequently to term *akrasia* is even possible.

As Plato sets it up in the dialog, the denial of *akrasia* actually follows
from a point on which Socrates and Protagoras are in agreement. They
have a common view of human motivation and action. Socrates asks
Protagoras:

> What is your attitude to knowledge? Do you share the common view about that
> also? Most people think, in general terms, that it is nothing strong, no leading
> or ruling element. They don't see it like that. They hold that it is not the
> knowledge a man possesses which governs him, but something else – now
> passion, now pleasure, now pain, sometimes love, and frequently fear. They
> just think of knowledge as a slave, pushed around by all the other affections.[7]

The common view is that the springs of action are, in effect, emotions and
sensations of pleasure and pain, which are perfectly capable of coming
into conflict with and overruling even the best thought-out plans and
commitments. But Protagoras, like Socrates, thinks that knowledge
alone is enough to explain action. As he puts it, "wisdom and knowledge
are the most powerful elements in human life."[8]

What Protagoras thinks he is agreeing to is most likely weaker than
what Socrates is trying to establish, however. My (unverifiable) suspicion
is that what Protagoras really means is that a wise man (i.e. a man suitably
trained by sophists such as himself) will always be able to act upon his

---

"lack of self-control" by Christopher Rowe and Sarah Broadie. See Wiggins 1978, Ackrill
1981, Irwin 1995, Broadie and Rowe 2002 respectively. The essays in Bobonich and
Destrée 2007 give an overview of how the phenomenon is understood from Socrates
through to Plotinus.

[6] Plato, *Protagoras* 353a. Translated by W. K. C. Guthrie in Hamilton and Cairns 1961, p.
344.
[7] Plato, *Protagoras* 352b/c. Translated by W. K. C. Guthrie in Hamilton and Cairns 1961, p.
344.
[8] Plato, *Protagoras* 352d. Translated by W. K. C. Guthrie in Hamilton and Cairns 1961, p.
344.

knowledge of what is good. His interlocutor, though, is after bigger game. Socrates begins:

> If they [i.e. "most men"] should ask us. 'What is your name for being worsted by pleasure?' I should reply, 'Listen, we take it that this happens to you when, for example, you are overcome by the desire of food, or drink, or sex – which are pleasant things – and though you recognize them as evil, nevertheless indulge in them.[9]

The next few pages argue that there is no such phenomenon. There is an inherent contradiction, Socrates claims, in the very idea of being "overcome by pleasure" or being "worsted by pleasure." And he concludes, when we appreciate the source of the contradiction, we see that what is really going on in apparent cases of *akrasia* is not really any type of mental conflict, but rather an error of calculation.

Socrates's key reason for claiming that it makes no sense to talk about "being overcome by pleasure" is his version of what is often called psychological hedonism.[10] In *Protagoras* Socrates argues (and convinces Protagoras) that the good is pleasure, and the bad is pain. Here is a representative passage (Socrates is addressing people in general):

> 'So you pursue pleasure as being good, and shun pain as evil?'
>
> He agreed.
>
> 'Then your idea of evil is pain, and of good is pleasure. Even enjoying yourself you call evil whenever it leads to the loss of a pleasure greater than its own, and lays up pains that outweigh its pleasures. If it is in any other sense, or with anything else in mind that you can call enjoyment evil, no doubt you could tell us what it is but you cannot.'
>
> I agree that they cannot, said Protagoras.
>
> 'Isn't it the same when we turn back to pain? To suffer pain you call good when it either rids us of greater pains than its own or leads to pleasures that outweigh them. If you have anything else in mind when you call the actual suffering of pain a good thing, you could tell us what it is, but you cannot.'
>
> True, said Protagoras.[11]

---

[9] Plato, *Protagoras* 353c. Translated by W. K. C. Guthrie in Hamilton and Cairns 1961, p. 345.

[10] Scholars disagree about whether the psychological hedonism in *Protagoras* is Socrates's considered view, or simply a dialectical tool that suited his purposes at the time. The former interpretation is defended (convincingly, to my mind) in Irwin 1995 §60 (pp. 85–87).

[11] Plato, *Protagoras* 354c–355e. Translated by W. K. C. Guthrie in Hamilton and Cairns 1961, pp. 345–46.

So, when people pursue what they take to be the good they are really pursuing it because of the pleasure that it is anticipated to bring, now or in the future (or both). And likewise, when they avoid what they take to be evil, they are really avoiding it because of the pain that it is anticipated to bring, now or in the future (or both).

But, in the context of psychological hedonism, it makes little sense to talk about doing something that one takes to be evil because one is overcome by pleasure, as Socrates immediately goes on to point out.

> The absurdity of this will become evident if we stop using all these names together – pleasant, painful, good, and evil – and since they have turned out to be only two, call them by only two names – first of all good and evil, and only at a different stage pleasure and pain. Having agreed on this, suppose we now say that a man does evil though he recognizes it as evil. Why? Because he is overcome. By what? We can no longer say by pleasure because it has changed its name to good. Overcome, we say. By what, we are asked. By the good, I suppose we shall say. I fear that if our questioner is ill-mannered, he will laugh and retort, What ridiculous nonsense, for a man to do evil knowing it is evil and he ought not to do it, because he is overcome by good.[12]

So, the traditional characterization of weakness of will (or what Aristotle later termed *akrasia*) is misplaced. What is really going on, according to Socrates, is an error of measurement. Weak-willed people standardly taken to be overcome by pleasure are really just misjudging the pleasure and pain that they will derive from their action (e.g. by attaching too much importance to short-term pleasure and too little to long-term pain).

Ultimately, then, weakness of will is a form of ignorance. And virtue, or the source of happiness, lies in a special kind of knowledge, what Socrates calls an *art of measurement*. The wise and virtuous person will be able correctly to assess the balance of pleasures and pains in every circumstance and situation. But the weak-willed person is not doing anything different. He is also calculating the balance of pleasures and pains, but just not doing so very well. For Socrates (at least in the *Protagoras*), decisions to act always result from the following process:

> So, like an expert in weighing, put the pleasures and the pains together, set both the near and distant in the balance, and say which is the greater quantity. In weighing pleasures against pleasures, one must always choose the greater and the more; in weighing pains against pains, the smaller and the less; whereas in weighing pleasures against pains, if the pleasures exceed the pains, whether the

[12] Plato, *Protagoras* 355b–355d. Translated by W. K. C. Guthrie in Hamilton and Cairns 1961, p. 346.

distant, the near, or vice versa, one must take the course which brings those pleasures; but if the pains outweigh the pleasures, avoid it.[13]

What separates the person with self-control from the person without self-control is their skill in this kind of analysis. What is standardly thought of as lack of self-control is failure to see through appearances because the appeal of the here and now obscures a correct assessment of how the different pleasures and pains balance out against each other. So really, then, from a Socratic perspective there is no such thing as self-control in the standard sense, where that requires an agent to exercise willpower in the face of temptation.

Of course, Socrates is not denying the behavioral facts. It is obviously the case that some people are more self-controlled than others. Some people stick to diets. Many more break them. And so on. But he is insisting that the usual way of thinking about the difference between the first group and the second group is mistaken. The first group do not have greater strength of will, or more power to resist temptation, than the second. They are just better at the science of measurement – better at what we might anachronistically term hedonic cost–benefit analysis.

Socrates does not go into any details in the *Protagoras* (or anywhere else, for that matter) about how to go about achieving that sort of accurate cost–benefit analysis. I will come back to that later, because I think that that's where framing comes into the picture. First, though, I'd like to turn to how the phenomenon of self-control looks from the modern perspective of decision theory and psychology. Interestingly, as I mentioned earlier, the decision-theoretic perspective on self-control is almost exactly the opposite of the Socratic perspective.

Sequential Choice and Self-Control

Decision theorists, like game theorists, like to work with very simple and schematic examples. They use these as blueprints or templates, stripping away the details in order to capture what a wide variety of decision situations and decision problems have in common. In Chapters 8 and 9 we will look at famous games such as Chicken, the Prisoner's Dilemma, and the Stag Hunt. They are famous because each seems to capture the structure of an important class of social interactions. Just as many social interactions arguably have the abstract structure of a Prisoner's Dilemma,

---

[13] Plato, *Protagoras* 356b–356c. Translated by W. K. C. Guthrie in Hamilton and Cairns 1961, p. 347.

and others have the abstract structure of a Stag Hunt, many intrapersonal decision problems have the abstract structure displayed by the simple sequential choice problem that I will now outline. This problem is very well suited to model weakness of will, self-control, and related phenomena. And so it has been widely discussed, in one form or another, both by decision theorists and by psychologists.

Suppose that at a given moment in time, an agent makes a plan or commitment. Let's call that time t_0. Sticking to the plan or commitment will bring a reward at some time in the future (say, t_2). It has become standard practice in the literature to label that reward LL, abbreviating Larger Later. LL is the long-term goal. At another time (say, t_1), earlier than the time of delivery of the long-term reward but later than the time of making the plan/commitment, the agent has the opportunity to abandon the plan. The reward at time t_1 is standardly termed SS (for Smaller Sooner). SS is the short-term temptation.

Now, in between time t_0, when the commitment/plan was originally made, and time t_1, when the option of SS appears, the agent's preferences change. At the earlier time, the agent prefers LL to SS (i.e. in the language of rational choice theory, she assigns greater utility to LL than to SS). That is why she originally makes the commitment to hold on for LL, even though she knows that she will have the opportunity to abandon the plan at time t_1. Between time t_0 and time t_1, however, the agent's utility function changes (in ways to be spelled out further below) and she comes to assign greater utility to SS than to LL, so that at time t_1 abandoning the plan seems more attractive than sticking to it.

Figure 7.1 shows the structure of the problem.

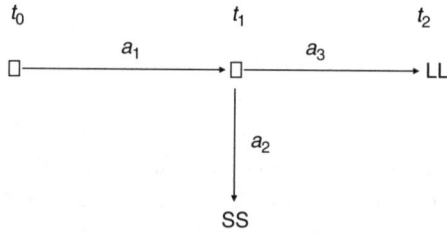

FIGURE 7.1 A paradigm case of self-control represented as a sequential choice problem
Note: The moment of planning is at time t_0 with the moment of choice at time t_1, when the agent chooses between the immediate Smaller Sooner temptation (SS) and the delayed Larger Later reward (LL).

The issue, then, is what should the agent do at time t_1? Should she stick to the plan and hold out for LL? Or should she follow her current utility assignment and opt instead for SS?

This schematic problem can easily be interpreted as an example of being overcome by temptation. The plan or commitment could be, say, the decision to stick to a diet, follow an exercise plan, or restrict oneself to driving-compatible quantities of alcohol at the bar. The long-term reward, LL, could be weight loss, physical fitness for a sporting event, or a safe and law-abiding journey home. The temptation is SS, which might be a cake, an hour's more sleep in the morning, or the drink that will put you over the drink-driving limit. To follow the plan, by continuing along the path a_3 that leads to LL, is to exercise self-control. To abandon the plan, by taking the path a_2 that leads to the SS reward, is to succumb to temptation.

On many occasions, to succumb to temptation in this way would be to display weakness of will, and so in that sense the sequential choice problem offers a classic example of precisely the phenomenon that Socrates and Protagoras were discussing. But the way the problem is set up is diametrically opposed to how Socrates ended up analyzing the phenomenon. The sequential choice problem hinges on precisely what Socrates declared could not happen. The agent who opts for SS at time t_1 seems clearly to be "overcome by pleasure." And in fact, the theoretical background to how the problem is standardly discussed makes it hard to see how the agent can be anything other than "overcome" by pleasure.

The key issue is about motivational strength. Decision theorists typically assume a broadly Humean view of practical reason and decision-making. As we have seen earlier, the basic principle of standard models of rational choice is Hume's view that reason is the slave of the passions, rather than the Socratic one that reason is the ruler of the passions. To exercise self-control at time t_1 in the sequential choice problem is to resist what is currently one's strongest desire or inclination. And from the decision-theoretic perspective, it is not clear that this is even possible, since decision theory envisages a cognitive economy where motivational strength is the only spring of action – or, alternatively, where rational agents act to maximize (expected) utility.

Within the framework of decision theory, therefore, the sequential choice problem depicted in Figure 7.1 raises two different problems.

- We have to explain the mechanisms that could allow an agent at t_1 to take path a_3 leading to the long-term goal of LL. How is this even possible, within a framework for understanding action based on the idea that choice always maximizes (expected) utility? At time t_1, the option that maximizes utility is to take path a_2, leading to the short-term goal of SS. So why is it not always taken?

- Suppose that an agent does act in a way that fails to maximize utility at time t_1, how can this be rational, if rational choice is understood to be choice that maximizes (expected) utility and taking path a_3 to secure LL is clearly not a maximizing option?

The first question, therefore, is about psychological mechanisms. And the second is about rationality.

Why Do Preferences Reverse?

The sequential choice problem on which I am focusing involves a conspicuous preference reversal. At time t_0, when the agent starts thinking about what to do, she assigns greater utility to LL than to SS. From the perspective of her t_0 self, in other words, $u(\text{LL}) > u(\text{SS})$. But, by the time the moment of choice at t_1 arrives, things have changed and $u(\text{SS}) > u(\text{LL})$. Since the influential work of George Ainslie, Howard Rachlin, and others, this preference reversal has standardly been viewed as the result of a particular way in which agents discount the future.[14]

To discount the future is to assign less utility to a future good than one expects to derive from it when it is eventually reached. A discounting function describes how the degree to which an agent discounts a future good is related to the temporal distance from that future good (i.e. the delay until the reward is received). There are two broad families of discount function. *Exponential delay discount functions* behave very differently from *hyperbolic delay discount functions*.

The key feature of exponential discount functions is that they remain constant over time. This means that the ratio between how much one discounts a future good at the start and the end of any given temporal interval is a function only of how long that interval is. So, the impact of a day's delay will be the same tomorrow as 25 years in the future. How near or how distant the future good is does not factor in at all. For that reason, exponential discounting is described as *time-consistent*.

Hyperbolic discount functions, in contrast, are *time-inconsistent*, because the ratio of the discount function is not constant. This means

[14] See Ainslie 1974, 1992, and Rachlin 2000 and 2018.

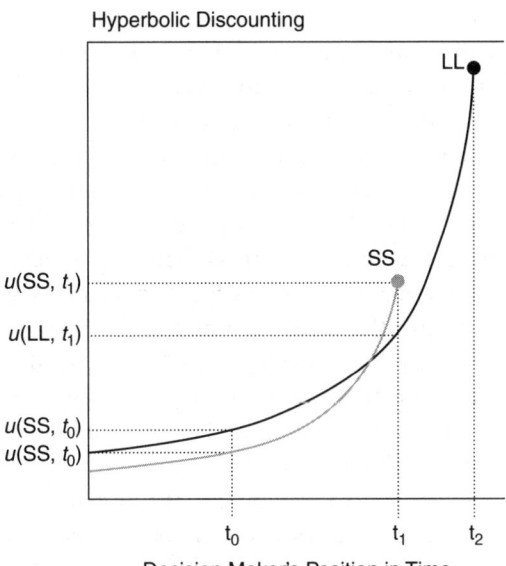

FIGURE 7.2 Hyperbolic discounting leading to self-control
Note: SS is an immediate benefit (Smaller Sooner), while LL is a long-term benefit (Larger Later). The vertical axis gives utilities while the horizontal axis gives times.

that the ratio between how much one discounts a future good at the beginning and at the end of a given temporal interval is affected by how far away the future good is. So, for example, a day's delay counts for more when the reward is nearer than when it is still a long time away. The difference between having $10 today and receiving $11 tomorrow is much greater than the difference between having $10 100 days into the future and having $11 in 101 days.[15] Figure 7.2 illustrates how the process of hyperbolic discounting might apply in our sequential choice problem.

As the moment of choice approaches, the hyperbolic discount function for SS steepens more rapidly than the discount function for LL (because SS is more imminent than LL) and so the utility assigned to SS surpasses the utility assigned to LL. That is what allows preferences to reverse between time t_0 and time t_1.

---

[15] Many people who would rather have $10 now than $11 tomorrow will be prepared to hold out that extra day for the extra dollar when the interval is sufficiently far into the future.

We can put aside interesting and important debates about the exact shape of delay discount functions.[16] For now we need only the basic idea that what opens up space for weakness of will is a contrast between how the utilities of the long-term reward LL and the short-term reward SS are discounted as a function of delay. This basic idea suggests an obvious mechanism for achieving self-control. You can exercise self-control by changing how the long-term reward is discounted. In Figure 7.2, weakness of will enters the picture at precisely the moment where the discount curve for SS crosses the discount curve for LL, because that is the point at which we first have $u(SS)$ > $u(LL)$. So, one way of achieving self-control would be to change one or other discount curve so that they no longer cross. An agent exercising self-control does not allow her discount curve for LL to be crossed by her discount curve for SS.

To say this, however, is to give the problem a name, not to provide a solution. How can an agent affect the shape and slope of her discount curves? No doubt this can be done in different ways. But one natural suggestion would be that the shape and slope of an agent's discount curves are (at least partially) driven by how she represents the relevant rewards. The idea that I will be developing is that we can model exercises of self-control in this type of case in terms of how the agent *frames* either or both the long-term reward LL and the short-term reward SS. After reviewing some very suggestive psychological evidence about the importance of goal representation and framing in self-control, I then show how this evidence supports, and can be incorporated within, a theoretical model of self-control that remains (broadly speaking) within the conceptual framework of contemporary rational choice theory.

The Delay of Gratification Paradigm

In the late 1960s and early 1970s, Walter Mischel and collaborators developed a disarmingly simple experimental paradigm for studying self-control in young children.[17] In the so-called delay of gratification paradigm, preschoolers are, in effect, offered a choice between SS and LL. The children are told that the experimenter needs to go away, but when the experimenter returns they will receive a delayed reward of, say, two cookies or two marshmallows (i.e. the LL). They can wait for LL or, at

[16] See, e.g., Green and Myerson 2018 for discussion and further references.
[17] For a review see, for example, Mischel, Shoda, and Rodriguez 1989.

any time, while the experimenter is away, they can ring a bell to receive an immediate reward of a single cookie or marshmallow (which is, of course, the SS). Various modifications of this paradigm enabled Mischel and colleagues to study different aspects of self-control and delayed gratification. Moreover, extensive longitudinal studies over the lifespan allowed the experimenters to establish the validity of performance in early childhood on delayed gratification tasks as a predictor of various social and cognitive competencies later in development, as well as scores on standardized tests such as the Scholastic Aptitude Test (SAT).[18]

One very interesting feature of the delayed gratification experiments that I want to focus on here is Mischel's hypothesis that patterns demonstrated in the experimental behavior can be explained through the interaction between "hot" and "cold" cognitive-affective systems – a version of the dual-process theory that we find in many areas of psychology.[19] Here is how Mischel and Ayduk state the contrast in a 2004 review article:

> Briefly, the cool system is an emotionally neutral, "know" system: It is cognitive, complex, slow, and contemplative. Attuned to the informational, cognitive, and spatial aspects of stimuli, the cool system consists of a network of informational, *cool* nodes that are elaborately interconnected to each other, and generate rational, reflective, and strategic behavior. . . . In contrast, the hot system is a "go" system. It enables quick, emotional processing: simple and fast, and thus useful for survival from an evolutionary perspective by allowing rapid fight or flight reactions, as well as necessary appetitive approach responses. The hot system consists of relatively few representations, *hot spots* (e.g. unconditioned stimuli), which elicit virtually reflexive avoidance and approach reactions when activated by trigger stimuli. This hot system develops early in life and is the most dominant in the young infant. (Mischel and Ayduk 2004, p. 109)

The precise details of the cold/hot cognitive-affective systems are not important, nor are hypotheses as to their respective neural underpinnings.[20] But I do want to emphasize a basic idea, common to most (if not all) dual-process approaches. This is that how an outcome or potential

---

[18] Not all of these claims have been replicated. The idea that the marshmallow test is a good predictor of SAT performance seems robust, but other claims have proved harder to replicate. See the recent replication studies reported in Watts, Duncan, and Quan 2018 (although these did not use exactly the same paradigm as Mischel's original experiment).

[19] As briefly discussed in Chapter 1. For a review of dual-process theories in reasoning, judgment, and social cognition, see Evans 2008. Kahneman 2011 offers an influential, book-length treatment aimed at a more general audience.

[20] For more discussion of the neural underpinnings of framing effects see the Appendix, "Frames in the Brain."

action is represented directly affects which of the two systems is engaged. Representing an outcome or an action in a cool way engages the cool system, while hot representations engage the hot system.

This dual-process theory connects up nicely with the earlier discussion of discounting functions. It gives a way of explaining why the two discount curves behave as they do. At time t_0, when SS is still at a safe (temporal) distance, the cool system dominates and so the utility attached to the two outcomes reflects the agent's considered preference for the added benefit of LL. That is why we have $u(LL) > u(SS)$. The closer the agent gets to SS, however, the more the hot system kicks in and so the slope of the valuation function steepens, until the SS discount curve eventually intersects the LL discount curve and paves the way for the weak-willed response.

So, from the perspective of promoting self-control, an obvious strategy is to ensure that hot representations of the short-term reward SS are counter-balanced and kept in check by cooler representations that might take into account, for example, the long-term consequences of succumbing to temptation. Another strategy would be to represent the long-term reward LL in ways that engage the hot system. This will steepen the LL discount function and prevent the SS discount function from crossing it.

Mischel and Ayduk make this very point, describing some of the early delay of gratification studies:

> it became clear that delay of gratification depends not on whether or not attention is focused on the objects of desire, but rather on just how they are mentally represented. A focus on their hot features may momentarily increase motivation, and unless it is rapidly cooled by a focus on their cool informative features (e.g., as reminders of what will be obtained later if the contingency is fulfilled) it is likely to become excessively arousing and trigger the "go" response. (2004, p. 114)

Here are some of the studies that they identify as pointing to what I will term the frame-dependence of discount curves.

- Mischel and Moore 1973 found that performance on the delay of gratification paradigm varied when children were presented with images of the rewards, as opposed to the rewards themselves. They reasoned that presenting an iconic representation of the reward would present the reward in a "cool" light, highlighting its cognitive and informational features, whereas presenting the reward itself would highlight its motivational features and engage the "hot" system. Children who had the actual reward in front of them performed much worse on the delay of gratification task than children who merely had a picture of the reward in front of them.

• Mischel and Baker 1975 went a step further, finding something that seems even more clearly to be a framing effect. Children undergoing delay of gratification experiments for marshmallows and pretzels were divided into two groups and cued to think about the rewards differently. One group, the "cold" group, was primed to think about the marshmallows as "white, puffy clouds" and the pretzels as "little, brown logs." Children in the second, "hot," group were cued to think about obvious motivational features of the marshmallows and pretzels – as "yummy and chewy" and "salty and crunchy respectively." As predicted, children in the cold group were significantly better able to withstand temptation than children in the hot group – a mean of 13 minutes before ringing the bell for the SS reward, as opposed to a mean of 5 minutes.

Both sets of results are highly suggestive of framing effects, but the Mischel and Baker experiment particularly so. Here it seems that the way in which the reward is framed directly affects rate of change of the SS discount curve, and so the point at which the SS discount curve crosses the LL discount curve. The language of "framing" is very natural here, because "white puffy clouds" and "yummy and chewy" are clearly different ways of describing the same reward – and likewise "little brown logs" and "salty and crunchy."

The Hidden Zeros Paradigm

A second, much more recent, illustration of how framing contributes to self-control comes from an interesting set of neuroimaging studies. These studies were explicitly designed to test the hypothesis that self-control can be achieved without the effortful exertion of willpower. They build on earlier studies suggesting that different brain areas are involved in valuing rewards, on the one hand, and exerting willpower, on the other.

How rewards are valued appears to be modulated by the ventromedial prefrontal cortex (vmPFC) and striatum areas, while willpower exertion is typically tied to the dorsolateral prefrontal cortex (dlPFC).[21] This is just a

---

[21] For the role of the vmPFC in reward valuation see, for example, Hare, Camerer, and Rangel 2009, and for the role of the dlPFC in the exercise of willpower see also Figner et al. 2010. The neuroscience of rewards and framing more generally is discussed in the Appendix, "Frames in the Brain."

fact about neuroanatomy. But it connects up suggestively with the idea
that one way to exercise self-control is to change the slopes of the discount
curves for SS and LL. To change the slope of the discount curve for a
reward is, in essence, to change how that reward is valued. So, if the neural
basis for reward valuation is distinct from the neural basis for effortful
willpower, then it seems at least in principle possible for self-control to be
exercised without engaging willpower. But how?

The hypothesis tested in Magen et al. 2014 is that self-control can be
enhanced by changing how the rewards are framed. The experimental
paradigm here does not depend upon any sort of dual-process theory,
unlike the Mischel experiments described above. Instead, Magen et al.
recruited an independently documented framing effect – the so-called
hidden zero effect.

Experiments designed to calibrate an individual's discount curve typically present subjects with choices such as the following: "Would you
prefer $5 today or $10 in a month's time?" This is plainly a choice
between SS and LL. It is described as being in *hidden zero* format, because
the question does not make explicit the fact that if you opt for $5 today,
you will receive $0 in a month's time and, correlatively, that if you opt for
$10 in a month's time you will receive $0 today. To include the relevant
non-rewards in the description of the choice is to frame the choice in an
explicit zero format – e.g. by asking: "Would you prefer $5 today and $0
in a month's time, or $0 today and $10 in a month's time?"

Consistent with the results of an earlier paper (Magen, Dweck, and
Gross 2008), the experimenters in the 2014 study found that participants
discounted the future at lower rates when outcomes were presented in the
explicit zero format than when they were presented in the hidden zero
format. This is plausibly described as a framing effect, since the outcomes
in the hidden zero and explicit zero outcomes can immediately be seen to
be equivalent.

The 2014 study contributed two new insights into how framing can
affect self-control.

- Subjects were given a valuation task in which, instead of being asked to
  choose directly between SS and LL, they are presented with the reward
  outcomes separately and asked to measure their satisfaction with the
  outcome – e.g. "How happy would you be to receive $10 in a month's
  time?" These outcomes were each presented in hidden zero and explicit
  zero format, so that it was possible to test whether the framing effect
  affected how both rewards were evaluated. It turned out that the

hidden/explicit format manipulation affected how SS was valued, but not how LL was valued. In other words, framing SS in the explicit zero format lowered the subjective value of immediate rewards (SS), but did not affect the subjective value of delayed rewards (LL).

* The neural data confirmed the hypothesis that the reframing is effective in enabling self-control without the exercise of effortful willpower. In particular, there was significantly less activation in the dlPFC (the area correlated with willpower) when LL was chosen in the explicit zero format than when it was chosen in the hidden zero format. Overall, in fact, variation in activity in the reward areas was sufficient to explain different valuations in the two conditions.

Combining the results of this study with the data from the delay of gratification paradigm discussed earlier strongly suggests that how outcomes are framed is directly relevant to the exercise of self-control. Self-control can be easier or more difficult, depending on the particular frame. These results are very suggestive. But still, one might wonder, are they of more than anecdotal significance? What lessons do they have for a more systematic account of self-control?

To focus the issues here, let me go back to the two questions that I posed in initially discussing the problem of self-control. The first question is, as it were, a descriptive question about the psychological mechanisms of self-control in the specific context of the sequential choice problem. If we assume a framework for understanding action on which choice is always based on maximizing (expected) utility, then how is it even possible for an agent to take the path that leads to the long-term goal of LL, as opposed to the utility-maximizing path, which leads to the short-term goal?

The second question is a normative question, about the rationality of exercising self-control. Suppose (as appears often to be the case) that an agent does act in a way that fails to maximize utility at time t_1, because exercising self-control leads them to forgo the utility-maximizing choice. Then, how can we think about this as rational behavior, within a general framework on which rational choice is taken to be choice that maximizes (expected) utility? It looks, on the face of things, as if exercising self-control in the sequential choice problem is either going to come out as irrational, or we are going to have to move away from the maximizing framework.

The psychological evidence just reviewed suggests that thinking about how outcomes can be differentially framed offers a way of answering the descriptive question about the psychological mechanisms of self-control in the sequential choice problem. We'll look at that in more detail in the next section. Then, in the final section, I'll turn to the normative question.

Framing in Self-Control

So, how might framing play a role in exercises of self-control in the sequential choice problem? The first step is to spell out in more detail the options and outcomes in the standard way of thinking about the problem. As portrayed in Figure 7.1, the agent at time t_1 is faced with two options, a_2 and a_3. The certain outcome of a_3 is LL and the certain outcome of a_2 is SS. Since SS will be reached sooner than LL let me make this even more explicit by terming these two outcomes *Delayed LL* and *Immediate SS* respectively. Correspondingly, we can label the two options *Wait for LL* and *Take SS*.

So, an agent who succumbs to temptation prefers *Immediate SS* to *Delayed LL* and, as a consequence, chooses *Take SS* over *Wait for LL*. That choice reflects his preference at time t_1. That much is clear enough. But how should we think about the agent who exercises self-control in the sequential choice? The natural suggestion would be that the self-controlled agent simply has the opposite pattern of preference and choice at time t_1. A self-controlled agent will choose *Wait for LL* over *Take SS* because she prefers *Delayed LL* to *Immediate SS*.

But, of course, that is not admissible, given how the sequential choice problem has been set up. What makes the sequential choice problem a problem is that the agent's preferences have reversed between t_0 and t_1. She did prefer *Delayed LL* to *Immediate SS* at the earlier time t_0. But by t_1, she prefers *Immediate SS* to *Delayed LL*. That's why she has a problem. If at t_1 she were to prefer *Delayed LL* to *Immediate SS*, then she won't need to exercise self-control at all.

But then, you might think, the sequential choice problem has become completely intractable, at least within the framework of expected utility theory. It looks as if an agent exercising self-control would have to have conflicting preferences and a completely incoherent utility function, because she would need simultaneously to prefer *Delayed LL* over *Immediate SS* (in order to explain why she exercises self-control) and to prefer *Immediate SS* to *Delayed LL* (in order to explain why she feels the pull of temptation).

This is where framing comes into the picture. It would be incoherent for her to prefer *Delayed LL* to *Immediate SS* and *Immediate SS* to *Delayed LL*. Those would be cyclical preferences, and there is not much to be said for cyclical preferences. But what if she had *quasi-cyclical preferences*? That would happen if she prefers LL to SS under one way of framing one or more outcome, but prefers SS to LL under a different framing. Incorporating frame-sensitivity into how we think about the available outcomes and options at time t_1, the moment of temptation, gives us a much richer decision problem.

We might imagine, for example, that the agent frames the *Delayed LL* outcome in a different way – as *Having Successfully Resisted SS*, for example. So, the agent now has a three-way choice, not a two-way one. With respect to goals, her choice is between *Delayed LL*, *Immediate SS*, and *Having Successfully Resisted SS*. Correspondingly, she now has three available options for action, where formerly she had two. The new option available at time t_1 is *Resisting SS*, which we can label a_4.

This would give the sequential choice problem a more complicated structure, as depicted in Figure 7.3.

Within this expanded version of the original sequential choice problem it is perfectly possible to preserve the key features of the original problem depicted in Figure 7.1. In particular, the agent still has the original (time-indexed) preferences and utility assignments. At time t_0, she prefers *Delayed LL* to *Immediate SS*, but her preferences reverse between t_0 and t_1, so that at the moment of temptation she comes to prefer *Immediate SS* to *Delayed LL*.

But we now have a new outcome over which utilities need to be defined. And this is where the differences emerge between the agent who succumbs to temptation and the agent who exercises self-control. The agent who

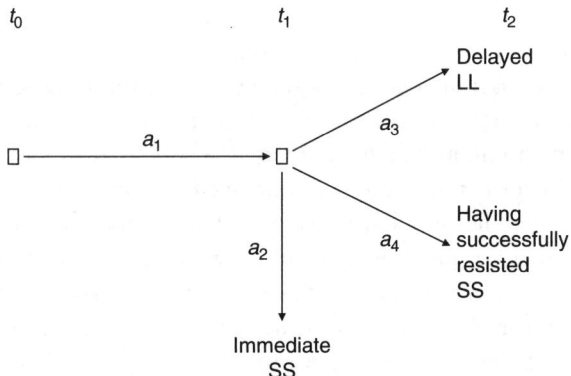

FIGURE 7.3 Reframing the decision problem in Figure 7.1

succumbs to temptation prefers to take the short-term reward, however the long-term alternative is framed. So, he prefers *Immediate SS* to *Having Successfully Resisted SS* and takes path a_2.

In contrast, the self-controlled agent finds the prospect of having successfully resisted temptation more attractive than the prospect of immediate gratification, and so she prefers *Having Successfully Resisted SS* to *Immediate SS*. Consequently, the option that maximizes expected utility for the self-controlled agent is *Resisting SS*, since that leads to the outcome *Having Successfully Resisted SS*, to which she assigns the most utility. Moreover, since *Having Successfully Resisted SS* and *Delayed LL* correspond to two different ways of framing the outcome of the agent eventually receiving LL, it follows that the agent does indeed successfully implement the plan that she formed at time t_0. And so, she exercises self-control.

This all suggests an important mechanism for exercising self-control, even within a framework where agents are assumed to maximize expected utility and where the agent values SS more highly than LL at the moment of choice (under one way of framing the outcomes). It is, of course, a special case of the general discussion of quasi-cyclical preferences and ultra-intensionality in Chapter 5. And it is very consistent with the psychological evidence discussed earlier in this chapter.

This is a good moment to revisit the ancient Greeks. As mentioned at the beginning of the chapter, Socrates was unimpressed by the idea that agents might be overcome by pleasure, which pushed aside their better judgment as to what they ought to do. And so, from his perspective, there is no need to exercise self-control in order to avoid being overcome by pleasure and to allow better judgments to rule. But that doesn't mean that Socrates denies that people behave in ways that we typically describe using the vocabulary of self-control and weakness of will. Some people manage to keep their New Year's resolutions, follow their diets, and so on. Others do not. It is not part of Socrates's strategy to deny those obvious facts. He is not taking issue with the existence of the phenomena, but rather with how we think about and interpret them.

The difference between the self-controlled person and the person who lacks self-control lies in what Socrates called the *art of measurement*. In *Protagoras* Socrates gives little detail on what exactly he means by this (and there is no guidance in other dialogs). But it seems clear that someone who properly applies the art of measurement correctly gauges how present pleasures and pains weigh up against future pleasures and pains. An agent in our sequential choice problem who applies the art of measurement correctly properly appreciates the long-term benefits of LL, and sees that

LL should not be outweighed by SS. In other words, they see both SS and LL correctly. And part of what is going on here is that the art of measurement allows an agent to compensate for the effects of immediacy. This emerges in the following important passage:

> Haven't we seen that the appearance leads us astray and throws us into confusion so that in our actions and our choices between great and small we are constantly accepting and rejecting the same things, whereas the metric art would have cancelled the effect of the impression, and by revealing the true state of affairs would have caused the soul to live in peace and quiet and abide in the truth, thus saving our life?[22]

You might reasonably ask, How exactly is this supposed to work?

Well, without of course presuming to attribute anything like it to Socrates, I would suggest that the model of framing and self-control that I have been proposing offers one possible answer. Given Socrates's analysis of what is really going on when an agent (unwisely) succumbs to the lure of SS, it is hard to see what resources the agent has available to them, besides different ways of conceptualizing or framing the relevant outcomes and options. By reframing LL as *Having Successfully Resisted SS* rather than simply as *Delayed LL*, the agent ends up with a valuation that recommends holding out for LL over succumbing to the temptation of SS. Surely, then, she has found a way of, as Socrates puts it, "cancelling the effect of the impression." And of course, further opportunities come from reframing SS – in a way, for example, that brings out how detrimental pursuing SS would be to one's deeply cherished long-term goals.

Rational Frames?

That still leaves us, though, with the second of the two questions identified earlier. Suppose that framing can and does play an important role in the psychology of self-control. That tells us about the psychological mechanisms for self-control. But it still leaves us with the question of rationality. Is an agent who achieves self-control through framing and reframing outcomes and options actually acting rationally?

Why is there even a problem here, you might ask? How could it not be rational to exercise self-control in pursuit of one's long-term interests? If reframing outcomes and options can help people save for retirement, stick to their exercise regimes, and achieve their weight loss goals, what could

---

[22] Plato, *Protagoras* 356d–e. Translated by W. K. C. Guthrie in Hamilton and Cairns 1961, p. 347.

possibly be wrong with that? Well, the answer should be clear. This could be a case where the rationality of the ends does not guarantee the rationality of the means. The problem, of course, is that our hypothetical agent is well aware that she is assigning different utilities to the same outcome framed in different ways. So doesn't the self-controlled agent have inconsistent preferences and an incoherent utility function?

Well, in the terminology of earlier chapters, she certainly has quasi-cyclical preferences. In Chapters 5 and 6, I argued that quasi-cyclical preferences can be rational, and we looked at a range of different examples. Those arguments do not automatically carry over to self-control, but they certainly point us in the right direction. In the remainder of this chapter, I show how the discussion in Chapter 6 can be generalized to apply to the case of self-control.

The first thing to say is that the discussion of how framing can work in self-control respects the two rationality constraints that I proposed on framing. I suggested there that it is rationally permissible to view situations and outcomes under multiple frames (knowingly and simultaneously), provided that those frames are complementary and consistent (i.e. they do not contradict each other) and that none of them are based on false beliefs or comparably dubious sources. Both constraints seem to be met when the agent simultaneously frames LL as *Delayed LL* and as *Having Successfully Resisted SS*. It is quite plainly true that holding out for LL will result in a delayed reward and will involve successfully resisting SS. And since both things can be true together, they are obviously consistent.

More generally, for the agent simultaneously to frame LL as *Delayed LL* and as *Having Successfully Resisted SS* fits the general picture I offered of the benefits and virtues of framing a single outcome in multiple ways – namely, that what should result is a richer and more nuanced understanding of a complex phenomenon, with each legitimate frame presenting a genuine aspect of the phenomenon.

Let me pick up on this last idea. What is it for a frame to present a genuine aspect of a complex phenomenon? The discussion and examples in Chapter 6 focused on emotional engagement and how emotional engagement can feed into valuations, and hence into preferences. The basic idea is that how one values something can be driven by how one interacts with it emotionally and, in turn, how one interacts emotionally with something can be driven by how one frames it. And so, framing a single outcome in different ways can lead to different valuations by way of different forms of frame-driven emotional engagement.

This is exactly what is going on, I think, when an agent exercises self-control in the sequential choice problem. At time t_1, the agent realizes that there is more at stake than a simple choice between *Immediate SS* and *Delayed LL*. Thinking about the long-term strategy brings home to her that there is more going on than simply the reward. She starts to think, as it were, not just about what lies at the end of the road, but also about the journey itself. Part of what it is to attain LL is to have successfully overcome the temptation of SS. This is not a new outcome. But it is a new way of framing the outcome. And that new way of framing the outcome brings into play different factors that are relevant to how the agent values the outcome (relative to that frame). As a function of those new factors, she can have good reasons for valuing the outcome differently in different frames.

Here are some examples of how that can work to create quasi-cyclical preferences.

- When the outcome of the long-term strategy is framed as *Having Successfully Resisted SS*, as opposed to simply in terms of the final reward, then it is being framed explicitly as an exercise of self-control. This opens the way for the agent to think of it as having practical consequences that she may well value highly. Knowing that self-control is typically self-reinforcing, she may think of *Having Successfully Resisted SS* as a way of strengthening her own willpower, and so as a way of diminishing the effort required to resist temptation in the future. When I force myself to do my early morning strength training routine, I don't just think about the end goal, but also about how conquering temptation today will make it easier to conquer temptation next week, and thereafter.

- The factors brought into play by framing the LL outcome as *Having Successfully Resisted* SS can also be symptomatic/diagnostic. In addition to the causal factors just referred to, attaining the *Having Successfully Resisted SS* outcome offers good evidence that I will be able to resist temptation in the future. That in itself could well be welcome news for the agent. It might, moreover, tell her something about her own personality and strength of will. The issue is not just hanging on in order to receive a larger reward later (as in the *Delayed LL* framing). It is doing something that will reveal aspects of one's character. So, for someone who values having the character traits that attaining that outcome would reveal, the *Having Successfully Resisted*

SS brings into play reasons that are simply not present in the *Delayed LL* frame.

- The *Having Successfully Resisted SS* frame opens up a symbolic dimension that is unlikely to be available under the simple *Delayed LL* framing. An outcome can be valued for what it symbolizes, and there is a clear opportunity for symbolism in the outcome of successfully resisting temptation. A devout Catholic, for example, might attach value to an outcome that parallels the result of the battle that St. Anthony waged and won in the desert. This third type of justifier would be an example of what Robert Nozick called symbolic utility.[23] It is distinct from the two types of reason already mentioned. Assigning symbolic utility to an outcome does not mean that one thinks that attaining that outcome will make it easier in the future to bring about that which it symbolizes, or even that it increases the evidence for one having the associated character trait.

Clearly, each of these three factors will emerge much more easily within the *Having Successfully Resisted SS* frame than the *Delayed LL* frame. And if they do then the agent will have reasons for assigning different utilities to the outcome depending on how it is framed. And so, because she has reasons for assigning different utilities to the different frames, she counts (I claim) as rational.

But still, a determined opponent is likely to put up a fight at this point. Surely, such a person might argue, the position I am proposing is not a stable one. If the agent I am envisaging is rational, then she must be committed to thinking that reasons will carry across different frames. Since *Having Successfully Resisted SS* is the same outcome as *Delayed LL*, and is known to be such by the agent, then a rational agent must think that any reason that applies to one must apply to the other.

I can see the appeal of this line of thought. It seems to me, however, to miss an important dimension of self-control. This is the dimension of mental conflict and struggle, which seems to be at the very heart of the phenomenon.[24] People who exercise self-control are often torn between

---

[23] See Nozick 1993. For a different framing of these three types of factor in terms of Nozick's distinction between causal, evidential, and symbolic utility see my paper "Frames, Rationality, and Self-Control" (Bermúdez 2018a). The first type of factor brings into play considerations of causal utility, while the second engages evidential considerations.

[24] This is vividly brought out in most of the ancient Greek discussions of *akrasia*. See Price 1995 and Lorenz 2006 for thought-provoking overviews of treatments of mental conflict in classical Greece. Socrates's account arguably fails to do justice to this aspect of the

the attractions of the immediate and the benefits of the future. But much of the struggle and conflict inherent in many typical cases of self-control is banished if there is indeed a rational requirement that reasons carry across frames. On the proposal that I am putting forward, the conflict in self-control arises because a single outcome is framed in different ways, each of which engages a different dimension of the agent's values, emotions, and motivation and so gives rise to a different utility assignment. The agent's utility function at the moment of choice includes both a preference for *Immediate SS* over *Delayed LL* and for *Having Successfully Resisted SS* over *Immediate SS*. That is why she is conflicted. If it were a requirement of rationality to standardize reasons across different frames, and if she felt the pull of the reasons I have sketched out, then she would either prefer *Delayed LL to Immediate SS*, or vice versa. But either way there would be no conflict. The agent would either not feel the pull of temptation, or she would be oblivious to the pull of the long-term reward.

So much the better, many would say. It is widely held that there should be no room for conflict and struggle in a theory of ideal rationality. I disagree. Conflict and struggle are simply part of psychological reality. What marks out rational agents is not that they are somehow exempt from the actions and passions of the *psyche*, but rather that they handle them well. And a rational agent can be conflicted and yet exercise self-control. An agent who can exercise self-control does so in the context of quasi-cyclical preferences, knowingly valuing an outcome differently according to how it is framed. What makes this pattern of valuation rational is, ultimately, that different frames bring into play different reasons, and relative to one such set of (frame-relative reasons), the self-controlled agent remains a rational maximizer of expected utility.

phenomenon. The importance of conflict and struggle in self-control has been emphasized more recently by Richard Holton and Al Mele. See Holton 2009 and Mele 2012.

8

Chickens and Chariot Races: Framing in Game Theory

So far we've been looking at frames and rational decision-making purely at the individual level. Agamemnon and Macbeth were grappling on their own account with issues of life and death. Our imaginary agent struggling with temptation was trying to control herself. Other people are involved, of course. Without Iphigenia, Duncan, and Lady Macbeth, Agamemnon and Macbeth would have been tackling very different problems, probably ones that we would not be talking about today. And although actually struggling with temptation can be a very private matter, there are often plenty of other people around ready to pass judgment and offer helpful (or unhelpful) advice. But still, all the decision-making we have been considering has been individual. We have not looked at any examples where multiple agents are making decisions simultaneously, with how things turn out for each agent depending not just on what they decide to do, but also on what other agents decide to do.

Now we turn to social decision-making, and in particular to what is often called *strategic decision-making*. A decision problem is strategic when the outcomes for each agent are a function, not just of what she herself does, but also of what other agents do. What we have been looking at up to now is standardly called *parametric decision-making*.[1] In parametric decision-making, the outcomes for an agent are fixed by what the agent does and by the state of the world. So, for example, to take Savage's classic example of deciding whether or not to add a sixth egg to the beaten eggs for the omelet, the relevant state of the world is whether or not the egg

---

[1] For more on the distinction between strategic and parametric decision-making, see Bermúdez 2015a and 2015b.

is rotten. In parametric decision-making, the agent only needs to take into consideration the probability of each of the different ways that things could turn out. For Savage, this would be the probability that the egg is rotten.

According to classical decision theory, rational agents solve parametric decision problems through calculating expected utility. But this can't work for strategic decision problems. Here's why. In strategic decision problems, the actions of the different agents are independent of each other, in the sense that what one agent does, does not constrain any other agent to act in a certain way. But, at the same time, different agents' actions are interdependent with respect to rationality. In other words, what it is rational for me to do depends upon what I think it would be rational for other agents to do, but what it would be rational for other agents to do depends upon what they think it is rational for me to do. And so on.

Take the game of Matching Pennies, for example. In Matching Pennies, two players both secretly turn a penny either heads or tails and then simultaneously reveal their choices. One player (Even) wins if the choices match, while the other (Odd) wins if they do not match. So, if I am Even, it is rational for me to play heads only if I think it is rational for Odd to play heads. But it is only rational for Odd to play heads if she thinks that I will think it rational to play tails. So, the key parameter (which for each player is what the other player will do) is inherently unstable, and it is difficult to see how to assign it a probability.

Things are completely different in parametric choice problems. There I am choosing against a fixed background, where the environment sets all the relevant parameters. What it is rational for me to do is fixed by a calculation of expected utility, which in turn depends only on my preferences and the probabilities that I assign to different ways that things can turn out. A rational omelet-maker needs to take into account the probability that he assigns to the egg being rotten – but that estimation does not need to take into account any thoughts the egg might have about what it is rational for an omelet-maker to do.

Game theory is the mathematical theory of strategic choice – more accurately, the mathematical theory of how to choose rationally in strategic interactions. Unfortunately, in a number of respects game theory is on a much less firm footing than expected utility theory. There are several well-known problems for game-theoretical analyses of some very fundamental kinds of strategic interaction. Looking at these problems will help us see how frames can be important in game theory.

Probably the most pressing problems have to do with the basic solution concept of orthodox game theory, which is the concept of *Nash equilibrium*. One of the most fundamental results of game theory, discovered by the mathematician John Nash, is that any (non-cooperative) strategic interaction involving a finite number of agents, each with a finite number of possible strategies, has at least one Nash equilibrium.[2] A Nash equilibrium is a set of strategies with the following key property. Each player has a strategy that is a *best response* to the strategies of the other players. It is a best response because none of the agents can unilaterally improve their position relative to the strategies of the other agents. So, they are in equilibrium.

An equilibrium state is stable for each agent. No agent has a (rational) reason to deviate from it. Nash's discovery that every (non-cooperative) game has an equilibrium solution is the cornerstone of game theory, and won him the Nobel Prize for economics in 1994. But game theorists, and others reflecting on game theory, have raised a number of important questions about the Nash equilibrium concept. I want to focus on two in particular. I'll state them briefly now and then explain what they have to do with framing, before going on to discuss them in more detail in the next section.

The equilibrium selection problem

Nash's theorem says that every strategic interaction satisfying some basic conditions has at least one equilibrium solution. But, it turns out that many games have multiple equilibrium solutions. There is no generally accepted method within game theory for identifying one solution as more rational than another, even in situations where it seems intuitively obvious that there is a unique rational solution.

The problem of non-equilibrium solutions

Game theory is a normative theory, telling agents how to interact if they want to be rational. It does not set itself up to describe how agents actually do solve strategic decision problems. But still, it seems reasonable to expect normative theories to have some predictive power, so that theories of rationality are anchored in the realities of practical

---

[2] A non-cooperative game is one where players are not able to make any binding agreements or alliances – as opposed to coalitional, or cooperative, game theory. For classic discussion of the differences between cooperative and non-cooperative game theory (in two-player games) see Luce and Raiffa 1957, chs. 5–6. Shoham and Leyton-Brown 2009 provide more up-to-date discussion.

decision-making. The problem, though, is that experimental and anecdotal evidence suggests that, in some fundamental types of social interaction, people often do not choose a Nash equilibrium solution. In fact, not only do they not choose it – they reject it when it is proposed. Often this is because, when Nash equilibrium points in a different direction from considerations of fairness, cooperation, and collaboration, people find the fair and/or cooperative outcomes more appealing. So, there seem to be non-equilibrium solutions.

These two problems have been much discussed, and many solutions proposed.[3] Some solutions lie, broadly speaking, within the standard framework of orthodox decision theory. I think it's fair to say that none of these has found general acceptance. But what I want to explore in this chapter is a bold proposal to move beyond that standard framework by incorporating frame-sensitive reasoning.

I will focus on the work of Michael Bacharach, a game theorist and economist from the University of Oxford, who died in 2002.[4] His posthumously published book *Beyond Individual Choice: Teams and Frames in Game Theory* (Bacharach 2006) makes a powerful case that thinking about how games are framed by players can solve the equilibrium selection problem in games where the rational solution does seem to be a Nash equilibrium, as well as explaining why in some games the rational solution seems not to be a Nash equilibrium at all. In particular, he emphasizes how individual agents can frame strategic interactions using a "we"-frame, instead of the "I"-frame that is implicit in orthodox game theory. Framing strategic interactions from a group perspective, rather than an individual perspective, opens up the possibility of what Bacharach calls *team reasoning*.

Bacharach shows how, in many of the problematic types of game, team reasoning can make a single equilibrium salient, pointing to a solution to the equilibrium selection problem. Moreover, he argues, we can make sense of how people actually interact with each other when they converge

---

[3] For a review of proposals to refine the Nash equilibrium solution concept see Govindan and Wilson 2008. Interesting historical fact: The game theorists John Harsanyi and Reinhard Selten were awarded the Nobel Prize for Economics at the same time as John Nash, and a few years earlier they had jointly published *A General Theory of Equilibrium Selection in Games* (Harsanyi and Selten 1988).

[4] Somewhat similar ideas about frames in game theory have been proposed by Robert Sugden. See, for example, Sugden 2000, 2003, and 2015. Bacharach is more focused than Sugden on the psychology of framing.

on non-equilibrium outcomes by thinking of them as engaging in team reasoning from within the "we"-frame.

The main task for this chapter is to present Bacharach's theory and show how it proposes to solve both the equilibrium selection problem and the problem of non-equilibrium solutions. I'll end the chapter by identifying two problems for how Bacharach thinks about frames in the context of game theory. These problems will set the agenda for Chapter 9, where I will develop my own account of framing in game theory. All this will become clearer, though, when we have some specific examples of strategic interactions in front of us. To that we now turn.

Strategic Interactions: Key Concepts

Game theorists study highly stylized forms of social interaction. But, highly stylized though they are, the games considered show a bewildering variety. They range from relatively simple two-person interactions that are symmetrical (every player confronts exactly the same set of options) to multi-player interactions where different players have different options open to them. In some games players choose simultaneously, while in others they choose sequentially. Some games are cooperative, so called because they allow players to form binding compacts and coalitions, while others are non-cooperative. In some games the pay-offs must sum to zero (so that a gain for one player can only come at the price of a corresponding loss for the other player(s)). Sometimes game theorists consider games that are only played once (one-off games). But they can also derive very different results from the same games when they are repeated, particularly if the exact number of repetitions is not known to any of the players.

That brief list really only touches the surface of the complexities of game theory. Fortunately, for the questions I want to raise we only need to consider some relatively simple games. Primarily we'll be looking at games that have the following characteristics. They are –

2 × 2

The games we will be considering all have two players. For reasons that will quickly become apparent, the players will be called Row and Column (unless they have real names). Row is female and Column is male. Row and Column each have two strategies to choose between, so that there are four possible outcomes (combinations of strategy).

Symmetrical
Row and Column both have exactly the same strategies open to them.

Non-cooperative
Row and Column choose their strategies at the same time, but independently. They have no way of making binding agreements.

We will be representing different games using what game theorists call *normal form* or *strategic form*. In essence, a game in normal form is represented as a matrix, with each box in the matrix representing the pay-offs to each player from a given combination of strategies. The matrices, usually known as *pay-off tables*, will look like this.

	Strategy 1	Strategy 2
Strategy 1	R_{11}, C_{11}	R_{12}, C_{12}
Strategy 2	R_{21}, C_{21}	R_{22}, C_{22}

The top left cell, for example, represents the pay-offs when both players play Strategy 1, with the pay-off to Row written first. I have written R_{11} to represent the pay-off to Row when both players play Strategy 1, with C_{12} representing the pay-off to Column when Row plays Strategy 1 and Column plays Strategy 2. And so on.

With these preliminaries out of the way, let's start to look at a specific game to introduce the two problems I mentioned – the equilibrium selection problem and the prediction problem. To make it easier to see what is really at stake here, I am going to start by giving a very specific example of the type of interaction that the game is intended to model, before showing how that type of interaction can be presented in normal form (as a pay-off table).

The game known as Chicken is often introduced through the famous film *Rebel Without a Cause*, starring James Dean. In the film, James Dean's character, Jimmie, plays a game of Chickie (which is what it is actually called in the film,) with a local gang leader, Buzz (played by Corey Allen). The game is for each of them to drive a stolen car at high speed towards a cliff edge. The first person to jump out of the car loses. As it happens, Jimmie loses, because Buzz's jacket gets caught in the door and he is unable to escape, going over the cliff edge with his vehicle. This is not a very good example, however. It is not clear how Chickie can be represented in a way that gives each player two strategies (since, presumably, driving a stolen car over the edge of a cliff is not a strategy that a rational player would consider). Relatedly, the outcome is determined by an accident, not by a combination of strategies.

A better example is one that has stood the test of time for somewhat longer – the famous chariot race in Book 23 of the *Iliad* during the funeral games that Achilles sets in motion to honor the memory of Patroclus. There are six competitors, but the part of the race that concerns us only involves two of them: Menelaös (husband of Helen, the cause of the war, and brother of Agamemnon, leader of the Greek forces) and Antilochos (son of Nestor, celebrated as the wisest counselor to the Greeks). Before the race, Nestor advises Antilochos to use his wits, because his horses are too weak to win in a straight contest. Here is how Antilochos interprets his father's advice, as he approaches the turning-point of the race, hard on the heels of Menelaös (in Peter Green's translation):

> Then, almost at once,
> Steadfast Antilochos sighted the narrow point where the road
> ran hollow: a gully had formed, where winter floods, collecting,
> had torn away part of the track, deepened the whole stretch –
> and here steered Menelaös, to avoid teams jostling abreast.
> But Antilochos now took his own whole-hoofed pair off-track,
> And began to overtake him, driving close in, side by side,
> And Atreus's son, in alarm, shouted out to Antilochos:
> "This is crazy driving, Antilochos! Rein in your horses!
> Here the track is narrow: it'll soon be wider for passing –
> This way you'll run into my chariot, wreck us both!"
>
> So he spoke; but Antilochos pressed on still more fiercely,
> Urging his team with the goad, as though not hearing. About
> As far as the range of a discus swung from the shoulder,
> That a young man throws when making trial of his strength
> So far they ran thus – but then the mares of Atreus's son
> Dropped back, as he'd decided he'd race them hard no longer,
> To avoid their whole-hoofed horses colliding on the track
> And upsetting the well-strapped chariots, and themselves
> Being thrown out in the dust, through their great lust to win.[5]

With the usual apologies to Homer and generations of classicists, I'd like to analyze the crux of this episode as follows. Menelaös and Antilochos are approaching the narrowing. Each of them has the same two options. Each can *Drop back* or *Press forward*. So, we have a strategic interaction that can be presented in a 2 × 2 matrix. In order to fill out the matrix we need to identify the pay-offs for Menelaös and Antilochos. I'll assume that these are the same for each of them, so that we have a symmetrical game.

---

[5] Homer, *The Iliad*, translated by Peter Green (Green 2015), Bk. 23, lines 418–37.

The best outcome for each chariot racer is that he should *Press forward* while the other *Drops back*. So, let's assign that 4 units of value. The worst outcome for each of them is that they should both *Press forward* – as Menelaös points out in the heat of the moment, they would then both crash since the track is too narrow for both chariots side by side. That outcome would seem to have 0 units of value. So, that leaves two possible outcomes. The first is *Dropping back* while the other racer *Pushes forward*, while the second is *Dropping back* while the other racer also *Drops back* (in effect, they agree to suspend hostilities until after the turn). Of these two outcomes, mutually suspending hostilities seems preferable. After all, if you are going to *Drop back*, then it's better for you if the other racer does the same. So, let's assign 2 units of value to *Drop back* when the other racer also drops back, and 1 unit of value to *Drop back* when the other racer *Presses forward*.

When we put the numbers in, the matrix looks like this:

		Menelaös	
		Press forward	*Drop back*
Antilochos	*Press forward*	0,0	4,1
	Drop back	1,4	2,2

In each cell, the pay-off for Antilochos is written first, and then the pay-off for Menelaös.

When we present the pay-offs in matrix form, it is relatively easy to identify the two Nash equilibria. Remember that we are trying to find pairs of strategies such that each strategy is the best response to the other. Look at it from Antilochos's point of view, first. If Menelaös chooses *Press forward*, then Antilochos is best off choosing *Drop back*, because that will secure him a pay-off of 1 as opposed to 0. Now, suppose that Antilochos chooses *Drop back* and consider things from Menelaös's point of view. Now, he is better off choosing *Press forward*, because that will secure a pay-off of 4 rather than 2. So, *Drop back* is a best response to *Press forward*, and *Press forward* is a best response to *Drop back*. In other words, *Drop back, Press forward* is a Nash equilibrium. And, since the game is symmetrical, you can run exactly the same argument with the players reversed to conclude that *Press forward, Drop back* is a Nash equilibrium.

In fact, those are the only two *pure strategies* Nash equilibria. The opposite of a pure strategy is a mixed strategy, where a player doesn't commit to a single strategy, but instead adopts a probabilistic mix of strategies. Take the game Rock, Paper, Scissors, for example. The game is typically played over several iterations. You would be most unwise to play a pure strategy (always choosing Paper, for example). A smart opponent would quickly work out your strategy and would beat you every time with Scissors. You are much better off playing a mixed strategy, playing each move with probability 1/3, for example.

In addition to the two pure strategy equilibria, Menelaös and Antilochos also have available to them a Nash equilibrium in mixed strategies. (In fact, Nash's theorem only holds if mixed strategies are included, because many games do not have any pure strategy Nash equilibria.) In the game described, the equilibrium in mixed strategies is reached when each player chooses *Press forward* with probability 2/3 and *Drop back* with probability 1/3.[6]

So – we have three Nash equilibria, one in mixed strategies and two in pure strategies. Problem solved? I don't think so. Even if we assume that Menelaös and Antilochos are game-theoretically rational and perfectly capable of working out the Nash equilibria, even as their chariots thunder across the Trojan plain, I don't think that this is going to help them very much. It's certainly true that, if they both happen to end up in a Nash equilibrium, then neither can benefit from changing strategy – because, by definition each is playing the strategy that is the best response to the strategy the other racer is playing. But

---

[6] The key to seeing where these numbers come from is remembering the point of randomizing. Menelaös needs to randomize in such a way that Antilochos has no reason to prefer one strategy over the other – or, in other words, so that his pay-off will be the same under each strategy. So, Antilochos's pay-off for *Press forward* must be the same as his pay-off for *Drop back*. Now, suppose that Menelaös chooses *Press forward* with probability p and *Drop back* with probability $1 - p$. Then Antilochos's expected pay-off for *Press forward* is given by the sum of his pay-offs in the two possible outcomes, each weighted by the probability that they will occur. The *Press forward*, *Press forward* outcome has a pay-off for him of 0 and occurs with probability p, while *Press forward*, *Drop back* has a pay-off for him of 4 and occurs with probability $1 - p$. So, Antilochos's expected pay-off for *Press forward* is $(0 \times p) + 4(1 - p)$. Reasoning in the same way gives Antilochos's expected pay-off for *Drop back* as $(1 \times p) + 2(1 - p)$. As far as Menelaös is concerned, therefore, if he wants to make Antilochos indifferent between *Press forward* and *Drop back*, he needs to find a value of p such that $(0 \times p) + 4(1 - p) = (1 \times p) + 2(1 - p)$. Solving the equation gives $p = 2/3$. Since the game is symmetrical, Antilochos will make Menelaös indifferent between his two pure strategies by playing the same value of p.

how are they supposed to get to a state of Nash equilibrium? Antilochos, of course, would much rather be in the Nash equilibrium in which he plays *Press forward* and Menelaös plays *Drop back*. By the same token, Menelaös would much rather be in the other Nash equilibrium, where *he* plays *Press forward*.

There seems to be no chance whatsoever that two rational chariot-racers will end up reasoning their way to one of the two pure strategy Nash equilibria. The difficulty is that the two pure strategy Nash equilibria are asymmetrical in a way that effectively rules out the two chariot-racers ever rationally converging on one of them. So, what about the mixed strategy Nash equilibrium, where each player plays *Press forward* with probability 2/3 and *Drop back* with probability 1/3? Is this more promising?

Well, the Nash equilibrium in mixed strategies is certainly symmetrical. That removes one obstacle. But still, randomizing in this way will strike many as a peculiar recommendation. One problem is that, if both players have a 2/3 probability of choosing *Press forward*, then there is a 2/3 × 2/3 = 4/9 probability of ending up in the least desirable outcome, where the two chariots collide because the track is too narrow for both. Are rational agents really going to converge on an equilibrium that yields almost even odds of disaster? It's certainly not obvious that that is the rational way to go, on a more intuitive understanding of what counts as rational. But I'm going to leave the equilibrium selection problem there, at least for the moment – because I want to turn now to the possibility that the rationally desirable outcome in a Chicken game may not be a Nash equilibrium at all.

Let's go back to the Iliad. The first thing to point out is that Antilochos and Menelaös did actually end up in a Nash equilibrium, because Antilochos chose *Press forward*, and Menelaös *Drop back*. But what actually happened could hardly be described by a dispassionate bystander as a sensible outcome for two rational agents. Menelaös was rightly furious, feeling that he had been bullied off his line going into the turn. After the race he complains in front of all the Greeks:

> Antilochos, once so sensible, consider what you've done!
> You insulted my manhood and you thwarted my horses
> By driving your own far ahead, although they are far inferior.[7]

---

[7] Homer, *The Iliad*, translated by Peter Green (Green 2015), Bk. 23, lines 570–72.

Antilochos then accepts that he is at fault:

> Wait a moment! Remember that I'm a good deal younger
> Than you, my lord Menelaös; you're my elder and better,
> You know what a young man's transgressions are likely to be –
> His mind's over-hasty, his judgments lack real substance.
> So bear with me in your heart: the mare that I won
> I'll willingly give you, and if you want something better
> From my house, I'd be only too glad to provide that as well,
> Here and now, Zeus's nursling, rather than spend my life
> Out of favor with you, and at fault in the eyes of the gods.[8]

In sum, neither participant was happy with the Nash equilibrium that they reached. Menelaös was outraged, and Antilochos full of remorse. They settled the matter by Antilochos handing his prize over to Menelaös, and then Menelaös giving the prize back to Antilochos. And it seems clear that both would have been equally unhappy had they reached the other pure strategies Nash equilibrium.

So, does that mean that they would have been happy with the mixed strategies Nash equilibrium? Hardly. As already mentioned, the mixed strategies Nash equilibrium has a 4/9 probability of mutual disaster, strongly dis-preferred by both chariot-racers. And it has a 4/9 probability of reaching one of the two pure strategies Nash equilibria, which neither of them wanted either. In other words, the probability is very high (8/9) that the Nash equilibrium in mixed strategies will lead to an outcome that neither of them wants. The only outcome that they would welcome from both randomizing is the outcome where both racers choose *Drop back*. But then, why bother with the mixed strategies at all? Why not converge on the non-equilibrium *Drop back*, *Drop back* outcome right from the beginning? Is that not the rational solution to the game, despite not being a Nash equilibrium?

I can imagine a game theorist immediately objecting: "No, you can't argue like that. You are redescribing the situation to make the cooperative outcome, where both players choose *Drop back*, seem the most rational. But when you do that you are changing the pay-offs, so that Antilochos and Menelaös are no longer playing the same game. You've turned it from a game of Chicken into a game where the most preferred outcome for both players is for both to choose *Drop back*. Your new game looks more like this:

---

[8] Homer, *The Iliad*, translated by Peter Green (Green 2015), Bk. 23, lines 587–95.

		Menelaös	
		Press forward	Drop back
Antilochos	Press forward	0,0	2,1
	Drop back	1,2	4,4

And in this new game, the *Drop back*, *Drop back* outcome is indeed the rational solution. But that's exactly what any game theorist would expect, because it's the unique Nash equilibrium."

This brings us, at last, back to framing. Because what I would reply to this imaginary game theorist is that the game has not changed at all. The pay-offs remain exactly the same. What I'm drawing attention to is different ways of framing that game. Under one frame, one of the Nash equilibria may well be the rational solution to the game. But under another frame, *Drop back*, *Drop back* comes out as the rational solution. To see how this might work, we'll look in the next section at how Michael Bacharach uses frames to shed light on game theory.

Bacharach on Frames and Team Reasoning

Michael Bacharach's book *Beyond Individual Choice* (Bacharach 2006) is driven by a single and extraordinarily insightful idea. This is that strategic interactions can be framed in different ways, with the rational solution varying according to the frame, even though the actual game remains constant. Bacharach focuses in particular on two frames, which I will call the "I"-frame and the "we"-frame, although this is not his standard terminology. What counts as a rational solution to a game is relative to how that game is framed. In the case of the Chicken game, the three Nash equilibria are rational solutions only relative to the "I"-frame. When a player adopts the "we"-frame, however, a different perspective opens up, so that it becomes possible for joint strategies that are not Nash equilibria to count as rational solutions (like the *Drop back*, *Drop back* combination considered at the end of the last section).

You might reasonably ask: How does one distinguish between a game and how that game is framed? Bacharach's definition of a game is entirely standard. A game is defined by three things:

- The players
- The players' strategies
- The pay-offs to each player from each combination of strategies

So, what are frames? Bacharach offers a technical account of frames in his *variable frame theory*, but for our purposes what really matters are the different types of reasoning operative within each frame.[9]

When a game is framed in the "I"-frame, standard, individualistic game-theoretic reasoning applies and determines what will count as a rational solution to the game. Agents framing the game in the "I"-frame, will look only at their own pay-offs. They seek an outcome that will provide the best pay-off for them, employing the type of best response reasoning that we looked at in the last section when explaining the concept of Nash equilibrium.

Adopting the perspective of the "we"-frame, however, makes available a different type of reasoning, which Bacharach terms *team reasoning*. A team reasoner thinks about the pay-off table from the perspective, not of an isolated individual, but instead from the perspective of a team member, or group member. The team reasoner needs to think, not just about her own pay-offs, but also about the pay-offs to others. There is no difference in the pay-off table when the game is framed in the "we"-frame. It is just that different aspects and properties of the pay-off table become salient.

Utilitarian team reasoners might be interested, for example, in the total pay-off, looking to make the total pay-off as large as possible (in order to achieve the greatest good for the greatest number). A differently motivated team reasoner might be interested in broad issues of fairness, looking for the combination of strategies that yields the most equitable outcome (relative, of course, to a particular understanding of equity and fairness). Or, as in Bacharach's own approach to team reasoning, team reasoners are primarily driven by the twin concepts of *Pareto-superiority* and *Pareto-optimality* (also known as *Pareto-efficiency*).

Pareto-superiority and Pareto-efficiency are concepts that apply to groups, and in particular to distributions of goods across groups. An outcome A is Pareto-superior to an outcome B for a given group just if the pay-off for each member of the group is at least as high in A as it is in B, and at least one member of the group has a higher pay-off in A than in B. In other words, A is Pareto-superior to B when everybody is at least as well-

[9] For more on variable frame theory see Bacharach 1993, 2001, Bacharach and Bernasconi 1997, and Bacharach and Stahl 2000.

off in A as in B, and at least one person is better off in A than in B. By extension, an outcome is Pareto-optimal when there is no Pareto-superior alternative.

So, for example, if a grandparent has left $51 in her will to be distributed between her five grandchildren, then a distribution that gives four of them $10 and one $11 would be Pareto-optimal. It is Pareto-optimal because nobody can be made better off without making someone worse off. Bear in mind that there is no requirement of uniqueness here. A given strategic problem can have multiple Pareto-optimal outcomes, as in fact does the grandparent bequest example. Each of the five children can be the recipient of the $11, which makes for five different Pareto-optimal outcomes. Economists call the range of Pareto-optimal outcomes for a given decision problem the *Pareto frontier*.

The simplest form of team reasoning that Bacharach considers is what he terms mode-P reasoning.[10] This has two stages. In the first stage, a player ranks all the available combinations of strategy according to broadly Paretian criteria. So, instead of looking purely at her own pay-off, she looks at the profile of pay-offs across all players, using the pay-off profiles for different combinations of strategies to rank those combinations. So, assuming that Row and Column are playing a symmetric two-person game, if the combination of strategies in which Row plays Strategy 1 and Column plays Strategy 2 leads to a pay-off profile that is Pareto-superior to the pay-off profile that results when Row and Column both play Strategy 1, then a team reasoner will rank the first combination of strategies higher than the second. This holds even if that combination of strategies is not a Nash equilibrium.

As it happens, every game has at least one Pareto-optimal combination of pure strategies, but often there are multiple Pareto-optimal outcomes. This, of course, creates a new equilibrium selection problem, but we'll put that to one side for the moment. In the second stage of mode-P reasoning, the team reasoner takes herself to have reason to perform her component of any Pareto-optimal combination of strategies. So, if the *Strategy 1, Strategy 2* combination is Pareto-optimal and Row is a team reasoner, then she will take herself to have reason to play *Strategy 1*. Likewise, Column, if he is a team reasoner, will take himself to have reason to play *Strategy 2*.

So far so good, you might say, but how does Row know that Column is a team reasoner, and vice versa? Team reasoning seems to make good

---

[10] See Bacharach 2006, pp. 59–60.

sense – if you can be confident in the other members of the team. But where does that confidence come from? Remember that we are talking here about non-cooperative game theory. Agents can't make binding commitments in non-cooperative game theory. So how can they count on other players being team reasoners? Surely, there are many situations in which it would benefit a rational agent *not* to be a team reasoner, precisely because they believe that the other player will be a team reasoner.

To put the point in terms of frames, from the perspective of the "I"-frame, the best response to a team reasoner in the "we"-frame may be *not* to be a team reasoner. Suppose that Row is a team reasoner and so is expected to play her part in a Pareto-optimal combination of strategies. Then Column, considering the game from an "I"-frame perspective, should play the strategy that is the best response to the strategy that Row is going to choose. And in many cases the best response to Row's team reasoning strategy will not be, as it were, the other half of the Pareto-optimal combination of strategies. When that's the case, how can any team reasoner count on another player being a team reasoner? And if they can't count on it, why doesn't that undercut their motivation to be team reasoners?

We can explore the dynamic here through another two-person game, the famous Prisoner's Dilemma. Continuing the Homeric theme, I will introduce the Prisoner's Dilemma through the interaction between Agamemnon and Achilles in Book 1 of the *Iliad*. This strategic interaction effectively sets the scene for the final stages of the siege of Troy. It stems from a classic problem in Homeric warrior culture – how to divide the spoils of war in a way that respects the honor and relative standing of the victors. It is the ninth year of the siege. The Greek forces have been beset by a plague. The prophet Calchas (the same Calchas who had interpreted the portent at Aulis for Agamemnon) identifies the source of the plague as Agamemnon having refused to return Chryseïs, a Trojan prisoner of war, to her father Chrysēs. Unwillingly, Agamemnon sends Chryseïs back home. But then, to make up for his loss, he commandeers Briseïs, who had been assigned to Achilles. Achilles is affronted, both at the loss of his slave and at the assault to his dignity and honor. After coming close to killing Agamemnon, restrained only by the goddess Athēnē, Achilles withdraws with his troops to his ships and vows to play no further part in the war against Troy.

I think that we can represent the strategic interaction between Agamemnon and Achilles as a 2 × 2 symmetrical game. They are, in fact, in a Prisoner's Dilemma. Each of them has the opportunity to

Cooperate. In Agamemnon's case, cooperation would take the form of giving up his claim upon Briseïs, while cooperation for Achilles would be to offer Briseïs to Agamemnon while continuing to fight with the Greeks. Each of them can also *Defect*, with defection for Achilles being to retreat with his troops back to their ships, while for Agamemnon defection would be to take Briseïs from Achilles. Here is what might be a familiar pay-off table:

		Agamemnon	
		Defect	Cooperate
Achilles	Defect	1,1	3,−3
	Cooperate	−3,3	2,2

Achilles's best outcome, given how little respect he is getting from Agamemnon, would be to retreat to his ships with his troops while Agamemnon abandons his claim to Briseïs. His worst outcome would be to offer Briseïs to Agamemnon and have the offer accepted, while continuing to fight for the Greeks. These two outcomes are (in reverse order) the worst and the best outcomes for Agamemnon. For Agamemnon, the best outcome would be to take Briseïs and not lose Achilles's participation in the war, while the worst outcome would be to abandon his claim to Briseïs and still have Achilles withdrawing from the army.

Looking at this from the perspective of the "I"-frame and best response reasoning, there is only one pure strategies Nash equilibrium. This is for both players to play the *Defect* strategy. Look at it from Achilles's point of view. If Agamemnon plays *Cooperate*, then he is better off playing *Defect* (to receive a pay-off of 3 as opposed to 2). While if Agamemnon plays *Defect*, then again he is better off playing *Defect* (to receive a pay-off of 1 as opposed to −3). So, *Defect* is Achilles's best response whatever Agamemnon does. As you can see from the table (and as you would expect, given that the game is symmetrical), things are exactly the same from Agamemnon's perspective. Whatever Achilles does, Agamemnon is better off playing *Defect*.

So now, back to Bacharach and the "we"-frame. Bacharach does not dispute that, from the perspective of the individualistic "I"-frame of traditional game theory, playing the *Defect* strategy is the unique rational solution to this type of strategic interaction. But, he thinks, things look very different when both participants engage in mode-P reasoning from within a "we"-frame perspective. Suppose that Achilles and Agamemnon think of themselves as members of a team (as well they might, being joint participants in the Greek army). Then they will look at the pay-off table from that perspective and (on Bacharach's model) seek out the profile of strategies leading to the Pareto-optimal outcome. As you can see from inspecting the pay-off table, there is only one Pareto-optimal outcome, which is for both players to *Cooperate*. Each player receives a pay-off of 2 when they both *Cooperate*, and neither can improve their position without making the other player worse off.

But now the problem should be clear. The combination of strategies leading to the Pareto-optimal outcome is inherently unstable. If one of the two players thinks that the other will play his part in the Pareto-generating combination of strategies, then he will certainly improve his pay-off by opting to *Defect* rather than *Cooperate* – in other words, by shifting back from the "we"-frame to the "I"-frame. And if one player is worried that the other person will not engage in mode-P reasoning, then his best option is surely to *Defect*, because the worst outcome for him would be to *Cooperate* while the other player plays *Defect*. The possibility of mode-P reasoning in the "we"-frame seems to require each player to be certain that the other player will also adopt the "we"-frame. But there can be no such guarantee from within non-cooperative game theory, since there are no binding commitments to be had.

Bacharach's solution to the difficulty is to develop a more sophisticated type of reasoning within the "we"-frame. It is more sophisticated because it takes into account the possibility that other player(s) might not actually be team reasoners. I will present what he calls *circumspect team reasoning* in the two-person case. The generalization to multi-player games is straightforward.

The key to circumspect team reasoning is that each player who frames the game within the "we"-frame assigns a certain probability ω to players playing their part in the Pareto-optimal profile of strategies (we'll assume that there is just one Pareto-optimal profile, to avoid unnecessary complexity). Each circumspect team reasoner assumes, therefore, that with probability $1-\omega$ the other player will play their best response strategy, in effect switching back from the "we"-frame to the "I"-frame. Moreover, they apply the same assumption to themselves – because team reasoning has to be accessible to, and reproducible by, all members of the team. In other words, each player takes a third-person perspective on the interaction, assessing it relative to the assumption that each player will play their part in the team with probability ω (and their best response strategy with probability 1–ω).

From a team reasoning perspective, the important thing is to work out, relative to a given value for ω, what is best for the team. If each player plays their part in the Pareto-optimal strategy profile with probability ω and applies best response reasoning with probability 1–ω, then it is possible to work out the expected value *for the group* of the Pareto-optimal strategy profile. This can then be compared with the expected value *for the group* of both players opting out of the "we"-frame and playing their best response strategies. (I will come back shortly to the significance of calculating expected values for the group, rather than for each individual on their own account.)

Let's see how this works for Agamemnon and Achilles. Here's the pay-off table again:

		Agamemnon	
		Defect	Cooperate
Achilles	Defect	1,1	3,–3
	Cooperate	–3,3	2,2

Suppose that each one of them is at heart a team reasoner. Their deepest allegiance is to the army besieging Troy, which they joined to make common cause against Paris and the Trojans. So, if they were completely confident that both were committed team reasoners, then they would each play their part in the Pareto-optimal strategy profile. Looking at the pay-off table, each can see that there is only one Pareto-optimal outcome. This is the outcome when both choose *Cooperate*. Each player receives 2 units of value and neither can improve their position without making the other player worse off. So, if each were totally confident in the other's commitment to the "we"-frame, then Achilles would offer Briseïs to Agamemnon and Agamemnon would give up his claim to Briseïs and decline the offer.

But still, the alliance has cracks in it and each man knows the other to be perfectly capable of putting their own honor before the collective cause. So, each needs to know what level of confidence they should have in the other before committing to play their role in the Pareto-optimal strategy – or, in other words, what the probability ω needs to be. To figure this out they need to start by recognizing that they have two joint strategy profiles to consider. The first is the Pareto-optimal strategy profile where both choose *Cooperate*. The second is the outcome that comes about when both players play their best response strategies – i.e. when both choose *Defect*.

If ω = 1, then it is obvious that the Pareto-optimal strategy profile is better for the team (yielding a total of 4 evenly distributed units of value, as opposed to 2 evenly distributed units of value). But we are assuming that ω < 1, so we need to start by considering the base line expected value when both players play their best response strategies from within the "I"-frame. If both players reason individualistically then the outcome is certain. Each will receive 1 unit of value, and so 2 units for the team. So, in order for team reasoning to make sense for the team, the expected pay-off from the *Cooperate, Cooperate* profile must be greater than 2. Only if the expected pay-off is greater than 2 does it make sense for both Achilles and Agamemnon to play their part of the Pareto-optimal strategy. And so, what they and we need to work out is what the probability ω needs to be in order for the expected pay-off for the team from team reasoning to be greater than 2. Here goes.

We know that the Pareto-optimal profile is *Cooperate, Cooperate*. But we also know that we are not guaranteed to be dealing with two fully committed team reasoners, so we need to consider the different ways that things could turn out (including all the ways that the team could fall apart). There are four possibilities:

(i)   Achilles and Agamemnon both play their roles in the team
(ii) Achilles plays his role in the team, but Agamemnon does not
(iii) Agamemnon plays his role in the team, but Achilles does not
(iv) Neither Achilles nor Agamemnon plays their role in the team

Since we know that Achilles and Agamemnon each play their role in the team with probability ω, we can calculate the probability of each of (i) through (iv). So, for example, we know that the probability of Achilles and Agamemnon both playing their role in the team is ω × ω = ω^2. And we can work out the pay-offs to the team of each of (i) through (iv) simply by summing the numbers in the relevant cell of the pay-off matrix. So, if Achilles and Agamemnon both play their roles in the team, then the team pay-off is 2 + 2 = 4.

The following table gives the possibilities and associated numbers.

Scenario	Team pay-off	Probability	Expected value
Achilles and Agamemnon both play their roles in the team	$2 + 2 = 4$	ω^2	$4\omega^2$
Achilles plays his role in the team, but Agamemnon does not	$-3 + 3 = 0$	$\omega(1 - \omega)$	$0(\omega - \omega 2) = 0$
Agamemnon plays his role in the team, but Achilles does not	$3 + -3 = 0$	$\omega(1 - \omega)$	$0(\omega - \omega 2) = 0$
Neither Achilles nor Agamemnon plays their role in the team	$1 + 1 = 2$	$(1 - \omega)^2$	$2(1 - \omega)^2$

So, putting everything together, Achilles and Agamemnon can figure out that the value for ω must be such that:

$$4\omega^2 + 0(\omega - \omega^2) + 0(\omega - \omega^2) + 2(1 - \omega)^2 > 2$$

if the expected pay-off from team reasoning is to be higher than the expected pay-off from both of them reasoning individually (from within the "I"-frame). Simplifying, we get $6\omega^2 - 4\omega > 0$, which puts the threshold of ω at $2/3$.

In other words, if Achilles and Agamemnon are both circumspect team reasoners and the probability of each of them following through on the "we"-frame strategy is greater than $2/3$, then the Pareto-optimal combination of strategies is indeed best for the team. Achilles should offer Briseïs to Agamemnon, and Agamemnon should withdraw his claim and reject the offer. But if the probability is $2/3$ or lower, then the team is better off if they each play their best response strategies.

The Rationality of Team Reasoning?

So, has Bacharach shown that it is rational to cooperate in the Prisoner's Dilemma? It might seem initially that he has, but that would be a mistake. The take-home message from Bacharach's model of circumspect team reasoning is much less dramatic. What he has shown (relative to our Trojan War example), is that *if* Achilles and Agamemnon are circumspect team reasoners and *if* the probability that each follows through on playing their part in the Pareto-optimal strategy is greater than 2/3, then it is rational *relative to the "we"-frame* for each to choose *Cooperate*. But that's a lot of qualifications.

Certainly, there is nothing in the preceding discussion that will persuade anybody operating within the "I"-frame that they should choose *Cooperate* in a Prisoner's Dilemma. If Achilles or Agamemnon is operating in the "I"-frame, then they will by definition be applying best response reasoning and, as we saw earlier, *Defect* is the best response whatever the other player does. In order to use circumspect team reasoning to identify the circumstances in which it is rational to play one's part in the Pareto-optimal strategy, one already has to have adopted the "we"-frame. And for that reason, the perspective of the circumspect team reasoner is completely alien to agents operating within the "I"-frame of standard game theory.

Bacharach himself is quite clear that he has no arguments to support the rationality of adopting the "we"-frame in a given situation. Instead, he takes it as given that people frequently do adopt the "we"-frame, and he is interested in solving the descriptive problem of explaining why they do so. People tend to adopt the "we"-frame when they confront strategic problems that have certain features. These features, as it were, prime for the "we"-frame, working to encourage people to think as members of a group or team, rather than as atomistic individuals. And so, people who recognize those features have a tendency to frame the strategic problem from a collective rather than an individual perspective.

Bacharach focuses on two priming features in particular.

Common interests
This holds (in a two-person game) when there are at least two states of affairs *s* and *s** and in one, *s**, the interests of both players are better served than in the other. In the Prisoner's Dilemma that Achilles and Agamemnon find themselves in, the state of affairs in which they both choose *Cooperate* is just such a state of affairs. For Antilochos and Menelaös playing Chicken, their common interests are best served in the state of affairs where both choose *Drop back*.

Strong interdependence
This holds when each player perceives that they will do well only if the other does something that is not guaranteed by standard,

individualistic reasoning (and, moreover, they perceive that the other player perceives the same thing, and so on). In the Prisoner's Dilemma, for example, strong interdependence holds because each player will do well only if the other player chooses *Cooperate*, which a standard game-theoretically rational player would not be expected to play.

That these two features prime for the "we"-frame is, in Bacharach's view, a matter of psychological fact.[11] And, as he brings out, the analysis certainly fits well with the psychological literature on group identification.[12]

Getting the psychology of strategic reasoning right is obviously important. And Bacharach is right that it helps us with the two basic problems of equilibrium selection and non-equilibrium solutions.

Equilibrium Selection

Many games have multiple Nash equilibria. Game theory tells us that these equilibria count as solutions, but there is no consensus method for selecting any particular one of these solutions, or for explaining how players might converge on a particular solution. Bacharach's psychological account goes some way to solving this problem, because it helps us to understand why and how players in multiple-equilibria

---

[11] See Bacharach 2006, particularly ch. 2. Bacharach discusses cognitivist theories such as the self-categorization theory developed by the social psychologist John Turner (see Oakes, Haslam, and Turner 1994 and, more recently, Turner and Reynolds 2012), as well as theories that assign a key role to common interests and interdependent goals (e.g. Rabbie, Schot, and Visser 1989). For a textbook survey of the literature on group identification and group identity, see Brewer 2003.

[12] There has been much less discussion of group identity within philosophy. However, there are definite connections with debates about group agency (List and Pettit 2011) and about the nature of collective intentionality. Philosophers have explored how groups can make decisions and have collective beliefs, and whether this type of collective intentionality can be reduced to individual intentionality (e.g. whether a group decision is ultimately just a collection of individual decisions). Bratman 2014 inclines to a reductionist approach to collective intentionality, while Gilbert 1989, List and Pettit 2011, and Tuomela 2013 hold that making sense of collective intentionality requires positing irreducible and ontologically basic group subjects/agents. Searle 1995 tries to steer a middle path, arguing that collective intentionality is conceptually irreducible to individual intentionality, but not ontologically reducible (Searle 1995). Petersson 2017 is the only article I am aware of trying to bridge between the literature on collective intentionality and Bacharach's views on team reasoning.

games with the two features he discusses might converge on a single equilibrium.

One of his favorite examples is the game of Hi-Lo, which has the following pay-off table:

		Column	
		Hi	*Lo*
Row	*Hi*	4,4	0,0
	Lo	0,0	1,1

The Hi-Lo game has two Nash equilibria – (*Hi*, *Hi*) and (*Lo*, *Lo*). The first is obviously preferable and almost invariably played when subjects play the game in the lab. Standard game theory cannot explain this, but Bacharach's theory can. The Hi-Lo game has the two features of Common interests and Strong interdependence, and so primes players for team reasoning in the "we"-frame. As team-reasoners, players converge on the unique Pareto-optimal solution, which is (*Hi*, *Hi*).

Another more complicated coordination game where Bacharach's framing hypothesis seems to have real explanatory leverage is the Stag Hunt game.[13] Hinted at by Rousseau in his *Discourse on the Origin and Basis of Inequality among Men*, the canonical version of the game asks us to imagine two hunters.[14] Each hunter has two options – *Stag* or *Hare*. Catching a stag is better than catching a hare, for obvious reasons, but will only happen if they both collaborate. Hunting hare is likely to lead to a successful outcome, but more so if there is only one player hunting hare (since there will be less competition when the other player is on a doomed solo stag hunt). The pay-off table looks like this:

[13] The Stag Hunt game has been increasingly discussed as a potentially better model for the emergence of cooperative behavior than the Prisoner's Dilemma, which was for a long time the almost exclusive focus of social scientists interested in game theory. See Skyrms 2012 for a book-length discussion.

[14] I say "hinted at" because it is not obvious how to derive a pay-off table from Rousseau's passing remark in the *Discourse on Inequality*: "If it was a matter of hunting a deer, everyone well realized that he must remain faithful to his post; but if a hare happened to pass within reach of one of them, we cannot doubt that he would have gone off in pursuit of it without scruple . . ."

		Stag	Hare
	Column		
	Stag	4,4	0,2
Row	Hare	2,0	1,1

There are two Nash equilibria in the Stag Hunt game – the equilibrium where both hunt stag and the equilibrium where both hunt hare. Only one of these equilibria is Pareto-optimal, however – the (*Stag*, *Stag*) equilibrium. Since the Stag Hunt game has the two features that prime for the "we"-frame, Bacharach's model of team reasoning predicts a tendency towards convergence on the Pareto-optimal equilibrium.

Non-Equilibrium Solutions

The Agamemnon and Achilles version of the Prisoner's Dilemma shows how team reasoners working within the "we"-frame can converge on non-equilibrium outcomes. There is only one Nash equilibrium in their strategic interaction – reached via each player playing *Defect*. The Pareto-optimal outcome (in which both players choose *Cooperate*) is not a Nash equilibrium, which means that rational agents operating within the "I"-frame and applying standard game-theoretic reasoning will never reach it.[15]

But nonetheless, as is well-documented anecdotally and experimentally, people do converge on *Cooperate, Cooperate*. In a review article published in 1995, David Sally offered a meta-analysis of 130 experiments from 37 studies over the period 1958 to 1992. He looked at a range of social dilemmas, but mainly the Prisoner's Dilemma. All of the social dilemmas shared the basic features of the Prisoner's Dilemma, which is that the cooperative outcome is not a Nash equilibrium, and choosing

[15] Despite the best efforts of some game theorists and more moral philosophers to argue that it can be rational to cooperate in a one-shot Prisoner's Dilemma. See, for example, Davis 1977 and 1985, and Hurley 1991. To emphasize, all the discussion in this chapter is on one-shot strategic interactions. Repeated interactions have a completely different dynamic, as described in any introduction to game theory (e.g. Shoham and Leyton-Brown 2009). Gauthier 1986 is one of the best-known philosophical analyses of repeated Prisoner's Dilemmas. For more popular discussion and many real-life examples see Axelrod 1984.

Cooperate is a dominated strategy. Sally found a mean cooperation rate across the studies of 47.4 percent, suggesting that a very significant proportion of people do indeed opt for non-equilibrium solutions in social dilemmas such as the Prisoner's Dilemma.[16]

Bacharach's model provides a neat explanation of what is going on here. The Prisoner's Dilemma has both of the features that prime for team reasoning. Players do have common interests and they are strongly interdependent. Yet the structure of the game militates against cooperation much more so than in the two games we just looked at – Hi-Lo and the Stag Hunt. Whereas there is almost no tension between the "I"-frame and the "we"-frame in Hi-Lo, the clash of frames is much starker in the Prisoner's Dilemma. Stag Hunt falls somewhere between the two. So, while Bacharach's model predicts that the game will prime for Pareto-optimality, it also predicts that the outcome of mutual cooperation will be harder to achieve than in either of the other two games.

Two Problems

We see, then, that Bacharach's introduction of framing into game theory can potentially solve both the equilibrium selection problem and the problem of non-equilibrium solutions. I close this chapter, however, by identifying what I think are two very significant difficulties for Bacharach's theory, as it currently stands.

The first shortcoming, to my mind, has to do with the rationality of adopting the "we"-frame and engaging in team reasoning. Bacharach explains how a rational agent, working within the "we"-frame, can use team reasoning to solve strategic, non-cooperative problems. And he points to psychological aspects of decision problems that will, in his words, *prime* for team reasoning – i.e. that will make it more likely that agents will engage in team reasoning. But he does not address the fundamental question of why it might be rational to switch from the "I"-frame to the "we"-frame.

What sort of reasons could there be to favor a group perspective over an individual perspective? Is there an overarching perspective from which the "I"-frame and the "we"-frame can be compared? The machinery developed in earlier chapters is helpful here too. Agents caught between the "I"-frame and the "we"-frame can have quasi-cyclical preferences.

---

[16] For more recent experimental work on one-shot Prisoner's Dilemmas, see Janssen 2008 and Pothos et al. 2011.

The agent might prefer outcome B (in the "I"-frame) to outcome A (in the "I"-frame), while preferring outcome A (in the "we"-frame) to outcome B (in the "I"-frame), despite knowing full well that there is just one single outcome framed in two different ways – or, to put it more game-theoretically, that there is a single pay-off table, construed from two different and incompatible perspectives. But is there a vantage-point from which rational agents can reason their way out of the "I"-frame to the "we"-frame?

This brings us to the second problem, which is how Bacharach thinks about team reasoning within the "we"-frame. He thinks that a team reasoner is primarily driven by the twin concepts of *Pareto-superiority* and *Pareto-optimality* (also known as *Pareto-efficiency*). But it seems unclear how considerations of Pareto-efficiency can support a case for rationality of team reasoning and the "we"-frame. For one thing, Pareto-optimality is completely useless in zero-sum interactions (i.e. interactions where a player can only gain a benefit if another player suffers a corresponding loss). In a zero-sum game, every distribution is Pareto-optimal by default, since no outcome can be Pareto-superior to any other.

Moreover, even when we are not in a zero-sum situation, applying Pareto-optimality reasoning within the "we"-frame often takes an agent to exactly the same (intuitively unacceptable) outcomes as applying standard, individualistic reasoning in the "I"-frame.

We've already looked in detail at a good example – the game of Chicken played by Menelaös and Antilochos in Book 23 of Homer's *Iliad*:

	Menelaös	
	Press forward	Drop back
Antilochos — Press forward	0,0	4,1
Antilochos — Drop back	1,4	2,2

There are two pure strategy Nash equilibria in this game. One equilibrium has Antilochos playing *Drop back* while Menelaös plays *Press forward*. The roles are reversed in the other equilibrium. Intuitively, this situation is not very satisfactory. It is true that in both equilibria each player is playing his best response to the other's strategy. But it is mysterious how rational players will converge rationally on one equilibrium rather than the other. Both are asymmetric, and so each significantly benefits one player and significantly disadvantages the other. We saw how Antilochos and Menelaös arrived at their Nash equilibrium, but that was hardly a paradigm of rational decision-making and neither competitor was happy either with the outcome or with the process.

There is an equilibrium in mixed strategies, where each player chooses *Press forward* with probability 2/3 and *Drop back* with probability 1/3, but that does not seem satisfactory either. In the mixed strategies equilibrium there is a 4/9 probability of both players choosing *Press forward*, a 4/9 probability of ending up in one of the asymmetric equilibria, and a 1/9 probability of ending up in the non-equilibrium outcome of both players choosing *Drop back*.

Can shifting to the "we"-frame in the way that Bacharach suggests help here? At first glance it might seem to. Recall that for Bacharach team reasoners look for Pareto-optimal outcomes. If we reject the two asymmetric Nash equilibria for the reasons just discussed, then that leaves the two symmetric outcomes. Of these the outcome resulting from both playing *Drop back* is clearly preferable. And inspection shows that this outcome is indeed Pareto-optimal. Each player receives a pay-off of 2. Each player can improve his pay-off to 4, but this can only be done by reducing the other player's pay-off to 1 – which would not be Pareto-superior. So, the intuitively rational solution is indeed Pareto-optimal. Problem solved?

Not quite! Look again at the pay-off table. Each asymmetric Nash equilibrium is also Pareto-optimal. Suppose that Menelaös plays *Press forward* and Antilochos plays *Drop back*. Then there are only two outcomes in which Antilochos can improve on his pay-off of 1. His pay-off will increase to 2 if both players choose *Drop back*, while it will increase to 4 in the other asymmetric outcome where he plays *Press forward* while Menelaös plays *Drop back*. But in each case, Menelaös's pay-off is diminished – from 4 to 2 and from 4 to 1 respectively. So, Antilochos's pay-off can't be increased without lowering Menelaös's pay-off, which means that this Nash equilibrium is Pareto-optimal. By exactly the same reasoning, so too is the other Nash equilibrium.

In this game of Chicken, therefore, every outcome is Pareto-optimal except the worst-case scenario where both players choose *Press forward* and end up crashing their chariots. We've now got a new (and even worse) version of the equilibrium selection problem. At least when we were choosing between Nash equilibria we only had two to choose between. But how are the players supposed to converge rationally on one of these three Pareto-optimal outcomes?

Clearly, we need to go beyond Pareto-optimality. If both players choosing *Drop back* is indeed the rational strategy profile, then this can't be just because it is Pareto-optimal. And in fact, its being Pareto-optimal might not in the last analysis even be relevant. So, how should we think about reasoning in the "we"-frame?

The next chapter will explore ways of tackling this problem that will also allow us to make progress on the other problem that we identified. This is the problem of explaining how rational agents might reason their way into the "we"-frame, as opposed to taking adoption of the "we"-frame in the way that Bacharach does – as a psychological fact, only explicable in terms of priming and other non-rational features of the decision problem and its context.

9

Fair's Fair: Framing for Cooperation and Fairness

Michael Bacharach has shown how framing is a powerful tool for reconceptualizing game theory. There are different ways of framing strategic interactions. One way is to frame them individualistically, in the "I"-frame. Agents reasoning in the "I"-frame pay attention only to their own pay-offs. They seek to identify best response strategies. Best response strategies produce the best outcome for the agent, whatever other players end up doing. When each player plays a best response strategy then we have a Nash equilibrium, which is a situation where nobody can benefit from changing strategy. Nash equilibrium is the solution concept for game theory considered within the "I"-frame.

The "I"-frame is almost omnipresent within traditional game theory. Only Michael Bacharach and a few others (such as Robert Sugden and Natalie Gold) have considered the possibility of alternative ways of framing strategic interactions.[1] When an interaction is viewed through the "we"-frame, players take a different perspective on the pay-off table. Instead of looking just at their own pay-offs, players in the "we"-frame look at the pay-offs for the group. The game itself does not change, because each player's pay-offs remain the same. What changes is what the agent finds important. Agents adopting the "we"-frame take into account the pay-offs to other players, because they are considering the pay-off table from the perspective of the group. This is team reasoning.

---

[1] See Bacharach 2006, Sugden 2000, 2003, and 2015, Gold and Sugden 2007, Gold 2012, 2013 and 2018.

Bacharach makes a strong case that broadening how we think about game theory to accommodate the "we"-frame can help resolve two very fundamental problems:

The equilibrium selection problem

Nash's theorem says that every strategic interaction satisfying some basic conditions has at least one equilibrium solution. But many games have multiple equilibrium solutions. And there is no generally accepted method within game theory for identifying one solution as more rational than another, even in situations where it might seem intuitively obvious that there is a unique rational solution.

The problem of non-equilibrium solutions

Experimental and anecdotal evidence suggests that, in some fundamental types of social interaction, people often do not choose a Nash equilibrium solution. In fact, not only do they not choose it – they reject it when it is proposed. Often, when a Nash equilibrium points in a different direction from considerations of fairness, cooperation, and collaboration, people find the fair and/or cooperative outcomes more appealing. So, there seem to be non-equilibrium solutions.

Allowing that agents might adopt the "we"-frame and engage in team reasoning can help solve both problems. In games with multiple Nash equilibria (such as Stag Hunt or Hi-Lo), a single outcome can be salient from the team reasoning perspective. And, as Bacharach claims to be the case in the Prisoner's Dilemma, a non-equilibrium outcome can be rational from the team reasoning perspective.

But still, Bacharach's discussion of framing in game theory, inspiring though it is, has two very significant shortcomings. The first has to do with the rationality of adopting the "we"-frame and engaging in team reasoning. Bacharach explains how a rational agent, working within the "we"-frame, can use team reasoning to solve strategic, non-cooperative problems. And he points to psychological aspects of decision problems that will, in his words, *prime* for team reasoning – i.e. that will make it more likely that agents will engage in team reasoning. But he does not address the fundamental question of why it might be rational to switch from the "I"-frame to the "we"-frame.

The second difficulty comes from how Bacharach thinks about team reasoning within the "we"-frame. He thinks that a team reasoner is primarily driven by the twin concepts of *Pareto-superiority* and *Pareto-optimality* (or *Pareto-efficiency*). These are concepts that apply to groups.

An outcome A is Pareto-superior to B when everybody is at least as well-off in A as in B, and at least one person is better off in A than in B. So, an outcome is Pareto-optimal (or, on the Pareto frontier) when there is no Pareto-superior alternative. But the Pareto concept has shortcomings. In some cases, applying Pareto-optimality reasoning within the "we"-frame takes an agent to exactly the same (intuitively unacceptable) outcomes as applying standard, individualistic reasoning in the "I"-frame. We saw that this is the case in the game of Chicken, where the two Nash equilibria are both intuitively irrational and Pareto-optimal. Moreover, Pareto-optimality is almost completely useless when it comes to zero-sum games (in which costs and benefits must add to zero, so that any benefit must be matched by a corresponding cost). Every distribution in a zero-sum game is Pareto-optimal.

These two difficulties in Bacharach's approach set the scene for this chapter. We'll see that they can both be solved – and, moreover, that the solutions are related. Ideas about fairness will be key to the discussion. I'll be suggesting that a rational agent might prefer to adopt the "we"-frame because it is fairer – and that considerations of fairness can be raised from within a perspective that includes both the "I"-frame and the "we"-frame and allows them to be compared to each other. But a fair distribution is often not Pareto-optimal. In many cases, fairness requires raising one agent's pay-off at the expense of another's, and this is not something that can ever be Pareto-superior to maintaining the status quo.

Before embarking on the positive discussion, however, we need to start by dispelling some worries that seem to threaten the entire project. These are worries about potential incommensurability – incommensurability of values across frames, and incommensurability of utilities across individuals.

Problems of Incommensurability?

Bacharach is very clear that he does not see any prospect of rationally justifying adoption of the "we"-frame over the "I"-frame (or vice versa, for that matter). He offers hypotheses about features of strategic interactions that will prime for the "we"-frame (common interests and strong interdependence), but priming and rational justification often come apart, as described in the previous chapter. It is unfortunate and misleading that, from a game-theoretic perspective, the cooperative outcome is often presented (framed, one might say) in a very prosocial way – as loyalty in a Prisoner's Dilemma, for example. But we have to remember that many of the most horrendous episodes in human history have emerged from collective group action in situations where participants have common interests and see that those common interests can only be achieved by joint action of a type that would not be promoted by purely individualistic reasoning. Think of the Nuremberg rallies, for example, or the Hutu genocide of the Tutsis in the Rwandan civil war.

Group identification can be a terrible thing – and in fact, the height of irrationality. So, why does Bacharach not try to distinguish between rational group identification and irrational group identification? Why does he hold back from discussing the circumstances in which it might be rational (or irrational) to adopt the "we"-frame? Bacharach doesn't say, but I think that many might find the following line of argument compelling.

Someone might say that the "I"-frame and the "we"-frame cannot be rationally compared, because they are *incommensurable*. This incommensurability is a consequence of the fundamentally instrumental nature of practical reasoning. If practical reasoning is instrumental then it must be guided by ends, values, or goals. Comparing the "I"-frame and the "we"-frame is only possible if there is some vantage-point independent of either frame from which those ends, values, or goals can be deployed. This is because comparing the "I"-frame and the "we"-frame is essentially a matter of comparing how well each does on promoting those values, ends, and goals. But ends, values, and goals have to be the ends, values, and goals of some agent. And this is where the incommensurability emerges, because the locus of agency differs between the "I"-frame and the "we"-frame. In the "I"-frame, the agent is the individual, while in the "we"-frame the agency is the group. In Bacharach's own phrase, the shift from the "I"-frame to the "we"-frame is essentially an agency transformation.

If this line of argument is sound, then the "I"-frame and the "we"-frame are incommensurable in a way that makes it impossible to theorize about how someone might reason their way from the "I"-frame to the "we"-frame, or back. That would justify Bacharach's focus on the psychology of the shift to team reasoning, as opposed to the rationality of the shift. But still, this type of (potential) incommensurability does not in itself stand in the way of tackling the second of the two problems identified in Bacharach's overall project by looking for an alternative to Paretian reasoning. After all, reasoning about alternatives to Pareto-efficiency takes place internally to the "we"-frame.

Nonetheless, there is a second type of potential incommensurability that would actually stand in the way of finding an alternative to Paretian

reasoning within the "we"-frame. To appreciate the problem, observe
that applying Paretian reasoning does not require being able to compare
different agents' utility functions. So, for example, distribution A is
Pareto-superior to distribution B just if every agent is at least as well off
under A as they are under B, and at least one person is better off under A
than under B. In order to establish that distribution A is superior to
distribution B, all we need to compare is how each individual fares
under A and under B. We just need to establish that each individual
weakly prefers their pay-off under A to their pay-off under B, and that
at least one person strongly prefers their pay-off under A to their pay-off
under B.[2] In other words, we can compare distributions A and B simply by
making *intrapersonal* comparisons of utility, and so without needing to
make any *interpersonal* comparisons.

One of the main reasons why Paretian efficiency is so popular among
economists, game theorists, and decision theorists is the thought (first
promoted, among others, by Pareto himself) that it is impossible to
make *interpersonal* comparisons of utility.[3] An interpersonal comparison
of utility would be a comparison of the utilities that different agents assign
to the goods that come to them within a given distribution. Here is a
simple example. In the last chapter we looked at the game of Chicken, as
played by the two charioteers, Menelaös and Antilochos. There are two
asymmetric outcomes, in each of which one chariot *Presses forward* while
the other *Drops back*. In the pay-off table, these two outcomes look very
similar – mirror images of each other, in fact. We wrote them down as (4,
1) and (1, 4), with Antilochos's pay-off coming first. Writing the two pay-
offs down like this can make it look, for example, as if Antilochos and
Menelaös assign exactly the same amount of utility to *Pressing forward*
while the other chariot *Drops back* – and hence, by extension, that the
total amount of utility is the same across the two outcomes, which differ
only in how that total amount of utility is assigned.

Unfortunately, that appearance is very misleading. The mathematical models of utility do not secure any kind of comparability across
individuals. The standard techniques (going back to Frank Ramsey

---

[2] Weak preference allows for the possibility of indifference, whereas strong preference does
not.
[3] Pareto was one of the prime movers in the so-called New Welfare Economics that emerged
in the 1930s, characterized (among other things) by a repudiation of the interpersonal
comparison of utilities. For a historical survey see Chipman and Moore 1978. Stigler
1950a and 1950b traces the tangled web of how the concept of utility evolved in this period
and earlier. For Pareto's own complicated views see Bruni 2010.

and John von Neumann) for assigning utility functions to individuals on the basis of their choice behavior provide absolutely no reason to think that there is an abstract quantity called utility, of which Antilochos and Menelaös each have equal amounts when they *Press forward* while the other *Drops back*. From the perspective of decision theory, utility functions are constructed from preferences, and preferences simply measure choice, provided that the choices are suitably consistent (where what counts as suitable consistency is determined by the relevant axiomatization).[4] For a given axiomatization of what counts as consistent choice, a representation theorem will prove that an agent's choices can be viewed as maximizing (expected) utility. Stepping back from the details, what all this shows is that the utility functions discussed by decision theorists and economists are really tools for representing a given individual's consistent choices. They are not measurements of an abstract quantity called utility that might be identified with pleasure, welfare, well-being, or some other desirable property.

The representation theorems of decision theory in themselves give us no reason to think, therefore, that utility can be compared across individuals. We can represent choices with numerical utility functions, but the numbers can be deceptive. They do not provide a common currency that will allow interpersonal comparison of utilities. So, for example, suppose that we are trying to compare the total utility available in the first two of the following distributions:

	A	B	C
Distribution 1	10	30	20
Distribution 2	30	20	10
Distribution 3	40	30	20

You might be tempted to think that Distribution 1 and Distribution 2 are equivalent, because the numbers in each row sum to 60. But that would be a mistake. We know that A assigns 30 units of utility to what she receives under Distribution 2, while C

---

[4] For further details see Chapter 1 of Bermúdez 2009, Chapter 4 of Resnik 1987, and Chapter 1 of Ahmed 2014. The original constructions are in Ramsey 1931, Von Neumann and Morgenstern 1944, and Fishburn 1970.

assigns 30 units of utility to what he receives under Distribution 1. But we have no information about how one of A's units of utility matches up to one of C's units. In other words, A's utility function is incommensurable with C's utility function.

On the other hand, we can give a clear reason for preferring Distribution 3 to Distribution 1, because it is Pareto-superior. A is better off, while B and C are no worse off in Distribution 3. Since we do not have to make any interpersonal comparisons of utility to justify preferring Distribution 3 to Distribution 1, the (putative) incommensurability of the utility functions is not a problem.

We can tie this all back to thinking about how to rank outcomes in the "we"-frame, since the pay-off table in a game really just presents an outcome as a distribution of utilities across the players. I cannot see any alternative to Paretian reasoning avoid having to make an interpersonal comparison of utilities. And so, if different individuals' utility functions really are incommensurable, then that would seem to rule out any non-Paretian rankings of outcomes in the "we"-frame.

Interpersonal Comparison of Utility

I will be focusing mainly on the first types of incommensurability – that supposed to hold between the "I"-frame and the "we"-frame. But I will start by saying something about the second, which is the incommensurability thought to hold between individual utility functions. This worry needs to be dispelled in order to open up the possibility of non-Paretian reasoning in the "we"-frame. And it will turn out that, when we have in front of us a particular type of non-Paretian reasoning, based upon considerations of fairness, we will be able to see how the alleged incommensurability between the "I"-frame and the "we"-frame might be overcome.

Here is a classic statement of the alleged impossibility of interpersonal comparisons of utility from the Chicago economist Roger Myerson (who won the Nobel Prize for Economics in 2007, jointly with Leonid Hurwicz and Eric Maskin):

> Interpersonal comparisons of utility cannot be given decision-theoretic significance. That is, there is no decision-theoretic meaning for a statement such as 'a movie gives me more utility than an opera gives you,' because neither of us could ever be forced to choose between being me at a movie and you at an opera. (Myerson 1985, 238–39)

It is probably true that none of us is ever forced to choose between being me at a movie and being you at an opera.[5] But why should one think that deciding whether a movie gives me more pleasure than an opera gives you requires anything of the sort? On the face of it, this is the sort of choice that I have to make all the time. I might possess a grand total of $10 in disposable income and then have to decide whether to keep it to myself and visit the cinema, or give it to you so that you can go to the opera. It's surely not inconceivable that I might decide that the opera means so much more to you than the movie does to me that I simply hand over the $10. And on a larger scale, an arts foundation that decides to support the local opera house over the local arts cinema would typically base its decision at least partially on the relative benefits to the community of opera vs. movies, and those comparisons of course rest on aggregating the benefits to individuals in the community.

But Myerson's point is really about whether we can make sense of such choices within decision theory. If there is to be an interpersonal comparison of utility, then there must be a single utility scale on which different people's utilities are ranked. But utility functions are derived from choices, as I have emphasized. So, what can the relevant choices be? How can I choose between my utilities and your utilities without choosing between being me and being you?

One plausible answer to these questions is very simple. It was first given a formal presentation by John Harsanyi, although its general ancestry goes back much further, at least as far back as eighteenth-century thinkers such as David Hume and Adam Smith. I have been particularly influenced by Ken Binmore's presentation in his book *Natural Justice*.[6]

Here is the basic idea in the two-person case: I can bring your utilities into my calculation by empathizing with you and then considering the choices that I would make if I were in your shoes. That will allow me to derive an empathetic utility function for you. The better empathizer I am, the more accurately I will predict the choices that you will make and so the better will be my approximation of your utility function. At the limit we can assume that I am a perfect empathizer and so will be able completely to predict your choices. That will allow me to derive an empathetic utility

---

[5] I say "probably" because there are ways of interpreting the devices of the original position and veil of ignorance as actually involving something like this choice.

[6] Binmore 2005. See also Binmore 2009b. Harsanyi's argument can be found in his book *Rational Behavior and Bargaining Equilibrium in Games and Social Situations* (Harsanyi 1986).

function for you that uses the same scale as my own, and so I can compare your utilities to mine. If I am a saintly person, I will treat each unit on my empathetic utility scale for you as equivalent to one unit on my own utility scale, and so in effect amalgamate the two scales. Or I might discount your utilities by a certain factor, which measures how close we are and how much I care about your well-being. Either way, your utilities and mine have become commensurable.

Moreover, if I can accurately predict your choices, and I know what your personal utility function is (i.e. I know the numbers that you assign to the different outcomes we are considering), then I will be able to map the utility function that emerges from my predictions of how you will choose onto your utility function. This is because any two utility functions derived from the same set of suitably consistent choices will stand to each other in the way that the centigrade scale stands to the Fahrenheit scale, or the liter scale to the gallon scale – since utility functions are, mathematically speaking, unique to positive affine transformation. This means that I can translate your utility units into the empathetic utility function that I have derived for you. If your utility function is on a scale from 0 to 100, while my empathetic function is on a scale from 32 to 212, then I know that I can convert your stated values into values on my empathetic utility function by multiplying by 9/5 and then adding 32. And once I have done that then I have made your utility function commensurable with mine.

Obviously, there is much more that might be said about commensurability and empathetic utility functions.[7] One might ask, for example, whether it is really plausible to assume that people can accurately think their way into other people's shoes in the manner needed to derive accurate empathetic utility functions. And even if it is plausible, are there good reasons to think that different people's empathetic utility functions will converge? Ken Binmore has interesting things to say about the potential evolutionary origins for empathetic reasoning, which dovetail nicely with ongoing psychological research into mindreading and related cognitive

---

[7] General issues of commensurability have been much discussed within philosophy. Influential discussions include Griffin 1986, Wiggins 1978, and the papers collected in Chang 1997. The idea behind what I am calling empathetic utility functions can be traced back to the extended sympathy preferences credited to Patrick Suppes (Suppes 1966). For critical discussions of extended preferences as a tool for tackling problems of commensurability see Greaves and Lederman 2017 and 2018. For a general review of economic approaches to interpersonal comparison, and an approach different from that proposed here, see Hammond 1991.

abilities.[8] As a matter of empirical fact, there is strong evidence that normal subjects are generally pretty good at reasoning about how others might choose and act. The basic capacity for mindreading is not in doubt. Most discussion in social psychology and developmental psychology focuses on different models of mindreading (does it involve implicit theorizing, for example, or is it an exercise in simulation?); on explaining how the relevant capacities emerge in normal development; and on understanding the different ways in which mindreading skills can break down or fail to develop.[9] The intersection between the science of mindreading and discussions of interpersonal comparisons of utility is almost completely unmined, but surely deserves close and detailed study.

For present purposes, though, what matters is that we can see a path to answering incommensurability concerns that might seem to block any application of non-Paretian reasoning within the "we"-frame. The device of empathetic utility functions allows us to aggregate utilities, for example. It would certainly be fallacious to conclude that Distributions 1 and 2 from the previous section both have the same total utility (60 units), but still I can calculate the total utility in each. If I am A, for example, then I simply use my own utility function for A. For B I use my empathetic utility function to translate her values into values in my personal utility function (and the result will be $20\beta + m$ for some β and some m in both Distribution 1 and Distribution 2). Likewise for C, whose utility assignments will come out as $30\gamma + n$ for some γ and some n in Distribution 1 and $10\gamma + m$ in Distribution 2. So, the total utility in the two distributions (calculated on my utility scale) comes out as:

Distribution 1: $10 + 20\beta + 30\gamma + m + n$
Distribution 2: $30 + 20\beta + 10\gamma + m + n$

If $\gamma < 1$, then there will be more utility in aggregate in Distribution 2, while if $\gamma > 1$ then Distribution 2 will have more total utility.

There seem to be no obstacles in principle, then, to using non-Paretian criteria within the "we"-frame. Let's turn now to the second alleged incommensurability – which is the incommensurability between the "I"-frame and the "we"-frame. It will turn out that seeing how and why the

[8] See Binmore 2005.
[9] For an introduction to the principal debates and guidance on further reading see Chapters 13 and 14 of my textbook *Cognitive Science: An Introduction to the Science of the Mind* (Bermúdez 2020).

"I"-frame and the "we"-frame are commensurable will point us towards alternatives to the Pareto-based reasoning favored by Bacharach, and also to seeing how one might argue for the rationality (in appropriate situations) of the "we"-frame over the "I"-frame.

Reasoning across Frames

Let's look again at the worry identified earlier. Here it is presented schematically.

1. Comparing the "I"-frame and the "we"-frame is a process of practical reasoning.
2. All practical reasoning is means–end, instrumental reasoning.
3. The "I"-frame and the "we"-frame can only be compared relative to how they promote some end, value, or goal.
4. Any end, value, or goal is the end, value, or goal of some agent.
5. The locus of agency is fundamentally different in the "I"-frame and the "we"-frame (the individual in the "I"-frame and the group in the "we"-frame).
6. Therefore, there can be no perspective or vantage-point from which instrumental reasoning can compare the "I"-frame and the "we"-frame.

Some of the premises in this argument would no doubt be challenged. There are many philosophers, for example, who would contest the claim that all reasoning is instrumental. But I think that even if we accept an instrumental way of thinking about practical reasoning the argument is invalid. The questionable move comes in the final step, where differences in agency between the "I"-frame and the "we"-frame are taken to rule out the possibility of instrumentally comparing the two frames.

There is a tacit assumption in the argument that needs to be brought out. This is the assumption that there can be no values, goals, or ends that are common to the two frames. Unless this is assumed, the argument plainly fails, because values, goals, or ends shared across the frames could in principle anchor the instrumental reflection required to compare. But why assume that values, goals, and ends must be frame-specific and non-shareable?

One important reason is that the contrast between the "I"-frame and the "we"-frame is often presented in a way that makes it look as if individualistic reasoning in the "I"-frame is purely selfish, while team reasoning in the "we"-frame is somehow altruistic. The standard terminology in the Prisoner's Dilemma is a good example, with the outcome of individualistic reasoning labeled as mutual *defection* and the outcome of team reasoning labeled as mutual *cooperation*. From an individualistic perspective, the optimal outcome is often described as being a *free-rider*, receiving the benefits without taking the costs. This is all loaded terminology, and it is easy to see why the contrast between the "I"-frame and the "we"-frame might come across as a contrast between selfishness and cooperation. And once one looks at it in these terms, then it quickly becomes persuasive that there is an incommensurability of values across the two frames.[10]

But this way of looking at things is confused. The defining feature of individualistic reasoning in the "I"-frame is that reasoners pay attention only to their own pay-offs – to the component of a joint outcome that concerns them. It is because of this that best response reasoning is appropriate within the "I"-frame. But that says nothing about what an individual's pay-off function should look like. It need not be self-regarding in any shape or form. An easy way to see this is by framing the Prisoner's Dilemma differently – as an Altruist's Dilemma.

Imagine, as a variant on a very famous scenario due originally to David Hume, that we are two altruistic farmers, each with a field to harvest before the rains begin.[11] As an altruist, my primary concern is to promote the success of your harvest. So, my preferred outcome is one where we both harvest your field. My least preferred outcome is the one where we both harvest my field. That leaves two possible outcomes. I know that you are better at harvesting your own field than I am, so from my altruistic perspective it is better for you to work on your field and me on mine than it is for me to work on your field and you on mine. Since you are an altruist also, your preferences are symmetrical. So, the pay-off table might look like this:

---

[10] And it also becomes persuasive to think that the "we"-frame is somehow intrinsically better than the "I"-frame. More on this misconception below.

[11] Hume's example, and pithy analysis, is in *A Treatise of Human Nature* at Book III, Part 2, section v. Game-theoretically, it is an asynchronous Prisoner's Dilemma (with the players playing sequentially). For an analysis of what is often called the Farmer's Dilemma see section 9 of Kuhn 2017. In an article in a special issue of *Business Ethics Quarterly* devoted to game theory, Kay Mathiesen proposed an altruist's dilemma even more closely modeled on the prisoner's dilemma than the dilemma in the text (Mathiesen 1999)

	You	

	Work on your field	Work on my field
Work on my field	2,2	−3,3
Work on your field	3,−3	1,1

Me

As you can confirm from the table, best response reasoning tells me to work on your field and it tells you to work on your field. So, exactly as in a standard Prisoner's Dilemma, we each end up with our third-best outcome by applying individualistic reasoning in the "I"-frame. But we remain altruists nonetheless.

And nor is it the case that team reasoners in the "we"-frame must be altruists. A team-reasoner, by definition, looks at an entire profile of pay-offs, rather than simply focusing on her own part of the profile. But that does not mean that she has to be altruistically motivated. A genocidal mob can be made up of what Bacharach calls circumspect team reasoners. Each of them assigns a probability to the other potential mob members being team reasoners and, on that basis, calculates that fulfilling his part in the team genocide is more rewarding for the team than engaging in best response reasoning (which might plausibly have called for each individual to live in peace with his neighbors). But the motivation for each member might be their purely individual hatred of an ethnic group. And there is certainly no reason to think that they would need to be altruistically minded towards each other.[12]

It is a mistake, therefore, to map the "I"-frame/"we"-frame distinction onto the selfish/altruistic distinction. This removes one possible reason for thinking that there might be an incommensurability of values between the two frames, and hence that it might be impossible to reason (instrumentally) to compare the two frames. To make further progress here we need to work through an example of how instrumental reasoning across frames might work. I'll close this section by giving a high-level

---

[12] Still, it is plausible to think that team reasoners in the "we"-frame must have a sense of collective identity and awareness of themselves *as a group*. For more on this see Schmitz 2018.

sketch. In the next section we'll work through the details using some of the tools developed in earlier chapters.

The key concept in the following is the concept of fairness. This is a hard concept to pin down, to put it mildly. In many contexts, the concepts of justice and fairness are used interchangeably, so that to talk about a fair outcome or a fair distribution is simply to talk about an outcome or distribution that is just. From a philosophical perspective, however, things are more complicated. At one end of the spectrum, John Rawls's monumental *A Theory of Justice* explicitly sets out to promote a conception of justice as fairness.[13] However, at the other end, there are theories of justice that abstract away from considerations of fairness, understood as a property of distributions of goods. Robert Nozick's book *Anarchy, State, and Utopia* is a good example. Nozick famously argues that the whole concept of distributive justice is an illusion, because justice is not a property of distributions at all. What are just or unjust are holdings of goods (economic or other), and a holding is just provided that it was acquired and transferred in the right sort of way.[14] Fairness seems, therefore, to be a narrower concept than justice.

The important point is that fairness is a property of distributions, whereas justice may not be. That is why it is potentially relevant to team reasoning. The characteristic of a team reasoner is that she takes into account the entire pay-off profile for a given outcome, rather than just her part of that pay-off profile, and a pay-off profile is really just a distribution of goods. So, fairness considerations are certainly possible candidates for an alternative way of ranking pay-off profiles to rankings reached by applying Paretian criteria. Relatedly, I shall argue, valuing fairness can be a powerful reason for adopting the "we"-frame. And moreover, since fairness can be valued even outside the "we"-frame, it potentially offers an anchor for reasoning into the "we"-frame.

To make progress we need some sort of definition of fairness. To avoid getting bogged down in fascinating but tangential discussions, I propose starting and finishing with Aristotle's *Nicomachean Ethics*, the first recorded discussion of these matters and still one of the best. Aristotle uses the concepts of fairness and equality interchangeably (using the term

---

[13] See Rawls 1971 and, for a later restatement of the theory, Rawls 2001. Rawls's theory of justice has been the subject of over 2,000 books and articles. A good place to start is the *Cambridge Companion to Rawls* (Freeman 2003).

[14] See Chapter 7 of Nozick 1974. Nozick has a trenchant discussion of Herbert Hart's fairness principle at pp. 90–95. He is not sympathetic.

to ison), and he defines a fair and equal distribution as one that is proportionate with regard to merit (*axia*), as opposed to any conception of absolute equality that abstracts away completely from individual differences.[15] In other words, differences between goods must correspond to differences in whatever merit is taken to consist in. Of course, as Aristotle immediately observes, merit is understood differently in different communities and different political systems.

The contemporary menu of merit-bestowing factors is of course rather different from Aristotle's, but for present purposes we can leave merit as a blank parameter. In the following I will take a distribution to be fair to the extent that it minimizes arbitrary inequality, where what counts as arbitrary is fixed by whatever criteria of merit are operative in that context. Leaving this important issue open makes sense, given that we are discussing how individual reasoners (and groups of reasoners) might reason their way into the "we"-frame and how they might rank distributions within the "we"-frame. Obviously, the members of the team need to agree on the criteria for team reasoning to get off the ground, but different teams (or the same team in different contexts) may well apply different criteria. Again, while I would not want to foreclose on the possibility that some subset of merit-bestowing criteria might be objectively preferable, we are currently working within a broadly instrumental framework.

Here is the basic idea to be developed more fully in the next section. Fairness can function as a frame-neutral value. We need to think about fairness (and other values) as things that lie behind and explain individual preferences and choices. It is true that, from the perspective of decision theory, preferences are revealed by choices. But still, choices are made for reasons. The representation theorems of decision theory assume a significant degree of consistency in choice behavior. That consistency is what makes it possible to define preferences from choices, and utility and probability functions from preferences. But there is no need to take that consistency as a brute fact. One reason that people make consistent choices is that those choices are guided by values and goals that hold across multiple-choice situations.

So, when we look at a pay-off table, we need to think not just about the individual pay-offs, but also what lies behind them. This holds in the "I"-frame no less than in the "we"-frame. And so, it is perfectly possible that considerations of fairness are what drive an individual agent's assignment

---

[15] See Aristotle, *Nicomachean Ethics*, Bk. V, Ch. ii. For an influential discussion of Aristotle's views on justice see Williams 1980.

of utilities. Consider the asymmetric outcomes in a game of Chicken, for example – like that played by Menelaös and Antilochos. For each player, the outcome in which he *Drops back* while the other *Presses forward* is their third preferred outcome. Each values it less than the symmetric outcome where they both play *Drop back* (which for each is their second preferred outcome). Why should this be? It is not hard to imagine that part of the explanation has to do with fairness. It is not just that the chariot that drops back is less likely to win the race (although that is no doubt true). What matters also is how the outcome has come about. The charioteer who plays *Drop back* has not been bested in a fair contest. The criteria of merit for a chariot race are, presumably, the strength and speed of the horses and the skill of the charioteer. So, a fair outcome for a chariot race is one that is determined by those factors. But when Antilochos plays Chicken with Menelaös, his underhand tactics force the merit-bestowing factors into the background.

Menelaös and Antilochos are both reasoning within the "I"-frame and, as the *Iliad* relates, they converge upon a Nash equilibrium. But they do so grudgingly. Imagine how things might have gone differently, had they perhaps had more time to reflect. Imagine that Menelaös, for example, had thought more carefully about his preferences over the outcomes. He might have realized that his strong aversion to the asymmetric outcome where he chooses *Drop back* is really based on concerns about fairness. And then, once that thought had taken a hold, he might have realized that it would be consistent for him to look at all the possible outcomes through the lens of fairness. It would be inconsistent, for example, to complain that one asymmetric outcome is unfair (because it is him who has to *Drop back*) while welcoming the other asymmetric outcome (in which he benefits because Antilochos chooses *Drop back*). If one is unfair then so too is the other.

Building on those thoughts, Menelaös might have realized that in general thinking about fairness requires him to look, not just at his own pay-off in each outcome, but also at Antilochos's pay-off. And now with this he has reasoned his way into the "we"-frame from the "I"-frame. Moreover, the way he has reasoned his way into the "we"-frame, gives him the tools for ranking the outcomes from a team reasoning perspective. He can develop a fairness ranking.[16] From the perspective of fairness, the

---

[16] Michael Schmitz made the helpful suggestion (in correspondence) that this process might be viewed as Menelaös's transition from a non-conceptual and undeveloped sense of fairness to a more developed and conceptual one.

optimal outcome is the outcome where both choose *Drop back*, clearly preferable to either of the two asymmetric outcomes. From a fairness point of view, moreover, the two asymmetric outcomes are equally undesirable. That still leaves open the question, though, of whether he prefers the outcome where both choose *Press forward* to the asymmetric outcomes. It is certainly fairer for both to crash out of the race, but still Menelaös may not want to take fairness quite that far. In any event, that's for him to think about. The important point is that, as a team reasoner motivated by fairness considerations, rationality tells him to play his part in the optimal strategy profile, which is where both charioteers choose *Drop back*.

We can qualify this, as per the discussion of circumspect team reasoning as in the last chapter. Even once Menelaös has thought his way into the "we"-frame, it may not be rational for him to be a team reasoner. It all depends on the probability that he assigns to team reasoning actually being implemented. If that probability is too low, then even from the perspective of the "we"-frame, best response reasoning would be appropriate. What counts as too low? The probability ω needs to be sufficiently high for the expected pay-off for the team (when each charioteer is a team reasoner with probability ω) to exceed the default pay-off for the team. The default pay-off occurs if both players play their "I"-frame best response strategy.

So, that's an illustration of the basic idea. One way that a rational agent can reason from the "I"-frame to the "we"-frame is by reflecting on the values that lie behind their "I"-frame preferences and choices. Doing so can lead them to see that those values can best be promoted by team reasoning within the "we"-frame. And then the switch to team reasoning can be rationally mandated (provided that there is sufficient reason to think that others will also be team reasoners). In the next section we will look at this in more detail using the tools developed in earlier chapters.

Quasi-Cyclical Preferences and Reasoning across Frames

Let's continue looking at the Chicken game for the moment. It has received far less attention across the social sciences than, say, the Prisoner's Dilemma. But in many ways it offers more fertile ground for comparing standard best response reasoning and team reasoning. This was spotted by Colin Camerer and Richard Thaler, who wrote in an article in 2003 that it is a game where "... the set of outcomes allowed by fairness is completely the opposite of the standard equilibrium outcomes. In this sense, Chicken is the best game to use to contrast fairness and pure self-interest, a better game than ultimatum bargaining, prisoner's dilemmas and other games that have been much more thoroughly studied."[17] The fairness outcome is neither a Nash equilibrium nor Pareto-optimal, whereas the unfair, asymmetric outcomes are both Pareto-optimal and Nash equilibria. So, the contrast between fairness and standard, individualistic game-theoretic reasoning is stark.

As with several of the symmetrical two-person games, Chicken can be framed in different ways. Another familiar way of presenting it is as a Hawk-Dove encounter, of the type made famous by Stanley Kubrick's film *Dr. Strangelove*. Less well known outside game theory is the so-called Snowdrift game. The pay-offs are exactly the same, but the context is collaborative rather than competitive. It is a simple enough scenario. Two people are stranded by a snowdrift in their car. Each has two possible courses of action. One option is to *Stay Inside* the car. The other is to leave the warmth of the car and *Dig Snow*. Obviously, if both players choose to *Stay Inside* then not much happens – giving each of them a utility of zero. If they both choose to *Dig Snow*, then they will certainly get out of the snowdrift, but they will have had to work for it, which would be worth, say, two units of utility for each. And then there are the two asymmetric outcomes, where one player chooses to *Stay Inside* while the other opts to *Dig Snow*. In each asymmetric case, the person inside the car stays nice and warm and gets out of the snowdrift, yielding four units of utility, while the person digging snow manages to escape the snowdrift but only at the cost of doing all the work, thus netting just one unit of utility.

So, the pay-off table should look familiar, because it is simply a relabeling of the pay-off table for Menelaös and Antilochos's chariot race:

		Column	
		Stay inside	Dig snow
Row	Stay inside	0, 0	4,1
	Dig snow	1,4	2,2

---

[17] Camerer and Thaler 2003, p. 164.

Let's look at this from the "I"-frame. Here is how Row and Column respectively rank the four possible outcomes (with Row's action coming first in each case), when they concern themselves solely with their individual pay-offs:

Row	Column
Stay Inside, Dig Snow	*Dig Snow, Stay Inside*
Dig Snow, Dig Snow	*Dig Snow, Dig Snow*
Dig Snow, Stay Inside	*Stay Inside, Dig Snow*
Stay Inside, Stay Inside	*Stay Inside, Stay Inside*

Things are different from the perspective of the "we"-frame. If Row and Column are team reasoners, motivated by fairness, then they will both rank the four outcomes the same way. (I'll assume that Row and Column's least favorite option is remaining stranded in the snowdrift, even though they might prefer that to either asymmetric outcome if they are exceptionally fair-minded.)

Row	Column
Dig Snow, Dig Snow	*Dig Snow, Dig Snow*
Dig Snow, Stay Inside	*Dig Snow, Stay Inside*
=	=
Stay Inside, Dig Snow	*Stay Inside, Dig Snow*
Stay Inside, Stay Inside	*Stay inside, Stay Inside*

Suppose now that Row has reasoned her way into the "we"-frame along the lines sketched out in the previous section. Then she will have available to her both sets of preferences – the "I"-frame set and the "we"-frame set. So, that means, for example, that she will have the following preferences (where the subscripts indicate which frame she is employing):

$$(\textit{Stay Inside, Dig Snow})_{\text{"I"-frame}} > (\textit{Dig Snow, Dig Snow})_{\text{"I"-frame}}$$
$$(\textit{Dig Snow, Dig Snow})_{\text{"We"-frame}} > (\textit{Stay Inside, Dig Snow})_{\text{"We"-frame}}$$

Neither of these preferences is hard to understand, since each is relative to a particular frame. However, given that Row has determined to her own satisfaction that the "we"-frame perspective is to be preferred over the "I"-frame, she also has this preference:

$$(Dig\ Snow,\ Dig\ Snow)_{\text{``We''-frame}}\ >\ (Stay\ Inside,\ Dig\ Snow)_{\text{``I''-frame}}$$

Plainly, Row has quasi-cyclical preferences, in the sense discussed in earlier chapters. She prefers mutual digging (in the "we"-frame) to the asymmetric outcome (in the "I"-frame) in which she benefits as a free-rider. And at the same time, remaining within the "I"-frame, she prefers the free-rider outcome to mutual digging. Of course, Row is perfectly well aware that mutual digging is mutual digging, which puts her (by the transitivity of preference) into the position of preferring mutual digging in the "we"-frame to mutual digging in the "I"-frame. In other words:

$$(Dig\ Snow,\ Dig\ Snow)_{\text{``We''-frame}}\ >\ (Dig\ Snow,\ Dig\ Snow)_{\text{``I''-frame}}$$

How can this make sense? And even if it can be made to make sense, how can it be rational?

At several points in earlier chapters we have explored the idea that one thing that makes a preference rational is its being based on a suitable reason. A rational agent can only prefer one thing to another if the first thing is different from the second thing in a way that justifies valuing it more highly. In the absence of such a justifying reason, there is what John Broome terms a "rational requirement of indifference."[18] So, first, we need to explain what difference there might be for Row between mutual digging in the "we"-frame and mutual digging in the "I"-frame. And then, second, we need to explain how that perceived difference can justify Row's not being indifferent between the same outcome framed in different ways.

One key difference when the (*Dig Snow, Dig Snow*) outcome is viewed in the two different frames is that the fairness of the outcome is salient in the "we"-frame in a way that it is not in the "I"-frame. Here is a way of understanding that. The hypothetical reasoning that I offered Menelaös in the last section and Row in this section does indeed depend upon one of the asymmetric outcomes being viewed as unfair within the "I"-frame. That is the anchor, as it were, that Menelaös and Row can use to bootstrap their way from the "I"-frame to the "we"-frame. But the perceived unfairness is self-regarding in the "I"-frame – unsurprisingly. What Menelaös and Row initially object to is the unfairness of the asymmetric outcome where they pay the cost and someone else takes the benefit. The process of reasoning

---

[18] See Broome 1991b, p. 104. I am confident, however, that Broome would think that there is a rational requirement of indifference when one knows that a single outcome has been framed in two different ways. See, for example, his discussion of putative counterexamples to transitivity principles at pp. 103–106 of Broome 1991b.

from the "I"-frame to the "we"-frame is one of moving from the narrow perspective in which they disvalue self-regarding unfairness initially to the broader perspective in which they come to disvalue even unfairness that benefits them and, as a consequence, to valuing a fair outcome positively. If this is right, then the fairness of the (*Dig Snow, Dig Snow*) outcome would not be a salient factor in the "I"-frame, which means that it could indeed serve as a reason-giving justifier within the "we"-frame.

You may not be convinced by this. Surely, you might say, rationality cannot permit the perceived fairness of an outcome to come in and out of focus. Even if I am right that the process of moving from the "I"-frame to the "we"-frame involves coming to see the fairness of the outcome where both players dig snow (or pull back from a potential clash of chariots when the path narrows), once someone has started to see the outcome as fair they can't and shouldn't stop seeing it that way. Once a player starts to view a social interaction from the "we"-frame, then from the perspective of rationality that new way of looking at things should *replace* her former way of looking at it, rather than provide an alternative and complementary perspective? So, perceived fairness can't be a justifier in the "we"-frame and not in the "I"-frame. Once it's in the frame (as it were), then rationality requires it to stay there.

This objection brings us back to some deep issues that have already come up in previous chapters and that we will look at in more detail in the next chapter. One recurring theme of this book is that it is a fundamental dimension of rational agency and rational decision-making that agents and decision-makers be able to hold in their minds, and move between, multiple ways of framing situations and outcomes. For the moment, let me make two points. The first is that the machinery of circumspect team reasoning depends upon an agent being able to evaluate the pay-off table from the "I"-frame and the "we"-frame simultaneously – because the basic idea is to compare the expected pay-off for the team, when it is not certain that the other players will apply team reasoning, to the expected pay-off when all play their "I"-frame best response strategy. And so, in order to apply circumspect team reasoning, the agent must be able, as it were, to compartmentalize the justifiers in the "we"-frame (and, for that matter, the justifiers in the "I"-frame), adopting a vantage-point independent of both frames.

Being able to apply circumspect reasoning is important, because of all the ways that things can go wrong with unqualified team reasoning. Team reasoners leave themselves open to exploitation, because team reasoning only works if other players play their parts in the optimal team strategy-profile. In many cases (such as a standard Prisoner's Dilemma) the worst outcome for a team reasoner occurs when she plays her part while the other player opts for best response reasoning. Circumspect team reasoning gives agents a way to incorporate this unwelcome possibility in their deliberations.

So much the worse for circumspect team reasoning, you might say. But in fact, there is much more at stake here than a formal model of team reasoning. Circumspect team reasoning is still team reasoning. That is to say, what matters for the circumspect team reasoner is still the pay-off for the group. And team reasoning is not an unqualified good thing. Many of the examples we have been looking at are ones where the team reasoning option seems less selfish and more appealing than best response reasoning. But that is itself a framing effect. Team reasoning can lead to highly questionable outcomes. This is unsurprising, since team reasoning can be the deliberative component of groupthink. Groupthink is often less than ideal even in mundane contexts – think of how the desire for consensus and to conform to (perceived) institutional culture can drive out good decision-making in companies, universities, and other large organizations. On a larger scale it can lead to truly catastrophic results. Recent political history presents some classic examples.[19]

You might think that team reasoning only goes astray when it is driven by values that are perverted in some way, as in a team reasoning genocidal mob. But that too would be a mistake. Let's look again at fairness. Here is an example of what might well have been fairness-based team reasoning from Homer. In Book 9 of the *Odyssey*, Odysseus tells Alcinous, King of the Phaeacians, what happened after he and his men left the ruins of Troy. In Robert Fagles's translation:

> The wind drove me out of Ilium on to
>   Ismarus,
> the Cicones' stronghold. There I sacked the city,
> killed the men, but as for the wives and plunder,
> that rich haul we dragged away from the place –
> so no one, not on my account,
> would go deprived of his fair share of the spoils.[20]

---

[19] Irving L. Janis's book *Groupthink: Psychological Studies of Policy Decisions and Fiascoes* goes through a number of examples where groupthink allowed US Presidents to make and implement what ended up being very bad policy, including Franklin D. Roosevelt's blindness to the Japanese threat to Pearl Harbor, Kennedy's invasion of the Bay of Pigs, and Nixon's Watergate cover-up.
[20] Homer, *Odyssey* IX, lines 44–49, translated by Robert Fagles (Fagles and Knox 1996).

If one were to attempt a hypothetical reconstruction of the decision-making after the sack of Ismarus, it is not hard to imagine that Odysseus and each of his men had utility functions that jointly converged on an unfair outcome, when best response reasoning was applied in the "I"-frame. It might have been collectively prudent for the men to renounce any claim on the plunder and Ciconian womenfolk, leaving the spoils all to Odysseus. But, reasoning as a team, with the background assumption of a sufficiently high probability that team reasoning applies, they rank the possible distributions by fairness criteria and choose the fairest distribution. (Homer uses the word *isos* to describe the fair outcome, the same word that Aristotle uses in his discussion of justice.)

For all these reasons, then, it is highly desirable to leave a space open for agents to reason their way out of the "we"-frame. And that in turn requires habits of thought and psychological skills that make it possible to hold multiple frames in mind simultaneously. Having quasi-cyclical preferences is almost universally taken as a sign of irrationality. In the appropriate contexts, however, it can be irrational *not* to have quasi-cyclical preferences, because having quasi-cyclical preferences is a sign of openness to the possibility of reasoning one's way out of a particular frame. That openness is a necessary condition of subjecting frames to rational comparison and evaluation.

And with that we come to the topic of the final two chapters – how to reason across frames.

IO

Getting Past No: Discursive Deadlock and the Power of Frames

It is not news that frames and framing play an important role in public discourse. Take party politics, for example. Political consultants use focus groups to work out how their clients' policies can be most beneficially framed (and how their clients' opponents can be framed in the worst possible light). Advertisers and spin doctors then translate those frames into images and slogans, which politicians, lobbyists, and partisan media can then use. This type of framing can be a tool for manipulation – for reinforcing prejudices and creating new ones. It is part of the political dark arts, a way of turning emotions, both positive and negative, into political capital. No doubt, this way of using framing is an important source of the widespread view that being subject to framing effects is a paradigm of irrationality.

This book has explored a very different side to framing. Instead of thinking of framing as either a tool for manipulation or as the paradigm example of a cognitive failing, I have suggested that framing can be a powerful tool for rational decision-makers. There are plenty of cases where it is irrational to be influenced by how an action or an outcome is framed. It certainly can often be irrational to be subject to a framing effect. But not always. I have proposed various examples where it can be rational to value actions or outcomes differently depending on how they are framed. Building on those examples I developed tools for thinking about frame-sensitivity and explained why I think they count as instances of rational decision-making.

In the final two chapters, in place of a simple summary of the main themes from earlier chapters, I will draw the principal threads of the argument together by showing how they can be applied to some of the complexities of contemporary public discourse. The topic is timely and important. Most commentators are agreed that the caliber and level of public discourse is currently at, or close to, an all-time low, with political partisanship replacing rational debate amid unprecedented levels of distrust and acrimony. It seems to be only mild hyperbole to talk of a crisis of democratic decision-making in both the United States and Great Britain, to take the countries I am most familiar with. So, it is pressing to explore whether the discussion of framing in this book can help us to understand why we are where we are. And whether this discussion yields any concrete suggestions about how to deal with, and perhaps remedy, the current situation.

To anticipate, it will turn out (unsurprisingly) that the power of frames is both part of the problem and part of the solution. I explore both by extending the discussions of framing and rationality in previous chapters to sketch a picture of what I call a model, frame-dependent reasoner. The model reasoner that I will depict is different in important respects from the archetypal rational decision-maker of classical decision theory. Most importantly, the model reasoner is able to engage rationally in frame-sensitive reasoning – to reason in other words, not just within a given frame, but also across frames. Since, I will suggest, some of the most intractable topics in contemporary public discourse are best viewed in terms of conflicts of frames, thinking about what a model, frame-sensitive reasoner would look like is an important counterpoint to the status quo, and suggests a blueprint for moving beyond it.

Some of the issues here are primarily theoretical. How might a model, frame-sensitive reasoner go about tackling problems that involve clashes of frames? What could we expect civil discourse to be like in a community of frame-dependent reasoners? But at the same time, there are important practical questions. It's plain that model frame-sensitive reasoning is honored more in the breach than in the observance. Why is this? Why are people so bad at dealing with clashes of frames? There must be obstacles and roadblocks standing in the way of frame-dependent reasoning. But what are they? And how can they be removed or alleviated?

The Limits of Frame-Neutrality

Almost all models of practical reasoning and rational decision-making hold that it is a sign of irrationality to allow the value one assigns to an action or outcome (or the preferences one has over actions and outcomes) to be influenced by how those actions and outcomes are framed. We explored this feature of classical decision theory in Chapter 4. Kenneth Arrow calls it *extensionality*. Daniel Kahneman and Amos Tversky term it *invariance*. I prefer the less technical *Juliet's principle*.

The first thing to be said about a model frame-dependent reasoner is that she must begin from a recognition that it is simply a mistake to take this type of frame-neutrality as a universal requirement of rationality. The examples in earlier chapters will hopefully have convinced you that there are many cases where it can be rational to have what I termed *quasi-cyclical preferences*. These occur when an agent or decision-maker prefers A to B and B to C, in the full knowledge that A and C are different ways of formulating the same outcome or action.

The case against Juliet's principle has been made through examples. And in a sense that is all that is needed. Nothing can be a universal rule if it has systematic exceptions. But still, Juliet's principle does hold much of the time. Not least, it holds of itself. It would be irrational to accept the principle of extensionality, while rejecting the principle of invariance. The same holds for many of the experimentally derived framing effects that we reviewed in Chapter 1 (the Asian disease paradigm, for example, or the ground beef that can be equivalently described as 25 percent lean or 75 percent fat).

So, can we say anything concrete about when Juliet's principle holds and when it does not hold? Is there a principled way of identifying the domain of frame-dependent reasoning and distinguishing it from the cases where being susceptible to framing effects does indeed count as irrational? A model frame-sensitive reasoner needs some principled way of distinguishing between these two domains, so that she can know when to engage frame-dependent reasoning, and when it is rationally appropriate to have quasi-cyclical preferences.

I am certain that the project of trying to give necessary and sufficient conditions is going to be just as unsuccessful for Juliet's principle as it is elsewhere. But still, there are certain indicators and clues to which a model frame-dependent reasoner needs to be sensitive.

I pointed out one important feature of the classical framing effect experiments in earlier chapters. Experimental subjects tend not to stick with their initial judgments when the framing effect is pointed out to them. Someone in the grip of the lean/fat framing effect might have quasi-cyclical preferences. She might, for example, prefer ground beef that is 25 percent lean to chicken breast, while preferring chicken breast to ground beef that is 75 percent fat. But once she realizes that any ground beef that is 25 percent lean is by that very fact 75 percent fat, then she will revise her quasi-cyclical preferences and take an unequivocal stand on the relative merits of chicken breast and this particular grade of ground beef. The simplest explanation is that such an agent recognizes the irrationality of her preferences and makes the necessary adjustments to restore rationality.

But Agamemnon-type cases are not like that at all. Agamemnon has quasi-cyclical preferences, despite being perfectly well aware that two of the outcomes are different framings of a single event. He does not revise his preferences – and even making a decision might not have removed his quasi-cyclical preferences (because they would still be reflected in subsequent regret and similar retrospective emotions). And this is not a peculiarity of his psychology, I argued. It reflects the fact that, in the terminology of Chapter 6, value is *ultra-intensional*, where that means that it is not a requirement of rationality that subjects assign the same value to different framings of a single event or action, even when they know that that is what they are dealing with. Agamemnon is rationally quasi-inconsistent, one might say. But still, this does not really solve our problem. When is it rationally permissible to be quasi-inconsistent?

To tackle this question let me start with two other ideas from Chapter 6. The first is that emotional engagement can be itself frame-dependent. Different ways of framing an outcome or course of action can bring different emotions into play. The very same military operation, for example, might be framed as an act of glorious self-sacrifice, or as a suicide mission. Each frame will bring a different set of emotions into play, and a decision-maker may well find himself oscillating between those two different emotional perspectives. Now, and this is the second idea, it is plausible that how one values an outcome or an action is a function of one's emotional engagement with it. Valuations have many sources, but typically they are informed by emotions, if not driven by them.

These points about how values and emotions are linked should not be controversial as claims about human decision-making. But we can build up from them to more substantive claims about rationality. In brief, I have argued throughout this book that it can be rationally permissible for how one values an outcome or scenario to be driven by how one responds to it emotionally. And, moreover, if one has rationally permissible valuations, then the resulting preferences are rationally permissible. If this is all correct, then what we need to consider is when it is rationally permissible to value the same outcome or action differently as a function of different emotional perspectives.

My proposal is that this holds when an action or outcome is sufficiently complex that no single frame-dependent, emotional perspective can be fully adequate to it. That in turn is likely to hold when viewing actions or outcomes through a single frame will inevitably leave out or underplay some dimensions potentially important to decision-making. So, for example, viewing issues of gun control in the United States solely through the lens of the right to keep and bear arms stated in the Second Amendment (as interpreted by the Supreme Court in the case of *District of Columbia vs. Heller* in 2008) is likely to leave out the concomitant duties, obligations, and restrictions that invariably accompany exercises of individual rights. Likewise, focusing exclusively on those duties, obligations, and rights may lead someone to neglect the framing of gun ownership in terms of individual security because they are concentrating exclusively on collective security.

One sign that a situation, action, or outcome has this level of complexity is that it generates multiple, internally consistent framings that yield conflicting prescriptions. To stick with the guns issue, there is a perfectly coherent world view that frames gun ownership in the United States through the lens of the quite extraordinary rate of gun violence in this country (relative to other countries in the G-8 group of industrialized nations for example). I have considerable sympathy with that view (as presented, for example, by advocacy groups such as the Brady Campaign to Prevent Gun Violence or Every Town for Gun Safety), and with the safety-based prescriptions for gun control that emerge from it. At the same time, however, focusing exclusively on it excludes or downplays some pieces of a highly complex situation. There is an equally coherent world view (associated with the National Rifle Association and the Second Amendment Foundation, most prominently) that frames the issue in terms of rights (the individual's rights to bear arms, and to defend oneself and one's family, for example) and arrives at a policy position that opposes all (or almost all) of the prescriptions of the groups working within the safety frame.

This is a good example of two frames that are incompatible in several dimensions. They are evaluatively and emotionally incompatible, because each typically engages different emotional responses and associated valuations. And they are prescriptively incompatible, because their associated policy recommendations cannot be simultaneously implemented. But I claim that, in a very important sense, they are not actually inconsistent. That is to say, someone can accept both frames and be conflicted, without being inconsistent (in what I will argue is the relevant sense of inconsistency). Certainly, there are individual propositions on which proponents of the different frames disagree. They might disagree, for example, on how to explain the apparent patterns in mass shooting revealed by investigations such as that carried out by the *Mother Jones* website.[1] Indeed, they might disagree about how to define a mass shooting, since there is no fixed definition in use (one issue of contention is whether to require a minimum number of deaths, usually four, or whether non-fatal gunshot wounds should be counted). But thinking about guns through the safety frame does not immediately rule out thinking about them through the frame of an individual's rights. The two frames can be consistent, despite being evaluatively, emotionally, and prescriptively incompatible. And ultimately that is because each frame reflects one dimension of a complex and multifaceted social problem (and corresponding decision problems), with neither of them able to do complete justice to the problem. (More soon on what I call *strict inconsistency*.)

So, when the overarching context for a given decision problem is sufficiently complex and multifaceted to generate conflicting and incompatible evaluations and prescriptions, what a model, frame-sensitive reasoner will do in such situations is go behind the evaluations and prescriptions to diagnose the conflict. More often than not, I claim, such conflicts can ultimately be traced to clashes of frames. Let's look at these conflicts and their sources in more detail.

Discursive Deadlock

We run into the limits of frame-neutrality (I claim) when we find ourselves in decision problems that are so complex and multifaceted that it is rationally permissible to view them in very different ways, engaging different types of emotional response, even though the result may be fundamental clashes in values and proposed resolutions. So far in this book I have focused primarily on *intrapersonal* cases – on cases where complex issues and decision problems are framed in multiple ways by a single individual. But there is an important extension to the *interpersonal* case, where we find evaluative and prescriptive conflicts between individuals and/or groups.

These evaluative and prescriptive conflicts typically involve what I call *discursive deadlock*. The defining feature of discursive deadlock is that standard tools for dispute resolution and collective decision-making are

[1] See the database at www.motherjones.com/politics/2012/07/mass-shootings-map/.

ineffective in securing agreement. Discursive deadlock is the interpersonal equivalent of the dilemmas and conflicts we have explored in earlier chapters. We are living in times where this type of deadlock is particularly widespread. It has become a platitude for contemporary political and social commentators to observe partisan deadlock and polarization on what are euphemistically called "values issues." Few are optimistic about the prospects for bridging the deadlock through reasoned discussion and rational argument.

Certainly, the evidence supports such pessimism, but there are some optimists, including groups such as the National Institute for Civil Discourse (NICD), founded after the mass shooting in Tucson, Arizona in May 2011 that killed six people and wounded thirteen others, including former Congresswoman Gabrielle Giffords. The NICD promotes a range of initiatives intended to ensure that "people with different values and political preferences can discuss their differences in a civil and productive manner."[2]

It is hard to take issue with initiatives designed to increase civility in public discourse, which is surely a commendable ideal. However, only so much can be achieved by taking personal pledges to be civil and by engaging in community conversations, laudable though these things are. The problem is not with the goal of increasing civility. The problem is with the diagnosis of the problem. It is true that contemporary public discourse displays unprecedented levels of incivility. A few years ago, it would have been hard to imagine a sitting President (or any other public figure) leading chants at a rally for opponents to be locked up. But incivility is surely more a symptom of the problem, than a cause. We need to dig deeper for a satisfying diagnosis.

One way of thinking about discursive deadlock is suggested by the widespread use of the language of values in contemporary politics. We have so-called values issues, which are the principal focus of so-called values voters. As a matter of sociological fact, what are typically identified as values issues (abortion, gun control, immigration, for example) are also the issues where discursive deadlock is most acute. And, one might think, this provides a very simple explanation for the deadlock. Values themselves cannot be rationally debated, which is why clashes of values cannot be rationally resolved. This way of thinking about values is a cornerstone of the Humean model of practical reasoning that we have looked at in

---

[2] For more on the NICD mission, inspiration, and ongoing initiatives, see their website at https://nicd.arizona.edu/, from which this quote comes.

earlier chapters. On the Humean picture, practical reasoning can only be about means. We have to start from an end that we take for granted, and we then reason about how best to achieve that end. Transposing to the language of values, we have to take values as given. All we can reason about is how to promote those values in particular contexts or situations.

There is a more nuanced view available here. Instead of the global thesis that reasoning about values is simply impossible, one might hold that some pairs of values are incommensurable. Someone who takes that view thinks that it is impossible to bring those values within a single scale, and, by extension, impossible to compare the actions or outcomes that reflect or express those values.[3] A version of this view has been developed within moral philosophy in an attempt to elucidate moral dilemmas. The characteristic of a moral dilemma, some have suggested, is that whatever course of action is chosen, there will remain an irreducible moral residue – a source of, as it were, moral regret. Whatever an agent does in a moral dilemma they will fail to do something that is morally required. And this in turn is thought to reflect the fact that moral dilemmas incorporate clashes of incommensurable values.[4] We can apply this way of thinking about intrapersonal moral dilemmas to the interpersonal case of discursive deadlock. This yields the diagnosis that discursive deadlock occurs when different groups espouse values that are incommensurable.

Now, while it is certainly true that discursive deadlock often involves clashes of values, I think that we need to go further to understand fully what is going on. Both of the views just considered think of values as a type of decision-making bedrock. Values are, as it were, where the process of explaining and justifying decisions and actions simply comes to an end. This, I want to suggest, is simply a mistake, because it neglects the role of frames. Once we bring frames into play, we both gain a richer perspective on discursive deadlock, and also see new possibilities for moving beyond deadlock.

A preliminary observation: Values often apply to things framed in a certain way. Values, emotions, and frames all interact in complex ways and we have seen numerous examples throughout this book of how this works and how it can lead to a single outcome or action being

---

[3] We explored themes of incommensurability in the different context of the relation between the "we"-frame and the "I"-frame in Chapter 9.

[4] For influential discussions of incommensurability, hard choices, and moral dilemmas see Wiggins 1978 and the various essays in Chang 1997. The relation between commensurability and reasoning about ends is pursued in Richardson 1994.

valued in different ways depending on the particular framing in play. Most of the examples we have looked at are intrapersonal, but the same point applies in the interpersonal case. So, we need to be thinking of discursive deadlock within a more complex framework. It over-simplifies and distorts the situation to describe it simply in terms of clashes of values. A decision-maker might see a particular outcome (say, unrest-ricted gun ownership) as exemplifying a given value (say, freedom) when framed one way, but not when framed another way (say, in terms of personal safety). Likewise, a group may fail to see an action as exemplify-ing a value that it holds dear as a function of how it is framed. At a minimum, therefore, we need to take into account that values are importantly frame-relative, which means that in order properly to char-acterize value-based reasoning we need to think of frame-relative values (values as applied under particular framings). By extension, intrapersonal conflicts and interpersonal discursive deadlock involve clashes of frame-dependent values, rather than simply clashes of values.

Still, that said, one might think that whenever there is a clash of frame-relative values, there must be a clash of values – or, in other words, that there cannot be a clash of frame-relative values unless there are (at least) two conflicting values. That would be a mistake, however. There can be deep and apparently irreconcilable conflicts between frame-relative values, even when there is a single value in play. For a nice example, consider the flat rate tax introduced by Margaret Thatcher in Scotland in 1989 and in England and Wales in 1990. In brief, Thatcher's idea was to replace the existing and variable property tax used to fund local govern-ment (the so-called rates system, based on the nominal rental value of a property) with a fixed tax charged to each adult resident.

The introduction of this tax was surely one of the most divisive political events in the United Kingdom in the last fifty years. It provoked a wave of public protest, including the famous Can't Pay! Won't Pay! campaign as well as widespread rioting, and bore much of the responsibility for Thatcher's resignation in November 1990 as Prime Minister and as Leader of the Conservative Party. As anyone who was present in the United Kingdom at the time will remember, this was a prime example of discursive deadlock. What brought about the demise of the flat rate tax and its replacement by the Council Tax was simply the weight of opposi-tion to it. Supporters of the flat rate tax were not brought by rational debate to see the error of their ways (if indeed they were in error). But nor was the opposition universal. The flat rate tax had, and continues to have, strong support in certain quarters.

One very interesting feature of the conflict over the flat rate tax is that it reflected two very different ways of framing the tax, each of which is encapsulated in a simple label. The official term for the tax was the Community Charge. This terminology reflected a framing on which local authority taxes are really charges to cover local services. In other words, they are user charges, similar to the charges that a homeowner in a particular development or subdivision might incur for shared services such as snow-clearing or maintenance of common green spaces. So, one consequence of this framing is that it starts to seem plausible that the charges be paid by all those who stand to benefit from local government services. And since pretty much everyone benefits in the community from at least some local government services (road maintenance and refuse collection, for example), it looks, on this framing, as if local authority taxes should be paid by all adults. One of the statistics that featured in early government discussions of the Community Charge was that, while there were 35 million people on the electoral roll in England, only 12 million were actually paying property-based rates.[5]

Moreover, for supporters of the Community Charge, it is not just that user charges for services should be paid by all beneficiaries of those services, it also follows that when a tax is a user charge, its rate should be fixed by the benefits that the tax-payer receives. In the case of local government, the benefits of the services provided are shared equally (just as all the residents in the subdivision benefit from having the sidewalks cleared of snow) – at least in the sense that everyone is *potentially* a beneficiary. And so, it seemed appropriate to those who framed local authority taxation as a user charge that all the recipients of the services should be charged an equal amount (with some relief built in for those having difficulty paying). Local authority services are provided equally to each member of the community and so each member of the community should contribute equally. That was an important part of the framing adopted and promoted by supporters of the flat rate tax, reflected in its official name, the Community Charge.

Opponents of the tax, in contrast, adopted a completely different framing, reflected in an alternative label. The Community Charge was more often known as the Poll Tax. This label echoed (no doubt at some point deliberately) the notorious tax imposed by John of Gaunt in 1377, requiring every non-beggar over the age of 14 to pay a groat (4 pence) to the Crown to help finance an ongoing war against France. John of Gaunt's

[5] For more details on the background to the Community Charge see Letwin 1993.

tax had nothing to do with local government and, unsurprisingly, opponents of the tax focused little if at all on the role of the tax in financing local government. Instead, their framing highlighted the regressive nature of the flat rate tax (the very feature that, in its earliest incarnation, had been a prominent cause of the Peasant's Revolt in 1381). For opponents of the Community Charge, it was a poll tax that deliberately and indiscriminately transferred the burden of paying for local services from well-off property-owners to the general population, including those least able to pay. Hence the Can't Pay! Won't Pay! rallying cry of the opposition.

The battle, then, was between proponents of the Community Charge and opponents of the Poll Tax, and the battle lines were drawn around two very different ways of framing the flat rate tax. What I want to emphasize, however, is that both frames were really driven by a single value. This is the value of fairness. At the 1987 Conservative Party conference, the Secretary of State for the Environment Nicholas Ridley introduced the Community Charge proposal with the statement: "People know that rates are unfair. We promised them a fair system and we shall not disappoint them."[6] The Community Charge framing highlights the perceived fairness of charging equally for equal benefits. Framing the tax as a charge for services makes salient one dimension of fairness – the idea of fairness as equality, with a fair treatment being an equal treatment. In contrast, the Poll Tax framing highlights the perceived unfairness of not tying tax rates to the capacity to pay. Framing the tax this way foregrounds a completely different dimension of fairness. This is the idea of fairness as equity, which in this context might seem to demand that taxes be proportional to overall wealth. So, this example illustrates how framings can be more fundamental than values, because the basic value of fairness is applied in different ways as a function of how the situation is framed.

Circling back to the main theme, the best clue alerting our model practical reasoner to the need for frame-sensitive reasoning is that she is working within a decision space sufficiently complex to generate some kind of decision-making or moral dilemma (in an intrapersonal context) or some kind of discursive deadlock (in an interpersonal context). The basic phenomena of dilemma and deadlock are familiar. From the perspective of demarcating the scope of frame-sensitive reasoning, it is the element of conflict that is important. Apparently irreducible conflict is important because it is a sign of the complexity of the decision situation

---

[6] Quoted in Letwin 1993, p. 227.

and decision problem. Dilemma and deadlock are often taken to be at bottom conflicts of values and to reflect forms of incommensurability and incomparability of values. This is at best only part of the story, however. Values are not basic. Applying values can be frame-relative, so that different ways of framing a given outcome or action can bring different values into play. And we have just seen how different framings can make salient different aspects of a single value – fairness as equality vs. fairness as equity, for example. So, even from a purely diagnostic and descriptive perspective, it makes sense to move away from simply talking about values to talking about frame-relative values.

In fact, though, broadening the discussion to incorporate the complex interplay between frames and values has a further and very significant benefit. When decision-making dilemmas are discussed in terms of clashes of incommensurable values, the clear message is one of irresolvable conflict. The basic idea of incommensurability is that it is impossible to have a rational preference for something that enshrines or reflects one value over something else that reflects a different (and putatively incommensurable) value. So, from the perspective of rationality, there is simply nothing to be done except find some non-rational way of solving the problem. The same holds when interpersonal discursive deadlock is understood as involving an irreducible clash of values. This way of describing the situation yields no clues as to how the deadlock might be broken.

As so-called moral dilemmas are standardly discussed by philosophers, they are typically presented in terms of a form of paralysis of action.[7] Agents in the grip of a moral dilemma are supposed to be unable to act, not because they are unable to move from thought to action (like Hamlet "sicklied o'er with the pale cast of thought"), but rather because they cannot even get started on the process of practical reasoning. Value incommensurability is a standard diagnosis. Practical reasoning cannot get started because there is no overarching framework within which conflicting values can be reconciled and so (in a more modern idiom) no possibility of deriving a preference ordering over the available actions. In the cases we have discussed, though, this misrepresents the situation. The problem is that agents have too many preference orderings, not that they

---

[7] I refer to so-called moral dilemmas because I am persuaded by Bernard Williams that the modern concept of morality, and hence of a moral dilemma, is a relatively recent invention (and, although Williams did not say this, no doubt culturally circumscribed as well). Agamemnon was certainly confronted with a dilemma, but to call it a moral dilemma is anachronistic and misleading. See Williams 1985.

cannot get started. They have multiple, frame-relative preference orderings, and the dilemma comes from not being able to narrow in on a single frame.

This is where frame-sensitive reasoning comes into the picture. For one thing, frames are more malleable than values. This holds intrapersonally. For many people it is almost impossible to change the values that different ways of looking bring into play. Frames can be easier to change – which is why framing can play such an important role in marketing and propaganda. Propaganda typically does not *create* values. Rather it *exploits* values by framing things in ways designed to bring already existing values into play. Because of that malleability it can be easier for me to reason about frames than it is to reason directly about values. It also holds interpersonally. I am probably not going to be able to change your values, but I may be able to change how you view a situation. And it will most likely be easier for me to think my way into your framing of the situation than it will be for me to think myself into a value that I completely fail to share. This can allow a model, frame-sensitive reasoner to exploit this malleability and flexibility to make headway on what might initially seem to be intractable conflicts. In the following I will focus mainly on the interpersonal case.

Rationality, Consistency, and Facts

One sign that frame-sensitive reasoning is needed in a particular decision problem is that the problem admits multiple framings. Each of these framings is internally coherent but they collectively yield different and often incompatible evaluations and prescriptions. But still, as I have emphasized, these multiple framings need not be inconsistent with each other, on the way that I propose to think about inconsistency.

I understand inconsistency extremely narrowly. To avoid confusion, let's call it *strict inconsistency*. To be strictly inconsistent is to contradict oneself on a point of fact. It is to assert p and *not-p* for some factual proposition p – in other words, to say, for some factual proposition, that it is both true and that it is false. What is a factual proposition? This is a term of art, which I am defining as follows. A factual proposition is a proposition that is straightforwardly true or false. And I am taking a proposition being straightforwardly true or false in a very commonsensical way. A proposition is straightforwardly true or false when its truth-value can be settled by employing standard methods. In other words, there are standard methods and techniques for determining whether it is true or false.

What counts as a standard method depends upon the context, of course. Sometimes firsthand experience in appropriate conditions is all that is required. So, for example, it is often easy enough to settle an argument about how to get to a particular place by actually going there, or looking at a map. Sometimes one needs additional techniques and appropriate calibration from experts. If the discussion about what the quickest way to get somewhere is, you might ask Google Maps. And, more generally, most people accept that there is a wide range of issues where we should defer to the authority of scientific and other experts.

Of course, there are gray areas that can be profitably discussed (on another occasion), and there are distressingly many people ready and willing to discount the role of experts. But still, it should not be controversial that there are standard methods for determining the truth-value of the proposition that a one-week-old fetus has a heart, or the proposition that there were fewer than n gun deaths in the United States in 2018 (once we have an agreed-upon definition of a gun death). These are factual propositions, clearly different from corresponding non-factual propositions. So, I don't think that it should be controversial that there are no standard methods for determining the truth-value of the proposition that a one-week-old fetus is a person, or the proposition that n gun deaths a year is an acceptable price to pay for the freedom to bear arms.

In any event, factual propositions are what matter for strict inconsistency. To be strictly inconsistent is to say, for some proposition where there are standard methods for determining whether it is true or false, that it is true and that it is false. So, for example, if you were to say that a one-week-old fetus has a heart and that it does not have a heart, you would be strictly inconsistent. However, if you were to say that a one-week-old fetus is a person and simultaneously to deny it is not a person, you would not be being strictly inconsistent, as I am defining it.

We can define a comparable notion of strict contradiction, so that only two factual propositions can be strictly contradictory. If a pro-life activist and a pro-choice activist agree on all factual propositions then they are not strictly contradicting each other, I claim. They disagree, of course, on many non-factual propositions, but they are not inconsistent. They might disagree, for example, on whether a one-week-old fetus is a person, but that would not be an example of strict contradiction. So, strict contradiction is a narrower notion than logical contradiction. There are logical contradictions that are not strict contradictions.

The same holds in the intrapersonal case. I claim that it is perfectly possible for me to think myself into a pro-life mindset and a pro-choice mindset simultaneously without strictly contradicting myself. If I were to do that, I would have multiple internal conflicts, both evaluative and prescriptive. And I may well have contradictory beliefs in a broader sense – by simultaneously believing, for example, that abortion is always wrong (when I am considering it through one frame) and also believing that it is not the case that abortion is always wrong (when I am considering the matter through a different frame). In that situation I would be logically inconsistent, even though not strictly inconsistent.

Do not read too much into this notion of a factual proposition. A factual proposition is one whose truth or falsity can be determined by standard techniques. But that does not mean that non-factual propositions *cannot* be true or false – that they are somehow meaningless, or simply ways of expressing one's approval or disapproval. Such views were suggested by the Logical Positivist philosophers in the first half of the twentieth century, because they thought that only propositions whose truth or falsity can be determined by standard techniques can be meaningful. This is the view known as verificationism. Logical positivism was very influential at the time, but its day has passed and very few philosophers nowadays would place such strict conditions on what it is for a proposition to be meaningful.

I am completely open to the idea that there are non-factual propositions with determinate truth-values. So, for example, I am happy to accept that there might be a fact of the matter about whether a one-week-old fetus is a person. A non-factual proposition can be true (by corresponding to the facts) or false (by failing to correspond to the facts). My point is just that there is a line between those propositions where we have (more or less) agreed-upon standard techniques for determining their truth-value, and those propositions where we do not. The truth-values of factual propositions are (relatively) easily accessible, whereas the truth-values of non-factual propositions are not.

The point of using the notion of a factual proposition to distinguish between strict inconsistency and logical inconsistency (and, correspondingly, between strict contradiction and logical contradiction) is that it defines a starting point for the model, frame-sensitive reasoner.

The most basic requirement of rationality on a model, frame-sensitive reasoner is that she not be strictly inconsistent – where this is understood to require, at a minimum, that she not accept any strict contradictions.

So, there can be no factual proposition p such that she accepts both p and *not-p*.

This is a weaker requirement than rationality is often taken to demand. So, for example, John Broome's book *Rationality through Reasoning* suggests that rational reasoners have to respect two basic consistency requirements, which he formulates as follows (Broome 2013, p. 155):

No contradictory beliefs
Rationality requires of N that N does not believe at time t that p and at t that *not-p*.

No contradictions
Rationality requires of N that N does not believe at time t that p and *not-p*.

These are actually distinct. I can fail to satisfy the first principle while still respecting the second. I believe both p and *not-p* for some proposition p, but not actually realize that that is what I am doing. And so I do not form the explicitly contradictory belief: p and *not-p*. This might hold if I am unaware that I have one or other of the beliefs at time t. In that case, I would fall foul of No Contradictory Beliefs, but not of No Contradictions.

Most philosophers would agree with Broome that these are minimal requirements of rationality.[8] On that view, if I believe that a one-week-old fetus is a person and that a one-week-old fetus is not a person then I am just as irrational as if I were to believe that a one-week-old fetus has a heart and that it does not have a heart. I do not accept this, however.

Broome's No Contradictory Belief principle cannot be a requirement of rationality, precisely because it is incompatible with frame-sensitive reasoning. In my reconstruction, Agamemnon at Aulis believed both the proposition *I must kill Iphigenia* and its negation *It is not the case that I must kill Iphigenia*. Likewise for Macbeth at Glamis Castle, who I claim believed the same two propositions of Duncan. Since, as I have argued, Agamemnon and Duncan were both rational in holding those

---

[8] There are holdouts, however. Some philosophers think that it is so common for people to have contradictory pairs of beliefs that counting doing so as irrational is unrealistic and imposes unreasonable demands upon a rational agent. Gilbert Harman falls into this camp – see Harman 1986. Philosophers inclined to the view known as dialetheism, in contrast, think that some contradictions (such as the Liar sentence, which says of itself that it is false) are actually true, and so proscribing belief in contradictions cannot be a universal requirement of rationality. See the essays in Priest, Beall, and Armour-Garb 2004. As will become clear from the following, I have some sympathy with the first group, but none with the second.

contradictory pairs of beliefs, No Contradictory Belief cannot be a general requirement of rationality.

Neither Macbeth not Agamemnon were dealing with what I am terming factual propositions. Propositions such as *I must kill Iphigenia* are great examples of non-factual propositions. As it happens, they are what philosophers call *deontic* propositions – propositions that have to do with requirements, obligations, permissions, and so forth.[9] There is a branch of logic devoted to the logical relationships between deontic propositions. It is widely accepted, however, that there are no standard techniques for determining in general whether deontic propositions such as this one are true or false.[10]

Given this, I propose restricting the principle that Broome calls No Contradictory Belief to factual propositions. It is not irrational to have contradictory beliefs *if those beliefs are non-factual*. On the other hand, I am prepared to accept that it is a fundamental requirement of rationality that a thinker should not explicitly believe a contradiction. Macbeth and Agamemnon have contradictory pairs of beliefs, but they do not explicitly believe the corresponding contradictions. They have contradictory beliefs, but are perfectly well aware that only one can be true. That's why they are conflicted.

So, that yields the following two basic requirements on a model frame-sensitive reasoner.

No contradictory beliefs (factual)
For any factual proposition p, rationality requires a model frame-sensitive reasoner not to believe at t that p and also to believe at the same time that *not-p*.

No contradictions
For any proposition p, factual or otherwise, rationality requires a model frame-sensitive reasoner not to believe at t that *p and not-p*.

You may wonder whether these really count as two different requirements. After all, if I believe that p and I also believe that *not-p*, does that

---

[9] Here is an example of the sort of logical relationship that might be captured in a deontic logic: If it is not obligatory for you to eat fish, then you are permitted not to eat fish. That seems reasonable enough.

[10] Actually, some deontic propositions will count as factual propositions, particularly those operating within very circumscribed boundaries. Consider, for example: *The law requires me to stop at a flashing red light*. This is a deontic proposition whose truth (in the United States) can be established by consulting the relevant part of the legal code. But unrestricted statements of obligation are generally (and surely correctly) held to be different. They may be truth-apt, but not in the same way as what I am calling factual propositions.

not rationally commit me to believing the explicit contradiction *p and not-p*? Well perhaps – but only if it is a general requirement of rationality that if I believe *p* and I believe *q* then I must believe their conjunction (i.e. *p and q*). This is what is called the requirement that beliefs be *closed under conjunction*. As it happens, though, there are good reasons not to accept that as a requirement of rationality.[11]

From an intrapersonal point of view, therefore, model frame-sensitive reasoners need to begin by ensuring that they do not believe either any explicit contradiction or any contradictory pairs of factual propositions. These are the minimal consistency requirements for frame-sensitive reasoning.

Moving beyond pure consistency, we should also mention the No False Belief requirement discussed in Chapter 6 and eloquently stated in a well-known passage from David Hume:

> In short, a passion must be accompany'd with some false judgment, in order to its being unreasonable; and even then 'tis not the passion, properly speaking, which is unreasonable, but the judgment. (Hume 1978 [1739–40], p. 416)

Hume is qualifying his famous claim that desires and other affective states (which he sees as the unique springs of action) cannot be assessed for rationality – what are rational or irrational are the means chosen towards the ends set by those desires and affective states. Desires can be irrational if they are "accompanied by" some false belief or judgment. Hume himself does not give much guidance as to what it takes for a belief to accompany a desire, and since desires are paradigmatically non-cognitive it is not obvious how this is supposed to work (since presumably the beliefs cannot be instrumental ones about how the desire is to be satisfied).

Fortunately, the framing framework gives us a more nuanced perspective on the springs of action. Actions and decisions do not emerge simply from calculations of how to satisfy desires and other "passions." The

---

[11] Take the lottery paradox, for example. Suppose that you are offered a ticket in a 1,000,000-ticket lottery. It would certainly be reasonable for you to believe that that ticket will not win. And the same will hold for any other ticket. Closure under conjunction would lead you (eventually!) to a (very long) proposition, conjoining all the individual propositions saying that each ticket will not win. Since you also believe that it is a fair lottery you believe that some ticket will win. By closure again, you are rationally committed to combining that belief with the long proposition that says, in effect, that no ticket will win. Hence the paradox – which disappears if the relevant closure principle is not accepted. Henry Kyburg was the first philosopher to press the lottery paradox as a counterexample to closure under conjunction (which he termed *agglomeration*). See Kyburg 1961 for the original discussion and Douven 2013 for a literature review on the lottery and related paradoxes, such as the preface paradox, which depends upon similar closure principles.

drivers instead are values and emotions that are modulated by frames. Framing a particular action or outcome often involves characterizing it (or its context) in certain ways. This process can involve judgments. Sometimes these judgments are explicit. Sometimes they are implicit. Moreover, as before, they can involve factual or non-factual propositions.

In line with earlier discussion of consistency, I think that we need to reject the idea that there is a universal No False Belief requirement. As I have said, it is perfectly possible for non-factual propositions to be true or false. And so, it might be false that one-week-old fetuses are persons. Or it might be true. Whichever one it is, one side of the abortion debate is likely to have a false belief. Does that mean that all the people on that side of the debate are irrational? It certainly would if there were a universal No False Belief requirement. But I think that would be unreasonable. If there are no generally accepted methods for determining truth or falsity, then it seems unfair to hold people accountable for not getting it right.

So, we need to have a narrower No False Belief requirement for frame-sensitive reasoning. What I propose is the requirement that frames not be grounded in false factual propositions. It is a simple matter of fact that one-week-old fetuses do not have a heart. Therefore, it is irrational to frame abortion in any way that presupposes or assumes that one-week-old fetuses have a heart.

This requirement applies both to explicit beliefs and implicit ones. A model frame-sensitive reasoner needs not simply to survey and verify the beliefs that she holds explicitly (the ones that she would be prepared to appeal to in an argument, for example), but also to explore the concealed presuppositions of how she is framing the outcome or action. Hence:

No false beliefs (factual)
Rationality requires a model frame-sensitive reasoner not to believe, implicitly or explicitly, any false <u>factual</u> propositions.

As before, the requirement is confined to factual propositions. Moreover, the definition of a factual proposition needs to be made relative to the reasoner's intellectual and cultural context. Something might count as a factual proposition in one context, but not in another. Take prophecies, for example. In the modern world we do not have generally agreed-upon techniques for determining the truth-value of prophecies, and so prophetic propositions do not count as factual. For Agamemnon and Macbeth, in contrast, prophecies were factual propositions. Thinkers count as rational or irrational relative to what were (or are) factual propositions for them – not by what counts as a factual proposition for us.[12]

In sum, therefore, I propose the following three basic rationality requirements on frame-sensitive reasoning:

No contradictory beliefs (factual)

For any factual proposition p, rationality requires a model frame-sensitive reasoner not to believe at t that p and also to believe at the same time that *not-p*.

No contradictions

For any proposition p, factual or otherwise, rationality requires a model frame-sensitive reasoner not to believe at t that p *and not-p*.

No false beliefs (factual)

Rationality requires a model frame-sensitive reasoner not to believe, implicitly or explicitly, any false <u>factual</u> propositions.

The crucial difference from standard ways of thinking about rationality is that the first and the last are relativized to factual propositions. They apply only to propositions where there are generally accepted techniques for establishing whether they are true or false.

Applying the Rationality Requirements

But there is more to rationality than being consistent and avoiding false beliefs. Back in Chapter 6 I identified a rationality requirement of due diligence. Here it is again, reformulated to match the other requirements.

Due diligence requirement

In setting up a decision problem, a model frame-sensitive reasoner needs to be appropriately sensitive to as many potential consequences of the different courses of action available to them as possible.

---

[12] Plainly, everything depends on what counts as a context. An extraordinarily large number of evangelical Christians in the United States appear to believe on the basis of biblical prophecy that the world will end with a Rapture, during which the souls of the saved will be taken up to heaven. Is this a factual proposition for them, given that evangelicals often live and worship in communities where the reliability of biblical prophecy is not seriously questioned? I say not – because the broader intellectual context, accessible to everyone whether they like it or not, includes an educational system and technologically ordered society where prophecy is not taken seriously as a source of reliable information about the future.

Applying the due diligence requirement in appropriately complex decision problems will lead the model frame-sensitive reasoner to be sensitive to multiple ways of framing outcomes and options. What does "sensitive to" mean? Well, the best way to be sensitive to a new or different frame is to try to think oneself into it. Let's look at an example.

Suppose that I am trying to make my mind up on a complicated and emotive issue, such as whether to support a political candidate whose views are broadly aligned with mine, except on the issue of the pledge of allegiance. He believes, while I do not, that children should have the opportunity to pledge allegiance to the flag of the United States every morning at the start of the school day.[13] Underlying the dispute is our framing the pledge in different ways. For him it is an expression of patriotism and a reverence for the values that he thinks underpin the American Constitution and the American way of life. In contrast, I, like many people who grew up in Europe, have an inherent distrust of flags, which I tend to frame from a historical perspective. Hitler, Mussolini, and Franco all came wrapped up in flags and the dominant image of a flag to my mind is of hundreds of thousands of people saluting the swastika at the Nuremburg rallies. How am I to proceed here?

The default option, of course, is simply to stay within my current framing of the issue. I have a strong preference against any pledges in schools and so all that I have to decide is whether that preference should ultimately be outweighed by the extent of my agreement with the candidate on the issues where we do agree. That would be a standard piece of practical decision-making, considering the trade-offs in order to come to a settled view. I claim, though, that this might be a sufficiently important issue for the due diligence requirement to come into play. If I aspire to being a model frame-sensitive reasoner, and this really is an important issue for me, then due diligence says that I am falling short on a commitment of rationality if I do not try to think myself into the candidate's very different way of framing the issue.

How might I do that? In very general terms, to frame a complicated situation or action is to make some aspect of it particularly salient, while other aspects become more recessive. So, one thing I can do is to try to focus on different aspects of the pledge in a way that will allow me to think

---

[13] It has been settled law in the United States since the Supreme Court decision in *West Virginia Board of Education vs. Barnette* in 1943 that making the pledge of allegiance compulsory is incompatible with the First Amendment right to freedom of speech.

my way into his preferences. The last five words of the pledge, for example, are "liberty and justice for all." If I make that the most salient part of the pledge, then I can start to understand why someone might think it important that children should have the opportunity to recite the pledge every morning. But that need not be the end of the story. I might shift frames again, making the "one nation, under God" phrase the most salient part of the pledge, which might then reinforce my initial preference. Taking both frames into account, then, I may end up in the familiar quasi-cyclical pattern. Relative to the "liberty and justice for all" frame, my preference is for children to have the opportunity to pledge allegiance, but relative to the "one nation, under God" my preference is for them not to have it.

The rationality requirements earlier identified place constraints on this frame-switching process, and in particular on how the different frames interface with values. To see this, consider a slightly different scenario, shifting from an intrapersonal context to an interpersonal one. Imagine two people at a meeting of the Parent-Teacher Association split down the middle on the pledge of allegiance. Flag and No Flag are on opposite sides. The heated discussion reveals that each of the two adopts a radically different frame. Both recognize their differences and aspire to resolving them rationally, but as yet have made little progress.

Flag frames the pledge of allegiance in terms of the core values of the US Constitution and the Declaration of Independence – the inalienable rights to life, liberty, and the pursuit of happiness. For children to recite it at the beginning of every school day is to bring those values alive and into their daily life. He sees similarities between the pledge and the core documents of the founding of the republic. His frame emphasizes heritage and continuity. For No Flag, on the other hand, the similarities go the other way. For No Flag what are salient are the discontinuities between the pledge and the founding documents. No Flag foregrounds the secular nature of the US Constitution and the separation of Church and State. In No Flag's framing, the heart of the Constitution is the principle of individual liberty and any ritualistic pledge flies in the face of that principle. This is a classic case of discursive deadlock. Is there room for rational debate between Flag and No Flag?

The No False Belief requirement certainly has traction here. No Flag might well point out that it is a misapprehension that the pledge of allegiance can somehow be traced back to the Founding Fathers (as opposed to having been written in 1892 by a Baptist minister who also happened to be a socialist). That is a straightforward factual proposition. Flag also may well be unaware that the phrase "under God" was added in 1954 in response to a campaign begun by the Catholic fraternal organization the Knights of Columbus. Another straightforward factual proposition.

In addition, there is the further, and more important, question of whether the pledge of allegiance is actually in the spirit of the founding documents. Plausibly, this is a factual proposition as well. We have generally accepted techniques for interpreting texts and for identifying whether and when they are in accord with each other. That, after all, is the foundation of the legal system. It is true, of course, that there is more room for dispute about the proposition "The pledge of allegiance affirms the basic values of the US Constitution" than about the proposition "The pledge of allegiance can be traced back to the Founding Fathers" – but that, to my mind, just means that the generally agreed-upon techniques for resolving such interpretive questions are harder to apply, rather than that they do not exist. One way of appreciating that is to compare the first proposition to "The basic values of the US Constitution are exactly the values we should accept," where I submit that there are no generally accepted techniques for determining whether it is true or false.

One of the techniques for establishing whether one text is in the spirit of an earlier one is to look at what is known about the intentions of the relevant authors.[14] And, as it happens, there is some evidence as to the particular vision of America that Francis Bellamy was seeking to promote. Bellamy, not unusually for his time, was deeply concerned by the increase in immigration from southern and eastern Europe that began in the 1890s. He saw these immigrants, many of whom were Catholic and Jewish, as being from inferior races and less hard-working and morally reliable than

---

[14] Many approaches to literature and literary criticism reject any move to bring authorial intentions into the picture. William Wimsatt and Monroe Beardsley famously denounced what they called the *intentional fallacy* in a jointly authored paper published in 1946. More dramatically, Roland Barthes declared the "death of the author" in a very influential essay of the same name (Barthes 1977). The disentangling of text and author is a cornerstone of deconstructionist approaches to literary criticism. There may be much of value in this approach to literature. However, it is unlikely to help much with the matter at hand, since an ineliminable part of what it means to say that one text is in the spirit of another is that the authors' intentions are appropriately aligned. That is certainly how it is interpreted in prominent approaches to jurisprudence, for example. Alternative approaches, clustered under the label of critical legal studies, have been more successful in law schools than in courts of law. For a thoughtful overview of the dialog between literary theory and legal studies see Norris 1988.

northern European immigrants. Bellamy was one of the editors of *The Illustrated American* magazine, and he contributed an editorial under his own name in August 1897 on the theme of "how far and along what lines immigration to this country should be restricted." There he wrote:

> A democracy like ours cannot afford to throw itself open to the world. Where every man is a law-maker, every dull-witted or fanatical immigrant admitted to our citizenship is a bane to the commonwealth. Where all classes of society merge insensibly into one another every alien immigrant of inferior race may bring corruption to the stock.
>
> There are races, more or less akin to our own, whom we may admit freely and get nothing but advantage from the infusion of their wholesome blood. But there are other races which we cannot assimilate without a lowering of our racial standards, which should be as sacred to us as the sanctity of our homes.[15]

With these statements in view, it is not hard to imagine that Bellamy himself saw the pledge of allegiance as a rallying call for a particular vision of white, Protestant America. That vision will strike many, probably including Flag and No Flag, as at odds with the spirit of the Constitution and the Declaration of Independence. That of course will not settle the question of whether the pledge of allegiance really is in the spirit of the founding documents, but it will certainly sharpen the discussion.

If the conversation between Flag and No Flag has progressed this far, then it is most likely about to transition beyond questions of fact to questions of principle. Applying the No False Belief requirement and the consistency requirements we have been discussing should, in theory, yield a form of factual common ground. But that, in itself, is unlikely to settle the issue between them. It can sometimes be the case that correcting factual errors can shift how someone frames a complex situation, but that is probably the exception rather than the rule. Processes of fact-finding and enforcing consistency are more likely to refine framings than dislodge them. So – how can progress be made?

One theme that has come up at several points in this book is how conflicting frames can express a single value. We saw how this might work with the value of fairness in the clash between the "I"-frame and the "we"-frame in game theory in Chapter 9 – and again with fairness earlier this chapter when we looked at two ways of framing the

---

[15] *The Illustrated American* 22 (August 28, 1897), p. 258. The full text can be accessed through the Hathi Trust digital library at https://babel.hathitrust.org. For more on Francis Bellamy and the history of the pledge of allegiance see Ellis 2005.

Community Charge in the United Kingdom. The point of bringing this up is that values shared across frames can anchor rational debate about framings. As Flag and No Flag go further into the murky history of the pledge of allegiance, the issue really becomes one about how the particular values are understood and how those understandings are applied in this context.

No doubt, Flag and No Flag can agree that they both support the abstract ideals of liberty and justice. They probably both promote religious freedom and believe that the United States is a nation of immigrants. It is actually pretty challenging (in this country) to find someone who explicitly rejects liberty, justice, or religious freedom, or who denies that America is a nation of immigrants. An important source of discursive deadlock, though, is that people are not very good at seeing how abstract values can be applied differently to the same thing. And one reason for that is that people are not very good at appreciating how values are refracted through frames. Nor are they very good at seeing how particular framings can express the same value differently – and indeed, bring out different aspects and implications of that value.

But if I am right that discursive deadlock often at bottom reflects a clash of frames, then the prospects for rationally resolving the deadlock will depend upon Flag and No Flag being able to reason across frames. In order to engage in constructive frame-sensitive reasoning, they will need to exercise some very fundamental intellectual skills. The way forward for Flag and No Flag, if they are to be model, frame-sensitive reasoners, is more complicated than simply keeping contradictions and false beliefs at bay. They need to develop and apply intellectual skills that are in short supply, and that are not usually discussed as part of the theory of rationality, formal or otherwise. These skills will allow them to engage on what I will call *non-Archimedean reasoning*. That will be the topic of the next and final chapter.

11

Opening the Door to Non-Archimedean Reasoning

In Book XXVI of *The Library of History*, written in the second half of the first century BCE, the historian Diodorus Siculus relates some enduring anecdotes about Archimedes, the famous Greek mathematician and inventor. Prominent among these is the story of Archimedes supposedly having often said: "Give me a place to stand and I shall move the whole world."[1] This may be a complete invention, but the phrase has stuck. Descartes famously refers to his *cogito ergo sum* as an Archimedean point. For Descartes the Archimedean point was the lever that would allow him to move the world. More generally, an Archimedean point is a fixed perspective that provides intellectual leverage.[2]

Standard models of rationality typically presuppose that each decision-maker starts from an Archimedean point. In the theory of expected utility, the Archimedean point is the decision-maker's utility function. Once the utility function is given, and probabilities assigned to the relevant states of the world, choosing an action becomes almost automatic – rational decision-makers just need to crunch the numbers to find the course of action with the highest expected utility. From a less quantitative perspective, the decision-making ideal for utilitarian ethical philosophers is a scale of value

---

[1] Diodorus Siculus's *Library of History* was written as a universal history, from the beginning of the world to Diodorus's own time. It is partially published in twelve volumes in Greek with a facing English translation by C. H. Oldfather in the Loeb Classical Library. The alleged quote from Archimedes is in Vol. 11 (section 18 of Book XXVI).

[2] Within contemporary philosophy in the analytic tradition, prominent discussions of the general Cartesian appeal for an Archimedean point include Bernard Williams's *Descartes: The Project of Pure Enquiry* (Williams 1978) and Thomas Nagel's *The View from Nowhere* (Nagel 1986). See also Moore 1997.

where, one might say, there is a place for everything and everything has its place. To take an extreme example, the first two sentences of Jeremy Bentham's *Introduction to the Principles of Morals and Legislation* read: "Nature has placed mankind under the governance of two sovereign masters, *pain*, and *pleasure*. It is for them alone to point out what we ought to do, as well as to determine what we shall do." Within this hedonistic calculus, the unitary scale of pleasure and pain functions as an Archimedean point.

Unfortunately, it is practically a defining feature of the type of case that we have been discussing that they arise precisely when Archimedean points stop being helpful. Looking at things from an intrapersonal perspective, the theory of expected utility gives no way of arbitrating quasi-cyclical preferences. And a good sign that we need frame-sensitive reasoning is that the decision-maker is in the grip of exactly the sort of clash of values that utilitarianism refuses to acknowledge.

Things do not improve when we switch to an interpersonal perspective. Flag and No Flag, for example, each have their own Archimedean points, and that is of course the source of the difficulty between them. Their ways of framing the pledge of allegiance function as Archimedean points, but their respective levers are, as it were, pushing the world in very different directions. More generally, frames can function as Archimedean points by fixing the way values are applied. We saw how this might work earlier in the context of Margaret Thatcher's flat rate tax for local authorities. On the one hand, framing local authority taxation as a user charge refracts the value of fairness through the lens of equality (so that a fair tax becomes one that charges equally for equal access to services) – while framing it as an equal tax makes salient the idea that a progressive tax is fair, in contrast to a flat rate tax, which is regressive.

So, whereas viewing an outcome or action through the lens of a single frame is a paradigm of Archimedean reasoning, frame-sensitive reasoning will have to be non-Archimedean. Frame-sensitive reasoners have to learn to operate without the safety net of a single fixed frame. And this is unlikely to be easy. The complex, multifaceted decision problems that we have been discussing are precisely the ones where most people feel the need for a fixed frame of reference. And yet the whole point of frame-sensitive reasoning is that there are no such fixed points. When frame-sensitive reasoning comes into play, the Archimedean paradigm ceases to apply.

There are two different ways in which frame-sensitive reasoning is non-Archimedean. First, model frame-sensitive reasoners have to be able to move away from any Archimedean points to which they might be attached. This is most obviously so in the interpersonal case. Both Flag and No Flag need to be able to suspend their attachment to their respective ways of framing the pledge of allegiance if they are to make any progress on settling their differences. But it also applies in the intrapersonal case. Doing justice to the due diligence requirement often requires coming to appreciate that an outcome or action can be framed in multiple ways – which in turn requires the ability to step back from one's own initial framing and then to develop alternative frames.

Second, once they have managed to disengage from their own Archimedean frames, model frame-sensitive reasoners need to be able to hold multiple frames in mind simultaneously. And then, once they have done that, they need to be able to find ways of evaluating those frames and the different sets of reasons that they bring with them. This second dimension is where the real difficulties lie.[3] It is all very well to encourage people to break loose from the confines of a fixed frame, but what will reasoning look like once this has been done? And what would count as reasoning rationally without the safety net of a single frame?

The consistency requirements that we have been exploring are all non-Archimedean (by design). The whole point of restricting the No Contradictory Belief and No False Belief requirements to factual propositions is so that it does not come out as irrational by definition to have the conflicting beliefs that will be inevitable in non-Archimedean contexts. A frame-sensitive reasoner may well end up with all sorts of conflicting beliefs, but they will be non-factual, rather than factual. Still, as we saw with the example of Flag and No Flag, these consistency requirements can only take us so far. A different approach is needed.

One promising strategy is to shift attention away from decision rules such as the expected utility principle, to focus instead on the general skills that a rational decision-maker might deploy in non-Archimedean reasoning. This is a different way of thinking about rationality. On this approach, what makes decision-makers rational is how they reason. To solve a decision problem rationally is to solve it using the appropriate skills and techniques *for that type of decision problem*. It may well be that for relatively straightforward decision problems, a broadly instrumental and/or rule-based approach is completely adequate. But, as we have seen

---

[3] Not least of these is the experimental evidence of how challenging a cognitive task this is. See below for more discussion.

repeatedly, complex and multifaceted problems present different challenges and require new techniques.

So, what are the framing techniques that a model frame-sensitive reasoner will need to deploy in the complex decision problems that we have been discussing? I think that we can derive them by working backwards from the requirements of frame-sensitive reasoning – from what it would take, for example, for Flag and No Flag to make progress on their discursive deadlock about the pledge of allegiance. And we can get at those requirements by thinking through the stages through which they might move to break the deadlock.

The first thing that Flag and No Flag have to do is recognize that they are each framing the pledge of allegiance issue in fundamentally different ways, and that these framing differences are the source of their disagreement and deadlock. In other words, they both need to move beyond the illusion of frame-neutrality. One might expect that it would typically be easier to see that someone else's perspective on the world is frame-relative than it is to see the same of one's own perspective. Be that as it may, the first step for Flag and No Flag is to be able to step outside their framing of the issue and recognize that they have been working within a particular way of framing the problem. Each of them needs, in other words, to turn their attention from what is actually at issue between them and focus it on how they themselves are framing that issue. The same holds for intrapersonal reasoning. A model frame-sensitive reasoner confronted with a sufficiently complex and multifaceted decision problem will need to start by stepping outside their own framing of an action or outcome in order to reflect upon the frame itself. Doing this brings into play the framing technique that I call *reflexive decentering*.

Once model frame-sensitive reasoners have used reflexive decentering to appreciate the frame-relativity of their perspective, the next step is to be open to different ways of framing the issue. In a situation like that of Flag and No Flag, the challenge is obvious. Each needs to be able to think their way into the other person's frame. Flag needs to be able to see how No Flag frames the pledge of allegiance, and vice versa. In this case, for each of them the alternative framing is, as it were, right in front of them. The same holds for many cases of interpersonal discursive deadlock. In other cases, including many intrapersonal ones, the effort is more difficult, because in them decision-makers might need to construct the alternative framing(s) themselves. In any event, this second aspect of frame-sensitive reasoning can be seen as an exercise in simulation. Frame-sensitive reasoners need to imagine what it would be like to frame things completely differently, and then to simulate actually being in that frame. Hence for this framing technique I will use the label *imaginative simulation*.

The whole point of reflective decentering and imaginative simulation is not, of course, to replace one frame by another. If Flag adopts No Flag's frame and No Flag adopts Flag's frame, then all that has been achieved is a framing version of musical chairs. Frame-sensitive reasoning requires being able to consider multiple frames simultaneously. Unless a decision-maker is able to do that the characteristic frame-sensitive pattern of quasi-cyclical preferences cannot arise. This is because a rational preference must be held for a reason and different frames bring different reasons into play. Being able to evaluate those reasons and see how they interact requires being able to adopt multiple frames simultaneously. This is one of the key ways in which frame-sensitive reasoners do justice to the complicated and multifaceted nature of the problems they are grappling with. And, in the interpersonal case, it is the first step in breaking discursive deadlock. This framing technique I will call *perspectival flexibility*.

It can be perfectly rational to have quasi-cyclical preferences. Ideally, though, model frame-sensitive reasoners will be able to come rationally to a settled position, with one set of frame-sensitive reasons winning out (as opposed to non-rationally resolving the issue, simply because a decision has to be made). For that to happen there has to be reasoning across frames. As we've discussed, reasoning across frames involves seeing how different frames bring different reasons into play. This can happen in multiple ways. One way is for the way an outcome or action is framed to foreground some reason-giving feature while downplaying another – as when Flag foregrounds one sentence in the pledge of allegiance while No Flag foregrounds a different one. Another way is for the framing to bring into play a reason-giving similarity to some other (appropriately framed) action or outcome. Genetic modification in agriculture is a good example. It can be viewed under the husbandry frame, which makes salient the similarity to thousands of years of agricultural selective breeding. Or it can be viewed under the monopoly capitalism frame, which makes salient the similarity to various types of predatory behavior by large corporations. Alternatively, framing an outcome a certain way can express a particular value in a particular way. The Community Charge frame for local authority taxation in Great Britain is a good example, bringing into play the equality interpretation of the value of fairness (if the tax is a charge on services, then it is fair to charge everyone the same for equal access to services, or so it might be claimed). All of these require the three framing techniques already discussed. But they also require a model

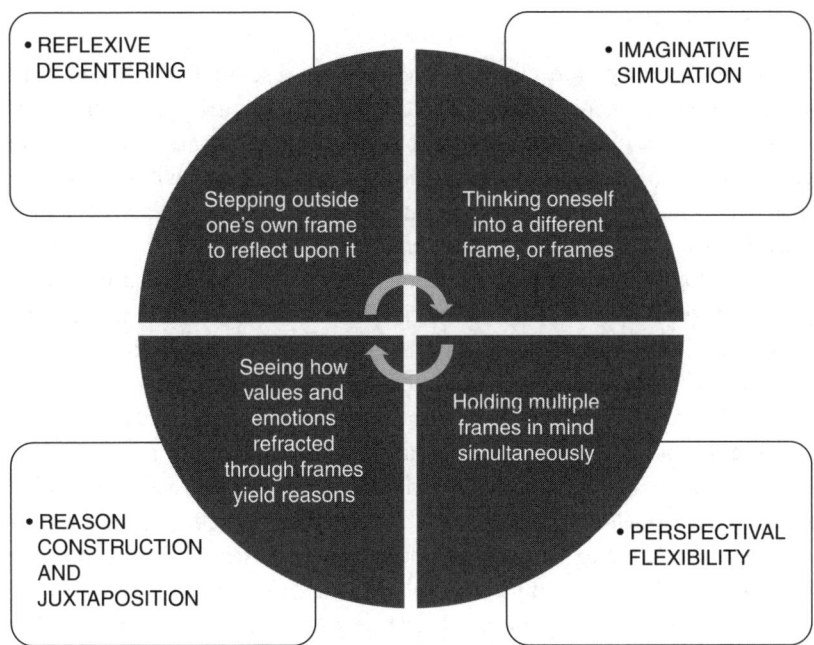

FIGURE 11.1 The key framing techniques for non-Archimedean, frame-sensitive reasoning

frame-sensitive reasoner to be able to see how values and emotions refracted through frames can yield reasons, and how different frames can yield different reasons. I will call this framing technique *reason construction and juxtaposition*.

So, we can think about non-Archimedean, frame-sensitive reasoning as having four different dimensions or aspects. To each of these dimensions there corresponds a different framing technique. Each framing technique is itself best viewed as a cluster of interrelated skills and abilities, as will emerge in the coming discussion. By way of summary and scene-setting for the rest of the chapter, Figure 11.1 is a diagram illustrating the basic structure of this type of non-Archimedean reasoning.

None of these skills and abilities have been discussed either as applied to frames or in the context of models of reasoning. However, there are interesting parallels and lessons from different areas of psychology, because some of them are analogs or developments of phenomena that have been well studied in different contexts.

Reflexive Decentering

Social, personality, and clinical psychologists discuss a number of constructs under the general label of *decentering*.[4] I'll start by sketching out
some of the key ideas of the relevant psychological literature, focusing in
particular on a three-part model of decentering. Then I will extrapolate
from the three-part model to spell out what I mean by *reflexive* decentering and how it functions in frame-sensitive reasoning.

Psychologists talk about decentering from both theoretical and clinical
perspectives. However, because it is more relevant to frame-sensitive
reasoning, I will primarily focus on the basic phenomena and techniques
of decentering, rather than on the role decentering is called upon to play in
forms of psychotherapy, such as mindfulness-based cognitive therapy.[5]

Decentering is conceptualized within psychology as a shift in one's
experiential perspective on the world. It is a movement away from being
immersed in one's experience of other people, oneself, and the world
towards being able to reflect upon the experience itself. Although it is not
typically put that way within psychology, one can think of decentering as
the shift from an outward-directed, first-person perspective on the world to
a more inward-looking, third-person perspective on one's own experience.
This basic idea has been developed in a number of different ways. One of
the most fundamental techniques in cognitive-behavioral therapy is *cognitive distancing* – the ability to step back from one's own thoughts and reflect
upon them as psychological events (as opposed to direct guides to the nature
of the world and the nature of one's self).[6] *Self-distancing* is a related
concept. Ethan Kross and Ozlem Ayduk say that it occurs when a person
takes "a step back when thinking about past experiences and reasons about
them from the perspective of a distanced observer, akin to a fly on the
wall."[7]

---

[4] See Bernstein et al. 2015 for a review of the literature and a model of decentering that I
have found very useful. Bernstein, Hadash, and Fresco 2019 review experimental techniques for studying decentering.

[5] See Chapters 6 and 7 of Safran and Segal 1990 for an early discussion of decentering in
psychotherapy.

[6] CBT was pioneered by the psychiatrist Aaron Beck (Beck 1976) and has now become a
dominant approach within clinical psychology for treating depression and a wide range of
other mental health disorders. Hofmann et al. 2012 review 269 meta-analyses of the
efficacy of CBT and conclude that the evidence-base for CBT is generally very strong.
See also Butler et al. 2006 and Kazantzis et al. 2018.

[7] Kross and Ayduk 2011, p. 187. There is some evidence that adopting a self-distanced
perspective helps people with depression analyze negative experiences adaptively (Kross et
al. 2012).

In a 2016 review article Arnit Bernstein and collaborators propose a model for unifying these and other decentering constructs. They see decentering as emerging from three interrelated psychological processes (with each of the several decentering constructs incorporating at least one process). Those processes are:

Meta-awareness

To be meta-aware of an episode of thinking is to be aware of the process of thinking itself (as opposed to its *content*, what it is about). To think about p is to be in a first-order state, with p as its object. To be meta-aware of that thought is to be in a second-order state, with the thought that p as its object. These thoughts can be about oneself or about the world. So, you might think a thought of self-loathing (a first-order state), or you might think about the fact that you are thinking negatively about yourself (a second-order state). Alternatively, in the case of emotional projection (when your emotional state colors your experience of the world), meta-awareness would allow you to see the role that your emotions are playing in structuring your experience.[8]

Disidentification from internal experience

Here is how Bernstein and colleagues characterize de-identification: "Disidentification from internal experience is the experience of internal states as separate from oneself. This experiential disidentification contrasts with the human tendency to identify with subjective experience and, therein, to experience internal states such as thoughts, emotions, and sensations as integral parts of the self. For example, when a person is identified with his or her experience of fear, he or she may verbally relate to it by noting 'I am afraid.' However, when disidentified from fear, he or she may relate to it by simply noting 'a feeling of fear.' Disidentification from internal experience is thus linked to experiencing sensations, emotions, and thoughts from a third-person perspective."[9] Disidentification in this sense is distinct from meta-awareness, although it presupposes it. I need to be able to think about my feeling of fear in a second-order way in order to take this kind of third-person perspective on it. However, I can take my feeling of fear as an object of thought without disidentifying

---

[8] In my book *Thinking without Words* (Bermúdez 2003a) I argued that metacognition in general requires language – that one can only think about thoughts to the extent that they are linguistically expressed, through inner speech, for example. See Bermúdez 2018b for more on the role of inner speech in metacognition.

[9] Bernstein et al. 2015, p. 602. I have left out multiple citations.

from it (as in the quoted example, where I conceptualize my feeling of fear as my being afraid).

Reduced reactivity to thought content

Decentering is not just a cognitive process, a matter of how one thinks about one's thoughts and relates to them. It also has an affective dimension. Decentering reduces the affective power of one's thoughts (and in many ways this is the key dimension from a mental health point of view). So, for example, a decentered person will be capable of thinking apparently negative thoughts without the emotional baggage that might normally accompany them. To take Bernstein et al.'s own example, such a person might think of themselves as fat without feeling the guilt or shame that they have always felt in the past. Or they might think that they are being insulted without feeling violent rage.

Back to non-Archimedean reasoning and the analogy between frame-sensitive reasoning and the psychological concept of decentering. Model frame-sensitive reasoners are able to step back from how they frame things in order to reflect upon the framing itself. This is a shift from a first-person perspective to a third-person perspective, broadly similar to that envisaged in psychological decentering. And in fact, reflexive decentering has three different components analogous to the three different aspects of decentering proposed by Bernstein et al.

First, model frame-sensitive reasoners will need to be capable of a high level of meta-awareness. They need to be able to shift perspective from their involved engagement with the world to the frame that is structuring that engagement. So, for example, for Agamemnon to be able to reason frame-sensitively about Iphigenia, he needs to be able to step back from the troops, the fleet, and Calchas's interpretation of the portent in order to make explicit the two very different frames that give rise to his quasi-cyclical preferences. One frame structures the decision problem privately, in terms of family affection and personal loyalties. The other frame makes salient the public dimension of his life as leader of the Greek forces and as brother of the insulted Menelaös. The decision problem looks very different under these two frames. That is the source of his difficulty (and what distinguishes him from Agamemnon-minus, or Abraham). In order to begin rationally confronting the problem, Agamemnon needs, first, to become aware that it is created by different framings, and then, second, to be able to see what those framings are.

Neither of these is easy, because the illusion of frame-neutrality is very powerful. Some frames are instilled through education and constantly culturally reinforced. The result, particularly evident for Agamemnon and other epic heroes, is that those frames become second nature, so that only a drastic shock can, as it were, shake them loose. The *Iliad* is full of characters who will never understand that the warrior ideal is a way of framing their options, not part of the furniture of the universe.[10] The same might hold for Flag, particularly if she herself grew up reciting the pledge of allegiance on a daily basis, with a particular framing inculcated by high school civics classes. And indeed, for No Flag, whose framing may be just as rigidly constructed.

What might make it possible for frame-sensitive reasoners to step back from their frames and bring them to light? The distinction between factual and non-factual propositions is very important here. We need to look for the influence of frames within the domain of non-factual propositions, that is, propositions where we do not have generally accepted techniques for establishing their truth or falsity. It is a factual proposition that a fetus does not have a heart one week after conception. It is a non-factual proposition that a fetus is a person one week after conception. So, frame-sensitive reasoners need to be able to draw the line between factual and non-factual propositions. Once they have done that, then they can start to be sensitive to what the way they evaluate non-factual propositions tells them about their frames. If a reflective, frame-sensitive reasoner thinks that it is false that a fetus one week after conception is a person, then he needs to be able to work backwards from that to make explicit some of the principles that are structuring his perspective on abortion, and related issues.

The idea of thick ethical concepts, as originally proposed by Bernard Williams in *Ethics and the Limits of Philosophy* is a useful tool here. A thick ethical concept, according to Williams, has both descriptive and evaluative components. The concept *cruel* is a good example. To call a person cruel is, roughly speaking, to say that he willfully causes some other person or sentient creature unnecessary and unjustifiable pain. But what counts as pain? Must it come from sticks and stones, or can it come from words? If so, which words? And how do we decide what counts as willful, unnecessary, and unjustified? It seems clear that propositions

---

[10] In fact, within the *Iliad* it is probably only Hector and Achilles (after the death of Patroclus) who are portrayed as understanding (what I would anachronistically describe as) the frame-relativity of the Homeric warrior ideal.

describing someone as cruel are non-factual. There are no generally accepted techniques for determining whether a significant minority of the population is correct or incorrect in thinking, for example, that horse-racing or boxing is cruel. The way in which this thick ethical concept is applied is often a function of how things are framed. People who think that boxing is cruel often frame it as a barbaric bloodsport catering to the tastes of people interested only in watching people being knocked senseless. Supporters of horseracing often frame it in terms of the idyllic conditions in which racehorses are raised and kept, all leading up to the race, which is the ultimate expression of the thoroughbred's innate passion for running. On the other hand, opponents have a narrative of exploitation that highlights malpractice at the track and what happens to many thoroughbreds once their racing days are done.

This brings us to the second and third aspects of the Bernstein et al. decentering model, because non-Archimedean reasoners will need to be able to disengage, at least partially, from the evaluative dimensions of their thick ethical concepts, in order to be able to focus on how that evaluative dimension is driven by their frame and its concomitant values and emotional perspective. Agamemnon needs to step back from his love for his daughter and associated characterization of the death of Iphigenia as murder in order to see that there are other possible frames. Flag needs to step back from the patriotic feelings instilled by the sight of the flag and the sound of the national anthem. In each case, there are two different tasks to perform.

The first task is to start to disidentify from the frame. Just as the patient undergoing cognitive-behavioral therapy learns to shift from internalizing to externalizing their feelings of their own worthlessness (the shift from "I am worthless" to "there is a feeling of worthlessness"), frame-sensitive reasoners need to put distance between themselves and the evaluative dimensions of the frame. This is the shift from thinking "This is how *I* frame the matter" to "This is a way of framing the matter." In short, a degree of dispassionate disidentification is required before a frame-sensitive reasoner can take a third-person perspective on how they are framing an issue, outcome, or action.

The second task is directly analogous to the reduced reactivity envisaged by psychological models of decentering. It is hard to bring your pro-choice frame clearly into view if you are overcome with rage and indignation at the thought of restrictions on abortion. Dispassionate disidentification must go hand in hand with emotional and affective distancing. The power of the frame must be neutralized, or at least weakened, before it can be seen clearly. This goes beyond disidentification from the evaluative dimension of a frame. Once again, looking at thick ethical concepts can be helpful. Philosophical discussions tend to present thick concepts as having only two dimensions – a descriptive dimension and an evaluative dimension. But that neglects their emotional/affective dimension. To describe someone as cruel is not simply to describe them as willfully inflicting unnecessary and unjustifiable pain while at the same time conveying disapprobation. It is also to express and invite strong sentiments of antipathy and repugnance.[11] Frames often work similarly, with particular framings both expressing and inviting strong affective reactions. A frame-sensitive reasoner needs to be able to disengage from those affective reactions.

There are multiple skills, then, included in what I term reflexive decentering. Reflexive decentering is the foundation of non-Archimedean reasoning. Through reflexive decentering, frame-sensitive reasoners are able to disengage from their frames so that they can take those frames themselves as objects of thought. Reflexive decentering makes possible the shift from thinking *through* frames to thinking *about* frames.

Imaginative Simulation

Frame-sensitive reasoning comes into play for decision problems too complex and multifaceted to be encompassed by a single frame. Looking at them through the prism of a single frame always leaves a residue. If frame-sensitive reasoners are to apply the due diligence requirement to such problems, then they will need to think about the decision problem under one or more new frames. The complex of skills and abilities in reflexive decentering sets the scene for this by, in effect, loosening the grip of the original frame. But in order to go further a model frame-sensitive reasoner needs to deploy a new range of framing techniques. The most fundamental of these I call *imaginative simulation*. As with reflexive decentering, imaginative simulation is more of a cluster of skills and

---

[11] My point here is restricted to discussions of thick ethical concepts. There are many views of ethical language which see it as primarily a device for expressing emotional attitudes. These expressivist views go back to the Logical Positivists in the first half of the twentieth century, most popularly Freddie Ayer in *Language, Truth, and Logic*. Such expressivists maintain that ethical sentences are not, strictly speaking, either true or false, which is not typically accepted by those who write about thick ethical concepts, and is not in the spirit of my own discussion. For influential discussions of how to incorporate truth-aptness within a broadly expressivist approach see Blackburn 1996 and 1998.

abilities than a unitary phenomenon. We can make a start by looking at important work on simulation and perspective-taking in developmental and social psychology.

Simulation receives a lot of attention from developmental psychologists and cognitive scientists interested in how young children acquire the complex of skills and representational abilities known as *theory of mind* or *mindreading*.[12] To have a theory of mind is to be able to understand and predict other people's behavior. It is to be able to apply psychological concepts to them – to understand that they have beliefs about how things are and desires about how they would like things to be; to appreciate that they respond emotionally and affectively to what they encounter; and to be able to predict what they will do on the basis of those beliefs and desires. In short, to have a theory of mind is to be able to navigate the social world. It is an ability that emerges gradually and in stages in the course of normal human development. One key indicator of possession of mindreading skills is the ability to pass the so-called false-belief test, originally proposed by Heinz Wimmer and Josef Perner (Wimmer and Perner 1983), and also known as the Sally-Anne test, after an influential variant proposed by Simon Baron-Cohen, Alan Leslie, and Uta Frith (1985). In the false-belief test, young children are presented with a fictional scenario and tested on their understanding that one of the characters has false beliefs about where an object is located. It is a very robust finding that young children start to succeed on this type of test at around four years of age.[13]

One popular account of what it is to have a theory of mind takes the word "theory" literally. The theory of mind is a body of lawlike generalizations, not really different from any other theory, and acquiring it is a process of testing hypotheses that eventually converges on the theory.

---

[12] For an overview of current debates about theory of mind in cognitive science see Chapters 13 and 14 of my textbook, *Cognitive Science: An Introduction to the Science of the Mind* (Bermúdez 2020). Each chapter has an annotated bibliography with guidance on further reading. I am following standard practice in using "theory of mind" and "mindreading" interchangeably. It would be more accurate, though, to use the term "mindreading" for the complex of skills and to reserve "theory of mind" for a particular way of thinking about what it is to possess those skills (namely, as having a tacit or folk theory of human behavior and psychology). For more discussion see Bermúdez 2003b.

[13] Nonverbal false-belief tasks have been proposed using the violation-of-expectations paradigm. These tasks test prelinguistic infants' sensitivity to false beliefs by using looking time as a measure of how surprised infants are (which is then interpreted as a sign of their expectations). See Onishi and Baillargeon 2005 for the original study and Perner and Roessler 2012 for discussion of the relation between nonverbal false-belief tasks and the standard false-belief task. Poulin-Dubois, Brooker, and Chow 2009 review studies on mindreading in infancy.

Infants and young children are, as the title of a popular exposition of the so-called "theory theory" has it, scientists in the crib.[14] The principal competition for the theory theory comes from what is known as simulation theory. According to simulation theory, we make sense of other people's behavior by simulating them. We run our own decision-making processes off-line, taking as inputs the beliefs and desires that we think another person has. That process tells us what we ourselves would do if we had that person's beliefs and desires. Assuming that they will react similarly gives us a prediction for how they will behave.[15]

What I call imaginative simulation goes beyond this type of simulation. Simulationist approaches to mindreading assume that mindreaders start off from their own beliefs, desires, and other emotional/affective states. The assumption behind simulation theory is that we all have a relatively secure grip on our own psychologies, which we can then use to make sense of other people. That may or may not be true in the normal course of things (I am inclined to think that it is *not* true, as it happens), but it is not helpful for thinking about frame-sensitive reasoning. Flag's problem is that he is struggling to understand No Flag's perspective on the pledge of allegiance. Extrapolating from his own beliefs, desires, and other emotional/effective states will be of limited use. The whole point of reflexive decentering, as just discussed, is to weaken the grip of one's own framing of the situation in order to make room for alternative framings. But extrapolating outwards from one's own perspective simply reinforces that perspective and the framing it reflects.

Part of the problem is that frames are often more fundamental than beliefs and desires. The distinction between factual and non-factual propositions is important. Factual propositions are frame-neutral. If we have generally accepted techniques for determining their truth-value, then believing particular factual propositions should not require framing actions or outcomes in any particular way, which is why factual propositions hold constant across frames. In contrast, non-factual beliefs tend to be frame-relative. An obvious example is No Flag's belief that it would be a bad idea to make the pledge of allegiance available to children at the start of the school day. But the same holds of Agamemnon's belief that the death of Iphigenia is a fitting sacrifice to placate Artemis – or Macbeth's

---

[14] Gopnik, Meltzoff, and Kuhl 1999.
[15] For influential anthologies summarizing the origins of the debate between theory theorists and simulation theorists see Davies and Stone 1995a and 1995b, and Carruthers and Smith 1996.

belief that the death of Duncan is the fulfillment of his (Macbeth's)
destiny. Having these (obviously non-factual) beliefs is a function of
framing each of the two deaths in a particular way. Framing the deaths
differently leads to different non-factual beliefs, which is why Macbeth
and Agamemnon both have quasi-cyclical preferences.

This means that a frame-sensitive reasoner needs to be able to
simulate frames and then, from within a simulated frame, be able to
simulate the beliefs, desires, and other emotional/affective states that
someone working within that frame might have. That in turn
requires, at a minimum, that a frame-sensitive reasoner be able to
appreciate that a single action or outcome can be apprehended from
different perspectival frames, and that different frames can generate
different non-factual beliefs (and other psychological states). This is
superficially similar to two important ideas in psychology, but importantly different from both. We can get at the phenomenon of imaginative simulation by looking at those differences.

The developmental psychologist John H. Flavell influentially discussed
visual perspective-taking as an aspect of how children develop mindreading skills, and in particular of how they come to understand the differences
between how things appear and how they really are. One route for understanding the appearance/reality distinction is through understanding that
people can have different visual perspectives on the world, with their
perspective determining what they see and how they see it. Flavell introduced an important distinction between two levels of visual perspective-
taking, suggesting that the transition between them marks a significant
milestone in children's cognitive development (one that he thinks occurs at
roughly the same time as children start to pass the standard false-belief
test, suggesting that it is a key component of mindreading).[16]

At the first level, young children have a very partial understanding of
visual perspective. They are only able to assess whether or not someone
can see an object. What they understand is essentially the idea of a line of
sight and of an object's being occluded or not occluded. At the second
level, in contrast, children are able to understand that a single object can
be seen differently from different perspectives. For example, in one
classic experimental paradigm, children are tested on whether they
understand that a picture of a turtle on a table in front of them will

[16] The distinction was originally proposed in Flavell 1977, with further evidence from
children's development presented in Flavell et al. 1981.

look upside-down to an experimenter sitting facing them on the other side of the table.[17]

What children learn when they become capable of level 2 perspective-taking is, in effect, that different environmental situations give people different types of information. Things look different from different visual perspectives because those different perspectives make available different types of information – the experimenter has different information about the turtle. But frames behave differently. No one can engage in frame-sensitive reasoning without understanding that things can look different to different people even when they have similar information, because they are operating within different frames. To put it another way, people can agree on all factual propositions while still differing on crucial non-factual propositions. That tells us something about the type of simulation that a frame-sensitive reasoner has to carry out. They have to be able to simulate having very different non-factual beliefs that are likely to be incompatible with their current non-factual beliefs. How can that be achieved?

The key lies in the complex relations between frames and emotions. These connections work in both directions. To frame the world is often to take a particular emotional perspective on it. A frame makes available a range of emotional responses – while ruling out others. Flag's emotional responses are clustered around feelings of patriotism and loyalty. Those who see human-caused climate change through the natural disaster frame probably have a different emotional perspective from those who view it through the future generations frame. The natural disasters emotions are probably "hotter" and more arousing than the "cooler" future genera-tions emotions, since the frame stresses immediate and easy-to-imagine costs to existing populations, rather than more intangible costs to people not yet in existence. This difference has not been lost on fund-raisers for environmental charities, who often try to make the future generations "warmer" by personalizing it to *your* children and *your* grandchildren. And Agamemnon's emotional state varies in obvious ways as he oscillates between the family and leadership frames.

But at the same time, particular emotions can also drive particular frames, so that the emotional response comes first and the frame second. Take immigration, for example, since this is a highly emotive subject. No doubt there are people whose attitudes towards immigration are driven by

[17] For the original turtle study see Masangkay et al. 1974. It is one of the paradigms used in Flavell et al. 1981. Moll and Meltzoff 2011 use a different test involving color filters and identify level 2 perspective-taking as early as 36 months.

abstract reasoning (for example, by calculations of how best to compensate for declining birth rates in the face of increasing costs for government entitlement programs such as social security and, in the United Kingdom, the National Health Service). But I would imagine that for a significant number of people their response has more visceral origins. It is not hard to imagine a supporter of open borders and a welcoming immigration policy whose first encounter with the issue was through some kind of image of extreme immigrant suffering – for example, the iconic photograph of a drowned Syrian toddler washed up on a beach in Turkey that was widely circulated on social media in late summer 2015, or one of the many photographs of children separated from their parents at the US/Mexico border.[18] Emotional responses to such images prime people for a particular narrative about immigration – one that stresses ordinary people in terrible straits desperately striving to improve their families' situation. A very different narrative is primed by the kind of story popular with Fox News and similar media outlets, where illegal immigrants are arrested in connection with, or convicted of, serious crimes, such as rape or murder.[19] Stories such as these encourage, some think intentionally, a climate of fear and distrust, with predictable consequences for how immigration in general is framed – as opening the door to predators who threaten the American way of life, and so forth.

This important emotional dimension of frames suggests a powerful tool for imaginative simulation of a novel frame. A frame-sensitive reasoner can think themselves into a new frame by simulating the type of emotions that give rise to that frame and that it typically generates. No Flag, for example, can work to simulate the feelings of patriotism and loyalty to the flag that motivate Flag. A supporter of immigration trying to understand the national insecurity frame for immigration needs to simulate the fear and distrust that might motivate someone to adopt that frame. But has this not simply pushed the problem back more or less to where we started? How can someone who does not feel fear and distrust at the idea of immigration simulate that emotional response? To solve this problem we need to think about how emotional responses are primed. A

---

[18] For the record, the drowned toddler was a three-year-old named Aylan Kurdi from Kobani in Syria, who died with his mother and one brother while trying to cross to the Greek island of Kos. A distressing transcript of an NPR story on the family can be downloaded at www.npr.org/sections/parallels/2015/09/03/437132793.

[19] For a typical example see www.foxnews.com/us/illegal-immigrant-with-criminal-history-arrested-in-california-womans-murder on the arrest of Carlos Eduardo Arevalo Carranza as a suspect in the murder of 59-year-old Bambi Larson.

model frame-sensitive reasoner will try to go behind the emotional responses of the frame that she is trying to understand to explore what those responses are responses to – by going out of her way to seek out, for example, stories about crimes perpetrated by immigrants (legal and illegal) and trying to imagine how someone with a different set of background sympathies might respond to them (or, coming at it from the other direction, someone might seek out depictions of the risks that immigrants take in order to try to understand the suffering that might have led them to expose themselves to heavy sacrifices).

This is just one set of techniques for imaginative simulation. Frames can be primed and generated in multiple ways and model frame-sensitive reasoners can exploit all or most of them to think their way into alternate framings. So, for example, they might have to think about different ways of responding to statistics, since frames are often tied to particular ways of interpreting statistics. Opponents of gun control, for example, who typically frame gun ownership as a personal security issue, tend to place a lot of weight on statistics about the frequency with which guns are used to prevent crimes. The instinctive reaction of supporters of gun control might be to challenge those statistics. From the perspective of frame-sensitive reasoning, however, they would be advised to start by suspending disbelief and instead think about how the statistics (as reported) might give rise to an alternative way of framing gun control. There is most likely an emotional dimension here too, but it will probably be harder to tease out. In any event, we have enough to go on to illustrate the type of skills in imaginative simulation that a model frame-sensitive reasoner will need to develop, cultivate, and maintain.

Perspectival Flexibility

Reflexive decentering allows a model frame-sensitive reasoner to detach and disengage from her own framing of a particular situation, action, or outcome. Then, through the techniques of imaginative simulation, she is able to step into one or more different ways of framing the decision problem. But the aim of the exercise is not for her to swap one frame for another. That may happen on occasion, of course, but a model frame-sensitive reasoner needs to be able to work simultaneously across two or more frames. Agamemnon is a skilled frame-sensitive reasoner to the extent that he can operate simultaneously within the family frame and the leadership frame. Flag and No Flag are not, I am assuming, skilled frame-sensitive reasoners and one sign of this is that they can only work uncritically within their respective frames. To move beyond this, they will each need to learn to consider and take into account the other person's framing, as well as their own. This requires the skills of what I term *perspectival flexibility*.

We can approach perspectival flexibility through the theory of role-taking developed by the Harvard educational psychologist Robert Selman. In studying social role-taking as a key indicator of social and cognitive development in children and adolescents, Selman was building on the work of distinguished predecessors including James Mark Baldwin, George Herbert Mead, and Jean Piaget. Selman used both cross-sectional and longitudinal studies to work out a taxonomy of five different stages of social role-taking that are typically traversed in the course of social development. Actually, Selman and his predecessors) are really talking about perspective-taking rather than role-taking. Their terminology implies that they are studying children's understanding of social roles. But what they actually offer is an account of how children develop increasingly sophisticated understandings of how different people can have different perspectives on social situations.

Selman developed his taxonomy by studying how children understand and react to social situations presented in short vignettes. The best-known involves a young girl called Holly, who is an expert tree climber. Here is the story that was given to the children:

> Holly is an 8-year-old girl who likes to climb trees. She is the best tree climber in the neighborhood. One day while climbing down from a tall tree she falls off the bottom branch but does not hurt herself. Her father sees her fall. He is upset and asks her to promise not to climb trees any more. Holly promises.
>
> Later that day, Holly and her friends meet Sean. Sean's kitten is caught up in a tree and cannot get down. Something has to be done right away or the kitten may fall. Holly is the only one who climbs trees well enough to reach the kitten and get it down, but she remembers her promise to her father.

Children were given the vignette and then interviewed for 20 minutes or so, with the interviewer using standard probe questions, such as:

- Does Sean know why Holly cannot decide whether or not to climb the tree?
- What does Holly think her father will think of her if he finds out that she climbed the tree?
- What does Holly think that most people would do in this situation?

On the basis of groups of interviews, both cross-sectional and longitudinal, Selman and collaborators came up with a taxonomy of levels of role-taking/perspective-taking.[20]

This taxonomy is illustrated in Table 11.1, which comes from the sixth edition of David R. Shaffer's textbook *Social and Personality Development* (Shaffer 2008). The table shows the different levels, together with the competencies (and limits) of each level and a brief description of typical responses to the Holly story at each level.[21]

However, even a normal and socially adept decision-maker capable of all of these types of perspective-taking will still fall short of the type of perspective-taking that skilled frame-sensitive reasoning requires. In

Table 11.1 *Selman's stages of social perspective-taking*

Stage of role-taking	Typical responses to the "Holly" dilemma
0. **Egocentric or undifferentiated perspective** (roughly 3 to 6 years) Children are unaware of any perspective other than their own. They assume that whatever they feel is right for Holly to do will be agreed with by others.	Children often assume that Holly will save the kitten. When asked how Holly's father will react to her transgression, these children think he will be "happy because he likes kittens." In other words, these children like kittens themselves, and they assume that Holly and her father also like kittens.
1. **Social-informational role taking** (roughly 6 to 8 years) Children now recognize that people can have perspectives that differ from their own but believe that this happens *only* because these individuals have received different information.	When asked whether Holly's father will be angry because she climbed the tree, the child may say, "If he didn't know why she climbed the tree, he would be angry. But if he knew why she did it, he would realize that she had a good reason."

(cont.)

---

[20] See Selman and Byrne 1974 and Gurucharri and Selman 1982 for the original studies. The earlier study looked at 40 children aged 4, 6, 8, and 10, while the later study reports three assessments over a five-year period of 41 adolescent and preadolescent boys.

[21] The levels are labeled differently in the table than in Gurucharri and Selman 1982, who use the following classification. Level 0 = Undifferentiated; Level 1 = Unilateral; Level 2 = Reciprocal; Level 3 = Mutual; Level 4 = Interdependent. I find Shaffer's labeling clearer.

Table 11.1 (cont.)

Stage of role-taking	Typical responses to the "Holly" dilemma
2. Self-reflective role-taking (roughly 8 to 10 years) Children now know that their own and others' points of view may conflict even if they have received the same information. They are now able to consider the other person's viewpoint. They also recognize that the other person can put himself in their shoes, so they are now able to anticipate the person's reactions to their behavior. However, the child cannot consider his own perspective and that of another person at the same time.	If asked whether Holly will climb the tree, the child might say, "Yes. She knows that her father will understand why she did it." In so doing, the child is focusing on the father's consideration of Holly's perspective. But if asked whether the father would want Holly to climb the tree, the child usually says no, thereby indicating that he is now assuming the father's perspective and considering the father's concern for Holly's safety.
3. Mutual role-taking (roughly 10 to 12 years) The child can now simultaneously consider her own and another person's points of view and recognize that the other person can do the same. The child can also assume the perspective of a disinterested third party and anticipate how each participant (self and other) will react to the viewpoint of his or her partner.	At this stage, a child might describe the outcome of the "Holly" dilemma by taking the perspective of a disinterested third party and indicating that she knows that both Holly and her father are thinking about what the other is thinking. For example, one child remarked: "Holly wanted to get the kitten because she likes kittens, but she knew that she wasn't supposed to climb trees. Holly's father knew that Holly had been told not to climb trees, but he couldn't have known about [the kitten]."
4. Societal role taking (roughly 12 to 15 and older) The adolescent now attempts to understand another person's perspective by comparing it with that of the social system in which he operates (that is, the view of the "generalized other"). In other words, the adolescent expects others to consider and typically assume perspectives on events that most people in their social group would take.	When asked whether Holly should be punished for climbing the tree, the stage 4 adolescent is likely to say "No" and claim that the value of humane treatment of animals justifies Holly's act and that most fathers would recognize this point.

particular, two key dimensions of frame-sensitive perspective-taking go beyond those attained in the normal course of Selman's developmental progression.

First, frame-sensitive reasoning requires deeper levels of engagement with different frames or perspectives than is envisaged in role-taking theory. The emphasis in role-taking theory is on recognizing the existence of other perspectives. So, children moving up through the role-taking levels come to understand that specific other people (in level 3) or a typical member of the social group (level 4) might look at and evaluate a particular situation in a different manner. Frame-sensitive reasoning goes beyond this, because it involves being able to simulate and/or adopt these alternative perspectives so that they become incorporated into one's own decision-making. If No Flag is to progress as a frame-sensitive reasoner then he needs to be able to think in and through Flag's framing of the pledge of allegiance and related issues. It is not enough just to recognize that Flag frames things differently – or even that Flag frames things in a typical way for someone from her social group. Those are important achievements, and doubtless necessary for frame-sensitive reasoning. But a frame-sensitive reasoner must be able to operate simultaneously in multiple frames, not just be aware that issues and decision problems can be multiply framed.

One way of thinking about the differences between perspectival flexibility and role-taking, as understood by Selman, is in terms of a shift in problem-solving manner and style. A Selmanian role-taker can treat people with different perspectives and frames as fixed features of the world with which she has to negotiate and, if necessary, compromise. Many books, academic and popular, offer strategies for this kind of social navigation. A very well-known and much discussed example is the strategy of principled negotiation and non-positional bargaining developed by Roger Fisher and William Ury in their best-selling 1981 book *Getting to Yes: Negotiating Agreement without Giving In*. To cut a long story short, Fisher and Ury propose four basic principles of negotiation. These are:

- Depersonalize the situation by separating the people from the problem;
- Focus on participants' interests rather than on antecedent positions;
- Generate a variety of options before trying to settle on an agreement;
- Insist that any final agreement be based on objective criteria.

No doubt this is sound advice. But the types of problems we are discussing are ones where following these four principles, or principles like them (there are plenty to choose from in the Business and Leadership section of the bookstore) is unlikely to be much help.

The differences that result in discursive deadlock are very different from those that might arise between, say, a real estate developer seeking financing and a banker trying to fix the terms of a loan. In financing-type cases it is not hard to understand what it would be to follow Fisher and Ury's principles – what it means to depersonalize the problem, for example, or to identify objective criteria to choose between a range of possible loan agreements. But things are very different in an example of discursive deadlock like that between, say, pro-choice and pro-life legislators trying to come to terms on regulation for abortion clinics. Here it is hard to imagine how to follow the instruction to depersonalize the problem, or to find objective criteria to assess agreement. The decision problem is too closely bound up with participants' deepest values and sense of their own identity for depersonalizing it to be a realistic instruction. And each participant's sense of what are going to count as objective criteria is determined by their frame (since we are squarely in the realm of non-factual propositions).[22]

So, to tackle discursive deadlock it is not enough for a frame-sensitive reasoner simply to understand that a particular action or outcome can be framed in multiple ways. She actually needs to frame it herself in multiple ways simultaneously. This transforms the type of problem-solving involved. Instead of engaging discursive deadlock on the model of inter-personal negotiation between separate individuals (or organizations), each of whom frames the problem in different and incompatible ways, we should think of it more as an exercise in intrapersonal negotiation. At the ideal limit, the participants would each have internalized the frames and perspectives of other participants (through reflexive decentering and imaginative simulation), so that each would be approaching the problem with the available conflicting framings already in play. Only when they have done that will they be in a position to start applying problem-solving principles such as those proposed by Fisher and Ury.

You might ask: How simultaneous is simultaneous? How literally should we take the requirement that frame-sensitive reasoners operate simultaneously in multiple frames? There is a huge amount of experimental evidence that people are actually really rather bad at doing more than one thing at a time. The phenomenon of *inattentional blindness* is a good

---

[22] As I emphasized in Chapter 10, it would be wrong to think that non-factual propositions cannot be true or false, and hence must be non-objective.

example, engagingly described in Chapter 8 of Nick Chater's book *The Mind is Flat*.[23] In one of the studies Chater describes, experienced pilots were using a heads-up display to land in cloud using instruments (a heads-up display projects the information onto the windshield so that pilots do not need to look down). Just before landing the clouds parted to reveal the runway with a large jet turning on to it. A significant number of the pilots were so focused on the information on the display that they did not notice the jet and continued the landing.[24] More humorously, Ulric Neisser's pioneering study showed participants a screen switching between two videos of separate teams of players throwing a ball between them. The participants were asked to count the number of passes made by just one of the teams. So intent were they on keeping track of the balls that 75 percent of the participants failed to notice a woman with an umbrella walking through the middle of the game in one of the videos.[25]

This literature shows convincingly that people have very limited bandwidth for dealing with perceptual information, and I'm sure that those limitations are even more acute when it comes to the demanding tasks of reasoning across frames. It may be the case that what I am describing as holding multiple frames in mind simultaneously is better understood as being able to switch very quickly from one frame to another. I don't think that really affects the argument, though. The fact remains that being able to switch between different frames is a skill that most people lack and frame-sensitive reasoners need to acquire. And frame-sensitive reasoners will still have quasi-cyclical preferences – we just need to think about preferences as being extended over time, rather than existing at an instant (which is in any case a much more psychologically realistic way of thinking about them).[26]

A final point about perspectival flexibility. This illustrates how the boundaries between interpersonal and intrapersonal reasoning can become quite fluid in frame-sensitive reasoning. When an individual decision-maker is holding multiple frames in mind simultaneously and trying to reason across them, then it can start to look almost like an interpersonal process. And conversely, when decision-makers tackling discursive deadlock do a good enough job of internalizing the perspectives

---

[23] Chater 2018. See also pp. 168–71 where Chater discusses multi-tasking, which he thinks is not really possible at all.

[24] The original study is Haines 1991.

[25] See Neisser 1979 and for many more examples Mack and Rock 1998.

[26] Thanks to an anonymous reader for Cambridge University Press for encouraging me to address this point.

and frames of other participants, then it can start to look as if the inter-personal debate has really become an intrapersonal one. But, you might ask, how can a frame-sensitive reasoner work across multiple frames simultaneously? How can perspectival flexibility be the basis for rational problem-solving? That takes us to the last of the four framing techniques.

Reason Construction and Juxtaposition

Skilled frame-sensitive reasoners are capable of reflexive decentering, imaginative simulation, and simultaneous perspective-taking. That allows them to disengage from their immediate framing of an action, outcome, or situation. They can think themselves into one or more alternative framings of that same action, outcome, or situation. And they are able to hold those multiple framings in mind (more or less) simultaneously. So now, with all the groundwork done, the final step in frame-sensitive reasoning is to extract reasons from those multiple framings, and then (if possible!) to settle on a single course of action. This is what I term *reason construction and juxtaposition*.

As the label suggests, there are two different things going on here. First, frame-sensitive reasoners need to be able to see how different frames can bring different reasons into play. Then, once they have done that, they need to be able to compare those reasons across frames. The ideal end-point here is that one reason wins out, as it were. But frame-sensitive reasoning is very different from normal decision theory. From a decision-theoretic standpoint, any decision-maker with a suitably consistent utility function and coherent probabilities will be able to rank-order available actions by their expected utility and there will either be a unique optimal action, or a tie. But there is no guarantee that frame-sensitive reasoning will be so well-behaved. Sometimes the frame-sensitive reasoner will end up with a clear winner, but at other times not. One index of this, as we saw in the case of Macbeth, is the persistence of rational regret and remorse. Macbeth murdered Duncan, of course, but it would be wrong to say that he came to a settled decision. He ended up acting on the reasons made most salient by one way of framing the situation (the personal ambition framing, as it were, rather than the kinsman/guest framing), but his ambiguous attitude to that action persists to the end of the play, as he himself recognizes when he asks the doctor for a "sweet oblivious anti-dote" for Lady Macbeth but not for himself. Macbeth feels regret that he does not want to eliminate. His quasi-cyclical preferences persist to the end of the play.

That is why I am talking about the juxtaposition of reasons. I reject the idea that rational decision-making is impossible in the type of hard choices for which frame-sensitive reasoning is required. But still, that does not mean that a settled decision is guaranteed. A rational choice, as I understand it, is a choice based on a rational preference. And a rational preference is a preference that is grounded in a reason (or more than one reason). So, Macbeth rationally prefers bravely taking the throne to backing away from his resolution to make the prophecy come true. The reasons here are the perceived bravery of the bold action, the perceived cowardice of failing to act on the witches' prophecy, and so on. These reasons make the decision rational. But they are frame-relative reasons, and on a different framing Macbeth has reversed preferences. He prefers fulfilling his double duty to Duncan to murdering the King, for example. This preference is rational, because it is grounded in reasons that become salient in the loyalty framing. So, if we define rational regret as regret that is grounded in reasons, then Macbeth feels rational regret after killing Duncan. Neither rational preference has won out. The reasons that ground those rational preferences all remain in play. They are juxtaposed, rather than ordered, which is sometimes the best that can be hoped for with quasi-cyclical preferences.

So, how does a model frame-sensitive reasoner extract reasons from frames? There are two processes here. The first I call frame decomposition, or frame deconstruction. The job here is to understand the perspectival nature of the individual frames – to extract the values that they express, for example, and the emotions that drive them. And then, once this has been done, the frame-sensitive reasoner needs to use that analysis to extract reasons from the frames and to use those reasons to make comparisons within and across frames.

A good place to start is with some ideas about frame analysis developed within political science and communication studies. The inspiration for frame analysis came from the sociologist Erving Goffman's 1974 book *Frame Analysis: An Essay on the Organization of Experience*, which we already looked at back in Chapter 1. As mentioned there, for Goffman, frames are "schemata of interpretation" that allow individuals "to locate, perceive, identify, and label."[27] Goffman's basic idea has been developed into a powerful set of tools for analyzing media communication, with the emphasis shifting from how individuals make sense of their own experience to how themes and messages are packaged in the media (and

---

[27] Goffman 1974, p. 21.

elsewhere). But whether one is thinking about frames as hermeneutic tools (tools for understanding) or thinking about them as tools for communication and/or manipulation, the fact remains that frames operate by highlighting selected dimensions of a complex situation and downplaying others – although in some contexts this is described more provocatively in terms of inclusion and exclusion (an illustration that the concept of a frame is itself up for framing).

Students of political communication have developed a theoretical framework for looking at the framing devices in news media. For example, Zhongdang Pan and Gerald Kosicki, in an article published in *Political Communication* in 1993, identify four different types of structure operative in constructing and processing news discourse. In each of these structures we can find devices that work to set up frames:

> *Syntactic structure* (understood broadly to include how headlines and other summary devices are used; how leads are used to set up stories; and how expert opinions are incorporated)
>
> *Script structure* (how news stories are constructed as narratives through answers to the familiar questions Who? What? Where? When? Why? And How?)
>
> *Thematic structure* (how attributions of causality are made or implied; how explanatory frameworks are suggested by the way the text is put together)
>
> *Rhetorical structure* (how word choices, symbols, metaphors, visual images, and other rhetorical devices work to promote particular affective responses)

A model frame-sensitive reasoner needs to be attuned to how framing works in news media, because this is a great tool for understanding both one's own way of framing an issue and that of other people. So, for example, someone approaching the issue of abortion from whatever perspective can learn plenty about their own framing and about alternatives from analyzing the very different framing devices used by, say, CNN and Fox News.

But clearly, the tools of news media frame analysis cannot be straightforwardly used for what I am calling frame decomposition. The framings we are considering are not primarily textual, and the way a frame works to structure and set up a decision problem is different from how it works to communicate a specific message or report a particular event. Moreover, the framings discussed in the context of media communication typically presuppose some degree of conscious communicative intent on the part of the framer, whereas the frames we are considering tend to have emerged through a much less intentional process – as a function of culture, background, social context, and associated types of affective and emotional responses. But, even though model frame-sensitive reasoners are working primarily with frames that lack explicit messages, there is a sense in which they are still engaged in the same kind of decoding activity. And news media frame analysis points to important dimensions of how frames work more generally.

So, for example, frames are often embedded in narratives, which are themselves constructed in particular ways.[28] Those narratives can be reason-giving. Narratives around climate change are a good example. A specific event such as the construction of a pipeline (the Keystone Pipeline, for example, or the Trans Mountain Pipeline) can be embedded in multiple different narratives. On one narrative the pipeline might be framed as part of a steady evolution towards energy independence and freedom from dependence on Middle Eastern oil. On another, the pipeline is a further step in raising standards of living by creating jobs and lowering fuel prices. A third narrative might see the pipeline as another step in the lengthy process of dispossessing Native American peoples of their land and heritage, while on a fourth narrative the pipeline is a further increase in environmental damage and environmental risk. Each of these narratives brings with it a different set of reasons. In part this is because each narrative tells a different causal/explanatory story – each narrative works to foreground some subset of the likely causal consequences of building the pipeline. And by bringing into play different comparison classes, each narrative engages with values and emotions in reason-giving ways – massacres of Native Americans at Wounded Knee, for example, or memories of the oil embargo imposed by OPEC upon the United States (and other countries) in retaliation for supporting Israel in the Yom Kippur War of 1973. And finally, as media frame analysis also stresses, each brings into play different symbols, metaphors, and visual imagery.

Something that media frame analysis does not typically emphasize, however, is the need to go behind a particular frame, as it were, to explore and uncover the values that it might express. This is very important from a reason-giving perspective. In order to do that a frame-sensitive reasoner will need to start by being very attuned to the distinction between factual and non-factual propositions. One of the principal dangers in dealing

---

[28] For a thought-provoking perspective on the importance of narratives in economics, see Schiller 2019, published just as this book was going to press. Schiller emphasizes how narratives, when they become embedded in the popular imagination, can have very significant economic consequences (e.g. in perpetuating recessions) precisely because they are such powerful mechanisms for engaging values and emotions.

intelligently with frames is taking non-factual propositions to be factual. We see many examples of this in discussions of abortion, where scientifically unfounded claims about the intellectual and emotional capacities of young fetuses are often presented as fact. A familiar example from America is television and newspaper advertisements that insert pictures of newborn infants into messages about second trimester abortion. For a European example, consider the successes of the lobby against genetically modified foods, which has managed to create a public perception that so-called "Franken-foods" present grave health risks, despite an almost complete absence of scientific evidence.[29] In both cases, non-factual propositions have been dressed up as factual propositions to spectacular effect. Even in the United States, for example, where the anti-GMO food campaign has been much less active than in Europe, a 2016 survey by the Pew Research Center found that 39 percent of adults thought that GM foods were more harmful to health than their non-GM equivalents.[30]

By and large, a frame-sensitive reasoner should not simply reject the views of those who believe that GM foods are dangerous to human health. This is not a productive way of dealing with discursive deadlock. A better strategy would be to treat purportedly factual claims about, say, the health risks of GM foods as non-factual propositions. This opens the door to a more constructive engagement, because it forces the frame-sensitive reasoner to focus not on what is being said, but on why it is being said and what lies behind the appeal to putative and questionable facts. This is a framing issue, and the appropriate response is to work backwards from the frame and its emotional and affective dimensions to the values that it incorporates and reflects. In the case of GM crops this is most likely to be a particular conception of what is natural, often wrapped up in a particular vision of agriculture and the rural lifestyle. In order to think one's way into the frame, one needs to be able to see the world from that perspective.

Bringing those implicit values into the open creates a space for identifying reasons and weighing them against each other. In the GMO case, for example, making explicit the particular conception of what is natural that might underlie someone's resistance to GM foods both opens that value

---

[29] For example, the interdisciplinary team who produced the 600-page report *Genetically Engineered Crops: Experiences and Prospects* for the National Academies of Science, Engineering, and Medicine in the United States in 2016 reviewed over 1,000 academic studies and found no significant evidence that GM foods were any more dangerous than their non-GM counterparts.

[30] A full report of the survey findings is available at pewresearch.org.

complex up to critical scrutiny on its own terms, and also allows it to be brought into dialog with other competing values. The issue is not so much one of "debunking" opposition to GM foods on health grounds by showing that this opposition lacks a scientific basis – if it were as simple as that then the anti-GM food movement would have expired long ago. The point is to shift the terms of the debate from non-factual propositions masquerading as factual propositions to a constructive discussion about the values that underlie those non-factual propositions.

Once that has been done, the frame-sensitive reasoner has arrived at the point that I am terming juxtaposition. Competing (frame-relative) values and reasons are available and open to scrutiny. To get to this point the frame-sensitive reasoner has been able to follow a fairly well-defined procedure, exploiting the techniques that I have been describing – reflexive decentering, imaginative simulation, perspective flexibility, and reason construction and juxtaposition. But at this point we are getting close to the end of the story that can be told about frame-sensitive reasoning in the abstract. We are now at a point where frame-sensitive reasoning becomes highly situational and context-dependent and its non-Archimedean nature becomes most clear.

The final stage of frame-sensitive reasoning can, broadly speaking, take several forms. It can involve bringing into dialog the different values and concomitant reasons that emerge in different frames. These values and reasons will most likely have given rise to preferences with a quasi-cyclical structure. Given that we are primarily interested in cases that generate discursive deadlock, the resulting dialog is most likely to be competitive. And if it is competitive, then in some cases one set of values and reasons might win out. This would happen if, for example, the juxtaposed reasons emerging from the processes outlined in this chapter turn out to be commensurable, allowing the reasons from one frame to outrank the reasons from another. In this sort of situation, frame-sensitive reasoners will have succeeded in eliminating the clash of frames. This would allow them to apply standard decision-making tools. They might be in a position to choose so as to maximize expected utility, for example. In those circumstances, the processes and techniques of frame-sensitive reasoning have effectively moved beyond discursive deadlock and brought decision-makers back to Archimedean reasoning.

One way this might happen would be, as it were, by a process of elimination. Applying the techniques already discussed might reveal the values underlying a frame and the reasons it brings into play to be so deeply repugnant that it effectively drops out of consideration. The

exercise of imaginative simulation and perspectival sensitivity can sometimes reveal an available frame to be completely unacceptable. It is true
that the first step in frame-sensitive reasoning is reflexive decentering, that
is, stepping back from identifying particular ways of framing a situation,
so that one can make the shift from thinking through frames to thinking
about them. But this is not supposed to be (and nor can it be) anything like
the type of reasoning that John Rawls envisaged as taking place behind
what he called the "veil of ignorance." Decision-makers behind the veil of
ignorance are supposed to reason in complete abstraction from any
knowledge of their intellectual, emotional, and social selves. They are
literally pure reasoners. Many philosophers and political theorists have
doubted that there could even be any such reasoning. Be that as it may,
however, it is certainly not even an aspiration in frame-sensitive reasoning. Frame-sensitive reasoners cannot completely decouple their affective
and emotional responses, or their valuational systems. Doing that would
make frame-sensitive reasoning impossible, given how important emotions and values are to engaging with frames. Frame-sensitive reasoners
must be able *partially* to disengage from their initial emotional and
affective responses, and also to be open to simulating unfamiliar and
even alien responses. But still, for many people there will be limits to
how far they can go in engaging with what they consider to be repugnant.

Can it be rational completely to reject a way of framing an outcome,
situation, or way of life in this manner? According to one extreme view, a
version of Humean instrumentalism, it can never be irrational to act in
accordance with one's most deeply felt values and affective attitudes – and
so it can never be irrational for one's values and affective attitudes to lead
one to reject an alien frame or perspective. That is what it means for
reason to be the slave of the passions. At the other extreme is the view that
it is a requirement of rationality to strive fully to understand all and any
way of framing actions or outcomes.

Neither extreme is plausible, from the perspective of rationality. The
Humean extreme falls foul of the due diligence requirement, because it
recommends persisting in discursive deadlock without trying to engage
with alternate perspectives and frames.

But nor can it be a requirement of rationality that a frame-sensitive
reasoner take every available frame on its own terms. Frame-sensitive
reasoners cannot be expected to step away from their own values and
emotions completely. There are people who have the ability and the will to
think their way into the perspective of torturers, child molesters, serial
killers, and genocidal murderers. And it is fortunate that they exist,

because their talents can be put to good use by law enforcement, the judicial system, and so on. But surely this level of reasoning goes far beyond what is required by rationality. The intellectual and emotional effort it requires effectively takes one outside the realm of frame-sensitive reasoning.

So what does rationality require in this regard? There are no cut-and-dried answers. The due diligence requirement effectively says that a model frame-sensitive reasoner should make appropriate efforts to understand multiple ways of framing complex decision situations. What counts as appropriate will vary by context. The four strategies (or families of strategies) we have been considering are ways of implementing the due diligence requirement. To the extent that reasoners fail to engage with them, it seems fair to say that they are falling short of model frame-sensitive reasoning. But falling short of model frame-sensitive reasoning is not the same as being irrational. Rationality is a scalar notion and there are degrees of rationality. So what should we make of a frame-sensitive reasoner who makes a good faith effort to think their way into a deeply alien perspective and then comes up against an internal wall of incomprehension and/or repugnance?

It seems to me that the real issue is how one evaluates the incomprehension and/or repugnance. The examples I have been discussing were deliberately chosen as eliciting repugnance within the vast majority of human social and cultural groupings, to the point where it seems reasonable to speak of a collective incomprehension and/or repugnance. My proposal, then, is that an individual's frame-sensitive reasoning falls short of rationality in this type of situation to the extent that their personal incomprehension and/or repugnance fails to map onto a collective incomprehension and/or repugnance. Incomprehension and repugnance can be rational when applied to serial killers and child molesters, in other words, but not when applied to abortion doctors, for example, or defenders of gun rights. It is reasonable to expect a rational frame-sensitive thinker to question their own incomprehension and repugnance when it is not shared by the overwhelming majority of the population (and I mean the population at large, not the particular circles a reasoner might happen to inhabit).

Another way in which one particular way of framing a decision problem can win out occurs when a decision-maker thinks their way through to an overarching frame that will subsume the formerly conflicting frames so that the reasons they generate can be weighed against each other on a single scale. For Agamemnon, for example, this would be a single way of framing the death of Iphigenia so that the costs of murdering his daughter could be directly weighed against the benefit of being able to lead the Greek fleet to Troy. I have no idea what such a frame might look like (and nor, I believe, did Aeschylus). But other examples seem more tractable. Different ways of framing the ill-fated Community Charge in Great Britain reflected different ways of framing the basic value of fairness. A frame-sensitive reasoner realizing that might evaluate and compare these different models of fairness. They might come to the view, for example, that fairness as equity subsumes fairness as equality (perhaps reasoning that equality is the limiting case of equity, arrived at when there are no significant differences across individuals on equity-relevant features such as income education, needs, and so forth).

But, of course, there is no guarantee of success. A frame-sensitive reasoner may do everything that can be reasonably be expected of them by way of reflexive decentering, imaginative simulation, perspectival sensitivity, and reason construction and juxtaposition without a single frame winning out in either of the two ways just described. Such reasoners cannot escape their quasi-cyclical preferences. Certainly, they can act – and indeed they may have to act, since not acting is often not an option. But that does not necessarily eliminate the quasi-cyclical preferences and consequent conflict. The quasi-cyclical pattern can persist, as reflected in regret, indecision, and backsliding. We saw an example of this in the case of Macbeth.

The rationality of frame-sensitive reasoning is determined by the process, rather than the result. And so lack of success does not necessarily show lack of rationality. A frame-sensitive reasoner is rational to the extent that they respect the basic consistency requirements discussed in Chapter 10 and engage in the techniques explored in this chapter. Moreover, it is perfectly rational to embark upon this type of dialog (whether internal or external), even though there is no guarantee of success. We are, by definition, discussing decision problems that cannot be solved by the "small world" techniques of, say, expected utility theory. These are problems that typically give rise to discursive deadlock. And they are also typically problems of a deeply fundamental and personal nature. How can it be more rational to persist in deadlock than to embark upon dialog? And if it is rational to embark upon the dialog, and the dialog respects the basic constraints upon model frame-sensitive reasoning that we have been exploring, then rationality will tend to be preserved. And the resulting state, even if it is one of persisting quasi-cyclicality, inherits the rationality of the process by which it was reached.

Appendix

Frames in the Brain

We can learn a lot about what drives framing effects by looking at the brain activity that underlies them – and in particular at how that activity is distributed across different parts of the brain. Technologies such as functional magnetic resonance imaging (fMRI) and electroencephalography (EEG) allow researchers to map out the different brain regions engaged when people carry out specific tasks. This offers a blueprint for exploring the neurobiology of framing effects.

So, for example, carefully reproducing experiments like those explored in Chapters 1 and 2 in an fMRI scanner can show which parts of the brain are active when subjects switch between being risk-averse for gains and being risk-seeking for losses. Tying framing effects to particular brain regions is not an end in itself, of course. What makes it interesting and important is that we can then calibrate these discoveries with other things that we know about those brain regions and what they do. So, for example, we can bring to bear what we know from neuropsychology about what happens when those brain regions are damaged, as well as integrate experimental work on related areas in primate brains. This Appendix shows how doing all this allows us to develop a much deeper picture of where framing effects come from and how they work.[1]

---

[1] For more detail on different techniques for brain mapping, as well as some of the theoretical and methodological challenges, see my textbook *Cognitive Science: An Introduction to the Science of the Mind* (Bermúdez 2020), particularly Chapter 9. I have drawn freely from that book in the following.

The Anatomy of the Human Brain: A Quick Primer

To appreciate the work that has been done on the neurobiology of framing, we need first to review the key elements of brain anatomy. As we do this I'll flag some of the principal brain areas that we will be looking at in the remainder of the chapter.

Neuroanatomists distinguish three different parts of the mammalian brain. The oldest (in evolutionary terms) is the *hindbrain*, popularly known as the reptilian brain. This is the part of the brain responsible for autonomic bodily systems such as breathing, sleep patterns, bladder control, and so forth. The next most recent part is the *midbrain*, which controls posture, walking, reflexes, temperature regulation, and basic sensorimotor coordination. The largest (and evolutionarily youngest) of the three parts of the brain is the *forebrain*. This is the most important part of the brain for cognitive and motor processing (thinking and acting, in other words) and everything that we will be discussing takes place within the forebrain.

The forebrain itself has a complex structure, illustrated in Figure A.1 (which also shows the midbrain and the principal structures of the hindbrain).

The largest part of the forebrain is the *cerebrum*, which is divided into two hemispheres (left and right). The two hemispheres are joined by the bundle of nerve fibers known as the *corpus callosum*. The corpus callosum allows the hemispheres to communicate with each other.[2] Each hemisphere has an outer layer (about 2–4 mm thick) known as the *cerebral cortex* (and popularly as "grey matter"). The cerebral cortex is the most recent part of the brain (in evolutionary

---

[2] It turns out that the corpus callosum has been very important in teaching us about what each of the two hemispheres actually does. In the 1950s and 1960s Roger Sperry (subsequently joined by Michael Gazzaniga) developed groundbreaking experimental techniques for studying "split-brain patients," whose corpus callosum has been severed (usually as a last-ditch attempt to control severe epilepsy). The fact that these patients do not have a corpus callosum transmitting information across the two hemispheres means that information can be presented separately to each hemisphere. In key areas, the left and right hemispheres respond differently. So, for example, since language is located in the left hemisphere, Sperry and Gazzaniga found that split-brain patients cannot verbally identify objects presented to the right hemisphere (see Gazzaniga 2005 for a review of forty-five years of split-brain research). Some of these textbook findings have recently been challenged (Pinto et al. 2017), but even these new studies found that split-brain patients are unable to tell whether objects presented separately to the two hemispheres are the same or different.

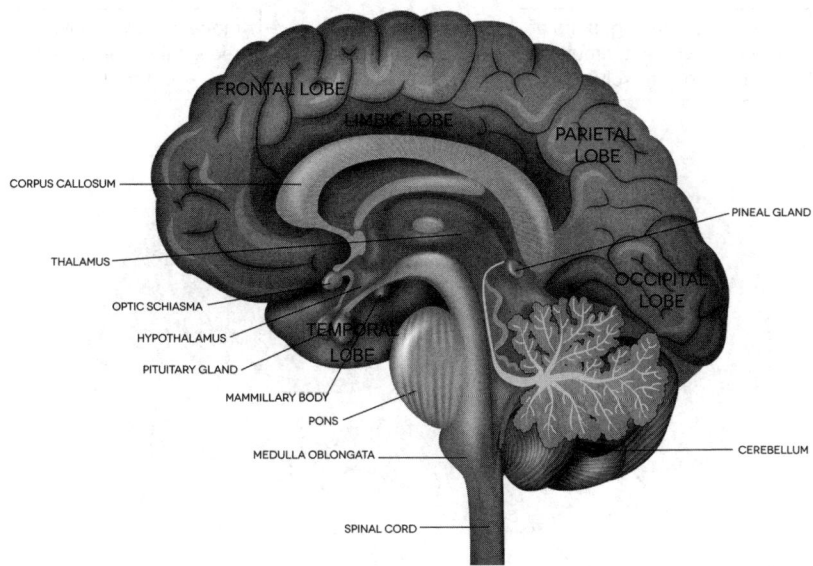

FIGURE A.1 A vertical cross-section of the human brain
Note: Principal structures of the cerebrum, including the four lobes (and the limbic lobe, postulated by Paul Broca, as described in the main text). The three principal structures of the hindbrain are the pons, medulla, and cerebellum. The midbrain is located immediately above the pons. *Credit*: TefiM / iStock / Getty Images Plus.

terms) and is associated with thought, language, reasoning, awareness, perception, and other higher-level cognitive functions.

Within each hemisphere the cerebral cortex is divided into four lobes. Each lobe has its own specific functions. Figure A.2 summarizes the functional specialization of the four lobes.

Within each lobe there is an even more fine-grained functional organization. The German neurologist Korbinian Brodmann proposed a much-used way of looking at this in 1909. He identified fifty-two different areas within the cerebral cortex. These areas are identified in anatomical terms (based on cytoarchitecture, or how the cells are organized), but many of the areas have been tied to specific cognitive and motor functions. Some of the cortical areas most relevant to the neuroscience of framing are located in the *frontal lobe*, specialized for executive functions such as reasoning and planning. We will be looking in particular at the *ventromedial prefrontal cortex* (vmPFC), which is

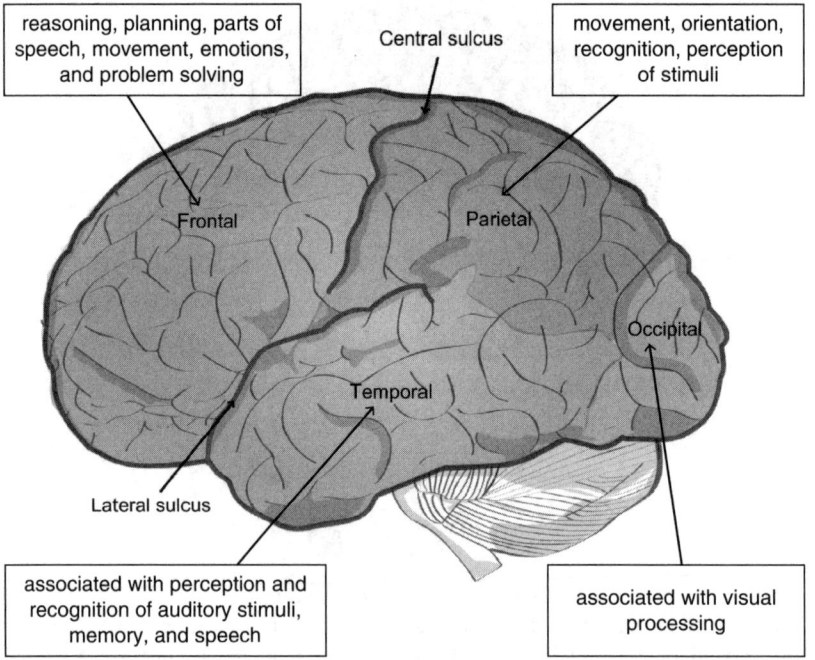

reasoning, planning, parts of speech, movement, emotions, and problem solving

Central sulcus

movement, orientation, recognition, perception of stimuli

Frontal

Parietal

Occipital

Temporal

Lateral sulcus

associated with perception and recognition of auditory stimuli, memory, and speech

associated with visual processing

FIGURE A.2 The division of the left cerebral hemisphere into lobes, showing the basic functions that each of the four lobes is believed to be specialized to perform
Note: These are Fig. 3.3 and Box 3.1 in Bermúdez 2020.

part of a network distributed across Brodmann areas 10, 11, 12, 25, and 32.

Moving inwards from the cerebral cortex we find the subcortex, composed of several distinct structures. These include the *basal ganglia*, the *limbic system* (composed of the *hippocampus* and the *amygdala*), and the *thalamus* and *hypothalamus*. Subcortical brain structures play two distinct roles. They function as relay stations between the cerebral cortex and the spinal cord. And they also play important roles in controlling movement, skill learning, emotion processing. The main subcortical structures within the cerebrum are illustrated in Figure A.3.

Subcortical areas have been less studied than the cerebral cortices, but there is some consensus among neuroscientists as to what they do in general. The basal ganglia work primarily in initiating and controlling movement and learning motor skills. They also form part of the reward

Limbic system

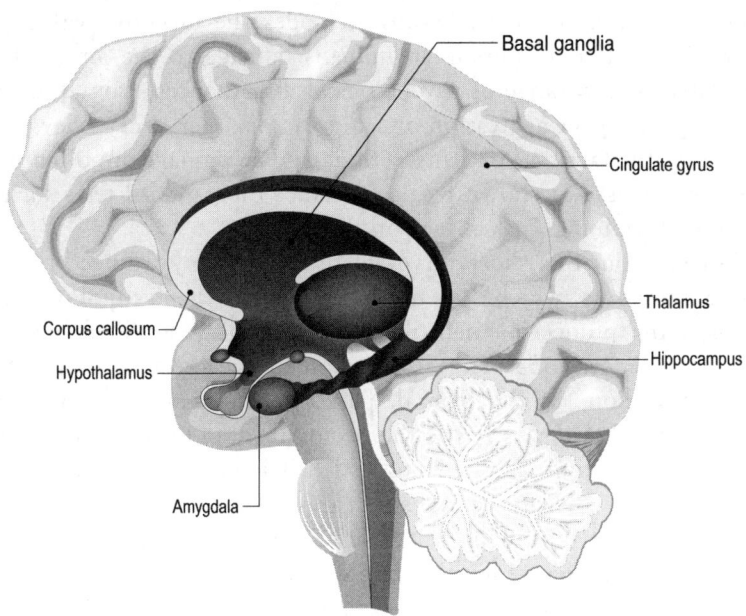

FIGURE A.3 The principal subcortical structures in the human brain
Credit: ttsz / iStock / Getty Images Plus.

and value system (to be discussed further below). The thalamus functions as a relay station and gateway for sensory and motor information coming into the cerebral cortex, while the hypothalamus is the link between the endocrine (hormone) system and the nervous system, responsible for regulating hormones that control a wide range of bodily functions such as sleep, attachment behaviors, temperature, hunger, thirst, and so on.

For this chapter the most important subcortical structure is the *limbic system*, usually taken to be composed of the hippocampus and the amygdala and generally thought to be responsible for emotion processing. The hippocampus is central to the development of memory, particularly the consolidation of short-term memories into long-term memories. The amygdala is very important in the neuroscience of framing. It is a small, almond-shaped structure within each hemisphere. It receives and integrates information from all the different senses, as well as from the major internal bodily organs. Studies from animals have shown that the amygdala is important for motivation, because it codes the incentive value (the valence) of different stimuli. In humans damage to the amygdala is correlated with a range of psychological disturbances, from addictive behaviors to hyper-aggression and bipolar disorder. Very relevant to framing is the fact that patients with amygdala damage are often poor at assessing risk, as shown by performance on standard tests such as the Iowa Gambling Task. More on this later.

To round out this short survey of brain anatomy we need to look at one more area, which does not fit neatly into the taxonomy so far. In 1878 the pioneering neurologist Paul Broca identified what he called the *limbic lobe*. This is a region of the cerebral cortex that includes sections of the frontal, parietal, and temporal lobes, but does not reach back as far as the occipital lobe. Even more so than the subcortical limbic system, to which it is closely connected, it is more of a set of interacting structures than a single, identifiable neural structure (and neuroscientists disagree about how exactly to draw its boundaries). Like the limbic system, the areas in the limbic lobe are very important in emotional processing. One part of the limbic lobe that plays a particularly significant role in the neurobiology of framing is the *anterior cingulate cortex* (ACC), distributed across Brodmann areas 24, 32, and 33 and looking rather like a collar around the frontal part of the corpus callosum. The ACC has strong connections both "downwards" to the amygdala and "upwards" to the frontal lobe, including the ventromedial prefrontal cortex. Its many roles include regulating affects (e.g. by managing uncomfortable emotions), modulating the emotional valence of different stimuli, and processing feedback from actions, both positive and negative.

Let's turn now from structure and organization to a more detailed look at function.

Technology and Methods for Studying the Brain

How does the brain represent value? This is the aspect of decision-making that has been most studied by neuroscientists. Researchers have looked at how the brain represents value in both monkeys and humans. Monkey brains and human brains are, of course, very different. And the experimental techniques used to study them operate at very different scales. Nonetheless, some common themes have emerged in the last ten or fifteen years, and neuroscientists are converging, at least in broad outline, on a map of how value is encoded in the brain.[3] The following sections will sketch out the basic landmarks on this map. First, though, a little background on how neuroscientists study decision-making in the brain.

We can start with animals. Researchers studying how monkeys make decisions typically use microelectrodes to track electrical activity in individual neurons. When neurons fire they send electrical impulses (called *action potentials*) down their axons. These action potentials are transmitted to other neurons at *synapses*. The details of how this works are complex, but the important point is that microelectrodes placed close to individual neurons can record the discharge of action potentials, and so allow researchers to make inferences about what individual neurons are responding to.

Studying individual neurons can only get us so far, however. It is too fine-grained a technique to tell us much, if anything, about how the brain is organized – about how different brain regions collaborate and coordinate with each other to solve different types of problem and process different types of information. To study the overall organization of the brain we need to look, not just at individual neurons, but at entire populations of neurons.

One way to do this is through human encephalography (EEG). This is a relatively uncomplicated and inexpensive technique for studying populations of neurons (not to be confused with ECG – which is an electrocardiogram, used to study the heart, not the brain!). EEG uses electrodes attached to the skull. Each electrode can pick up the electrical activity of thousands of neurons. The firing patterns of neural populations look like waves. These waves oscillate at different frequencies, divided up into bands typically labeled with letters from the Greek alphabet. Slow wave sleep takes place in the delta band, for example. The great advantage of EEG is that it is very accurate with respect to time. EEG is typically used to record the electrical activity provoked by a specific stimulus (what neuroscientists call *event-related potentials*). The changing shape of an

---

[3] There are useful reviews in Kable and Glimcher 2009 and Louie and Glimcher 2012. Rangel et al. 2008 discuss some of the theoretical/methodological issues in studying decision-making in the brain. Bartra, McGuire, and Kable's 2013 article is a meta-analysis of 206 published fMRI experiments showing how very different methodologies and experiments have converged upon a "subjective value network" incorporating the vmPFC and the ventral striatum, as described further on in this section.

event-related potential can be measured at the level of milliseconds (thousandths of a second). But the major limitation of EEG is that, despite its exceptional temporal accuracy, it is not a very fine-grained tool for understanding where exactly in the brain the electrical activity it is measuring takes place. To get a higher spatial resolution we need to switch from looking at patterns in the brain's electrical activity to looking at what the flow of blood in the brain tells us about which different parts of the brain are active during a particular task or activity.

This brings us to functional neuroimaging (more popularly known as brain-scanning). This is the technology that has launched a thousand breathless headlines, with journalists often writing as if neuroimaging allows us directly to observe what the brain is doing, so that we can find the neural basis for romantic love, for example, or schizophrenia. The brightly colored pictures that typically accompany these reports encourage the perception that neuroimaging is a picture of emotion or of thought. The reality, unfortunately, is quite a bit messier and a lot less newsworthy. The basic assumption behind neuroimaging is that the more work cells are doing in a particular region of the brain, the more blood flows there. So neuroscientists can track blood flow in order to get an indirect measure of activity in populations of neurons. Positron emission tomography (PET) scanning was the original form of neuroimaging. It directly measures blood flow through tracking the movement of radioactive water in the brain. But PET scanning has now largely been superseded as a research tool by functional magnetic resonance imaging (fMRI), which actually measures blood flow indirectly. So fMRI is really an indirect measure of an indirect measure! What it actually measures is levels of oxygen in the blood. It works because oxygenated and deoxygenated blood have different magnetic properties. The powerful magnetic field in an MRI scanner detects the contrast between oxygenated and deoxygenated blood and gives a measure of the so-called BOLD signal ("BOLD" stands for Blood Oxygen Level Dependent, in case you are wondering).

Goals and Value in the Monkey Brain

I mentioned earlier that there is growing consensus among neuroscientists about how value is coded and computed in the brain, and about which brain areas are primarily responsible. An important part of this consensus has come from animal studies. So in this section we will look at an important and influential study using single neuron recordings to study how individual neurons in the monkey brain respond to rewards. This will give us a framework for looking at fMRI experiments in humans, which we will do in the next section. These imaging experiments have gone a long way towards identifying a neural network for valuing different actions and outcomes.

In a pioneering set of studies published in the journal *Nature* in 2006, Camillo Padoa-Schioppa and John Assad used single neuron recording techniques to study the choice behavior of rhesus monkeys.[4] A number of earlier studies had suggested that the orbitofrontal cortex (OFC) is very important for choice and decision-making in monkeys, and they confined their recordings to a highly specific region of the OFC. Recall that neuroscientists often describe the topography of the brain in terms of Brodmann areas. In non-human primates the OFC spans three Brodmann areas (11, 12, and 13). Padoa-Schioppa and Assad focused on Brodmann area 13. What they were interested in was how monkeys actually make comparisons between different rewards. In this case, as often in monkey experiments, the rewards were quantities of juice. (Actually juice A was water and juice B was unsweetened Kool-Aid. It turns out that monkeys prefer water to Kool-Aid. More on this below.)

As we've seen on several occasions, economists, psychologists, and decision theorists use different formal theories to describe, predict, and explain choice behavior and decision-making. These theories diverge in many respects. Prospect theory, as developed by Kahneman and Tversky, is very different from classical utility theory. But both theories share a single fundamental assumption. This is the assumption that different outcomes can be compared relative to a single, "common currency." Standard utility theory has the name that it does because it employs the common currency of utility. In prospect theory the common currency is called value. The two theories are agreed, though, on two basic ideas. The first is that (as it were) the "desirability" of different outcomes can be represented relative to some abstract measure. And the second is that the process of decision-making involves some sort of comparison between the desirabilities of different outcomes.

So, that's the theory. But what is the neural reality? Economists and decision theorists are typically rather coy about what utility theory is actually a theory of. They usually describe utility theory as a representation of choice. What they mean is that, provided decision-

[4] Padoa-Schioppa and Assad 2006.

makers make choices in ways that respect certain basic principles of consistency, then those choices can be represented as maximizing expected utility. It follows that economists and decision theorists are not in any sense committed to their talk of utility mapping cleanly onto anything that actually takes place in the brain. As they typically see it, utility theory offers an elegant and useful framework for describing the choices of ideally rational decision-makers. But that doesn't mean that it explains why decision-makers make the decisions that they do – still less that it actually describes any specific method or mechanism for comparing different options and outcomes.[5] So it certainly would be a very interesting result indeed if it turned out that we can find neurons behaving as if they are measuring the value/utility of outcomes.

Yet that is exactly what Padoa-Schioppa and Assad's monkeys seemed to be doing in their ingeniously constructed experiment! The first thing the experimenters did was to work backwards from the monkeys' choices between juices to their "value function." They did this by offering different quantities of water and Kool-Aid and seeing how much extra Kool-Aid the monkeys would require before switching their preference away from water. It turned out that monkeys are more or less indifferent between one unit of water and just over four units of Kool-Aid. So, at least in this highly restricted domain, the monkeys could plausibly be described as comparing the two juices in a common currency that assigns a different value to quantities of each juice. Following the standard terminology in this literature, let's term this common currency *subjective value* (SV).[6] The starting point for the experiments, therefore, is that SV(water) ≈ 4.1 SV (Kool-Aid).

So now, if we know how much monkeys value water relative to how much they value Kool-Aid, then we can work out the value for each option when they are offered a specific amount of water vs. a specific amount of Kool-Aid. Just plug in the quantities!

---

[5] Milton Friedman's influential 1953 article "The methodology of positive economics" explicitly states that assumptions about utility in economics are not intended to be psychologically realistic. All that matters is that they generate useful predictions of how ideally rational agents would behave. This is the "official" view within economics. But of course one might reasonably ask how utility can be predictively accurate if it is not psychologically realistic, and many non-economists have tended to view utility in more psychological terms. For further discussion from a more philosophical perspective see Broome 1991a, Bermúdez 2009, and Okasha 2016.

[6] The authors themselves use the terminology of *value*, but "subjective value" is better because it is neutral between different theoretical frameworks. Recall that Kahneman and Tversky use the term "value" for the common currency of prospect theory.

So, for example, given a choice between 2 units of water and 6 units of Kool-Aid, we would expect the monkeys to choose the water (which has 8.2 units of SV – i.e. 4.1 × 2) to the Kool-Aid (which only has 6 units of SV). But if we add three more units of Kool-Aid then we would expect the monkeys to switch their choice. The important point is that it is the overall amount of SV that determines choice, irrespective of whether it comes from water or Kool-Aid. That is what we mean by saying that it is a common currency for comparing options.

The next thing the researchers did was investigate the neurons in area 13 of the OFC to see whether there were any whose firing rates correlated with SV. In fact, they found three different types of neuron, sensitive to different aspects of the decision-making process. The first class of neurons they termed *offer value neurons*. These neurons fired in response to the SV of one of the offered rewards – i.e. their firing rates were correlated with the total SV associated either with the offered water or with the offered Kool-Aid. So, they seem to be computing the costs and benefits of the different possible outcomes. Padoa-Schioppa and Assad also found neurons correlated with the process of comparing the different options and selecting one. They called these neurons *chosen value neurons*. These are neurons that fire in response to the total SV of the selected reward, abstracting away completely from whether what was chosen was water or Kool-Aid. Finally, they identified *taste neurons* that fired in response to the particular type of juice chosen. So, for example, if a monkey on one trial opted for 2 units of water with a total of 8 units of SV, and then on a later trial selected 8 units of Kool-Aid, the *chosen value neurons* would have a similar profile across the two trials, but the taste neurons would differ. According to Padoa-Schioppa and Assad, around 80 percent of all the neurons in OFC area 13 were either offer value neurons, chosen value neurons, or taste neurons.

From the Monkey Brain to the Human Brain

So, it looks as if the Padoa-Schioppa and Assad experiment reviewed in the previous section shows that there are neurons whose job it is to measure the value/utility of outcomes in a common currency. This common currency allows different outcomes to be compared. But they were working on the monkey. How can we extend this work to the human brain?

Well, we certainly can't use the same techniques. Since single cell recording is highly invasive, it is typically only carried out in non-human animals.[7] Researchers studying decision-making in humans have primarily employed imaging technologies, particularly fMRI. And they have also looked in a slightly different place. In the monkey the neurons responsible for measuring value/utility have been identified primarily in the OFC. Imaging researchers have tended to focus primarily on a nearby area, the ventromedial prefrontal cortex (vmPFC).[8] In fact, in humans the vmPFC is adjacent to the OFC. Both are parts of the ventral prefrontal cortex.

There is a reason for starting with the vmPFC. Research on brain-damaged patients suggests that, when it comes to humans, the vmPFC is the place to look for comparisons and calculations of subjective value across different possible outcomes and actions. A number of studies have tested decision-making in patients with damage to the vmPFC using a version of the Iowa Gambling Task, developed by Antoine Bechara, Antonio Damasio, and colleagues at the University of Iowa.[9] Subjects can click one of four cards on a screen, leading either to a (financial) loss or to a gain. Experimenters can vary the proportion and size of losses and gains in different "decks," so that some decks have both large losses and large gains, while others much less variance, offering a safer route, with smaller gains but even smaller losses. Normal subjects quickly learn to spot the "risky" decks, and develop physiological responses to them (e.g. galvanic skin responses) even before they are consciously aware of what is going on. Patients with damage to the vmPFC tend to behave in exactly the opposite way to normal subjects. Whereas normal subjects tend to avoid the "risky" decks and settle instead for the boring strategy of small gains interspersed with even smaller losses, the vmPFC subjects deliberately seek out the high-risk, high-reward option. So, experimenters conclude, the vmPFC must be playing an important role in evaluating the riskiness of different outcomes.

Further experiments carried out by Natalie Camille and colleagues (and published in the *Journal of Neuroscience* in 2011) suggest that the vmPFC

---

[7] There have been single neuron studies in humans. These have typically involved epileptic patients, who have had a tungsten electrode inserted during surgery. For an overview and review see Rey et al. 2015.

[8] It is no easy matter to extrapolate from monkey studies to humans. Wallis 2011 discusses some of the anatomical and methodological challenges specifically in the context of studies on the role of OFC in decision-making. Öngür and Price 2000 is a classic discussion of the comparative anatomy of the prefrontal cortex in rats, monkeys, and humans. For a general review of the role of prefrontal cortex in decision-making see Kennerley and Walton 2011.

[9] Bechara et al. 1994 and 1999 were pioneering studies. See also Fellows and Farah 2007.

has a key role to play, not just in evaluating different outcomes, but also in comparing outcomes across different choices. One index of whether patients can compare outcomes in different choice situations is whether or not they are consistent. It turns out that patients with damage to the vmPFC have problems in this domain. Camille et al. found that vmPFC-damaged patients often make choices that are internally inconsistent in basic ways. They would make intransitive choices for example, choosing C over A even though they had just chosen A over B and B over C.[10]

So, the evidence from neuropsychology points to the role of the vmPFC in humans in assessing risk and evaluating and comparing different outcomes. The monkey experiments just reviewed identified neurons that code for subjective value. Is there a connection here?

Well, a number of fMRI experiments suggest a bridge between these two lines of research. These experiments have found patterns of BOLD activation suggesting that the distinctive contribution of the vmPFC may lie in measuring and comparing the subjective value of different outcomes. (Recall that fMRI studies track levels of blood oxygen through the BOLD signal, rather than the actual electrical activity of neurons.)

Joseph Kable and Paul Glimcher carried out an influential study that was published in *Nature Reviews Neuroscience* in 2007. They examined how people choose between immediate and delayed monetary rewards. Before putting subjects in the fMRI scanner Kable and Glimcher tested their preferences between an immediate reward of $20 and different delayed rewards (varying both in the size of the reward and in the length of the delay). They used these preliminary behavioral experiments to calculate a *psychometric discount function* for each subject. A discount function essentially measures how the subjective value of money decreases the further away in the future it is. (Describing this discount function as psychometric just means that it reflects how subjects subjectively experience the rewards).

Once they had identified ten subjects with stable discount functions (i.e. ten individuals who were internally consistent in their choices between immediate and delayed rewards), Kable and Glimcher then tested the subjects again on similar choices between immediate rewards and delayed rewards. Because they had already calculated a discount function for each subject, they were able to estimate the subjective value of both immediate and delayed rewards. They then used this information to identify brain regions that seemed to be measuring subjective value. The

[10] Camille et al. 2011.

two regions that they ended up focusing on were the vmPFC and the *ventral striatum* (VS). The ventral striatum is a subcortical brain region that forms part of the basal ganglia and is thought to play an important role in reinforcement learning (and, relatedly, in drug and other addiction behaviors). In both the vmPFC and the VS Kable and Glimcher found a significant correlation between neural activity (as reflected in the BOLD signal) and the subjective value of the presented rewards, as that subjective value varied across different trials.

In fact, they found two different types of correlation. The first is the most obvious. The two regions showed increased neural activity when subjective value increased, and decreased neural activity when subjective value decreased. In addition, though, they found a much more subtle correlation. The subjective value of a reward decreases with delay. The rate and shape of that decrease is measured, for a specific individual, by the psychometric discount function that was calculated before the imaging part of the experiment began. Kable and Glimcher were able to map the rate and shape of this psychometric discounting onto the rate and shape of the decrease in neural activity in the vmPFC and the VS. To illustrate, imagine someone who very much prefers a reward now to a delayed reward. That means that they have a steep discount curve. In other words, the value of the reward to them drops drastically the further into the future it lies. For these subjects, the shape of their discount curve maps onto the rate of decrease in neural activity in the vmPFC and VS, so that neural activity also drops drastically with the length of the delay. As Kable and Glimcher put it, the neurometric discount functions that describe how neural activity decreases with delay map into the psychometric discount functions that measure how subjective value decreases with delay. Less technically, the rate at which these two brain areas fire in response to rewards matches the rate at which the subjects lose interest in the rewards.

So, in certain respects the vmPFC and VS behave similarly. In both we see neural activity correlated with the subjective value of rewards. Yet, the two areas seem to play different roles in decision-making. We have already looked at the vmPFC and its role in evaluating risk (as revealed, for example, in the tendency of patients with vmPFC damage to engage in riskier behavior than most people would be comfortable with). The VS seems to be more involved in calculating and predicting rewards. There is a pleasing symmetry here. Calculating rewards and evaluating risk are complementary activities and decision-making involves both.

One final point – about how learning takes place in the brain. Most theories of learning emphasize the importance of dopamine, which is the neurotransmitter thought to be primarily responsible both for normal reward-seeking behavior and for abnormal behaviors such as addiction. There are important populations of dopaminergic neurons (i.e. neurons that increase dopamine-related activity) projecting from the midbrain to both the vmPFC and the VS. This is exactly what one would expect, given that these areas seem to code for subjective value and subjective value is largely a function of expected reward. But the VS seems to have a distinctive role to play, tied to a distinctive feature of dopaminergic neurons that was first discovered in the late 1990s.

Wolfram Schultz, Peter Dayan, and Read Montague, in a very influential paper published in *Science* in 1997, reviewed a range of behavioral and animal studies and proposed a model on which dopaminergic neurons do not respond directly to rewards as they are presented or consumed, but instead measure what they called a "reward prediction error."[11] That is to say, dopaminergic neurons respond to the difference between the reward that is expected and the reward that is actually received. They are strongly inhibited when the reward falls a long way short of expectation and strongly excited when it greatly exceeds expectation. Firing and inhibition are correspondingly lower when the prediction error is lower and, it turns out, dopaminergic neurons show very little response when the reward is as predicted. The point here, of course, is that error is what matters for learning. The brain needs to keep track of the reward prediction error because the point of learning is to close the gap between what one expects to happen and what actually happens. And this is where the VS comes into the picture, because it is thought to be an important location for coding the reward prediction error.[12]

Gains and Losses in the Brain

And now (finally!) to framing effects. Remember that the first framing effect we looked at back in Chapter 1 was the Asian disease paradigm. What that showed was that people are generally risk-averse for gains and risk-seeking for losses. In other words, people can be induced to react to

[11] See Schultz, Dayan, and Montague 1997 and Schultz 1998. Bromberg-Martin, Matsumoto, and Hikosaka 2010 is a comprehensive review of subsequent research on dopamine. For Schultz's most recent thoughts see Schultz 2016.

[12] See Haber 2011 for more on the neuroanatomy of the VS.

an event differently depending on how it is described. If it is described positively or as a gain (in terms, for example, of the number of lives that would be saved by a particular treatment) then people will typically behave in ways that are risk-averse. They are less likely to take chances than they would be if that very same event was described negatively or as a loss (e.g. in terms of the number of lives that would be lost if the very same treatment was adopted).

There have been some fMRI experiments that actually use versions of the Asian disease paradigm, but this has not received as much traction as a financial decision-making task developed by Benedetto de Martino and colleagues in an article published in *Science* in 2006.[13] Like the Asian disease experiment, De Martino et al. constructed their task so that subjects were presented with a single outcome in two different frames – a loss frame and a gain frame. Unlike the original Asian disease experiments, however, these experiments were within subjects (i.e. each subject had the opportunity to make choices in both the loss frame and the gain frame, which were randomly interspersed). You might think that subjects in a within-subjects paradigm would be able to figure out what was going on, but interestingly when the subjects were debriefed the majority were completely unaware that they had succumbed to a framing effect!

At the start of each trial subjects were shown a slide telling them that they would receive a certain sum of money – say, $50. They were then given a choice. They could either settle for a fixed portion of the starting sum, which they would be allowed to keep. This was the sure option. Or they could choose the gamble option. The gamble option had two possible outcomes – they would either keep the entire starting sum, or walk away with nothing. Obviously, the sure option is the risk-averse choice, while the gamble option is the risk-seeking choice.

The subjects were presented with a slide showing both options. The left hand side of the slide showed the sum that they would be guaranteed to keep if they took the sure option, while the right hand side showed the gamble option in the form of a pie-chart, depicted in Figure A.4.

The experimenters varied the amount of the sure option across trials, but they were careful to make corresponding adjustments to the probabilities to ensure that within each trial the sure option and the

[13] See De Martino, Kumaran, Seymour, and Dolan 2006. Zheng, Wang, and Zhu 2010 is an example of a study using the Asian disease paradigm. Yu and Zhang 2014 compares the Asian disease paradigm to the De Martino financial decision-making task.

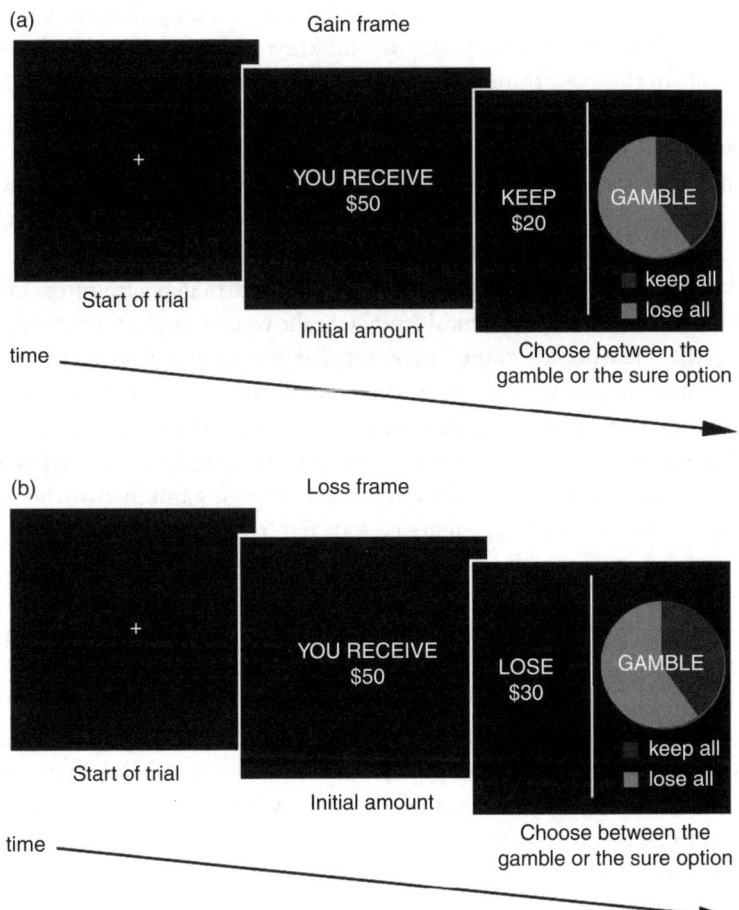

FIGURE A.4 The experimental set-up in De Martino et al. 2006
Note: Subjects are initially given a fixed sum of money and then offered a choice between the (risk-averse) option of keeping some portion of the money for sure, or a (risk-seeking) gamble between keeping all of the money and losing all of it. The probabilities in the gamble are represented visually in a pie-chart. In all trials the expected value of the sure option is exactly the same as the expected value of the gamble.

gamble option had the same expected value (although, since the subjects were not given the precise numerical probabilities, it is unclear that they were in a position to figure this out for themselves exactly). But the principal variation across trials was in how the sure option was framed.

In some of the trials the sure option was framed as a Gain. That is, subjects were told how much money they would keep from the original allocated amount. In the Loss frame, in contrast, they were told how much money they would lose from the original sum. So, as illustrated in Figure A.4, the sure option in the Loss frame was presented as losing $30, while in the Gain frame it was presented as keeping $20. Of course, if you start with $50, then losing $30 is exactly the same as keeping $20. And so the gamble option was exactly the same in both cases.

Unsurprisingly, given how robust this particular framing effect generally is, the experimental subjects showed a robust tendency to make the "textbook" choice of going for the sure option in the Gain frame and the gamble option in the Loss frame. On average across the population of 20 subjects, subjects only chose to gamble in 42.9 percent of the Gain frame trials, while in the Loss frame they gambled in 61.6 percent of the trials. Every subject showed an increase in gambling in the Loss frames, with the percentage increase varying from a low of 7 percent to a high of 40 percent. In other words, both as a population and as individuals, they were risk-averse for Gains and risk-seeking for Losses. So, given that all of these trials were taking place in an fMRI scanner, everything was in place to investigate the neural basis of this classic framing effect.

To explore the neurobiology of framing, De Martino and his colleagues asked two related but importantly different questions. The first was a question about the population as a whole. When one looks across all of the subjects, is there a distinctive "neural signature" for choices that show the framing effect? In other words, can the framing effect be pinned down to one or more specific brain areas? This across-subjects question is the sort of question most typically asked in fMRI experiments. But it does not take into account the wide variance across individuals in how susceptible they are to the framing effect. And looking at individual differences can give a more precise picture of what is going on. So they also asked a second, within-subjects question. Is there a distinctive neural signature, for each subject, of what happens when a given person does *not* succumb to a framing effect?

To answer the first question the experimenters looked at the contrast between patterns of brain activation in choices that showed the framing effect (framing effect choices) and patterns of activation in non-framing effect choices. Here all roads led to the amygdala, which is a key part of the subcortical limbic system. Analyzing the brain scans showed significant activation in the amygdala in both cerebral hemispheres when subjects chose the risk-averse option in the Gain frame and the risk-seeking option in the Loss frame. To confirm that this bilateral amygdala activation was not disproportionately concentrated in one frame rather than the other (because then it might be just a function of how subjects reacted to the prospect of a loss or a gain, rather than driving different choices across frames), De Martino et al. studied the activation contrast in each frame independently and found strong amygdala activation in both.

So, what does that tell us about this particular framing effect? Well, one conclusion that can immediately be drawn is that the framing effect is driven, at least in part, by emotional responses to the different frames. There are literally decades' worth of studies showing that the amygdala is a key part of an "impulsive" system generating emotional responses to stimuli.[14] For a long time the amygdala was thought to be primarily dedicated to negative emotions, particularly fear. In fact, the amygdala has been described as a "fear module," and this characterization has found its way into the popular investment literature.[15] In his book *Neuroinvesting: How to Build a New Investing Brain*, Wai Yee-Chen dramatically describes the amygdala as "the engine room of fear."[16] Jason Zweig's influential *Your Money and Your Brain: How the New Science of Neuroeconomics Can Help Make You Rich* manages to go a step further: "The amygdala seems to act like a branding iron that burns the memory of financial loss into your brain."[17] A Google search on "amygdala," "fear," and "investing" will turn up many more examples in the same genre. This sort of talk is probably not a bad way of selling books or gaining clicks, but it cannot possibly be correct. For one thing, as we've just seen, if the amygdala was focused solely on the fear of loss then one would expect it only to be active in the Loss frame, whereas De Martino and colleagues found equal levels of activation in the Gain frame.

Current neuroscientific thinking on the role of the amygdala is more nuanced (but, sadly, less dramatic). What the amygdala is thought to do is track the emotional valence of immediate outcomes. This valence can be positive or negative. One very interesting feature of current thinking on the amygdala is that it is thought to respond primarily to learned valence. To help see what is going on here, consider how a rat might respond to something that it immediately recognizes as a predator – to a snake, for example. This would be a good example of what one might call an

---

[14] For a review with many references see Gupta et al. 2011.
[15] The "fear module" hypothesis is proposed in Ohman and Mineka 2001, for example.
[16] Chen 2013.   [17] Zweig 2007, p. 163.

instinctive valence (and, in fact, it turns out that rats with amygdala damage lose their fear of predators). Instinctive valences are automatic. But people can make automatic responses to valences that are learned. The concepts of *winning* and *losing* fall into this category. They are not innate (in the way that a rat's fear of snakes might be), and yet people seem to respond to them in a visceral and immediate way. According to Antoine Bachara, Antonio Damasio, and colleagues at the University of Iowa, the amygdala has a special role in tracking this kind of learned valence. Much of their work is based on the Iowa Gambling Task and, as already mentioned in the context of the vmPFC, normal subjects quickly learn to distinguish the "safer" decks from the "risky" decks. Before they are consciously able to discriminate, normal subjects show different physiological responses to the different decks (as indicated by galvanic skin response, for example). Patients with lesions to the amygdala, however, do not show these responses to anything like the degree of normal subjects.[18] They are failing to respond to the learned valences associated with winning, losing, and risk. Other work on the amygdala has highlighted its role in tracking the learned valences involved in social cognition – working out why people are doing what they do and predicting how they are going to behave. Much social cognition is driven by emotional responses to facial expressions, body language, and so on.[19]

So, looking across the subjects in the De Martino et al. fMRI experiments, activation in the amygdala seems to be the distinctive neural signature of the framing effect. Susceptibility to framing effects goes hand in hand with the intrusion of a certain kind of emotional responsiveness into decision-making. But what happens when subjects make decisions that do not show the framing effect? Is there a distinctive neural signature associated with resisting the framing effect by, for example, choosing the gamble option in the Gain frame or the sure option in the Loss frame? It turns out that there is, and that it involves three of the brain areas that we have already looked at – the anterior cingulate cortex (ACC), the orbitofrontal cortex (OFC), and the ventromedial prefrontal cortex (vmPFC).

Recall that De Martino et al. looked both at the entire population (between-subjects) and at individual responses (within-subjects). Whereas at the between-subjects level, the amygdala was the principal

---

[18] Bechara et al. 1999.
[19] For a review of the role of the amygdala in social cognition see Adolphs 2006.

area associated with risk-aversion for gains and risk-seeking behavior for losses, the opposite pattern of choices was accompanied by increased activation in the ACC. As indicated earlier, the ACC has strong connections both to the amygdala in the cortex and to the vmPFC in the cortex. It is thought to be particularly involved in monitoring conflict and in what clinicians call affect regulation (i.e. modulating the effects of painful emotions). In other words, part of the job of the ACC is to evaluate and, where necessary, modify the effects of emotional valence on decision-making.[20]

But De Martino et al. were able to go a step further than this, because of the within-subjects design of their experiment. The fact that the non-framing effect choices were primarily correlated with activation in the ACC across the population as a whole does not mean that the ACC is somehow responsible for a given individual resisting the frame effect. After all, if an individual chooses the gamble option in the Gain frame and the sure option in the Loss frame, that doesn't mean that she is somehow immune to how the outcomes are framed. Quite the contrary, in fact. It seems that she has just succumbed to a different kind of framing effect. After all, she is still switching from one option to another purely as a function of how the scenario is described. She is just not making the switch in the same direction that most people do. So, to frame it in terms of rationality, there is no sense in which choosing the gamble option in the Gain frame and the sure option in the Loss frame makes you more rational than someone who displays the classic framing effect of choosing the sure option in the Gain frame and the gamble option in the Loss frame. And yet some people do seem more resistant to any kind of framing effect than others. Does that resistance have a distinctive neural signature?

To get at that more subtle question the researchers calculated what they called a "rationality index" for each of the 20 subjects. In essence, the rationality index is inversely proportional to susceptibility to the framing effect. The less susceptible you are, the higher your rationality index. (Of course, the assumption here is that susceptibility to framing effects is invariably irrational. We have been challenging that assumption throughout this book.) In order to measure susceptibility to the framing effect, De Martino and colleagues looked at how much more frequently subjects chose the gamble option in the Loss frame than in the Gain frame, since that switch is the classic framing effect. Every subject showed the framing effect to some degree, and so there was always an increase in the

---

[20] For overviews of the ACC see Botvinick 2007 and Stevens, Hurley, and Taber 2011.

frequency of choosing the gamble option when the frame was switched from Gain to Loss. But the dimension of the increase varied significantly, with the least susceptible subject only showing an increase of around 7 percent, and the most susceptible subject gambling in 40 percent more of the trials in the Loss condition than in the Gain condition.

De Martino et al. then looked at the patterns of neural activation to see if any areas correlated with the rationality index – that is, they looked to see if there were any brain areas whose level of activation in individual subjects during the trials correlated with each individual subject's rationality index. What they found was that the subjects with the highest rationality indices showed correspondingly higher activation levels in two prefrontal areas that we have already looked at – the OFC and the vmPFC. We have already looked at evidence from animal studies and neuropsychological patients implicating both areas in calculating the subjective value of different options. So, for example, the three different types of value-computing neurons that Padoa-Schioppa and Assad discovered (offer value neurons, chosen value neurons, and taste neurons) were all located in the monkey OFC. And the Kable and Glimcher studies on how people evaluate delayed rewards highlighted the role of the vmPFC in calculating the expected benefit of a reward. Calibrating the Kable and Glimcher experiments with evidence from neuropsychological patients suggests that the distinctive contribution of the vmPFC lies in evaluating risk. There is considerable evidence from brain-damaged patients that damage to the vmPFC manifests itself in significant impairments in managing risk.

The De Martino et al. experiments, then, point to a distinctive way of thinking about the classical framing effect in which changing the frame leads subjects to flip from risk-aversion for gains to risk-seeking for losses. It is starting to look like a classic example of what is often termed *hot* cognition. People typically describe cognition as hot when it is strongly influenced by emotion and other affective states. The key role of the amygdala is what makes the framing effect look like a prime example of hot cognition. And yet this cannot be the whole story. The activity of the amygdala is tempered and modulated by brain areas more often associated with *cold* cognition – i.e. with attenuating the effects of emotion on judgment and decision-making. These areas include the ACC, the OFC, and the vmPFC. Whereas hot cognition is driven by emotion and affect, cold cognition is the domain of reason, rationality, and control. Looking at the neural underpinnings of this particular framing effect, therefore, seems to reinforce the basic idea behind the litany of irrationality – the idea that framing effects are fundamentally irrational. The narrative that seems to emerge (neatly encapsulated in De Martino et al.'s use of the phrase "rationality index") is of irrational emotional responses battling with the cool, calm forces of calculation, and region – the subcortical limbic system dueling with the more recently evolved prefrontal cortex.

The Neural Basis of Loss-Aversion

Think back to the discussion of loss-aversion in Chapter 2. We looked at it there in the context of a very specific framing effect common in investors – the disposition effect. The disposition effect is the tendency to "sell winners and ride losers" – or, in other words, the tendency to sell investments that have done well, rather than ones that are doing badly. The disposition effect is powerful in investors of all levels of skill and competence. One reason often suggested for this is that people tend to be loss-averse. A person is loss-averse when her negative reaction to a given financial loss is much greater than her positive reaction to a corresponding financial gain. People who are loss-averse feel the pain of loss much more than they feel the joy of gain. In fact, as we saw in the context of the disposition effect, there are robust data suggesting that the average "coefficient of loss" is around 2 – i.e. that losses are roughly twice as psychologically impactful as gains.[21]

Loss-aversion is not the same as risk-aversion. People who are risk-averse prefer to receive a sum of money for sure, rather than taking a gamble with an equivalent expected (financial) value. So, if you would rather take $5 than flip a coin to receive $10 if it lands heads and $0 if it lands tails, then you are risk-averse. Strictly speaking, this type of gamble does not involve any loss or potential loss, since the worst case scenario is that you end up exactly where you started, namely with $0. It is pretty much what it says on the label. Risk-aversion is about your attitude to risk. Loss-aversion is about your attitude to loss. These are separate things, even though they can combine in interesting ways (e.g. when a risky gamble involves the prospect of loss).

Loss-aversion *per se* is not an example of a framing effect. Framing effects occur when one values a given outcome differently depending on how it is framed (as a loss or as a gain), which is very different from finding that losses are more psychologically impactful than gains. But still, loss-

---

[21] See Kahneman, Knetsch, and Thaler 1990 and Carmon and Ariely 2000.

aversion is thought to play an important role in driving framing effects such as the disposition effect. And it turns out that the neural underpinnings of loss-aversion involve some of the key neural areas that we have been looking at. This emerges very clearly in a neuroimaging study by Sabrina Tom, Craig Fox, Christopher Trepel, and Russell Poldrack that was published in *Science* in 2007.[22] As with many of the studies in this area, Tom and her colleagues used a simple financial decision-making task. They presented subjects with a series of gambles in which there was a 50:50 chance of a loss or a gain, rather like the simple coin-tossing example considered a couple of paragraphs ago. But they made it into a test of loss-aversion by doing two things. First, they gave subjects a sum of money to start with that they would be allowed to keep. And second, the "bad" outcome in each case was an actual loss, rather than a zero outcome. A further interesting twist was that the subjects were asked not just to accept or reject the gambles, but also to indicate how firm they were in their judgments. They were given a choice between *strongly accept, weakly accept, weakly reject,* and *strongly reject.* All of the experiments were carried out in an fMRI scanner.

As in other experiments we have looked at, the first step in analyzing the data was to get clear on the behavioral phenomena. The experimenters took the acceptability judgments, calibrated them to the magnitude of the losses and gains in the relevant gambles, and then used that to identify a loss-aversion coefficient for each subject. There was significant individual variation across the 16 individual participants, ranging from a low of 0.99 to a high of 6.75. But, consistent with existing data, the median was 1.93. So, on average, the participants were nearly twice as sensitive to losses as to gains.

With the behavioral data in hand, Tom and her collaborators turned to the neural data. The first thing they looked for was whether there were any areas in the brain that seemed to be measuring the size of the relevant gains and losses across the different trials. In other words, are there any brain areas where levels of activation correlated directly with the amount of money that subjects stand either to gain or to lose? It turned out that, if you look just at the size of prospective gains, then a number of the brain areas we have been looking at are directly engaged. These include the anterior cingulate cortex (ACC) and the orbitofrontal cortex (OFC) as well as the ventral striatum (VS) and the ventromedial prefrontal cortex (vmPFC). The picture looks a little different, though, if

---

[22] Tom et al. 2007.

you look at the size of prospective losses as well as the size of prospective gains. The first thing to note is that there did not seem to be any neural areas showing increased activation in response to prospective losses. There are no parts of the brain that fired more strongly in response to the prospect of loss. But there were two regions that saw systematic *decreases* in activation mapping onto the size of prospective losses. These were (as you might have guessed!) the VS and the vmPFC. These two areas showed increased activation correlated with the size of prospective gains and decreased activation correlated with the size of expected losses. This is exactly what one would expect if, as research from many different directions appears to show, the VS and the vmPFC are key components in a neural network responsible for computing the subjective value of different possible outcomes.

But that is not all! Looking at the patterns of activation in these two areas revealed another very interesting feature. It's not just that neural activity in the vmPFC and the VS decreased in the face of prospective losses. The rate of decrease was also significant. To appreciate how and why, think back to the basic definition of loss-aversion. To be loss-averse is to attach greater *disvalue* to a given loss than one attaches value to a gain of corresponding magnitude. So, someone who is loss-averse will be much more troubled by a $1,000 loss than they are gratified by a $1,000 gain. A good way of visualizing this is through a graph that charts the value/disvalue of gains and losses, as in Figure A.5. The tell-tale sign of loss-aversion in the graph is that the slope of the curve is steeper for losses than it is for gains.

Now, back to the vmPFC and the VS. Tom et al. looked at how quickly activation decreased in these two areas when subjects were confronted with a range of prospective losses of increasing amounts. They then compared the rate of decrease with the corresponding rate of increase for gains – i.e. the rate at which activation increased when subjects were faced with the prospect of gains of increasing amounts. What they found was that activation decreased more for losses than it increased for gains. In other words, if you were to draw a graph like that in Figure A.5, but with the y-axis showing levels of activation in the vmPFC and the VS, then it would have roughly the same shape as Figure A.5. In the words of the experimenters, these two neural areas show patterns of "neural loss-aversion"![23]

---

[23] Compare Frydman et al. 2014 for similar results on the vmPFC and the VS.

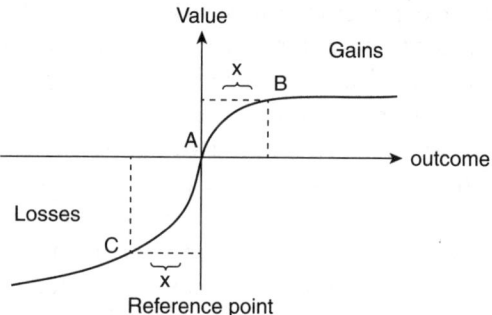

FIGURE A.5 Representing loss-aversion
Note: If *x* is a given magnitude of change (say, $1,000), then the value the agent attaches to gaining *x* is represented by the vertical distance from B to A, while the value the agent attaches to losing *x* is represented by the vertical distance from C to A. People have a general tendency to attach a greater disvalue to losing a given sum than the value they attach to gaining that same sum. This is reflected in the fact that the curve is steeper for losses than it is for gains.
Drawing by Marc Oliver Rieger.

One final point. As I have already noted, loss-aversion is deeply implicated in framing effects such as the disposition effect, but it is not itself a framing effect. Disvaluing losses more than one values gains is one thing. Attaching different (dis-)values to a single outcome depending on whether it is framed as a loss or a gain is something completely different. So, one would not expect to see a complete match between the neural correlates of loss-aversion and the neural correlates of framing effects involving gains and losses. And again this is what emerges from the Tom et al. experiments. The vmPFC and the VS are both heavily implicated in gain/loss framing effects. And, as we saw in the previous section, those framing effects also show significant involvement from the subcortical limbic system, particularly the amygdala. But this piece of the puzzle is completely absent from the basic phenomenon of loss-aversion as explored in the Tom et al. experiments, where the experimenters failed to find any significant engagement of the amygdala.

This offers a further twist to the neural narrative of framing developed in the previous section. The suggestion there was that framing effects emerge from a clash between "hot" emotion-driven mechanisms and "cold", reason-driven mechanisms. The hot mechanisms are subcortical, while the cold mechanisms are cortical. Looking at the neural correlates of loss-aversion adds more detail to this picture. Engaging the hot, subcortical mechanisms seems to require more than simply the prospect of financial loss. Loss-aversion is a function of the subjective value that one assigns to outcomes. It is the result of cold cognition. It is not driven simply by an emotional reaction to the prospect of financial loss. If it was so driven then one would expect to see the limbic system involved when loss-aversion is displayed. Since the limbic system is not involved in loss-aversion, that emotional reaction so important in framing effects must be triggered by other aspects of how the outcomes are framed.

Bibliography

Ackrill, J. L. 1981. *Aristotle the Philosopher*. Oxford University Press.

Adolphs, R. 2006. How do we know the minds of others? Domain-specificity, simulation, and enactive social cognition. *Brain Research* 1079, 25–35.

Ahmed, A. 2014. *Evidence, Decision, and Causality*. Cambridge University Press.

Ahmed, A. 2017. Exploiting cyclic preference. *Mind* 126(504), 975–1022.

Ainslie, G. 1974. Impulse control in pigeons. *Journal of the Experimental Analysis of Behavior* 21, 485–89.

Ainslie G. 1992. *Picoeconomics*. Cambridge University Press.

Ainslie, G. 2001. *Breakdown of Will*. Cambridge University Press.

Allais, M. 1979. Criticism of the postulates and axioms of the American school. In M. Allais and O. Hagen (Eds.), *Expected Utility Hypotheses and the Allais Paradox*. Dordrecht: Reidel.

Allingham, M. 2002. *Choice Theory: A Very Short Introduction*. Oxford University Press.

Anderson, M. 1990. *The Adaptive Character of Thought*. Hillsdale, NJ: Lawrence Erlbaum Associates.

Anscombe, G. E. M. 1958. Modern moral philosophy. *Philosophy* 33, 1–19.

Ariely, D. 2008. *Predictably Irrational: The Hidden Forces That Shape Our Decisions*. New York. HarperCollins.

Aristotle, *Nicomachean Ethics*. See Broadie and Rowe 2002.

Arrow, K. J. 1982. Risk perception in psychology and economics. *Economic Inquiry* 20, 1–9.

Attridge, N. and M. Inglis. 2013. Advanced mathematical study and the development of conditional reasoning skills. *PLoS ONE* 8(7), e69399.

Axelrod, R. 1984. *The Evolution of Cooperation*. New York: Basic Books.

Bacharach, M. 1993. Variable universe games. In K. Binmore, A. Kirman, and P. Tani (Eds.), *Frontiers of Game Theory*. Cambridge, MA: MIT Press.

Bacharach, M. 2001. Superagency: beyond an individualistic theory of games. In J. van Benthem (Ed.), *Theoretical Aspects of Rationality and Knowledge*. San Francisco, CA: Morgan Kaufmann.

Bacharach, M. 2006. *Beyond Individual Choice: Teams and Frames in Game Theory*. Princeton University Press.

Bacharach, M. and M. Bernasconi. 1997. The variable frame theory of focal points: an experimental study. *Games and Economic Behavior* 19(1), 1–4.

Bacharach, M. and D. Stahl. 2000. Variable-frame level-n theory. *Games and Economic Behavior* 32, 220–46.

Barberis, N. and M. Huang. 2008. The loss aversion/narrow framing approach to the equity premium puzzle. In R. Mehra (Ed.), *Handbook of the Equity Risk Premium*. Amsterdam: Elsevier.

Barberis, N. and W. E. I. Xiong. 2009. What drives the disposition effect? An analysis of a long-standing preference-based explanation. *The Journal of Finance* 64, 751–84.

Barnes, J. 1979. *The Presocratic Philosophers*. London: Routledge.

Baron-Cohen, S., A. M. Leslie, and U. Frith. 1985. Does the autistic child have a 'theory of mind'? *Cognition* 21(1), 37–46.

Barthes, R. 1977. The death of the author (S. Heath, Trans.). In *Image, Music, Text*. New York: Hill & Wang.

Bartra, O., J. T. McGuire, and J. W. Kable. 2013. The valuation system: a coordinate-based meta-analysis of BOLD fMRI experiments examining neural correlates of subjective value. *Neuroimage* 76, 412–27.

Battaly, H. 2008. Virtue epistemology. *Philosophy Compass* 3(4), 639–63.

Baumeister, R. F., T. F. Heatherton, and D. M. Tice. 1994. *Losing Control: How and Why People Fail at Self-Regulation*. San Diego, CA: Academic Press.

Bechara, A., A. R. Damasio, H. Damasio, and S. W. Anderson. 1994. Insensitivity to future consequences following damage to human prefrontal cortex. *Cognition* 50, 7–15.

Bechara, A., H. Damasio, A. R. Damasio, and G. P. Lee. 1999. Different contributions of the human amygdala and ventromedial prefrontal cortex to decision-making. *Journal of Neuroscience* 19, 5473–81.

Beck, A. T. 1976. *Cognitive Therapy and the Emotional Disorders*. Oxford: International Universities Press.

Benartzi, S. and R. H. Thaler. 1995. Myopic loss aversion and the equity premium puzzle. *The Quarterly Journal of Economics* 110, 73–92.

Ben-David, I. and D. Hirshleifer. 2012. Are investors really reluctant to realize their losses? Trading responses to past returns and the disposition effect. *Review of Financial Studies* 25, 2485–532.

Bermúdez, J. L. 2003a. *Thinking without Words*. Oxford University Press.

Bermúdez, J. L. 2003b. The domain of folk psychology. In A. O'Hear (Ed.), *Minds and Persons*. Cambridge University Press.

Bermúdez, J. L. 2009. *Decision Theory and Rationality*. Oxford University Press.

Bermúdez, J. L. 2014. *Cognitive Science: An Introduction to the Science of the Mind* (2nd edition). Cambridge University Press.

Bermúdez, J. L. 2015a. Prisoner's dilemma cannot be a Newcomb problem. In M. Peterson (Ed.), *The Prisoner's Dilemma*. Cambridge University Press.

Bermúdez, J. L. 2015b. Strategic vs. parametric choice in Newcomb's problem and the prisoner's dilemma: reply to Walker. *Philosophia* 43(3), 787–94.

Bermúdez, J. L. 2018a. Frames, rationality and self-control. In J. L. Bermúdez (Ed.), *Self-Control, Decision Theory, and Rationality*. Cambridge University Press.

Bermúdez, J. L. 2018b. Inner speech, determinacy, and thinking consciously about thoughts. In P. Langland-Hassan (Ed.), *Inner Speech*. Oxford University Press.

Bermúdez, J. L. (Ed.). 2018c. *Self-Control, Decision Theory, and Rationality*. Cambridge University Press.

Bermúdez, J. L. 2020. *Cognitive Science: An Introduction to the Science of the Mind* (3rd edition). Cambridge University Press.

Bernstein, A., Y. Hadash, and D. M. Fresco. 2019. Metacognitive processes model of decentering: emerging methods and insights. *Current Opinion in Psychology* 28, 245–51.

Bernstein, A., Y. Hadash, Y. Lichtash, G. Tanay, K. Shepherd, and D. M. Fresco. 2015. Decentering and related constructs: a critical review and metacognitive processes model. *Perspectives on Psychological Science: A Journal of the Association for Psychological Science* 10(5), 599–617.

Binmore, K. 2005. *Natural Justice*. Oxford University Press.

Binmore, K. 2007. *Game Theory: A Very Short Introduction*. Oxford University Press.

Binmore, K. 2009a. *Rational Decisions*. Princeton University Press.

Binmore, K. 2009b. Interpersonal comparison of utility. In D. Ross and H. Kincaid (Eds.), *The Oxford Handbook of the Philosophy of Economics*. Oxford University Press.

Blackburn, S. 1996. *Spreading the Word*. Oxford University Press.

Blackburn, S. 1998. *Ruling Passions*. Oxford University Press.

Blavatskyy, P. R. and G. Pogrebna. 2009. Myopic loss aversion revisited. *Economics Letters* 104, 43–45.

Blavatskyy, P. R. and G. Pogrebna. 2010. Reevaluating evidence on myopic loss aversion: aggregate patterns versus individual choices. *Theory and Decision* 68, 159–71.

Bobonich, C. and P. Destrée (Eds.). 2007. *Akrasia in Greek Philosophy: From Socrates to Plotinus*. Leiden: Brill.

Botvinick, M. M. 2007. Conflict monitoring and decision making: reconciling two perspectives on anterior cingulate function. *Cognitive, Affective, & Behavioral Neuroscience* 7, 356–66.

Bratman, M. E. 1999. Toxin, temptation, and the stability of temptation. In *Faces of Intention: Selected Essays on Intention and Agency*. Cambridge University Press.

Bratman, M. E. 2014. *Shared Agency: A Planning Theory of Acting Together*. Oxford University Press.

Brewer, M. 2003. *Intergroup Relations*. Buckingham: Open University Press.

Brewer, M. and Kramer, R. M. 1986. Choice behavior in social dilemmas: effects of social identity, group size, and decision framing. *Journal of Personality and Social Psychology* 50, 543–49.

Broadie, S. and C. Rowe. 2002. *Aristotle: Nicomachean Ethics: Translation, Introduction, Commentary*. Oxford University Press.

Bromberg-Martin, E. S., M. Matsumoto, and O. Hikosaka. 2010. Dopamine in motivational control: rewarding, aversive, and alerting. *Neuron* 68, 815–34.

Broome, J. 1991a. Utility. *Economics and Philosophy* 7, 1–12.

Broome, J. 1991b. *Weighing Goods: Equality, Uncertainty, and Time*. Oxford: Basil Blackwell.

Broome, J. 2013. *Rationality through Reasoning*. Chichester: Wiley-Blackwell.

Bruni, L. 2010. Pareto's legacy in modern economics. *Revue Européenne des Sciences Sociales* 48, 93–111.

Butler, A. C., J. E. Chapman, E. M. Forman, and A. T. Beck. 2006. The empirical status of cognitive-behavioral therapy: a review of meta-analyses. *Clinical Psychology Review* 26(1), 17–31.

Camerer, C. and R. H. Thaler. 2003. In honor of Matthew Rabin: winner of the John Bates Clark Medal. *The Journal of Economic Perspectives* 17(3), 159–76.

Camille, N., C. A. Griffiths, K. Vo, L. K. Fellows, and J. W. Kable. 2011. Ventromedial frontal lobe damage disrupts value maximization in humans. *Journal of Neuroscience* 31, 7527–32.

Carmon, Z. and D. Ariely. 2000. Focusing on the foregone: how value can appear so different to buyers and sellers. *Journal of Consumer Research* 27, 360–70.

Carruthers, P. and P. K. Smith (Eds.). 1996. *Theories of Theory of Mind*. Cambridge University Press.

Chang, R. (Ed.). 1997. *Incommensurability, Incomparability, and Practical Reason*. Cambridge, MA: Harvard University Press.

Chater, N. 2018. *The Mind Is Flat: The Remarkable Shallowness of the Improvising Brain*. New Haven, CT: Yale University Press.

Chen, W.-Y. 2013. *Neuroinvesting: How to Build a New Investing Brain*. Singapore: John Wiley & Sons.

Cheng, P. W., K. J. Holyoak, R. E. Nisbett, and L. M. Oliver. 1986. Pragmatic versus syntactic approaches to training deductive reasoning. *Cognitive Psychology* 18(3), 293–328.

Chipman, J. S. and J. C. Moore. 1978. The new welfare economics 1939–1974. *International Economic Review* 19(3), 547–84.

Cohen, L. J. 1981. Can human irrationality be experimentally demonstrated? *Behavioral and Brain Sciences* 4, 317–70.

Cosmides, L. 1989. The logic of social exchange: has natural selection shaped how humans reason? Studies with the Wason selection task. *Cognition* 31(3), 187–276.

Cosmides, L. and J. Tooby. 1992. Cognitive mechanisms for social exchange. In J. H. Barkow, L. Cosmides, and J. Tooby (Eds.), *The Adapted Mind: Evolutionary Psychology and the Generation of Culture*. Oxford University Press.

Dancy, J. 2000. *Practical Reality*. Oxford University Press.

Davidson, D. 1969. How is weakness of the will possible? In J. Feinberg (Ed.), *Moral Concepts*. Oxford University Press.

Davies, M. and T. Stone (Eds.). 1995a. *Folk Psychology*. Oxford: Basil Blackwell.

Davies, M. and T. Stone (Eds.). 1995b. *Mental Simulation*. Oxford: Basil Blackwell.

Davis, L. H. 1977. Prisoners, paradox, and rationality. *American Philosophical Quarterly* 14(4), 319–27.

Davis, L. H. 1985. Is the symmetry argument valid? In R. Campbell and L. Sowden (Eds.), *Paradoxes of Rationality and Cooperation*. Vancouver: University of British Columbia Press.

Davis, M. A. and P. Bobko. 1986. Contextual effects on escalation processes in public sector decision making. *Organizational Behavior and Human Decision Processes* 37, 121–38.

Degomme, O. and D. Guha-Sapir. 2010. Patterns of mortality rates in Darfur conflict. *The Lancet* 375, 294–300.

De Martino, B., D. Kumaran, B. Seymour, and R. J. Dolan. 2006. Frames, biases, and rational decision-making in the human brain. *Science* 313, 684–87.

Dhar, R. and N. Zhu. 2006. Up close and personal: investor sophistication and the disposition effect. *Management Science* 52, 726–40.

Dimson, E., P. Marsh, and M. Staunton. 2002. *Triumph of the Optimists: 101 Years of Global Investment Returns*. Princeton University Press.

Douven, I. 2013. The lottery and preface paradoxes. *Oxford Bibliographies*. DOI:10.1093/obo/9780195396577-0196.

Druckman, J. N. and R. McDermott. 2008. Emotion and the framing of risky choice. *Political Behavior* 30(3), 297–321.

Duchon, D., K. J. Dunegan, and S. L. Barton. 1989. Framing the problem and making decisions: the facts are not enough. *IEEE Transactions on Engineering Management* 36, 25–27.

Durand, R., H. W. Tee, and P. Lloyd. 2004. Myopic loss aversion and the equity premium puzzle reconsidered. *Finance Research Letters* 1, 171–77.

Ellis, R. J. 2005. *To the Flag: The Unlikely History of the Pledge of Allegiance*. Lawrence, KS: University Press of Kansas.

Elster, J. 1979. *Ulysses and the Sirens: Studies in Rationality and Irrationality*. Cambridge University Press.

Enderton, H. 1977. *Elements of Set Theory*. New York: Academic Press.

Entman, R. M. 1993. Framing: toward clarification of a fractured paradigm. *Journal of Communication* 43, 51–58.

Eriksen, K. W. and O. Kvaløy. 2010. Do financial advisors exhibit myopic loss aversion? *Financial Markets and Portfolio Management* 24, 159–70.

Evans, J. S. 2008. Dual-processing accounts of reasoning, judgment, and social cognition. *Annual Review of Psychology* 59, 255–78.

Fagles, R. 1977. *Aeschylus: The Oresteia*. London: Penguin Classics.

Fagles, R. and B. Knox. 1996. *Homer: The Odyssey*. Harmondsworth: Penguin.

Fellows, L. K. and M. J. Farah. 2007. The role of ventromedial prefrontal cortex in decision making: judgment under uncertainty or judgment per se? *Cerebral Cortex* 17, 2669–74.

Figner, B., D. Knoch, E. J. Johnson, A. R. Krosch, S. H. Lisanby, E. Fehr, and E. U. Weber. 2010. Lateral prefrontal cortex and self-control in intertemporal choice. *Nature Neuroscience* 13, 538–39.

Fishburn, F. C. 1970. *Utility Theory for Decision-Making*. New York: John Wiley.

Fisher, R. and W. L. Ury. 1981. *Getting to Yes: Negotiating Agreement without Giving In*. London: Penguin.

Flavell, J. H. 1977. The development of knowledge about visual perception. *Nebraska Symposium on Motivation* 25, 43–76.

Flavell, J. H., B. A. Everett, K. Croft, and E. R. Flavell. 1981. Young children's knowledge about visual perception: further evidence for the Level 1–Level 2 distinction. *Developmental Psychology* 17(1), 99–103.

Freeman, S. (Ed.). 2003. *The Cambridge Companion to Rawls*. Cambridge University Press.

Friedman, M. 1953. The methodology of positive economics. In *Essays in Positive Economics*. University of Chicago Press.

Frydman, C., N. Barberis, C. Camerer, P. Bossaerts, and A. Rangel. 2014. Using neural data to test a theory of investor behavior: an application to realization utility. *The Journal of Finance* 69, 907 46.

Garvey, R. and A. Murphy. 2004. Are professional traders too slow to realize their losses? *Financial Analyst's Journal* 60, 35–43.

Gauthier, D. 1986. *Morals by Agreement*. Oxford: Clarendon Press.

Gauthier, D. 1997. Resolute choice and rational deliberation: a critique and a defense. *Noûs* 31, 1–25.

Gazzaniga, M. S. 2005. Forty-five years of split-brain research and still going strong. *Nature Reviews Neuroscience* 6, 653–59.

Genesove, D. and C. Mayer. 2001. Loss aversion and seller behavior: evidence from the housing market. *The Quarterly Journal of Economics* 116, 1233–60.

Gigerenzer, G. 1991. How to make cognitive illusions disappear: beyond "heuristics and biases." *European Review of Social Psychology* 2(1), 83–115.

Gigerenzer, G. and W. Gaissmaier. 2011. Heuristic decision making. *Annual Review of Psychology* 62(1), 451–82.

Gigerenzer, G. and R. Selten. 2001. *Bounded Rationality: The Adaptive Toolbox*. Cambridge, MA: MIT Press.

Gigerenzer, G., P. M. Todd, and T. A. R. Group. 1999. *Simple Heuristics That Make Us Smart*. New York: Oxford University Press.

Gilbert, M. 1989. *On Social Facts*. London: Routledge.

Gneezy, U. and J. Potters. 1997. An experiment on risk taking and evaluation periods. *The Quarterly Journal of Economics* 112, 631–45.

Goffman, E. 1974. *Frame Analysis: An Essay on the Organization of Experience*. New York: Harper Colophon.

Gold, N. 2012. Team reasoning, framing, and cooperation. In S. Okasha and K. Binmore (Eds.), *Evolution and Rationality: Decisions, Co-Operation and Strategic Behaviour*. Cambridge University Press.

Gold, N. 2013. Team reasoning, framing, and self-control: an Aristotelian account. In N. Levy (Ed.), *Addiction and Self-Control*. Oxford University Press.

Gold, N. 2018. Putting willpower into decision theory: the person as a team over time and intrapersonal team reasoning. In J. L. Bermúdez (Ed.), *Self-Control, Decision Theory, and Rationality*. Cambridge University Press.

Gold, N. and R. Sugden. 2007. Collective intentions and team agency. *The Journal of Philosophy* 104(3), 109–37.

Gopnik, A., A. N. Meltzoff, and P. K. Kuhl. 1999. *The Scientist in the Crib: Minds, Brains, and How Children Learn*. New York: William Morrow.

Govindan, S. and R. B. Wilson. 2016. Nash equilibrium, Refinements of. In *The New Palgrave Dictionary of Economics*. London: Palgrave Macmillan.

Greaves, H. and H. Lederman. 2017. Aggregating extended preferences. *Philosophical Studies* 174(5), 1163–90.

Greaves, H. and H. Lederman. 2018. Extended preferences and interpersonal comparisons of well-being. *Philosophy and Phenomenological Research* 96 (3), 636–67.

Green, L. and J. Myerson. 2018. Preference reversals, delay discounting, rational choice, and the brain. In J. L. Bermúdez (Ed.), *Self-Control, Decision Theory, and Rationality*. Cambridge University Press.

Green, P. 2015. *The Iliad, Homer: A New Translation*. Oakland, CA: University of California Press.

Griffin, J. 1986. *Well-Being: Its Meaning, Measurement and Moral Importance*. Oxford: Clarendon Press.

Gross, L. 1982. *The Art of Selling Intangibles: How to Make Your Million($) by Investing Other People's Money*. New York Institute of Finance.

Gupta, R., T. R. Koscik, A. Bechara, and D. Tranel. 2011. The amygdala and decision-making. *Neuropsychologia* 49(4), 760–66.

Gurucharri, C. and R. L. Selman. 1982. The development of interpersonal understanding during childhood, preadolescence, and adolescence: a longitudinal follow-up study. *Child Development* 53(4), 924–27.

Haber, S. N. 2011. Neuroanatomy of reward: a view from the ventral striatum. In J. A. Gottfried (Ed.), *Neurobiology of Sensation and Reward*. Boca Raton, FL: CRC Press.

Hagger, M. S., C. Wood, C. Stiff, and N. L. Chatzisarantis. 2010. Ego depletion and the strength model of self-control: a meta-analysis. *Psychological Bulletin* 136, 495–525.

Haigh, J. 2012. *Probability: A Very Short Introduction*. Oxford University Press.

Haigh, M. S. and J. A. List. 2005. Do professional traders exhibit myopic loss aversion? An experimental analysis. *The Journal of Finance* 60(1), 523–34.

Haines, R. F. 1991. A breakdown in simultaneous information processing. In G. Obrecht and L. W. Stark (Eds.), *Presbyopia Research: Perspectives in Vision Research*. Boston, MA: Springer.

Hamilton, E. and H. Cairns. 1961. *Plato: The Collected Dialogues*: Princeton University Press.

Hammond, P. J. 1991. Interpersonal comparisons of utility: why and how they are and should be made. In J. Elster and J. E. Roemer (Eds.), *Interpersonal Comparisons of Well-Being*. Cambridge University Press.

Hand, D. J. 2008. *Statistics: A Very Short Introduction*. Oxford University Press.

Hardin, G. 1968. The tragedy of the commons. *Science* (13 December), 1243–48.

Hare, T. A., C. F. Camerer, and A. Rangel. 2009. Self-control in decision-making involves modulation of the vmPFC valuation system. *Science* 324, 646–48.

Harman, G. 1986. *Change in View*. Cambridge, MA: MIT Press.

Harsanyi, J. 1977. Advances in understanding rational behavior. In R. E. Butts and J. Hintikka (Eds.), *Foundational Problems in the Special Sciences.* Dordrecht: D. Reidel.

Harsanyi, J. 1986. *Rational Behavior and Bargaining Equilibrium in Games and Social Situations.* Cambridge University Press.

Harsanyi, J. and R. Selten. 1988. *A General Theory of Equilibrium Selection in Games.* Cambridge, MA: MIT Press.

Hofmann, S. G., A. Asnaani, I. J. J. Vonk, A. T. Sawyer, and A. Fang. 2012. The efficacy of cognitive behavioral therapy: a review of meta-analyses. *Cognitive Therapy and Research* 36(5), 427–40.

Holton, R. 2009. *Willing, Wanting, Waiting.* Oxford University Press.

Hume, D. 1978 [1739–40]. *A Treatise of Human Nature.* With text revised and notes by P. H. Nidditch. Oxford: Clarendon Press.

Hurley, S. L. 1991. Newcomb's problem, prisoners' dilemma, and collective action. *Synthese* 86(2), 173–96.

Hurley, S. and M. Nudds. 2006. *Rational Animals?* Oxford University Press.

Hursthouse, R. 1999. *On Virtue Ethics.* Oxford University Press.

Irwin, T. 1995. *Plato's Ethics.* Oxford University Press.

Ishiguro, H. 1990. *Leibniz's Philosophy of Logic and Language* (2nd edition). Cambridge University Press.

Janis, I. L. 1983. *Groupthink: Psychological Studies of Policy Decisions and Fiascoes.* Boston, MA: Houghton-Mifflin.

Janssen, M. A. 2008. Evolution of cooperation in a one-shot prisoner's dilemma based on recognition of trustworthy and untrustworthy agents. *Journal of Economic Behavior & Organization* 65(3), 458–71.

Kable, J. W. and P. W. Glimcher. 2007. The neural correlates of subjective value during intertemporal choice. *Nature Neuroscience* 10, 1625–33.

Kable, J. W. and P. W. Glimcher. 2009. The neurobiology of decision: consensus and controversy. *Neuron* 63, 733–45.

Kahneman, D. 2011. *Thinking, Fast and Slow.* New York: Farrar, Straus & Giroux.

Kahneman, D., J. L. Knetsch, and R. H. Thaler. 1990. Experimental tests of the endowment effect and the Coase theorem. *Journal of Political Economy* 98, 1325–48.

Kahneman, D. and A. Tversky. 1972. Subjective probability: a judgment of representativeness. *Cognitive Psychology* 3, 430–54.

Kahneman, D. and A. Tversky. 2000. *Choices, Values, Frames.* Cambridge University Press.

Kazantzis, N., H. K. Luong, A. S. Usatoff, T. Impala, R. Y. Yew, and S. G. Hofmann. 2018. The processes of cognitive behavioral therapy: a review of meta-analyses. *Cognitive Therapy and Research* 42(4), 349–57.

Kennerley, S. W. and M. E. Walton. 2011. Decision making and reward in frontal cortex: complementary evidence from neurophysiological and neuropsychological studies. *Behavioral Neuroscience* 125, 297–317.

Kross, E. and O. Ayduk. 2011. Making meaning out of negative experiences by self-distancing. *Current Directions in Psychological Science* 20, 187–91.

Kross, E., D. Gard, P. Deldin, J. Clifton, and O. Ayduk. 2012. "Asking why" from a distance: its cognitive and emotional consequences for people with major depressive disorder. *Journal of Abnormal Psychology* 121(3), 559–69.

Kühberger, A. 1995. The framing of decisions: a new look at old problems. *Organizational Behavior and Human Decision Processes* 62, 230–40.

Kuhn, S. 2017. Prisoner's dilemma. *The Stanford Encyclopedia of Philosophy* (Spring 2017 Edition), Edward N. Zalta (Ed.). https://plato.stanford.edu/archi ves/spr2017/entries/prisoner-dilemma/.

Kyburg Jr., H. E. 1961. *Probability and the Logic of Rational Belief.* Middletown, CT: Wesleyan University Press.

Lakoff, G. 2004. *Don't Think of an Elephant: Know Your Values and Frame the Debate.*White River Junction, VT: Chelsea Green Publishing.

Lee, B. and Y. Veld-Merkoulova. 2016. Myopic loss aversion and stock investments: an empirical study of private investments. *Journal of Banking and Finance* 70, 235–46.

Letwin, S. R. 1993. *The Anatomy of Thatcherism.* New Brunswick, NJ: Transaction Publishers.

Levi, I. 2002. Money pumps and diachronic books. *Philosophy of Science* 69, S235–S247.

Levin, I. P. 1987. Associative effects of information framing. *Bulletin of the Psychonomic Society* 25(2), 85–86.

Levin, I. P. and G. J. Gaeth. 1988. How consumers are affected by the framing of attribute information before and after consuming the product. *Journal of Consumer Research* 15, 374–78.

Levin, I. P., S. L. Schneider, and G. J. Gaeth. 1998. All frames are not created equal: a typology and critical analysis of framing effects. *Organizational Behavior and Human Decision Processes* 76, 149–88.

Leyton-Brown, K. and Y. Shoham. 2008. *Essentials of Game Theory: A Concise Multidisciplinary Introduction.* San Rafael, CA: Claypool & Morgan.

Linville, P. W., G. W. Fischer, and B. Fischoff. 1993. AIDS risk perception and decision biases. In J. B. Pryor and G. D. Reeder (Eds.), *The Social Psychology of HIV Infection.* Hillsdale, NJ: Lawrence Erlbaum Associates.

List, C. and P. Pettit. 2011. *Group Agency: The Possibility, Design, and Status of Corporate Agents.* Oxford University Press.

Lomberg, B. 2001. *The Skeptical Environmentalist: Measuring the Real State of the World.* Cambridge University Press.

Lorenz, H. 2006. *The Brute Within: Appetitive Desire in Plato and Aristotle.* Oxford University Press.

Louie, K. and P. W. Glimcher. 2012. Efficient coding and the neural representation of value. *Annals of the New York Academy of Sciences* 1251, 13–32.

Luce, R. D. and H. Raiffa. 1957. *Games and Decisions: Introduction and Critical Survey.* New York: John Wiley.

McClennen, E. F. 1990. *Rationality and Dynamic Choice.* Cambridge University Press.

McClennen, E. F. 1998. Rationality and rules. In P. A. Danielson (Ed.), *Modeling Rationality, Morality, and Evolution.* Oxford University Press.

McDowell, J. 1980. The role of eudaimonia in Aristotle's ethics. In A. O. Rorty (Ed.), *Essays on Aristotle's Ethics*. Berkeley, CA: University of California Press.

McDowell, J. 1995. Might there be external reasons? In J. E. J. Altham and R. Harrison (Eds.), *World, Mind and Ethics: Essays on the Ethical Philosophy of Bernard Williams*. Cambridge University Press.

MacIntyre, A. 1981. *After Virtue: A Study in Moral Theory*. London: Duckworth.

Mack, A. and I. Rock. 1998. *Inattentional Blindness*. Cambridge, MA: MIT Press.

McKirahan, R. 2010. *Philosophy before Socrates: An Introduction with Texts and Commentary* (2nd edition). Indianapolis: Hackett.

McRaney, D. 2011. *You Are Not So Smart*. New York: Gotham.

Magen, E., C. S. Dweck, and J. J. Gross. 2008. The hidden-zero effect: representing a single choice as an extended sequence reduces impulsive choice. *Psychological Science* 19(7), 648–49.

Magen, E., B. Kim, C. S. Dweck, J. J. Gross, and S. M. McClure. 2014. Behavioral and neural correlates of increased self-control in the absence of increased willpower. *Proceedings of the National Academy of Sciences* 111 (27), 9786–91.

Mandel, D. 2013. Do framing effects reveal irrational choices? *Journal of Experimental Psychology: General* 143, 1185–98.

Mankiw, N. G. and S. Zeldes. 1991. The consumption of stockholders and nonstockholders. *Journal of Financial Economics* 29(1), 97–112.

Masangkay, Z. S., K. A. McCluskey, C. W. McIntyre, J. Sims-Knight, B. E. Vaughn, and J. H. Flavell. 1974. The early development of inferences about the visual percepts of others. *Child Development* 45(2), 357–66.

Mehra, R. 2007. The equity premium in India. In K. Basu (Ed.), *The Oxford Companion to Economics in India*. Oxford University Press.

Mehra, R. 2008. The equity premium puzzle: a review. *Foundations and Trends in Finance* 2, 1–81.

Mehra, R. and E. Prescott. 1985. The equity premium: a puzzle. *Journal of Monetary Economics* 15, 145–61.

Mele, A. R. 1987. *Irrationality: An Essay on Akrasia, Self-Deception, and Self-Control*. Oxford University Press.

Mele, A. R. 2012. *Backsliding: Understanding Weakness of Will*: Oxford University Press.

Mellor, D. H. and A. Oliver. 1997. *Properties*. Oxford University Press.

Mischel, W. and O. Ayduk. 2004. Willpower in a cognitive-affective processing system. In R. F. Baumeister and K. D. Vohs (Eds.), *Handbook of Self-Regulation: Research, Theory, and Applications*. New York: Guilford Press.

Mischel, W., O. Ayduk, M. G. Berman, B. J. Casey, I. H. Gotlib, J. Jonides, E. Kross, T. Teslovich, N. L. Wilson, V. Zayas, and Y. Shoda. 2011. 'Willpower' over the life span: decomposing self-regulation. *Social Cognitive and Affective Neuroscience* 6, 252–56.

Mischel, W. and N. Baker. 1975. Cognitive appraisals and transformations in delay behavior. *Journal of Personality and Social Psychology* 31(2), 254–61.

Mischel, W. and B. Moore. 1973. Effects of attention to symbolically presented rewards on self-control. *Journal of Personality and Social Psychology* 28, 172–79.

Mischel, W., Y. Shoda, and M. I. Rodriguez. 1989. Delay of gratification in children. *Science* 244, 933–38.

Moll, H. and A. N. Meltzoff. 2011. How does it look? Level 2 perspective-taking at 36 months of age. *Child Development* 82(2), 661–73.

Montier, J. 2010. *The Little Book of Behavioral Investing: How Not To Be Your Own Worst Enemy*. Hoboken, NJ: John Wiley & Sons.

Moore, A. W. 1987. *Points of View*. Oxford University Press.

Myerson, R. B. 1985. Bayesian equilibrium and incentive compatibility: an introduction. In L. Hurwicz, D. Schmeidler, and H. Sonnenschein (Eds.), *Social Goals and Social Organization*. Cambridge University Press.

Nabi, R. L. 2003. Exploring the framing effects of emotion. *Communication Research* 30, 224–47.

Nagel, T. 1986. *The View from Nowhere*. Oxford University Press.

Neale, M. A. and M. H. Bazerman. 1985. The effects of framing and negotiator overconfidence on bargaining behaviors and outcomes. *Academy of Management Journal* 28, 34–49.

Neisser, U. 1979. The control of information pick-up in selective looking. In A. D. Pick (Ed.), *Perception and its Development: A Tribute to Eleanor J. Gibson*. Hillsdale, NJ: Lawrence Erlbaum Associates.

Nisbett, R. E. and E. Borgida. 1975. Attribution and the psychology of prediction. *Journal of Personality and Social Psychology* 32, 932–43.

Norris, C. 1988. Law, deconstruction, and the resistance to theory. *Journal of Law and Society* 15(2), 166–87.

Nozick, R. 1974. *Anarchy, State, and Utopia*. New York: Basic Books.

Nozick, R. 1993. *The Nature of Rationality*. Princeton University Press.

Oakes, P., A. Haslam, and J. C. Turner. 1994. *Stereotyping and Social Reality*. Hoboken, NJ: John Wiley.

Oaksford, M. and N. Chater. 2007. *Bayesian Rationality: The Probabilistic Approach to Human Reasoning*. Oxford University Press.

Odean, T. 1998. Are investors reluctant to realize their losses? *Journal of Finance* 53, 1775–98.

Ohman, A. and S. Mineka. 2001. Fears, phobias, and preparedness: toward an evolved module of fear and fear learning. *Psychological Review* 108, 483–522.

Okasha, S. 2016. On the interpretation of decision theory. *Economics and Philosophy* 32, 409–33.

Öngür, D. and J. L. Price. 2000. The organization of networks within the orbital and medial prefrontal cortex of rats, monkeys and humans. *Cerebral Cortex* 10, 206–19.

Onishi, K. H. and R. Baillargeon. 2005. Do 15-month-old infants understand false beliefs? *Science* 308(5719), 255–58.

Orwell, G. 1957. *A Collection of Essays*. Garden City, NY: Doubleday.

Owen, G. E. L. 1960. Logic and metaphysics in some early works of Aristotle. In *Logic, Science, Dialectic: Collected Papers in Greek Philosophy*. Ithaca, NY: Cornell University Press.

Padoa-Schioppa, C. and J. A. Assad. 2006. Neurons in the orbitofrontal cortex encode economic value. *Nature* 441, 223–26.

Pan, Z. and G. M. Kosicki. 1993. Framing analysis: an approach to news discourse. *Political Communication* 10(1), 55–75.

Parfit, D. 1997. Reasons and motivation. *Aristotelian Society Supplementary Volume* 71, 99–130.

Pears, D. 1984. *Motivated Irrationality*. Oxford University Press.

Perner, J. and J. Roessler. 2012. From infants' to children's appreciation of belief. *Trends in Cognitive Sciences* 16(10), 519–25.

Peterson, M. 2009. *An Introduction to Decision Theory*. Cambridge University Press.

Petersson, B. 2017. Team reasoning and collective intentionality. *Review of Philosophy and Psychology* 8(2), 199–218.

Pinto, Y., D. A. Neville, M. Otten, P. M. Corballis, V. A. Lamme, E. H. de Haan, N. Foschi, and M. Fabri. 2017. Split brain: divided perception but undivided consciousness. *Brain* 140(5), 1231–37.

Plato, *Collected Dialogues*. See Hamilton and Huntingdon Cairns 1961.

Pothos, E. M., G. Perry, P. J. Corr, M. R. Matthew, and J. R. Busemeyer. 2011. Understanding cooperation in the prisoner's dilemma game. *Personality and Individual Differences* 51(3), 210–15.

Poulin-Dubois, D., I. Brooker, and V. Chow. 2009. The developmental origins of naive psychology in infancy. *Advances in Child Development and Behavior* 37, 55–104.

Price, A. W. 1995. *Mental Conflict*. New York: Routledge.

Priest, G. 2000. *Logic: A Very Short Introduction*. Oxford University Press.

Priest, G., J. Beall, and B. P. Armour-Garb (Eds.). 2004. *The Law of Non-Contradiction: New Philosophical Essays*. Oxford University Press.

Rabbie, J. M., J. C. Schot, and L. Visser. 1989. Social identity theory: a conceptual and empirical critique from the perspective of a behavioural interaction model. *European Journal of Social Psychology* 19(3), 171–202.

Rachlin, H. 2000. *The Science of Self-Control*. Cambridge, MA: Harvard University Press.

Rachlin, H. 2018. In what sense are addicts irrational? In J. L. Bermúdez (Ed.), *Self-Control, Decision Theory, and Rationality*. Cambridge University Press.

Ramsey, F. P. 1931. Truth and probability. In R. P. Braithwaite (Ed.), *Foundations of Mathematics*. London: Routledge & Kegan Paul.

Rangel, A., C. Camerer, and P. R. Montague. 2008. Neuroeconomics: the neurobiology of value-based decision-making. *Nature Reviews Neuroscience* 9, 545–56.

Rawls, J. 1971. *A Theory of Justice*. Cambridge, MA: Harvard University Press.

Rawls, J. 2001. *Justice as Fairness: A Restatement*. Cambridge, MA: Harvard University Press.

Read, S. 1995. *Thinking About Logic*. Oxford University Press.

Resnik, M. D. 1987. *Choices*. Minneapolis: University of Minnesota Press.

Rey, H. G., M. J. Ison, C. Pedreira, A. Valentin, G. Alarcon, R. Selway, M. P. Richardson, and R. Quian Quiroga. 2015. Single-cell recordings in the human medial temporal lobe. *Journal of Anatomy* 227, 394–408.

Richardson, H. S. 1994. *Practical Reasoning about Final Ends*. Cambridge University Press.

Safran, J. D. and Z. V. Segal. 1990. *Interpersonal Processes in Cognitive Therapy*. Lanham, MD: Jason Aronson.

Sally, D. 1995. Conversation and cooperation in social dilemmas: a meta-analysis of experiments from 1958 to 1992. *Rationality and Society* 7(1), 58–92.

Salmon, W. C. (Ed.). 2001. *Zeno's Paradoxes*. Indianapolis: Hackett.

Sartre, J.-P. 1948. *Existentialism and Humanism*. Translated with an Introduction by Philippe Mairet. London: Methuen.

Savage, L. J. 1954. *The Foundations of Statistics*. New York: John Wiley.

Savage, L. J. 1972. *The Foundations of Statistics* (2nd revised edition). New York: Dover Publications.

Schick, F. 1986. Dutch bookies and money pumps. *The Journal of Philosophy* 83, 112–19.

Schick, F. 1991. *Understanding Action*. Cambridge University Press.

Schick, F. 1997. *Making Choices*. Cambridge University Press.

Schick, F. 2003. *Ambiguity and Logic*. Cambridge University Press.

Schiller, R. 2019. *Narrative Economics*. Princeton University Press.

Schmidt, U. 2004. Alternatives to expected utility: formal theories. In S. Barberà, P. J. Hammond, and C. Seidl (Eds.), *Handbook of Utility Theory, Volume 2: Extensions*. Boston, MA: Springer.

Schmitz, M. 2018. Co-subjective consciousness constitutes collectives. *Journal of Social Philosophy* 49, 137–60.

Schultz, W. 1998. Predictive reward signal of dopamine neurons. *Journal of Neurophysiology* 80, 1–27.

Schultz, W. 2016. Dopamine reward prediction-error signalling: a two-component response. *Nature Reviews Neuroscience* 17, 183–95.

Schultz, W., P. Dayan, and P. R. Montague. 1997. A neural substrate of prediction and reward. *Science* 275, 1593–99.

Searle, J. 1995. *The Construction of Social Reality*. New York: Free Press.

Selman, R. L. and D. F. Byrne. 1974. A structural-developmental analysis of levels of role taking in middle childhood. *Child Development* 45(3), 803–806.

Setiya, K. 2004. Against internalism. *Noûs* 38, 266–98.

Shaffer, D. R. 2008. *Social and Personality Development*. Belmont, CA: Wadsworth.

Shefrin, H. 2002. *Beyond Greed and Fear: Understanding Behavioral Finance and the Psychology of Investing*. Oxford University Press.

Shefrin, H. and M. Statman. 1985. The disposition to sell winners too early and ride losers too long: theory and evidence. *The Journal of Finance* 40, 777–90.

Sher, S. and C. R. McKenzie. 2006. Information leakage from logically equivalent frames. *Cognition* 101, 467–94.

Sher, S. and C. R. McKenzie. 2008. Framing effects and rationality. In N. Chater and M. Oaksford (Eds.), *The Probabilistic Mind: Prospects for Bayesian Cognitive Science*. Oxford University Press.

Sher, S. and C. R. McKenzie. 2011. Levels of information: a framing hierarchy. In G. Keren (Ed.), *Perspectives on Framing*. New York: Psychology Press.

Shields, C. 1999. *Order in Multiplicity: Homonymy in the Philosophy of Aristotle*. Oxford University Press.

Shoham, Y. and K. Leyton-Brown. 2008. *Multiagent Systems: Algorithmic, Game-Theoretic, and Logical Foundations*. Cambridge University Press.

Skyrms, B. 2012. *The Stag Hunt and the Evolution of Social Structure*. Cambridge University Press.

Smith, M. 1995. Internal reasons. *Philosophy and Phenomenological Research* 55, 109–31.

Smith, M. 2004. Humean rationality. In P. Rawling and A. R. Mele (Eds.), *The Oxford Handbook of Rationality*. Oxford University Press.

Sober, E. 1978. Psychologism. *Journal for the Theory of Social Behavior* 8, 165–91.

Sosa, E. 1991. *Knowledge in Perspective*. Cambridge University Press.

Stanovich, K. E. and R. F. West. 2000. Individual differences in reasoning: implications for the rationality debate. *Behavioral and Brain Sciences* 23, 645–726.

Starmer, C. 2000. Developments in non-expected utility theory: the hunt for a descriptive theory of choice under risk. *Journal of Economic Literature* 38, 332–82.

Stein, E. 1996. *Without Good Reason*. Oxford: Clarendon Press.

Stevens, F. L., R. A. Hurley, and K. H. Taber. 2011. Anterior cingulate cortex: unique role in cognition and emotion. *Journal of Neuropsychiatry and Clinical Neurosciences* 23, 121–25.

Stich, S. 1990. *The Fragmentation of Reason*. Cambridge, MA: MIT Press.

Stigler, G. J. 1950a. The development of utility theory. I. *Journal of Political Economy* 58(4), 307–27.

Stigler, G. J. 1950b. The development of utility theory. II. *Journal of Political Economy* 58(5), 373–96.

Strotz, R. H. 1956. Myopia and inconsistency in dynamic utility maximization. *The Review of Economic Studies* 23, 165–80.

Sugden, R. 2000. Team preferences. *Economics and Philosophy* 16(2), 175–204.

Sugden, R. 2003. The logic of team reasoning. *Philosophical Explorations* 6(3), 165–81.

Sugden, R. 2004. Alternatives to expected utility: foundations. In S. Barberà, P. J. Hammond, and C. Seidl (Eds.), *Handbook of Utility Theory, Volume 2: Extensions*. Boston, MA: Springer.

Sugden, R. 2015. Team reasoning and intentional cooperation for mutual benefit. *Journal of Social Ontology* 1(1), 143–66.

Suppes, P. 1960. *Axiomatic Set Theory*. New York: Van Nostrand.

Suppes, P. 1966. Some formal models of grading principles. *Synthese* 6, 284–306.

Temkin, L. S. 1987. Intransitivity and the mere addition paradox. *Philosophy and Public Affairs* 16, 138–87.

Temkin, L. S. 1996. A continuum argument for intransitivity. *Philosophy and Public Affairs* 25, 175–210.

Thaler, R. H. 1999. Mental accounting matters. *Journal of Behavioral Decision Making* 12, 183–206.

Thaler, R. H. and E. J. Johnson. 1991. Gambling with the house money and trying to break even: the effect of prior outcomes on risky choice. *Management Science* 36, 643–60.

Tom, S. M., C. R. Fox, C. Trepel, and R. A. Poldrack. 2007. The neural basis of loss aversion in decision-making under risk. *Science* 315, 515–18.

Tuomela, R. 2013. *Social Ontology: Collective Intentionality and Group Agents.* Oxford University Press.

Turner, J. C. and K. J. Reynolds. 2012. Self-categorization theory. In P. A. P. Van Lange, A. W. Kruglanski, and E. T. Higgins (Eds.), *Handbook of Theories in Social Psychology*. London: Sage.

Turri, J., M. Alfano, and J. Greco. 2011. Virtue epistemology. *The Stanford Encyclopedia of Philosophy* (Winter 2011 Edition), Edward N. Zalta (Ed.). https://plato.stanford.edu/archives/win2011/entries/epistemology-virtue/.

Tversky, A. and D. Kahneman. 1981. The framing of decisions and the psychology of choice. *Science* 211, 453–58.

Tversky, A. and D. Kahneman. 1986. Rational choice and the framing of decisions. *The Journal of Business* 59. S251–S278.

von Neumann, J. and O. Morgenstern. 1944. *Theory of Games and Economic Behavior.* New York: John Wiley & Sons.

Voorhoeve, A. 2013. Vaulting intuition: Temkin's critique of transitivity. *Economics and Philosophy* 29, 409–25.

Wallis, J. D. 2011. Cross-species studies of orbitofrontal cortex and value-based decision-making. *Nature Neuroscience* 15, 13–19.

Watts, T. W., G. J. Duncan, and H. Quan. 2018. Revisiting the marshmallow test: a conceptual replication investigating links between early delay of gratification and later outcomes. *Psychological Science* 29(7), 1159–77.

Weber, J. 1998. The resilience of the Allais paradox. *Ethics* 109, 94–118.

Wiggins, D. 1978. Weakness of will, commensurability, and the objects of deliberation and desire. *Proceedings of the Aristotelian Society* 79, 251–77.

Williams, B. 1978. *Descartes: The Project of Pure Inquiry.* London: Penguin.

Williams, B. 1979. Internal and external reasons. In R. Harrison (Ed.), *Rational Action.* Cambridge University Press.

Williams, B. 1980. Justice as a virtue. In A. O. Rorty (Ed.), *Essays on Aristotle's Ethics.* Berkeley, CA: University of California Press.

Williams, B. 1985. *Ethics and the Limits of Philosophy.* Cambridge, MA: Harvard University Press.

Wimmer, H. and J. Perner. 1983. Beliefs about beliefs: representation and constraining function of wrong beliefs in young children's understanding of deception. *Cognition* 13, 103–28.

Wimsatt, W. K. and M. C. Beardsley. 1946. The intentional fallacy. *Sewanee Review* 54, 468–88.

Yu, R. and P. Zhang. 2014. Neural evidence for description dependent reward processing in the framing effect. *Frontiers in Neuroscience* 8.

Zagefka, H. and T. James. 2015. The psychology of charitable donations to disaster victims and beyond. *Social Issues and Policy Review* 9, 155–92.

Zagefka, H., M. Noor, R. Brown, G. R. de Moura, and T. Hopthrow. 2011. Donating to disaster victims: responses to natural and humanly caused events. *European Journal of Social Psychology* 41, 353–63.

Zheng, H., X. T. Wang, and L. Zhu. 2010. Framing effects: behavioral dynamics and neural basis. *Neuropsychologia* 48, 3198–204.

Zweig, J. 2007. *Your Money and Your Brain: How the New Science of Neuroeconomics Can Help Make You Rich*. New York: Simon & Schuster.

Index